the Lewis & Clark
~ trail ~

the Lewis & Clark

~ trail ~

T 22000

TRAVEL * HISTORIC * AMERICA

Fodor's

First Edition

Fodor's Travel Publications
New York | Toronto | London | Sydney | Auckland
www.fodors.com

Fodor's Travel Historic America: The Lewis and Clark Trail

Editor: William Travis

Writers: Gina Bacon (Oregon, Washington), Thomas D. Griffith (South Dakota), Suzanne G. Fox (Introduction), Pat Hansen (Montana), Candi Helseth (North Dakota), Diana Lambdin Meyer (Iowa, Illinois, Kansas, Missouri, Nebraska), Carole Smolinski (Idaho)

Design: Tina Malaney

Cover Images: Top: *A Map of Lewis and Clark's Track, across the Western Portion of North America from the Mississippi to the Pacific Ocean copied by Samuel Lewis from the original drawing of Wm. Clark, 1814* (Library of Congress Geography and Map Division Washington, D.C.). Bottom: *Missouri River Breaks National Monument, Montana* (Chuck Haney).

Maps: David Lindroth Inc., Mapping Specialists, *cartographers*; Rebecca Baer, Robert Blake, *map editors*

Production/Manufacturing: Robert B. Shields

First Edition

ISBN 1–4000–1297–X

ISSN 1543–1053

Important Tip

Although all prices, opening times, and other details in this book are based on information supplied to us at press time, changes occur all the time in the travel world, and Fodor's cannot accept responsibility for facts that become outdated or for inadvertent errors or omissions. So always confirm information when it matters, especially if you are making a detour to visit a specific place.

Special Sales

Fodor's Travel Publications are available at special discounts for bulk purchases for sales promotions or premiums. Special editions, including personalized covers, excerpts of existing guides, and corporate imprints, can be created in large quantities for special needs. For more information, contact your local bookseller or write to Special Markets, Fodor's Travel Publications, 1745 Broadway, New York, NY 10019. Inquiries for Canada should be directed to your local Canadian bookseller or sent to Random House of Canada, Ltd., Marketing Department, 2775 Matheson Boulevard East, Mississauga, Ontario L4W 4P7. Inquiries from the United Kingdom should be sent to Fodor's Travel Publications, 20 Vauxhall Bridge Road, London SW1V 2SA, England.

PRINTED IN THE UNITED STATES OF AMERICA

10 9 8 7 6 5 4 3 2 1

Contents

ix **Traveling through History**

How to Use This Guide...x

1 **Journey of Discovery**

Map: The Lewis and Clark Trail...4–5

An Expedition Time Line...12

23 **Illinois, Missouri, and Kansas**

Illinois...23

Driving Tour: Preparations for Discovery...25

Illinois Town Listings...25

Map: Illinois, Missouri, and Kansas...26–27

Missouri...33

Driving Tour: Trail Beginnings...35

Driving Tour: We Proceed On 36

Missouri Town Listings...37

Kansas...64

Driving Tour: Traversing Kanza Territory...65

Kansas Town Listings...67

75 **Nebraska and Iowa**

Nebraska...75

Driving Tour: Nebraska Journey...77

Map: Nebraska and Iowa...78

Nebraska Town Listings...79

Iowa...95

Driving Tour: The Loess Hills...97

Iowa Town Listings...99

109 **South Dakota**

Driving Tour: Traversing South Dakota...111

Map: South Dakota...112

South Dakota Town Listings...113

133 **North Dakota**

Driving Tour: North Dakota Journey...135

Map: North Dakota...136

North Dakota Town Listings...137

153 **Montana**

Driving Tour: Tracing the Trail through Montana...155

Map: Montana...156

Driving Tour: Through Native American History...159

Montana Town Listings...160

195 **Idaho**

Driving Tour: In the Land of the Agai-dika...197

Map: Idaho...198

Driving Tour: In the Land of the Nez Percé...199

Idaho Town Listings...200

219 Washington and Oregon

Washington...219

Map: Washington and Oregon...222–223

Driving Tour: From Plateau to the Pacific...224

Washington Town Listings...226

Oregon...244

Driving Tour: From Desert to Dunes...248

Oregon Town Listings...251

Portaits of Discovery

Captain William Clark...6–7

Captain Meriwether Lewis...8–9

The Lewis and Clark National Historic Trail...19–20

Fort Kaskaskia...32

Paw Paws...34

The Katy Trail...42

The Journey Continues...50–51

A Musical Journey...52

The Construction of Fort Clark...56

Discipline on the Expedition...66

Celebrating Independence Day...70

Medical Care on the Trail...72

A Journey of Freedom...80

Gifts of Peace...84

Barking Squirrels...94

The Men's Best Friend...98–99

Sergeant Charles Floyd...104

A Changing River...114–115

Meeting the Yankton

Sioux...118

The Powwow Experience...126

The Long Winter: Fort Mandan...140

Sacagawea and the Knife River Indian Villages...148–149

Montana's Native Americans...161

Lewis' Return Trip...169

Camp Disappointment...177

Yellowstone River...187

Yellowstone National Park...189

Sacagawea at Home...203–204

The Lolo Trail...207

Hells Canyon Fish Hunt...211–212

Getting Acquainted with the Nez Percé...217

Lewis and Clark Among the Nez Percé...227–228

Pacific Northwest Cuisine: Lewis and Clark Style...235–236

O! How Horriable Is the Day...245–246

Columbia River, Then and Now...249–250

Columbia River Tribal Culture...259–260

Astoria's Colorful Past...265–266

269 Resources

283 Important Numbers and On-line Info

287 About Our Writers

289 Regional Directory

291 Index

<u>A Memorandum of Articles in readiness for the Voyage</u>

14 Bags of Parchmeal of 2 bu: each about	1200
9 do - Common do - do - NB do	800
11 do - Corn Hulled - do - do	1000
30 half Barrels of flour } - (gross 3900ᵂ) do	3400
3 Bags do - do }	
7 do - of Biscuit } (gross 6500) do	5600
4 Barrels do }	
7 Barrels of Salt of 2 bus: each + (270) do	750
50 Kegs of Pork - (gross 4500) do	3705
2 Boxes of Candles (one of which has 50ᵂ of Soap) do	170
1 Bag of Candle-wick - do	8
1 do - Coffee	50
1 do - Beens & do Pees	100
2 do - Sugar - do	112
1 Keg of Hogs Lard - do	100
4 Barrels of Corn hulled (650) do	600
1 do - of Meal 170 do	150

600ᵂ Grees
40 bushels Meal
24 do. Natchus Corn Hulled
21 Bales of Indian Goods
Tools of every Description & &ᶜ

<u>our party</u>

2 Capᵗˢ 4 Sergeants, 3 Inttpᵗᵉʳˢ 22 Amⁿ 9 or 10 French & york also 1 Corpˡ & Six in a Perogue with 40 Days provision for the party as far as they provisions last

"A Memorandum of articles in readiness for the voyage," by William Clark
(Yale Collection of Western Americana, Yale University)

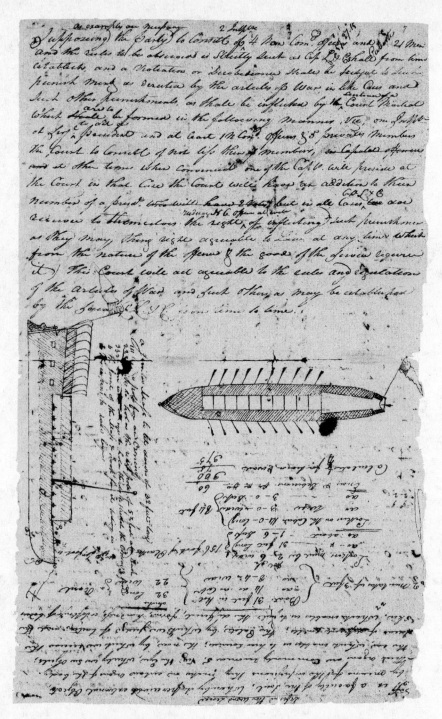

Drawing of a keelboat by William Clark, January 20, 1804
(Yale Collection of Western Americana, Yale University)

Traveling through History

rom the beginning, America has been a land of travelers—settlers on the move in sailing ships, wagon trains, canal barges, railroad cars, and pack-coaches—and there has never been a better time than now to partake of that tradition. There is a grand excitement in going to the very sites where the nation's character was formed and actually setting foot in momentous places you've until now only read about. When you're there you discover new things about the country's past, in the process deepening your understanding of America's historic events.

If you want to get to know what the United States is all about, nothing beats visiting the places where the nation's life story unfolded. When you stroll the streets of heritage-rich towns or gaze across prairies and plains where destiny was determined, you travel back in time. Before your eyes, the past sheds its dusty mantle and becomes new again, a fresh and even thrilling experience for you to relive. You imagine you can see Lewis and Clark and the Corps of Discovery heading west, watch a herd of buffalo rumbling across the plains, and hear the thundering rapids of the Missouri River. Whether you are a great-grandparent who's heard (and perhaps told) the story over and over, or a third-grader who's finding out about it for the very first time, a trip into the past can leave you with a whole new perspective on the people and events that made America what it is today.

And what about that third-grader (or sixth-grader or tenth-grader)? Even if your kids yawn their way through their history homework, a field trip to a place they've learned about in school is almost guaranteed not to bore them. Leave behind the textbook and head for the trail, and what they've read about immediately becomes real. Take the lesson out of the classroom and into the cabin, and suddenly even the most reluctant students can't resist the urge to join in. When you're face-to-face with the America of long ago, history bursts to life before your eyes, in illuminating and often unexpected ways. It makes for an unforgettable vacation.

Keeping a travel guide fresh and up-to-date is a big job, and we welcome any and all comments. We'd love to have your thoughts on places we've listed, and we're interested in hearing about your own special finds. Our guides are thoroughly updated for each new edition, and we're always adding new information, so your feedback is vital. Contact us via e-mail in care of editors@fodors.com (specifying the name of the book on the subject line) or via snail mail in care of *Travel Historic America: The Lewis and Clark Trail*, at Fodor's, 1745 Broadway, New York, NY 10019. We look forward to hearing from you. And in the meantime, have a wonderful trip.

HOW TO USE THIS GUIDE

▼▼

Travel Historic America: The Lewis and Clark Trail contains everything you need to know in order to plan and enjoy your trip into the American past. For a family on summer vacation, a retiree traveling the country by RV, a college student on break, or simply anyone who wants to be immersed in our country's history up close and in person, the book that you hold in your hands is a great tool. With it as your guide you can tour an old fort, examine pioneer artifacts in a museum, or grab a bite in a historic saloon. Whatever your interests, this book will help you make the story of America part of your personal history.

✦ WHAT'S INSIDE

For each of the 11 states that was part of the Lewis and Clark Trail, you will find information on the cities, villages, and sites where you can still glimpse the American frontier the way Lewis and Clark saw it. *Travel Historic America: The Lewis and Clark Trail* includes as many attractions, events, restaurants, and lodgings as space allows, focusing on delivering to you the kind of in-depth, expert knowledge that you won't get anywhere else. The guide opens with an introduction to that historic journey, accompanied by a time line that highlights the pivotal moments of the story. A map of the region shows the cities and highways of today as well as the original trail.

Following the trail from east to west, state by state, the chapters of the guide contain everything you need to know to plan a fun and fulfilling Lewis and Clark Trail adventure. Whether you are trying to decide which part of the trail to explore or have already chosen a destination, the opening sections of each chapter can answer your questions. A brief historical overview of Lewis and Clark events is contained in each state's introduction. On a regional map are marked the towns listed within the chapter, plus major roads and landmarks and the routes of the state driving tours.

We the subscribers do acknowledge to have received of the several sums set opposite to our Names, the same being due us from the War department, pursuant to an act of Congress bearing date March the 3d. 1807. entitled "an act making compensation to Messrs. Lewis & Clark and their companions" — Signed Duplicate.

No.	Names	Rank	Commencement of service, and settlement as per pay Roll	Ending of pay as per pay Roll at the September of Service	Time paid for Months	days	pr Months	Amount of Pay Received Dollars	Cents	Signers Names	Witness
1	John Ordway	Sergeant	1st January 1804	10th October 1806	33	10	8	266	66 ⅔		
2	Nathaniel Pryor	ditto	20th October 1803	10th October 1806	35	20	33⅓	278	50		
3	Charles Floyd	ditto	1st August 1803	20th August 1804	12	20	8	86	33 ⅓		
4	Patrick Gass	ditto	1st January 1804	10th October 1806	33	10	5⅓	243	66 ⅔		
5	William Bratton	Private	20th October 1803	10th October 1806	35	20	5	178	33 ⅓		
6	John Collins	do	1st January 1804	ditto ditto	33	10	5	166	66 ⅔		
7	John Colter	do	15th October 1803	do	35	26	5	179	33 ⅓		
8	Pierre Cruzatte	do	16th May 1804	do do	28	25	5	144	16 ⅔		
9	Joseph Fields	do	1st August 1803	do do	38	10	5	191	66 ⅔		
10	Reubin Fields	do	1st August 1803	do do	38	10	5	191	66 ⅔		
11	Robert Frazier	do	1st January 1804	do do	33	10	5	166	66 ⅔		
12	Silas Goodrich	do	1st Jany 1804	do do	33	10	5	166	66 ⅔		
13	George Gibson	do	19th October 1803	do do	35	21	5	178	50		
14	Thomas Proctor Howard	do	1st Jany 1804	do do	33	10	5	166	66 ⅔		
15	Hugh Hall	do	1st Jany 1804	do do	33	10	5	166	66 ⅔		
16	Francis Labiche	do	16th May 1804	do do	28	25	5	144	66 ⅔		
17	Hugh McNeal	do	1st Jany 1804	do do	33	10	5	166	66 ⅔		
18	John Shields	do	19th October 1803	do do	35	21	5	178	50		
19	George Shannon	do	19th October 1803	do do	35	21	5	178	50		
20	John Potts	do	1st Jany 1804	do do	33	10	5	166	66 ⅔		
21	John Baptiste Lepage	do	2nd Nov 1804	do do	22	9	5	111	50		
22	John B. Thompson	do	1st Jany 1804	do do	33	10	5	166	66 ⅔		
23	William Werner	do	1st Jany 1804	do do	33	10	5	166	66 ⅔		
24	Richard Windsor	do	1st Jany 1804	do do	33	10	5	166	66 ⅔		
25	Peter Weiser	do	1st Jany 1804	do do	33	10	5	166	66 ⅔		
26	Alexander Willard	do	1st Jany 1804	do do	33	10	5	166	66 ⅔		
27	Joseph Whitehouse	do	1st Jany 1804	do do	33	10	5	166	66 ⅔		
28	Richard Warfington	Corporal	14th May 1804	1st June 1805	12	17	7	99	16 ⅔		
29	John Newman	Private	14th May 1804	1st June 1805	12	17	5	62	83 ⅓		
30	George Drewlier	Interpreter	1st January 1804	10th October 1806	33	10	25	833	33 ⅓		
31	Touissant Charbono	ditto	7th April 1805	17th August 1806	16	11	25	409	16 ⅔		

Receipt for compensation of members of the expedition by William Clark

The driving tours mapped out for each state are an excellent trip-planning tool. Each is an efficient yet adventurous itinerary for a road trip, complete with recommendations on which routes to take for a great drive and interesting places to stop along the way. The towns visited on the driving tours are listed east to west, south to north within the chapters, following Lewis and Clark's journey westward. As you peruse the town listings you will also come across boxes filled with fascinating anecdotes and legends that will enrich your Lewis and Clark experience.

The final chapter of the guide, "Resources," directs you to a wealth of sources for further information on the history of the Lewis and Clark Trail and contacts who can help you plan your trip. There are both general sources, which can inform you about the Lewis and Clark Trail as a whole, and state-specific sources, which can tell you what you need to know about the state you plan to visit. Organizations listed under "Historical and Tourism Organizations" specialize in supplying information, and those under "History Tours and Packages" can set you up on a preplanned trip or can customize a guided itinerary for you. Under "Further Reading" are the kind of solidly researched yet enjoyably readable books that can put you in the mood for your Lewis and Clark Trail adventure months ahead of time—or prolong the excitement for months afterward.

Where to Find It Town by Town

▼▼▼

It's easy to find the city you are looking for in *Travel Historic America: The Lewis and Clark Trail,* because the towns within each state are listed from east to west, as they follow the trail

✦ TOWN LISTINGS
A brief description of each town summarizes its place in the Lewis and Clark journey and its character today. You can get more information before you visit by contacting the organizations—chambers of commerce, visitor bureaus, historical associations, and the like—listed below the town introduction.

✦ ATTRACTIONS AND EVENTS
From historic sites to festivals, the historically oriented things you can see and do in and around each town are all here, and it's all true to history. You won't find hokey theme parks or bogus roadside attractions in these pages: every destination listed is of genuine historical significance. You'll learn about museums, walking tours, hands-on activities, state and national parks, theatrical performances, and annual events. Note that attractions in smaller nearby towns are sometimes listed under larger towns, and that when a nearby town is of interest in its entirety but is too small to have its own heading, it may appear as an attraction under a larger town.

✦ HISTORIC DINING AND LODGING

In this section you will find reviews of dining and lodging options of historical interest in and near the town. Not every town has such accommodations, but those that do are worth considering as a stopover for lunch, dinner, or a night's sleep. These distinctive restaurants, hotels, inns, bed-and-breakfasts, and watering holes have been selected for their combination of authenticity and quality. Some of these properties have served the public continuously; others have been restored after years of disuse, or converted from other uses, with meticulous respect for history. Furnishings may be antiques or reproductions and food may be old-fashioned or updated, but your overall experience will be transporting, allowing you to remain immersed in the past even when your day of touring is done. Of course, every review provides all the practical information you will need, such as phone numbers, prices, and the policies (such as seasonal closings and whether credit cards are accepted) of each property.

A Topogra
of the Missouri and U
Exhibitin
the various Nations and Tribe
Copied from the Original Sp

Unknown

Country

Chippewian
Indians

145 140 135 130 125 120 115

60

55

50

45

40

35

Beaver Indians

Black footed Indians

Country of the

Sturgeon L.

Wintering
Place of the
English 1786

M. Ful

Brochet
L.

Jupas R.

Swan R.

An English
Fort

S.t Jacques

Odmabin
Ind.

Crestenoes

Boisettur M.

Discovered
by J.o de Fuca

Gande Ind.s

Manitou

Mountain of Rock
the Piney Mountains

Country

of

the

Snake

Indians

THE

Grand Peel Indians

ROCKY

Placote L.

The Osnaboins

Osnaboin Ind.

Turtle M.ts

Elk Mount.

Chart Ind.

The
Grand
Detour

Acton
Ind.

Bouch.

Discovered by d'Aguillar

oregan, or R. of the West

M

Sioux Ind.

River Missouri

O

Arctche Ind.

Mandan
Mountain Ind.

Crow Indian

U

Aras an Ind.

Ricard Ind.

The Little Missouri R.

The Little Big Bend Ind.

Chaquiens Ind.

N

The River

PACIFIC

Unknown

T

Redbed Ind.

Country

A

Notes

I

N

N. Fork of the Plate

S

Wandering Nations

The Plate Mountain

Fixed & permanent d.o

OCEAN

S.t Fra: Drake staid
5 weeks in this port

The line formed thus, divides
the United States from Canada

signifies the route pursued
by the English traders among the
Indian Nations

N.B. The narrowest
part of the neck of the
Grand Detour, or Great
Bend of the Missouri
is only 20 miles across

Knife River

130 125 120 115

Note: The no.
Grand Detou.
Mackingie, lie

Journey of Discovery

magine setting out on the greatest adventure of your life. You have accepted the challenge of charting a path across a vast wilderness, unexplored and unknown by anyone in your society. Many of your contemporaries believe the land you are to traverse holds great wealth for the nation and great fame for the explorers who first understand, document, and exploit the area's minerals, plants, and animals, as well as the land itself. You are trained to observe the natural wonders you will certainly encounter, have acquired the best supplies and equipment, and have even planned ahead by bringing presents and diplomatic gifts for the people who already inhabit the region. Yet it is these people who call your unexplored wilderness home that pose perhaps your greatest challenge. How will they view you and your companions as you cross the lands that have belonged to them for generations, for which their forebearers, and they themselves, have fought and died?

Welcome to the odyssey that was the Lewis and Clark expedition. Over the course of nearly 2½ years, Captains Meriwether Lewis and William Clark led a small band of adventurers across more than 8,000 mi of rivers, prairies, and mountain passes in search of a commercial trade route across the North American continent. Along the way they documented plants and animals new to science and met the area's Native American inhabitants. Moreover, their journey opened a door to a new era of American westward expansion and settlement—much to the dismay of those who already lived there.

The Shaping of an Idea

The massive swath of land that Louisiana once encompassed today straddles all or part of 13 states. As part of Spain, the Louisiana Territory languished quietly under the rule of a crumbling empire. When Spain suddenly turned the lands over to France in 1801, President Thomas Jefferson immediately began negotiating to purchase New Orleans, the region's primary trading hub, from Napoleon.

As negotiations progressed Jefferson saw the need for an expedition to cross all of Louisiana. The idea was not new. Traders and politicians from several countries had long theorized about the existence of a navigable route across the continent. The nation that opened up such a passage to the Pacific would instantly gain a lock on trade from the Orient, to say nothing of a major foothold on lands in the vast unexplored area. Jefferson was well aware of the journey of Scotsman Alexander Mackenzie, whose overland trek in 1793 had taken him across Canada and to the Pacific. Although Mackenzie's route was unsuitable for trade, Jefferson knew that if the much sought-after route existed, the British would soon be searching for it.

Jefferson also recognized the scientific significance of the journey, which could yield important discoveries for naturalists around the world. A noted natural scientist in his own right, the president had little doubt that the Corps of Discovery, as he called it, might rewrite, or help others rewrite, the very tenets of what was known about the natural world. After all, this group of explorers would be encountering plants and animals that Europeans had never before seen, living under conditions and in environments that had never been previously documented in the annals of natural science. Who knew what they might encounter? Jefferson had very specific ideas about how the Corps of Discovery would operate in the field. It is little wonder, then, that he selected his own personal secretary to lead the expedition.

Assembling the Corps

Meriwether Lewis was 29 years old in 1803. Born in the Piedmont region of Virginia on August 18, 1774, Lewis came from an aristocratic family and was educated by a series of private tutors. As a member of the landed gentry of Virginia, he met Jefferson and President George Washington and at the age of 20 joined the militia, eventually rising to the rank of captain. Serving as a regimental paymaster for troops stationed along the western territories of the Ohio River country, he traveled up and down the rivers and into the wilderness. He learned about the hazards of travel in the West and the skills required to survive there. He also learned about diplomacy and warfare with the Indians of the Ohio River country.

Shortly before his inauguration as the nation's second president, Jefferson offered Lewis employment as his personal secretary. Lewis leaped at the offer. For the next two years he served the president and was in turn tutored by Jefferson in the ways of science. He learned how to use a sextant and the tools of a surveyor. He studied maps and scientific works from Jefferson's personal library. He became, in short, Jefferson's protégé, and when Congress approved funding for the Missouri River expedition, he begged to lead it. Jefferson agreed, then sent Lewis to Philadelphia for a crash course in scientific methodologies by the prominent scholars of the American Philosophical Society. Returning to Washington, D.C., for his final instructions for the expedition, Lewis was ready to begin.

To assist him on his journey across the continent, Lewis requested and received the assistance of his friend and former army commander, William Clark. Four years older than Lewis, Clark was born in Virginia on August 1, 1770, but moved with his family to Kentucky at an early age. He was raised on the frontier and grew up a tough backwoodsman, a fine waterman, and an excellent leader of men. He was also an experienced surveyor and mapmaker. The two had known each other for only about six months while Lewis served in Clark's elite company of riflemen, but that was long enough for each man to learn and come to respect the other's abilities. Clark had afterward resigned his military commission and gone into business with his brother in the Indiana Territory. Despite their relatively brief acquaintance, the trust between the two men was such that Lewis requested that Clark be recommissioned into the army with the same rank as his own and be appointed co-commander of the expedition. Clark spread the word through the settlements of the lower Ohio that a company of explorers was being drawn together for an expedition.

On July 4, 1803, as Lewis prepared to depart for Pittsburgh, Pennsylvania, and the beginning of the expedition, he received a stunning piece of news. Napoleon had just sold the entire Louisiana Territory to the United States for $15 million. The purchase was a bold and controversial move by Jefferson, one that secured America's hold on the North American continent and challenged England's dominance of the Northwest. It also made the Lewis and Clark expedition critically important to Jefferson. Now, besides Jefferson's desire to find a trade route to the Pacific coast and his recognition of the potential scientific value of the journey, he wanted to demonstrate to the American people (and their representatives in Washington, D.C.) that the land he had obtained from Napoleon was more than a vast, expansive wasteland, as opponents to the purchase charged.

Lewis traveled from Pittsburgh to Clarksville, Indiana, just across the Ohio River from Louisville, Kentucky, where he met up with Clark. Here the captains began recruiting for the journey. Many local men looking for adventure and the possibility of claiming lands in the newly acquired territory volun-

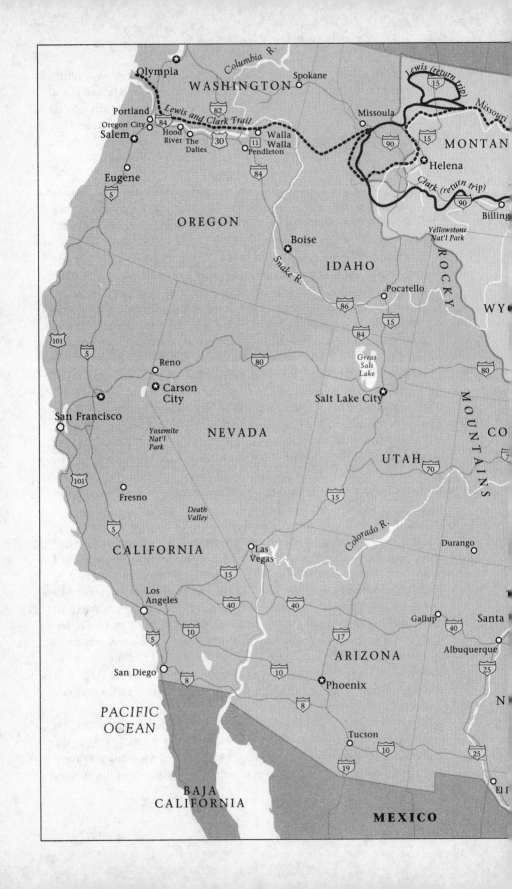

William Clark by Charles Willson Peale, 1807–1808
(Independence National Historic Park)

Captain William Clark

"Outgoing," "gregarious," and "optimistic" describe the man Meriwether Lewis chose to co-captain the Corps of Discovery. William Clark was a leader of men, unquestionably brave and honorable in all he set forth to accomplish.

Four years older than Lewis, Clark was born in August 1, 1770, in the same area in Virginia as Lewis. Tall and red-haired, Clark was educated by a local schoolmaster, and although he was clearly lacking in many skills, his inquisitiveness and efforts to communicate his experiences stood out. The journals kept by William Clark during the Corps of Discovery expedition give the greatest insight into the personalities of the men, the daily struggles, and the impressions of the land and its beauty.

His military experience in the Indian Wars established his reputation as a leader and a diplomat. He honed his scouting skills and frontier survival tactics at this time, which would prove invaluable later in life. He was the one who was often sent forward to meet with the native chiefs, who later called him the "red-haired chief."

During the winter of 1803, while Lewis was in Cahokia and St. Louis doing business, Clark drilled, disciplined, trained, and inspired the men. Although he was officially a second lieutenant, Lewis considered him his equal and the members of the Corps granted him the respect and honor as co-leader of the expedition.

Upon safely returning to St. Louis in September 1806, Clark married Julia Hancock and settled in St. Louis. As well as having children of their own, the couple cared for and provided education to Sacagawea's son, Jean-Baptiste Charbonneau. Clark served as an administrator of Indian Affairs from 1807 to 1812. During this time, he returned upriver near Independence, Missouri, to supervise the construction of what is today known as Fort Osage, which served as a trading post for the U.S. government with area Osage.

After Lewis's untimely death in 1809, Clark took over the task of completing the journals and preparing a report to Congress. The large map of the West that Clark drafted for the report is considered a landmark in the geographic understanding of the area. President Madison appointed Clark governor of the Missouri Territory from 1813 to 1821 until the state joined the union. He then became superintendent of Indian Affairs from 1822 until his death on September 1, 1838. His funeral remains the largest ever held in the city, with a procession more than a mile long. Many of his personal items are held today by the Missouri History Museum in St. Louis.

Meriwether Lewis by Charles Willson Peale, 1807
(Independence National Historic Park)

Captain Meriwether Lewis

"Serious," "reserved," even "aloof" describe Meriwether Lewis, the man Thomas Jefferson chose to lead his most ambitious dream as president—to find a navigable water passageway to the Pacific.

Born August 18, 1774, near Charlottesville, Virginia, Meriwether Lewis was just 28 years old when the expedition began. Raised in wealth and tutored at home, Lewis was considered well educated. He joined the Virginia militia and fought in the Whiskey Rebellion of 1794 and later fought against Native Americans in the Ohio Valley. This is where he met and served briefly with William Clark. Lewis also spent time living alone in the wilderness, learning survival skills and how to speak native languages. A slight man, bow-legged, and with blond hair, Lewis was a healthy man for his day, despite bouts of depression and hypochondria.

Lewis was dedicated, precise, and loyal, and these qualities were recognized by President Jefferson, who knew Lewis as a friend of the family. In 1801, he asked Lewis to serve as his personal secretary. At this time, Jefferson had begun planning the expedition to the Pacific and quickly included Lewis in his plans. Lewis was sent to Philadelphia to study medicine, botany, and celestial navigation in preparation for the journey.

As the Corps began to take shape, Lewis's role continued to be one of planner, manager, and visionary. He often traveled ahead of or separate from the crew, walking the riverbanks alone, climbing bluffs and exploring caves, at times creating great risk to himself and the mission.

Lewis was above all the scientist of the expedition. His journals were filled with drawings, charts, and images of all that was encountered. Despite his distance from the men in both physical and emotional capacity, Lewis was greatly admired by his men for his courage, intellect, and vision.

Upon the successful return of the Corps of Discovery, Meriwether Lewis seemed to lose focus and purpose. His promise to Thomas Jefferson to publish journals went unfulfilled. Nonetheless, the president appointed Lewis governor of the Louisiana Territory in 1807 and continued to pressure him regarding the publication of materials from the expedition. Yet Lewis continued to suffer from bouts of depression, about which he wrote to William Clark, and his personal finances suffered as well. Meriwether Lewis never married, and while en route to Washington, D.C., in October 1809, he died at a roadhouse in Tennessee from two self-inflicted gunshot wounds. Meriwether Lewis was 35 years old.

teered for the trip. Then the Corps of Discovery set out for the far-flung trading center of St. Louis. The party consisted of Lewis; Clark; Clark's manservant and slave, York; Lewis's Newfoundland dog, Seaman; 25 soldiers and recruits; and George Drouillard, who served as an interpreter and scout.

The Corps set up winter camp northeast of St. Louis at Wood River, Illinois, where the captains took stock of the goods and supplies they had brought from America and supplemented them with purchases from St. Louis merchants. Lewis used his authority as Jefferson's representative freely, distributing federal IOUs for supplies. Huge stores of provisions were purchased, as well as trade goods and gifts for the Native Americans they expected to meet along the way. They would use a collection of boats of various sizes—a 55-foot-long keelboat, two large canoes, and two smaller, flat-bottomed boats known as pirogues.

The Expedition Begins

On May 14, 1804, members of the Corps pointed the bows of their boats north from Camp Dubois, their Wood River camp, and began ascending the Missouri. Along the way they observed and recorded the weather, geography, plants, and animals they encountered. Theirs were, in fact, the first accounts of much of the plains' flora, fauna, and animals such as prairie dogs (which they called barking squirrels) and pronghorn antelope, which they described as "very shy." Over the course of their 28-month odyssey, the Corps lost only one man, Sergeant Charles Floyd, who died of what they thought was probably appendicitis. They buried him on a hillside overlooking the Missouri River. Lewis himself killed two Indians, Blackfeet he encountered on an ill-fated side trip up the Marias River in present-day Montana.

Upon its departure from European civilization, the Corps of Discovery began another critical part of its mission: for its members to serve as diplomatic ambassadors to the hundreds of Native American tribes that lived in the territory they were to cross. Their success was mixed. The captains' past experiences with the native tribes of the Ohio River valley provided only so much preparation for dealing with the peoples they would encounter. Lewis and Clark distributed presents freely—ribbons, hats, parts of military uniforms, mirrors, flags, and presidential peace medals that bore an image of Jefferson on one side and the clasped hands of a Euro-American and a Native American on the other, with the legend "Peace and Friendship."

Although the captains gained the support of several tribes, they were not always successful. The Sioux and Blackfeet in particular were not impressed with their presents; the trespassing Euro-Americans thought them hostile and dangerous from their first encounters. The United States may have purchased Louisiana from France, but the regional people who had fought for supremacy in this land had not been consulted on the transaction. Lewis and Clark were ill prepared to negotiate with the tribes. Their understanding of the cultural and political organizations of the people they encountered was marginal at best, as was their appreciation of the deep-seated and historic rivalries that existed among tribes, bands, and clans of Native Americans spread across the continent.

Hostile encounters notwithstanding, the explorers marveled at the scenery. Rolling prairies spread from horizon to horizon, bisected by the river they traveled on. Massive herds of elk, deer, buffalo, and pronghorn antelope lined the edges of the river, and migratory birds filled the skies. Lewis took time at the end of his day's work to walk out onto the plains, often accompanied only by his dog, Seaman, or a couple of human companions.

Near present-day Washburn, North Dakota, the Corps of Discovery built Fort Mandan for its winter quarters. The location was good—just across the river stood a sizeable village of friendly Mandan Indians, whose supply of corn kept the explorers from going hungry that winter. Here the captains hired French-Canadian trader Toussaint Charbonneau, a onetime trapper who now lived among the Hidatsa. Charbonneau was hired less for his own expertise than for that of his two Shoshone wives, one of whom, Sacagawea, was hired to accompany the expedition. As a young girl, Sacagawea had been kidnapped from her people and eventually presented to the man who would become her husband as payment of a gambling debt. About 15 years old at the time of the journey, she and her newborn son, Jean-Baptiste, would now accompany the travelers. Serving as translator, navigator, and diplomat, Sacagawea would be critical to the success of the expedition. By the spring of 1805 it was clear to everyone in the Corps of Discovery that without the help of the Native Americans, they could never expect to reach their objective.

Moving Westward across Montana

On April 7, 1805, the expedition continued up the Missouri. The cumbersome keelboat was sent back to St. Louis and four canoes were added to the fleet. They paddled north, then nearly due west into what is now Montana, caching some supplies and one of their pirogues at the mouth of the Marias River, and more supplies and the remaining pirogue at Great Falls. The explorers portaged their canoes and equipment over an exhausting route around the falls. Lewis had brought along a collapsible iron boat frame, an experimental item the captain hoped to cover with elk and buffalo hides and use as the river narrowed above the falls. But not every experiment was successful. After much effort, the boat leaked, foundered, and was abandoned. Now short of carrying capacity for equipment and provisions, the Corps had to spend several days constructing two dugout canoes from cottonwood trees.

An Expedition Time Line

August 1, 1770 William Clark born in Virginia.

August 18, 1774 Meriwether Lewis born in Virginia.

February 23, 1801 Thomas Jefferson offers Lewis a position as his personal secretary.

Spring 1801 Jefferson learns that Spain has ceded the Louisiana Territory back to France.

Fall 1802 Jefferson informs Lewis that he will lead an expedition to the Pacific Ocean.

March 17, 1803 Lewis leaves Monticello for Harpers Ferry, West Virginia, for the first leg of the journey.

July 4, 1803 In Washington, D.C., Lewis learns that Napoleon has sold the Louisiana Territory to the United States for $15 million.

October 15, 1803 Lewis meets Clark at Clarksville, Indiana Territory, across the Ohio River from present-day Louisville, Kentucky.

Fall 1803 William Clark establishes winter headquarters at Camp Dubois.

March 1804 The French and Spanish officially transfer the Louisiana Territory to the United States in March.

May 14, 1804 The Corps of Discovery leaves Camp Dubois and begins ascending the Missouri River.

August 1804 Lewis and Clark explore Nebraska as a part of the Louisiana Territory. The first council with Native Americans is held. Sergeant Charles Floyd, the only man lost on the two-year journey, dies near Council Bluffs. During a council with the Yankton Sioux, Lewis names an infant boy, Struck by the Ree, the first Sioux citizen of the United States.

August 27, 1804 The party encounters the Yankton Sioux at Calumet Bluff, near Yankton, South Dakota.

September 25, 1804 Lewis and Clark meet the Teton Sioux.

October 26, 1804 The expedition arrives at the Mandan villages for the winter.

November 4, 1804 Toussaint Charbonneau, a French-Canadian fur trader and husband of Sacagawea, introduces himself and offers his services as an interpreter.

April 7, 1805 The Corps leaves Fort Mandan and continues up the Missouri.

April 25, 1805 The Corps arrives at the confluence of the Missouri and Yellowstone rivers.

June 13, 1805 The Corps arrives at the Great Falls in what is now Montana—the portage takes one month.

July 25, 1805 The Corps arrives at the Missouri River headwaters at Three Forks.

August 12, 1805 Lewis and three others cross the Continental Divide at Lemhi Pass, becoming the first Euro-Americans to enter what is now Idaho. Lewis has his first glimpse of the western Bitterroot mountain range.

August 13, 1805 Lewis meets the Shoshone led by Cameahwait, the brother of Sacagawea.

October 10, 1805 The Corps reaches the confluence of the Clearwater and the Snake rivers at what is today Lewiston, Idaho.

October 16, 1805 The Corps of Discovery reaches the Columbia River, where the Snake empties into it, at present-day Pasco, Washington.

October 31, 1805 On a rainy Thursday morning, Lewis and Clark spot Beacon Rock, today Beacon Rock State Park, as they prepare to portage the last Columbia River rapid. They note tidal influences in the river beyond Beacon Rock.

November 7, 1805 Clark writes in his journal: "Ocian in view! O! the joy."

November 18, 1805 Having finally arrived at the Pacific, Lewis and Clark ask everyone in the party to vote where to set up a permanent winter camp. For the first time in America, a black slave (York) and a woman (Sacagawea) are allowed to vote.

December 30, 1805 Fort Clatsop, built near present-day Astoria, Oregon, is completed.

March 23, 1806 The Corps of Discovery sets out back up the Columbia River toward home.

June 14, 1806 The Corps makes its first attempt to cross the Lolo Trail.

June 23, 1806 Guided by Nez Percé, the Corps begins crossing the Lolo Trail for the second time.

June 30, 1806 The Corps arrives at Travelers' Rest. Lewis and Clark separate for the return trip across Montana.

July 15, 1806 Clark arrives at the Yellowstone River near Livingston.

July 22, 1806 Lewis ends his exploration of the Marias River at Camp Disappointment near Glacier Park.

July 25, 1806 Clark engraves his name on Pompeys Pillar, near Billings.

August 12, 1806 The expedition reunites near what is now New Town, North Dakota.

September 21, 1806 The Corps reaches the European settlements just north of St. Louis, concluding its expedition.

March 1807 Lewis is appointed governor of the territory of Louisiana.

October 11, 1809 Lewis commits suicide at Grinder's Inn, outside Nashville, Tennessee.

1813 William Clark is appointed governor of the Missouri territory.

1838 William Clark dies in St. Louis.

Members of the expedition now found themselves on the high plains of today's central Montana, heading south as they followed the Missouri toward its headwaters in the Continental Divide. They could see the snow-capped peaks in the distance while they baked in the midsummer sun on the mostly treeless plains. They encountered buffalo, herds of 10,000 at a time, and discovered and described the first bighorn sheep and western meadowlark known to western science.

As they ascended the narrowing tributaries of the Missouri, the Corps of Discovery began to grow anxious. Soon they would have to abandon their canoes to cross the great mountains before them. To accomplish this they would need the horses that they hoped to obtain from Sacagawea's people, the Shoshone. Lewis, together with his sign-language-fluent guide, Drouillard, and two other men, set out to make contact with the Shoshone. Four days after setting off into the mountains, the party crossed present-day Lemhi Pass into present-day Idaho. Standing atop the Continental Divide, Lewis looked out over a vast sea of rippling mountain ranges. From this vantage point the possibility of Jefferson's navigable route across the continent must have appeared entirely hopeless.

The party soon encountered the Shoshone and was led to the camp of Chief Cameahwait. Through Drouillard's sign language Lewis explained his situation as best he could, and the Shoshone agreed to assist him. Providing a selection of fine horses, which even the Piedmont Virginian admired, Cameahwait and a party of Shoshone accompanied the captain and his men back over the pass to find Clark and the rest of the expedition.

Their meeting, at a site later named Camp Fortunate, became one of the most important in the history of Native American/Euro-American relations. Shortly after the first conference between the captains and the Shoshone delegation began, Sacagawea suddenly jumped to her feet, ran over to Cameahwait, and embraced him. She had recognized her brother. Clearly this was good fortune for the explorers. Using a translation chain that went from the Shoshone through Sacagawea to Charbonneau in the Hidatsa language, from Charbonneau to Private Francis Labiche in French, and finally to the captains in English, arrangements to transport the explorers over the Bitterroot Mountains were made. Cameahwait had never journeyed west into the country of the Nez Percé, but he had a guide on hand who could take the strangers where they wanted to go.

Returning to the Shoshone village, the Corps of Discovery rested, hunted, and restocked provisions. Then they pressed on. As the Corps continued westward they encountered members of the Salish tribe, crossed another pass in the Bitterroot Mountains, and then trekked down the treacherous Lolo Trail. They were now surrounded by dense forests, and even their Shoshone guide, nicknamed Old Toby by the captains, became disoriented from time to time. They followed an ancient Indian path that crossed innumerable canyons, which made for terrifying and dangerous climbs on rocky terrain. At high altitudes the party encountered snow and freezing temperatures, an unwelcome, though not unusual, occurrence for mid-September. Finally, as the travelers resorted to eating their pack animals, they emerged into a flattening river valley, where they encountered two villages of friendly Nez Percé. Here they rested and reconnoitered with the Nez Percé, trading their trinkets for dried fish and the camas roots that were a primary food source for the tribe.

"Ocian in View!"

▼▼

While recovering from their exhausting trip across the Bitterroots, the explorers sought advice from Twisted Hair, the chief of the Nez Percé. He took the party to his people's village along the banks of the Clearwater River, where the men constructed dugout canoes for the next leg of their journey. Setting out on October 9, 1804, in five unwieldy canoes, they navigated the rapids of the Clearwater River and continued down the Snake. They left the mountains behind them, traveling through the deep canyon of the Snake as it twisted through the treeless plain of what is now eastern Washington. The Corps passed through the lands of the Nez Percé, often stopping to camp, trade, and visit with the bands the men encountered along the waterway. They soon reached the Columbia River, where they came across a new type of watercraft: a Chinookan canoe, smaller, lighter, and far more maneuverable than their bulky dugouts. Lewis traded with a riverside band of Nez Percé for one.

Farther downriver the corps entered the lands of the Chinook people, enemies of the Nez Percé and members of a Native American culture unlike any the captains had encountered. They lived in wooden houses, ate a diet primarily of dried fish, and spoke a language unlike any the travelers had ever heard. Even Drouillard's sign language was of little use. Despite the language barrier, the Euro-Americans and Chinooks were soon trading vigorously, the captains distributing their trade goods and the natives introducing their visitors to the delicacies of their abundant homeland. The Corps of Discovery then traveled down the valley of the Columbia River, a fertile and rolling swath of land stretching from the plains of eastern Washington and Oregon through the Cascade Range, and finally down to the Pacific. They encountered wild rapids and portaged around these on several occasions. As they passed through the Cascades, the expedition entered great forests that were very different from those in the Rocky Mountains. As the travelers approached the Pacific, they found themselves in a portion of North America's only temperate rain forest, the dark and wet home of the Clatsops, a branch of the Chinookan people.

On November 7, 1805, William Clark wrote in his journal: "Ocian in view! O! the joy."

Returning Home

▼▼▼

The Corps wintered on the Pacific coast, building Fort Clatsop, near today's Portland, Oregon. They had hoped that a ship might stop in the mouth of the nearby Columbia River, affording them the opportunity to send word of their achievement back to the United States, or perhaps even to transport some members of the Corps home. But no ship appeared, and the party spent a cold, dreary winter in the company of members of the Clatsops. The captains complained that these Native Americans had had too much contact with Europeans and failed to be sufficiently impressed with the presents the Americans gave them.

In March 1806 the explorers headed for home. At that point they had exhausted most of their supplies, which made them more dependent than ever on the people they met along the way. They paddled back up the Columbia, where they found little game and hungry and curious Native Americans all along the way. Upon passing The Dalles they found they could go no farther up the river, so they set out on foot. The explorers were eager to get back to the Nez Percé camps to obtain horses for the treacherous passage over the Bitterroots. Near the junction of the Columbia and Snake rivers, the company encountered the Walla Walla, relatives of the Nez Percé, whom the explorers had met the previous year. Here the Corps rested, visited with the Walla Walla and their neighbors the Yakima, and traded for horses and what food the men could obtain.

Setting out once more, they endured cold rain and hail in a spring storm. Upon reaching Twisted Hair's village near the base of the Bitterroots, they encountered several more of the Nez Percé leaders, including Cut Nose and Broken Arm, who came to investigate the visitors. Here the Corps of Discovery waited for the snows on the Lolo Trail to melt. They met with the leaders of the Nez Percé and pledged the friendship of the United States, inviting several tribe members to visit Washington, D.C., to meet Jefferson.

Of more immediate interest to the Nez Percé, however, was the captains' offer to broker a peace between them and their traditional enemies, the Blackfeet. Such an arrangement would have given the Nez Percé the right to hunt on the buffalo grounds east of the Rocky Mountains, an enticing prospect for the hungry tribes. In the end, however, little was agreed to except to assist the Euro-Americans on their way eastward.

Despite the advice of their hosts the party set out to cross the Lolo Trail in early June. They soon turned back, recognizing that the journey would have been foolhardy without guides. Obtaining these, they again set off, crossing the mountains in about half the time it had taken to cross them the previous fall. At the camp the captains had named Travelers' Rest, the party split up, Clark heading south to take a route along the Yellowstone River and Lewis heading north along the Blackfoot River, then over land to the Great Falls of the Missouri. Dividing the command was dangerous, but the captains wanted to gather as much information about the region as possible before taking the final trip down the Missouri.

The captains parted ways on July 3 and did not meet again until August 12. Lewis crossed the beautiful central section of present-day Montana, an area of heavily wooded mountains surrounding rolling grass-covered valleys. Once again, he was on the high plains and the group feasted on the buffalo they found in abundance. Lewis's party reached the portage above the Great Falls, where they had cached supplies the previous fall. Lewis then led a portion of this group on a reconnaissance of the Marias River, ultimately traveling north nearly to the boundaries of today's Glacier National Park. An encounter with a small band of Piegan hunters, one of the three divisions of the Blackfeet, turned sour when Lewis, discovering that the Indians intended to steal their weapons and horses, killed two of the Native Americans.

Lewis's actions ended any hope of bringing the Blackfeet into the American fold along with the Shoshone and Nez Percé and furthermore made a speedy departure from the area essential. Lewis and his men raced back to the Missouri, loaded the boats they had left there, and headed east for their planned rendezvous with Clark and his party at the mouth of the Yellowstone.

Meanwhile, Clark had used Sacagawea as a guide over the landmark now known as Bozeman Pass in an effort to find the Yellowstone River. Despite having half of his horses stolen by Crow Indians along the way, Clark and his party had found the river, constructed dugout canoes, and traveled nearly 800 mi downstream to the Missouri. Their route took them through mountain passes, and then across rolling grass-covered plains, which flattened into a sea of sagebrush prairie. The vistas were ringed by impressive pine forests and outcroppings of multihued stone.

At the confluence of the Yellowstone and Missouri, Lewis's party found that Clark had already proceeded downriver. Six days later on August 12 the Lewis and Clark parties were reunited along the banks of Missouri. The meeting was not as joyous as one would imagine. Lewis, who had been wounded in a hunting accident a few days before, was in considerable pain. Still, all of the members of the expedition were present and accounted for and eager to continue toward St. Louis. Most of them were, at any rate: when the group camped two days later at Fort Mandan, one of the soldiers, Private John Colter, requested permission to accompany two fur trappers, who were heading back up the Missouri and were interested in obtaining a guide. The captains allowed him to detach himself from the Corps of Discovery; he later gained fame as America's premier mountain man and the first Euro-American to discover what is today known as Yellowstone National Park. Also parting ways

with the expedition at Fort Mandan were Toussaint Charbonneau, Sacagawea, and the now one-year-old Jean-Baptiste. The remainder of the company
set sail for St. Louis on August 17.

The group stopped to visit with the Arikara and hunted buffalo. They
avoided meeting the Teton Sioux, but they ran across a band of Yantoni Sioux
who had sent one of their chiefs to Washington, D.C., the previous year. Despite
the missteps of some of their encounters with the Native Americans, Lewis
saw this as an indication that perhaps the Corps of Discovery's diplomatic
mission would yield fruit in the future. As the group continued downriver,
they encountered traders heading in the opposite direction. The expedition
was now completely out of any European goods, except for a few cooking
pots and scientific instruments. They happily traded with the river men for
tobacco, a small barrel of whiskey, and a keg of flour.

On September 21, 1806, the Corps of Discovery reached the European settlements north of St. Louis, and the expedition was over.

Aftermath and Interpretation

▼▼▼

Upon their return, the captains were hailed as heroes. Jefferson named Lewis
governor of the Louisiana Territory and the scientific world waited for the
publication of the expedition's report. Three years later, however, in the winter
of 1809, Lewis committed suicide, taking with him any hope of a full account-
ing of the amazing discoveries he and his team of explorers had made.
Current historians speculate that had the report been published, Lewis would
now hold a place alongside Charles Darwin as a titan in the field of natural
science. As it happened, bits and pieces of the Corps' documents were
published over the years and many of the originals were dispersed or lost.
Portions of the expedition's maps and papers that were published served as
guidebooks for those who dared venture into the strongholds of the Sioux,
Blackfeet, and Crow. Subsequent expeditions rediscovered the plants and
animals that Lewis and Clark had seen and dutifully documented in their
journals. To most Americans, Lewis and Clark were known as the adventurers who had traversed the continent, but as little more.

Clark was appointed governor of Louisiana in Lewis's place and created
the base for an American empire that would use St. Louis as its headquarters. He was also appointed to lead the United States' efforts at trading and
negotiating with the Native Americans of the Louisiana Territory. In this role
he continued to put forth the Jefferson administration's ideal of trading with
the Native Americans, gradually bringing them into the American fold
through trade and friendship while protecting their lands from the illegal
encroachment of American settlers. In this, as in the Corps of Discovery's
negotiations with the Indians, he ultimately failed. The tribes that had

The Lewis and Clark National Historic Trail

In the 200 years since the Corps of Discovery traveled westward, much along their original route has changed. The rivers they traveled on, always dynamic from season to season, changed courses or were changed by subsequent human intervention. Settlements were abandoned and others erected; new trails were forged with iron and asphalt.

During the 1960s, officials in the states that the original route passed through identified highways and roads that most closely followed the progress of the Corps of Discovery. In 1978, this system of approximately 2,700 miles of highway was designated as the Lewis and Clark National Historic Trail under the oversight of the National Park Service. This modern-day "trail" system starts in Wood River, Illinois, and passes through Missouri, Kansas, Iowa, Nebraska, South Dakota, North Dakota, Montana, Idaho and Washington before ending in Oregon at the site of the Corps' winter quarters at Fort Clatsop. Across its length, the Lewis and Clark National Historic Trail is marked with distinctive highway signage.

Though the Park Service maintains oversight of the trail, the highways, historic sites, and access routes to them are all owned, managed, and maintained by a constellation of federal, state, local, and private entities. The National Park Service, National Forest Service, Bureau of Land Management, and historical and tourism boards in the individual states all maintain Web sites and offices that can provide further information about museums, historic sites, and information centers along the Lewis and Clark National Historic Trail.

It is estimated that over the course of the four-year celebration of the Bicentennial of the Corps of Discovery's journey, between 4 and 10 million people will walk, bike, paddle, horseback ride, and drive along the Lewis and Clark's original route and the Lewis and Clark National Historic Trail. It is important to treat the sites on the trail with respect, so that future generations can retrace the journey as effectively as we can today. Some sections of the Corps' original route, as well as some trail-related historical sites, are on private property. Be sure to receive the landowner's permission before venturing onto it. It is likewise critically important that you exercise care when using public lands associated with the Corps of Discovery's route. Follow posted signage, stick to established trails, and leave any plants, animals, or artifacts as you find them.

Although much is known about the travels of Lewis and Clark, archaeological, geographical, and biological studies of the areas you will encounter are ongoing. Future researchers rely on your thoughtfulness and respect to ensure that these sites remain as much like what Lewis and Clark saw as is possible. For more information, see the Resources section in the back of the book.

controlled the high plains before the expedition crossed the territory maintained their positions, and the Shoshone and Nez Percé, whom the captains had invited onto the buffalo grounds, stayed to the west and south of the Rockies. With the exception of the occasional visit of a wandering mountain man or trapper, little changed for Lewis and Clark's Native American allies until the wagon trains of the invading settlers began to make their appearance nearly 40 years later.

The Native Americans had no way of knowing it, but they had aided the leaders of a tribe that would one day overwhelm them in a way that the Blackfeet or Sioux had never approached. Within little more than a generation, all of the people who had aided the Corps of Discovery would find themselves impoverished and exiled from their homelands; their cultures condemned as savage; their languages, religions, and lifestyles denounced and slated for eradication. The other regional peoples that the Corps of Discovery had encountered would fare little better; some, like the Sioux, were to fare even worse.

The Corps of Discovery was made up of Euro-Americans imbued with the knowledge and prejudices of their day. They braved the elements and their own ignorance of the lands and peoples they encountered, made friends, and returned home with wondrous tales. They lived the adventure of their generation yet took time along the way to record a world that Euro-Americans had never dreamed of: 10,000 buffalo in a single valley; hot springs; great waterfalls; mountains with towering alpine spires; blazing sun-drenched days followed by nights when the water froze in the cooking pots; dark, rain-soaked forests. They met Native Americans who lived in great houses constructed of wooden slabs and covered with exotic painted animals, others who lived on roots and wild game, and all of whom spoke languages strange to the European ear. Lewis and Clark hardly opened the lands of the American West to settlement, but instead they enticed a nation of adventurers and entrepreneurs to explore the region.

It was nearly a century before scholars rediscovered the scientific work of the Corps of Discovery and not until the last few years that a definitive reconstruction of its journals was assembled. The publication of James Ronda's *Lewis and Clark Among the Indians* and Stephen Ambrose's *Undaunted Courage* has introduced millions of Americans to the contributions made by the Lewis and Clark expedition. The commemorations of the 200th anniversary of the journey may engage the imaginations of countless others around the globe.

Over the past 200 years much along the route of the expedition has changed. The descendants of the Native Americans who guided and fed the expedition still live across the high plains and along the Missouri and the Columbia, though on minute fractions of the lands they once roamed. Highways now crisscross the route, and cities and towns dot the landscape where buffalo once grazed. The voyage that took the Corps of Discovery nearly 2½ years can today be made in a few hours by air and a few weeks by car. Yet the broad plains, the mighty rivers, and the towering peaks remain. The prairie dogs bark and the antelope still course across the oceans of sagebrush. And for those who know the story of the Lewis and Clark expedition, the adventure and anticipation of a great journey are as real as they were two centuries ago.

Illinois, Missouri, and Kansas

On May 14, 1804, Lewis and Clark departed from their winter head-quarters at Camp Dubois, near Wood River, Illinois, and began their expedition west. The Corps of Discovery spent most of their time crossing the state of Missouri, with little exploration in Illinois and Kansas. The state introductions that follow detail the history of their time in the area. Today's route passes through towns and cities, many of which include sites that provide a sense of the land and river the Corps of Discovery experienced as well as museums, monuments, and scenic overlooks. Driving tours for each state show you the way.

Illinois

If the overall encompassing image of the Lewis and Clark expedition is one of adventure and hardship, endurance and survival, then the communities of St. Clair County, Illinois, played an insignificant role. Encounters with grizzly bears, raging waters, ice-covered mountains, and Native Americans are certainly more romantic, more rugged, and more "American" images of their journey. However, the elements of a successful mission—strategic planning, teamwork, discipline, and scientific understanding—came together in Illinois.

The Corps of Discovery spent 154 days during the winter of 1803–04 at Camp Dubois on the south bank of the Wood River, where it flows into the Mississippi at the confluence of the Missouri. Their initial training, however, began weeks before as the earliest members of the Corps traveled the waters of the Ohio River, then worked upstream against the overpowering current of the Mississippi River to reach the Missouri. Sometimes making as little headway as 8 mi a day, Lewis and Clark quickly realized that more men and sturdier boats were needed. Two of those men were recruited at Fort Massac in southern Illinois, but 11 more came when the Corps arrived at Fort Kaskaskia, about 45 mi south of St. Louis. This was the westernmost outpost for the U.S. military at this time, and the men here had mastered the survival skills necessary for the journey into unfamiliar territory. Lewis and Clark spent the better part of a week at Fort Kaskaskia, reassessing their needs, employing the services of French riverboat handlers, and securing the final pirogue.

In all, 13 men came to the Corps from Illinois, more than from any other state, including Sergeants John Ordway and Patrick Gass. Many consider these men as significant to the success of the expedition as Lewis and Clark themselves. Both men kept journals that contributed greatly to the body of knowledge that resulted from the journey.

The people of western Illinois in 1803 were of varied cultures, religions, educational levels, and experience, and this mixture benefited Lewis and Clark as they gathered their troops. Much of the expedition's work was to be diplomatic in nature, as Lewis told leaders of the Illinois community and nearby St. Louis. Relying on their friendship and expertise, Lewis laid the foundation for political success while Clark worked with the troops. The men were all enlisted army personnel, so it was imperative that they function on a day-to-day basis with discipline and focus. Most were chosen for their marksmanship and survival skills, and Clark subsequently drilled them in shooting, marching, and hunting. They practiced navigating a river and charting the stars at night. At the same time, Clark instilled in them a sense of duty and honor and emphasized the vital importance of the cooperation that would be essential to their lives as they faced the harshest, most unimaginable conditions. As a team, they discovered each other's strengths and built upon them, uncovered weaknesses and buoyed them, and developed a trust and sense of purpose that would carry them safely more than 8,000 mi to the Pacific Ocean and back.

The inhabitants of Illinois, either knowingly or not, contributed to these developments as well. The people who lived in what is now Alton, Cahokia, and Wood River were accustomed to coming and going on the river. Even though its fate was unknown, the Corps of Discovery had a purpose and vision far beyond those who had come before it. For nearly six months, the civilian residents observed and interacted with the Corps, offered advice and distractions, and on May 14, 1804, shouted their farewells as the Corps of Discovery left Illinois for the beginning of one of the greatest exploratory journeys ever known to humankind.

Preparations for Discovery
A DRIVING TOUR FROM CAHOKIA TO HARTFORD

▼▼▼

Distance: 35 mi   **Time:** 2 days
Breaks: Spend the night in Alton.

West-central Illinois is where the Corps of Discovery came to prepare for its journey, both mentally and physically. Although the region the men covered is small in comparison with other states, they spent more time in Illinois than in any other state on the trail.

Start your journey in **Cahokia,** where Meriwether Lewis arrived first, in December 1803, and where he spent much time corresponding with Thomas Jefferson. Here, at the Old Courthouse, is where much of Lewis's official business was conducted. Other business was perhaps done at the home of Nicholas Jarrot, who at the time owned the land on which Camp Dubois was built. Lewis's and Clark's journals both refer to the Cahokia Mounds, 3 mi northeast of town. The site was once home to more than 20,000 Native Americans and is now a United Nations World Heritage Site.

After spending several hours touring sites in Cahokia, travel north on Route 3, which is designated as the Great River Road National Scenic Byway. In addition to overlooks where you can view the Mississippi River, you'll see the St. Louis skyline to the west. Route 3 takes you to **Alton,** where you can book a riverboat cruise or learn about the changes in the river region at the Alton Museum of History. Make reservations for the evening at the Beall Mansion and consider springing for a Lewis and Clark package, which includes dinner and a limousine drive to historic sites.

On your second day, retrace your trip on Route 3, driving south 5 mi to **Wood River.** The Wood River Museum houses original notes in Meriwether Lewis's handwriting to members of his family and a replica of Camp Dubois. Continue just a few more miles to **Hartford,** home of the Lewis and Clark State Historic Site, a 60-acre complex that includes a view of the confluence of the Missouri and Mississippi rivers, a life-size Camp Dubois, and a visitor center displaying a life-size keelboat.

CAHOKIA

▼▼▼

Founded by French-Canadian missionaries in 1699, Cahokia is the oldest town in Illinois. It was a central point for administrative, political, and judicial

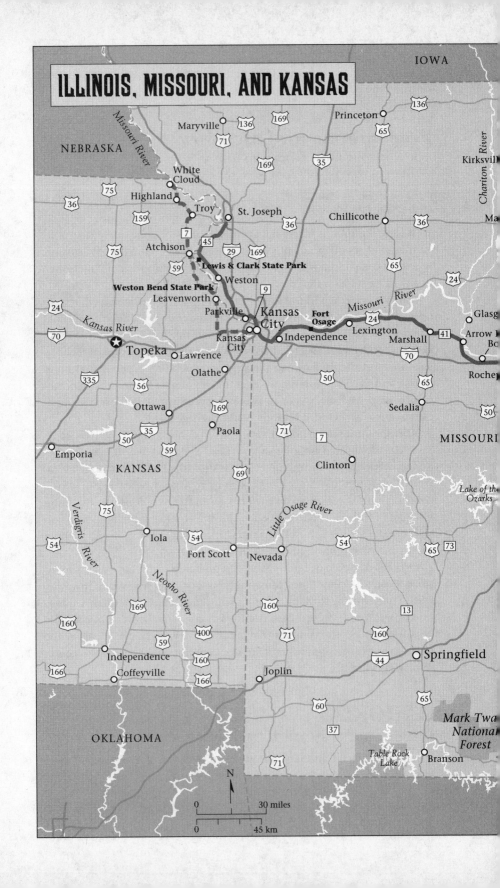

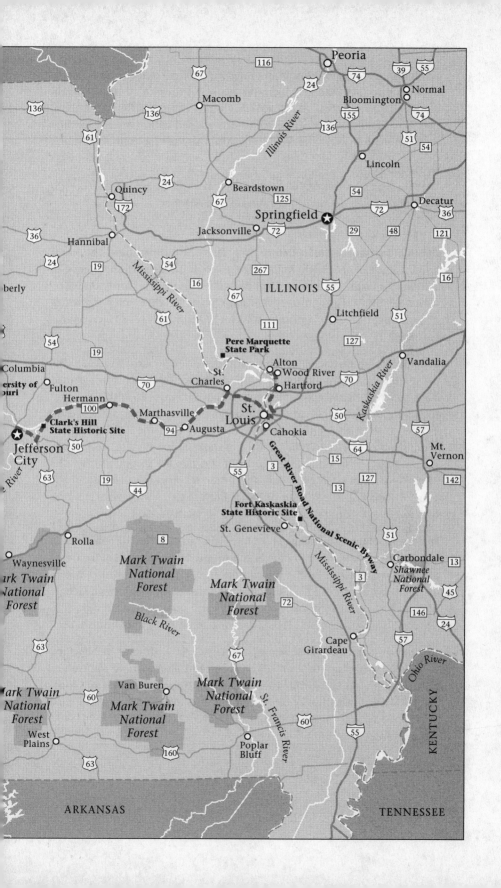

activities for a large portion of the American frontier, which was bordered by Britain on the north and Spain on the west. People of all races and religions came to and through Cahokia, including Lewis and Clark in December 1803. Here, the captains recruited and trained men, gathered supplies and information, and in general prepared themselves for their expedition.

◆ INFORMATION
Cahokia Area Chamber of Commerce | 905 Falling Springs Rd., 62206 | 618/332–1900 | www.norcom2000.com/users/cahokia.

SITES TO SEE

Cahokia Courthouse State Historic Site. This 1740s courthouse, the oldest building in Illinois, is where Clark received and sent correspondence to Thomas Jefferson. An exhibit includes quotes from that correspondence. Other exhibits trace the history of Illinois from its Native American beginnings through the 21st century. | 107 Elm St. | 618/332–1782 | Free | Wed.–Sun. 9–5.

Cahokia Mounds Historic Site. Several entries in Clark's journals mention the many Indian burial mounds in and around the winter camp. Now a United Nations World Heritage Site, this area was once home to 20,000 people and includes more than 60 mounds of dirt as burial areas. Exhibits here cover all aspects of the Cahokian way of life, including their food gathering and social structure, as well as the building of the mounds. Pottery, stone tools, and wood products found in the digs of the region are also on display. The center holds numerous educational lectures and programs throughout the year. | 30 Ramey St., Collinsville, 62234 | 618/346–5160 | www.cahokiamounds.com | $2 | Wed.–Sun. 8–dusk, Interpretive Center Wed.–Sun. 9–5.

The Church of the Holy Family. In summer you can tour this log church built in 1699, the oldest church in Illinois. It is believed that members of the Corps attended services here during the winter of 1803. In the adjacent cemetery are the remains of the 52 members of the parish who fought with George Rogers Clark in the Revolutionary War. A Latin mass is held Sunday. | 116 Church St. | 618/337–4548 | Free | June–Aug., daily or by appointment.

Great River Road National Scenic Byway. The Great River Road parallels the Mississippi River for 3,000 mi from its source in Minnesota to the Gulf of Mexico. In Illinois, the corridor winds through 18 counties. Numerous roadside markers tell the history of the communities along the route. The road is identified by green circular signs. | Rtes. 3 and 100 | 217/782–7820 | Free | Daily.

Jarrot Mansion State Historic Site. Nicholas Jarrot, a prominent Cahokia businessman, served as an interpreter for Meriwether Lewis in his communications with the Spanish. It is believed the Corps wintered on land owned by Jarrot, who also supplied wood planks to the Corps, possibly to enclose the upper deck of the keelboat. Although this house was built in 1810, it provides great insight to an individual who aided the Corps of Discovery. This imposing Federal-style brick building reflected Jarrot's idea of American simplicity. Today the home retains almost all of its original features, including plaster, flooring, woodwork, and even some window sashes. Original family portraits hang in the parlor. | 124 E. 1st St. | 618/332–1782 | www.state.il.us/hpa | Free | Variable hrs.

Martin-Boismenue House State Historic Site. Built in the 1790s by a Revolutionary War veteran, this house reveals the lifestyle of western Illinois during the Lewis and Clark era. The house's French-Creole floor plan allows for two rooms on the first floor and a basement cooking area. Furnishings are simple, including a bed, table, and a few chairs. The large open porches were used as living space during warm weather. | 2110 1st St., Prairie du Pont | 618/332–1782 | Free | Sat. 10–4 or by appointment.

✦ ON THE CALENDAR

July Liberty Bell of the West. This patriotic program in Kaskaski includes the Louisiana Purchase and the Corps of Discovery with period reenactors, food, and period music. | 618/859–3741.

Nov. Landing Reenactment. This annual program on the riverfront in Kaskaskia reenacts the team's arrival at Fort Kaskasia. Period crafters demonstrate their work, and there are food booths and carnival games. | 618/859–3741.

Dec. Native American/French Fête. Ceremonies involving the departure of Lewis and Clark from Kaskaskia are a part of this festival, which also includes music, parades, and period games for the children. | 618/859–3741.

ALTON

▼▼

Founded in 1818, Alton soon became a bustling town on the Mississippi. In winter 1803, the area that would become Alton was heavily forested and occupied by hardy trappers, traders, missionaries, free blacks, and Native Americans. They were curious about the developments at Camp Dubois on the Wood River and often entertained themselves in hunting outings or shooting competitions with the Corps. Today, Alton is a modern, industrial community in the shadow of St. Louis and is still dominated by the traffic along the Mississippi River.

✦ INFORMATION

Greater Alton/Twin Rivers Convention and Visitors Bureau | 200 Piasa St., 62002 | 618/465–0491 or 888/227–9612 | www.visitalton.com.

SITES TO SEE

Alton Museum of History. Discover what the Mississippi River was like in the 1800s when Lewis and Clark were crossing to and from St. Louis. The Pioneer Room exhibit includes maps, tools, and clothing from the period. | 2809 College Ave. | 618/462–2763 | www.altonmuseum.com | $2.50 | Weekdays 10–4, weekends 1–4.

River Boat Cruises. The *Grampa Woo* Excursion Boat takes passengers from the Lewis and Clark Historic Site in Hartford to St. Charles, Missouri. Dinner cruises are available. | 1 Henry St., in the Alton Marina | 618/462–7256 seasonal; 251/981–8241 | www.grampawoo.com | $27 and up | Variable hrs.

✦ ON THE CALENDAR

May 2004 **Bicentennial Concert Series.** This family-oriented musical entertainment includes patriotic songs and fireworks at the Gateway International Raceway. | 618/465–0491.

HISTORIC DINING AND LODGING

My Just Desserts. American/Casual. Roasted bison, smoked salmon chowder, and succotash are just a few of the items on the menu here that would make Lewis and Clark feel right at home. Be sure to try the homemade bread and Ozark berry pie. | 31 E. Broadway | 618/462–5881 | Closed Mon. and Tues. | $6–$12 | MC, V.

Beall Mansion. This home was built in 1902 by Z. B. Job, who owned the land from which the Corps departed Illinois into Missouri. A Lewis and Clark package includes a narrated limousine ride to historic sites and dinner at an area restaurant. Leaded-glass and stained-glass windows are found throughout the mansion. Antiques and Oriental rugs embellish each guest room. Some rooms have fireplaces and whirlpools. Cable TV, Internet; no smoking. | 407 E. 12th St., 62002 | 618/474–9100 or 800/990–2325 | fax 618/474–9090 | www.beallmansion.com | 5 rooms | $89–$260 | MC, V.

WOOD RIVER

▼▼

By the time the Corps reached Wood River in December 1803, only farmland and forest occupied the land that is now the town of Wood River. Nicholas Jarrot owned the land where the Corps cleared forest to build five simple cabins on the south side of the Wood River. No town actually developed here until 1900, when Standard Oil built a refinery nearby. The refinery is gone but 1,200 residents remain today within sight of the St. Louis skyline.

✦ INFORMATION

City of Wood River | 111 N. Wood River Ave., 62095 | 618/251–3100 | www. woodriver.org.

SITES TO SEE

Camp Dubois. Authentic construction techniques were used to reconstruct the cabins the Corps of Discovery built here to prepare for its journey. As you walk through the cabins, you can examine the construction process and imagine the lives of the explorers here. Tent camping is available at a nearby lake. | Rtes. 143 and 3 | 618/254–1993 | Free | By appointment.

Wood River Museum. Original notes from Meriwether Lewis to family members are among the exhibits here, which also include a replica of Camp Dubois, a compass, and other material used by the Corps. | 40 E. Ferguson Ave. | 618/ 254–1993 | Free | Thurs. and Fri. 1–4, Sat. 10–4.

✦ ON THE CALENDAR

May **Camp Dubois Rendezvous.** Canoe races, black-powder shoots, and a drum-and-fife corps are among the attractions at this three-day event on the grounds of the museum. | 618/254–1993.

May **Frontier Discovery Games.** This two-day contest of heritage skills includes black powder shooting, tomahawk throwing, archery, and log cutting. | 618/ 251–5811.

HARTFORD

▼▼▼

Snow was falling in December 1803 as Lewis and Clark first came to this area along the Wood River. The land was relatively flat and covered with ash and elm trees. They immediately began to fell trees and subsequently built five cabins and a stockade fence, and Camp Dubois came to life. For five months during the winter of 1803–04, Clark trained and prepared nearly 40 men for the adventure ahead, while Lewis traveled to Cahokia and St. Louis to gather information and provisions. During their winter here, the Corps members improved upon the boats, learned to work together as a team, and developed the skills necessary to survive in the wilderness.

Today, the tiny community of Hartford has the distinction of being the first site on the Lewis and Clark National Historic Trail. Unincorporated until 1910, Hartford remains a quiet rural community, as greatly influenced by the course of the river today as it was 200 years ago.

Fort Kaskaskia

As they interviewed candidates for the Corps of Discovery, Lewis instructed Clark to "accept no soft-palmed gentlemen dazzled by dreams of high adventure." The men who would make the journey with Lewis and Clark were as instrumental to the expedition's success as its leaders, and finding them was among the first challenges the leaders faced. They sought disciplined men with experience on the frontier, men who were also good hunters and marksmen.

On November 29, 1803, Lewis and Clark and 24 other men arrived at Fort Kaskaskia on the Mississippi River, about 45 mi south of St. Louis. Here they acquired the expedition's third boat, the red pirogue, and selected 11 men to serve as permanent members of the Corps. They also hired local Frenchmen, called engagés, to help with the boats moving upriver. Those men would return to St. Charles after spending the winter in the Mandan villages of North Dakota.

Two companies were based at Fort Kaskasia, one artillery and the other infantry. Artillery men who volunteered included John Dame, John Robertson, Ebenezer Tuttle, and Alexander Hamilton. From the infantry were John Ordway, Patrick Gass, John Boley, John Collins, Peter Weiser, and Richard Windson. Not only is a good deal of the expedition's success attributed to these men, but to them must also be credited the body of knowledge that was documented. Of the six known surviving journals, two were written by Patrick Gass and John Ordway, both of whom who were recruited at Fort Kaskaskia.

Today, Fort Kaskasia State Historic Site provides an expansive view of the Mississippi and a detailed look into the lives of the men who were instrumental in the success of the Corps of Discovery.

✦ **INFORMATION**
Village of Hartford | 140 W. Hawthorne, 62048 | 618/251–2681 | www.hartfordillinois.net.

SITES TO SEE
Lewis and Clark State Historic Site. These 60 acres at the confluence of the Missouri and Mississippi rivers provide a comprehensive look at the overall mission of the Corps of Discovery and the challenges it faced in preparing

for the journey. A 12-minute video links camp preparations and later events in the journey. Twenty acres of prairie and wetlands have been returned to their original condition. At the **Historic Marker** you can see the confluence of the two rivers where Lewis and Clark began their journey. The monument, on the river's edge, consists of 11 stone pillars—one for each state the explorers passed through on their route to the Pacific Ocean. In the **Visitor Center,** the focal point is a 55-foot full-scale replica of the keelboat with mast and sail. A cutaway section enables you to see how provisions for the journey were carried. Navigational maps exemplify the body of knowledge brought back by the expedition team. Five log cabins connected by exterior structures make up **Camp Dubois,** a re-creation that allows visitors an opportunity to explore the world in which the Corps team trained for its mission. | 1 Lewis and Clark Trail, 3 mi north of I–270 on Rte. 3 | 618/251–5811 | www.campdubois. com | Free | Wed.–Sun. 9–5.

✦ ON THE CALENDAR

May **National Signature Event.** This four-day festival includes educational programs, heritage displays, and period entertainment on the grounds of the Lewis and Clark State Historic Site. | 618/251–5811.

Dec. **Arrival of the Corps.** Each December 12, a celebration recognizes the date that William Clark and the Corps arrived at Camp Dubois. A small reenactment, parade, and military exercises mark the occasion. | 618/251–5811.

Missouri

Perhaps no other state is more synonymous with the Lewis and Clark expedition than Missouri. Although Lewis and Clark spent more time actually exploring the land that became other states, Missouri is where much of the planning took place and where the expedition ended successfully two years and four months later. It is a state that was so loved by Clark, who was born a Virginian, that he chose to make Missouri his home after the expedition and serve as the territory's first governor.

The Missouri River takes its name from the Missouri Indians, a name that means "dwellers of the big muddy." Many of the health problems of the Corps, specifically dysentery, were attributed to drinking the water of the Missouri, which journals noted as half mud and half water. "The Water we drink or the common water of the missourie at this time, contains half a comn wine glass of ooze or mud to every pint." From its source in southwestern Montana, the Missouri is 2,540 mi long.

Clark was the first of the team's leaders to arrive in the St. Louis area, followed by Lewis, who stayed on to make arrangements after Clark returned

Paw Paws

"We gathered paw paws beside the trail . . ." was a frequent entry in the journals, indicating that papaws were a regular part of the Corps' diet, at least in the early weeks of the journey along the Missouri. The fruit's nickname is the Missouri banana because of its taste, although it is a member of the custard apple family.

A papaw fruit is edible and highly nutritious, grows to between 2 and 5 inches long, and turns yellow-orange when ripe. Its yellow, fan-shape leaves are sometimes used in recipes, such as for papaw bread, for the fruit's bananalike flavoring. The custardy pulp is sweet with several dark oval seeds. The fruit is dark brown, with soft orange flesh. An unripe fruit, however, is unpalatable. Typically, the papaw ripens in September; journal entries of Corps members report that they were picking the fruit in early summer. Perhaps eating the fruit too soon contributed to some of the intestinal problems the Corps experienced during this part of the journey.

The papaw has high amino acid content, and anti-carcinogens are present in the leaves. Extracts from the twigs and leaves have some insecticidal properties. However, the papaw is not viable as a commercial crop today because of its short shelf life.

Pere Marquette State Park in Illinois, not far from Camp Dubois, is home to a large papaw grove.

to Camp Dubois. Clark and the rest of the Corps spent the winter of 1803–04 at Camp Dubois, on the Illinois side of the Mississippi, making regular journeys into St. Louis to meet with trappers and traders who had traveled portions of the river and gathered provisions. As the official transfer of the Louisiana Territory from Spanish to French and then to U.S. control took place, Lewis and some eight members of the Corps joined Clark and the rest of the men upon their arrival in the St. Louis area.

The Corps reunited, the men set off from St. Charles on May 21, 1804, amid farewells from townspeople and prayers for the Corps' safe return. The last civilized settlement the Corps encountered was just a few miles upriver in the little community of Marthasville. For nearly two months, the Corps struggled upriver, remaining in present-day Missouri most of the time. Records indicate 51 outward-bound campsites in present-day Missouri and 14 homeward-bound camps.

Unfortunately, all expedition route maps from St. Louis to present-day Omaha are lost, so it is difficult to pinpoint some of the remarkable geological points mentioned in the journals. The river's course has altered over the years, but major outcroppings such as Sugar Loaf Rock, Manitou Bluff, and Bull Rock remain dominant geological features on the river's main channel. Only a tour along the Katy Trail or via water up the Missouri River lets you experience up close some of the rock outcroppings and views mentioned in Corps members' journals.

Upon returning safely to St. Louis in September 1806, Corps members were treated as celebrities and recognized with parades, balls, and celebrations. Each of the Corps members was awarded acreage in the Louisiana Territory as partial compensation for his service. Several members chose to stay in Missouri, near the river that brought them fame and adventure.

In the meantime, the people of Missouri honored Thomas Jefferson for his vision of the American West by naming the state capital, Jefferson City, in his honor. And in 1839, the first public land-grant college in the Louisiana Territory was founded in Columbia, based on Jefferson's model of the University of Virginia.

In 1963, construction began on the Jefferson National Expansion Memorial, better known as the Gateway Arch, on the exact spot where the Corps of Discovery concluded its journey. Completed in 1965, the arch pays tribute to the pioneers who explored the American West and who often began their journey on the banks of the Mississippi and Missouri rivers. Underneath the arch, in the Museum of Westward Expansion, is a comprehensive tribute to the Corps of Discovery.

The people of the state so identify with this great adventure that they chose to incorporate the Corps of Discovery on the U.S. Mint's state quarter, released in 2002. The image shows three men paddling a canoe up a tree-lined Missouri River with the Gateway Arch in the background. Under the name of the state are stamped the words "Corps of Discovery" and the dates 1804 to 2004, signifying Missouri's role in westward expansion and the bicentennial celebration, a celebration that has its beginning and end in the state of Missouri.

Trail Beginnings

A DRIVING TOUR FROM ST. LOUIS TO JEFFERSON CITY

▼▼▼

Distance: 132 mi   **Time:** 3 days
Breaks: St. Charles and Hermann are good choices for an overnight stay.

Start your journey in **St. Louis.** The city demands an entire day, beginning with the Jefferson National Expansion Memorial, better known as the Gateway Arch. The adjoining Museum of Westward Expansion details the growth of the western United States. Next, visit the Missouri History Museum, where you can see the many artifacts owned by Clark and the original copy of the Louisiana Purchase transfer papers. As the day ends, follow Interstate 70 for 20 mi to **St. Charles** and spend the evening with Peter Geery at Geery's Bed and Breakfast. Geery is a reenactor who has made the modern trip via keelboat.

Begin your second day with a walking tour of historic St. Charles, with visits to the Lewis and Clark Boat House and Frontier Park, a trailhead for the Katy Trail State Park. If the weather is good, walk or bike a few miles along the Katy Trail for a close-up experience of the Missouri River. Enjoy lunch at any of a number of historic cafés in Olde Towne St. Charles before heading south on U.S. 94 toward **Augusta** and **Marthasville.** Across the river from Augusta is Tavern Cave, where members of the Corps scratched their names in the rock. This area is also the last point of civilization the Corps encountered as it headed upriver. Continue on U.S. 94 another 26 mi and cross south of the river on Route 19 at **Hermann,** where you can spend the evening at the White House Hotel. Owner Bob Plummer is a member of the Corps of Discovery reenactment team and is pleased to share with you his experiences along the river.

On your third day, follow Route 100 as it meanders close to the Missouri River banks for 42 mi to **Jefferson City.** Missouri's newest state park, Clark's Hill/Norton State Historic Site, is 3 mi east of the state capital, on a bluff overlooking the river where the Corps explored in the spring of 1804. The Military History Museum is an important stop in understanding the role of the U.S. Army in this expedition, and the Jefferson Landing State Historic Site provides insight into the changing role of the river in the last 200 years.

We Proceed On . . .

A DRIVING TOUR FROM COLUMBIA TO ST. JOSEPH

▼▼

Distance: 184 mi   **Time:** 3 days
Breaks: Spend the first night in Arrow Rock, a community listed on the National Register of Historic Places; your second in Kansas City; and your third upriver in St. Joseph.

By the time the Corps reached mid-Missouri, the men were beginning to see parts of the region that weren't yet documented. Today, most travelers going west from Columbia to the small villages of Rocheport and Arrow Rock have Interstate 70 to follow to Kansas City.

Start your tour in **Columbia** at the University of Missouri, which serves as the caretaker of Thomas Jefferson's original gravestone. Begin your day with a walking tour of the campus, whose design resembles Jefferson's for the University of Virginia. The campus also houses the State Historical Society of

Missouri and the Museum of Art and Archaeology, which displays items from the exploration period of the Missouri River valley.

Leaving Columbia, travel 16 mi west on Interstate 70 to **Rocheport,** a quiet hamlet in the middle of the Katy Trail State Park. Plan on having lunch at any of several casual eateries, but allow plenty of time to walk or bike at least a few miles of the trail for magnificent views of the river, the bluffs, and the foliage, all of which are noted in the Lewis and Clark journals. Continue 17 mi west on Interstate 70 to Exit 98 for **Arrow Rock,** which is 6 mi north on Route 41. Spend a couple of hours at Arrow Rock State Historic Site Visitor Center, with its detailed explanation of exploration of the Missouri River valley, beginning with the Louisiana Purchase. Stay overnight at one of the several bed-and-breakfasts in Arrow Rock, many in 19th-century buildings.

On the second day, take Interstate 70 from Arrow Rock to the junction of Route 41. Drive 10 mi north on Route 41 to the intersection of U.S. 65. Continue east on U.S. 65 for 17 mi to the intersection of U.S. 24. This 41-mi route follows the Missouri to **Fort Osage,** where river views approximate what the Corps saw. Originally known as Fort Clark, Fort Osage was designed by Clark and was the second U.S. outpost west of the Mississippi.

Drive east on U.S. 24 for another 14 mi to **Independence** and the National Frontier Trails Center. After a tour of the center, drive west on Interstate 70 into downtown **Kansas City.** Your first stop is the Arabia Steamboat Museum, where the cargo of a steamboat that sank near Parkville in 1856 tells river history. Just 10 mi north of downtown on Route 9, **Parkville** has two B&Bs along Interstate 29.

On the third day, take Route 45 into antebellum **Weston,** where both the Weston Bend State Park and Lewis and Clark State Park provide views of the river and interpretive markers of the Corps' time in this area. Continuing north, Route 45 turns into U.S. 59, which takes you into **St. Joseph.** Spend the rest of your day touring exhibits at the St. Joseph Museum and the Glore Psychiatric Museum. End your day with dinner at the Sunset Grill and spend the night at the River Towne Resort.

ST. LOUIS
▼▼▼

New Orleans fur trader Pierre Laclède selected this ideal spot, where the Missouri River meets the Mississippi, for the new settlement of St. Louis in 1764 in what had just become Spanish-colonial territory. The Lewis and Clark expedition would help earn the city its moniker as Gateway to the West, for it was here that they provisioned their famous expedition while wintering in Camp Dubois. In the years that followed, St. Louis became a manufacturing center for wagons, guns, blankets, saddles, and everything else the pioneer would need on a journey west.

By 1860, the city's population exceeded 160,000. Because of its size and location, St. Louis became a center for government offices and financial trade. The 1904 World's Fair brought increasing growth and global diversification to the St. Louis marketplace. Its significance to the Lewis and Clark Bicentennial was accentuated when the Bicentennial Commission moved its offices from Oregon to St. Louis in 2002.

✦ INFORMATION

Lewis and Clark Bicentennial Commission | 5700 Lindell Blvd., 63112 | 314/454–3124 | www.lewisandclark200.org. **St. Louis Convention and Visitors Commission** | 1 Metropolitan Sq., 63102 | 314/421–1023 or 800/916–0040 | www.explorestlouis.com/visitors/itin_lewclrk.asp.

SITES TO SEE

Bellefontaine Cemetery. William Clark and some of his family are buried on the rolling, tree-lined hills of this cemetery. Maps are available at the office to guide visitors to the sites. | 4947 W. Florissant Ave. | 314/381–0750 | Free | Daily 8–5.

Delta Queen Steamboat Company. America's only authentic paddle-wheel steamboats carry passengers on overnight trips from 3 to 14 nights along the Missouri and Mississippi, departing from the St. Louis riverfront. Historic tours bring reenactors, storytellers, and period musicians on board to enrich the experience. | 30 Robin St. Wharf, New Orleans, LA 70130 | 504/586–0631 or 800/543–1949 | www.deltaqueen.com.

Fort Belle Fontaine County Park. A fort was established on the banks of the Missouri River here in 1805 while Lewis and Clark were on their expedition. It was the first military post in the new Louisiana territory and served as a trading post with Native Americans. Shifts in the Missouri River channel have long since buried the site of the fort where Lewis and Clark spent their last night on September 22, 1806. In 1808, the military moved the fort to higher ground, then abandoned it in 1826. The land was farmed for more than 100 years, and in 1985 it became a county park. Although archaeological digs uncovered the foundation of the officers' quarters, no buildings remain. Interpretive markers describe the Corps' stay here, and a walking tour of up to 3 mi takes you past former barracks, cannons, and Works Progress Administration (WPA) structures. | 13300 Bell Fontaine Rd. | 314/615–7275 | www.co.st-louis.mo.us/parks/ftbellefontaine | Free | Daily.

Jefferson National Expansion Park. This 91-acre park, which stands on the spot of Lewis and Clark's return, is home to St. Louis's famous Gateway Arch as well as the Museum of Westward Expansion and the Old Courthouse, which is two blocks away from the arch. Named for President Thomas Jefferson, this monument honors his vision of a continental United States. Don't miss the tram ride in four-passenger capsules 630 feet to the top of the **Gateway Arch** for expansive views of the river, Illinois farmland, and the St. Louis metro below. Below the Arch you'll find the **Museum of Westward Expansion** ($2 | Memorial Day–Labor Day, daily 8 AM–10 PM; Labor Day–Memorial Day, daily 9–6), which has interactive exhibits on the Lewis and Clark expedition, Native Americans, and animals of the West. Included in the exhibit is a peace medal that Lewis and Clark presented to Native Americans along the route. The bookstore here sells an extensive collection of Lewis and Clark research materials, including maps and various journal interpretations. At the **Old Courthouse,** built in 1839, restored courtrooms appear as they did at the time. Other exhibits showcase the history of St. Louis and the French and Spanish heritage in the region. | Memorial Dr., on the riverfront | 314/655–1700 | www.nps.gov/jeff | Free; tram to top of arch $2 | Daily 8 AM–10 PM.

Laclède's Landing. Horse-drawn carriages clatter over cobblestone streets past 19th-century brick warehouses in this historic nine-square-block neighborhood northwest of the Gateway Arch. Now filled with restaurants, galleries, shops, and nightspots, this is the earliest settlement of St. Louis and the area where William Clark would have met with many trappers and traders in winter 1803–04. | 1st, 2nd, and 3rd Sts. between Washington and Carr | 314/241–5875 | www.lacledes-landing.com | Free | Daily.

Missouri History Museum. William Clark's sword, rifles, maps, and other artifacts from his days as federal Indian agent in St. Louis are on display. Another exhibit houses the original Louisiana Purchase transfer papers, which includes the signature of Meriwether Lewis. | 5700 Lindell Blvd., in Forest Park | 314/454–3124 | www.mohistory.org | Free | Tues. 10–8, Wed.–Mon. 10–6.

Powder Valley Conservation Nature Center. A model of the Lewis and Clark keelboat, built to half-size scale, is on display at this 112-acre Department of Conservation center. Elsewhere on the grounds, the center identifies and explains the flora and fauna of the region as noted by the Corps of Discovery. Trail markers indicate which plants and animals were documented by Lewis, sometimes quoting entries from his journal. More than 3 mi of hiking trails let you view wild turkeys, deer, and small mammals. | 11715 Cragwold Rd., Kirkwood, 63122 | 314/301–1500 | www.conservation.state.mo.us/area/cnc/powder | Free | Memorial Day–Labor Day, daily 8–8; Labor Day–Memorial Day, daily 8–6.

Walk of Fame. William Clark adopted St. Louis as his hometown and is honored with a star and biographic sidewalk plaque in the neighborhood known as the Loop, where more than 100 St. Louis greats are recognized along five blocks of Delmar Blvd. | 6619 Delmar Blvd. | 314/727–7827 | www.stlouiswalkoffame.org | Free | Daily.

✦ ON THE CALENDAR

Aug. 2003–Aug. 2004 Lewis and Clark: Great Journey West. The St. Louis Science Center hosts this exhibition of the scientific and technical aspects of the expedition. Use a compass and navigate via the stars as the Corps did during the journey. | 314/289–4444.

Jan.–Mar. 2004 Plant Life of the Expedition. The Missouri Botanical Garden hosts this exhibition highlighting the 150 species of plant life documented by Lewis and Clark. | 314/577–9400 or 800/642–8842.

Jan.–Sept. 2004 Lewis and Clark: The National Bicentennial Exhibition. This is the opening venue of this traveling exhibition organized by the Missouri Historical Society at the Missouri History Museum in Forest Park. You can step into a lost America to explore historic and ethnographic treasures. | 314/454–3124.

Feb.–Dec. 2004 Beyond York. This exhibit at the Black World History Museum focuses on York, William Clark's slave, who was a member of the Corps of Discovery. | 314/241–7057.

HISTORIC DINING AND LODGING

Meriwether's. American/Casual. Set on the top floor of the Missouri History Museum with a spectacular view of Forest Park, this casual restaurant is best known for its Plainsman chili, made from Missouri-raised buffalo and crawfish tail, and for its sweet corn-cakes sandwich. | 5700 Lindell Blvd., in Forest Park | 314/361–7313 | No dinner | $5–$12 | AE, D, DC, MC, V.

Drury Plaza Hotel. Originally the International Fur Exchange, this 1919 building and its two neighboring structures now house an expansive hotel. In the lobby are bronze life-size statues of Lewis, Clark, Sacagawea, and several animals encountered on the trail. The statue display also includes a river scene on which the sun appears to rise and set throughout the day. Rooms have modern amenities, and most provide views of the Gateway Arch and Riverfront. 2 restaurants, microwaves, refrigerators, cable TV with movies and video games, indoor pool, exercise equipment, business services, meeting rooms, parking (fee). | 4th and Market Sts., 63102 | 314/231–3003 | fax 314/231–2952 | www.druryhotels.com/properties/druryplazahotel | 367 rooms, 55 suites | $129–$159 | AE, D, DC, MC, V | BP.

Napoleon's Retreat B&B. This B&B in the historic Lafayette Square neighborhood pays homage to Emperor Napoleon, who ruled the territory before selling it to the Americans. The house is French Second Empire in style with Victorian furnishings and modern amenities. Some rooms have fireplaces. Some refrigerators, cable TV; no kids under 12, no smoking. | 1815 Lafayette

Ave., 63104 | 314/772–6979 or 800/700–9980 | fax 314/772–7675 | www. napoleonsretreat.com | 5 rooms | $95–$135 | AE, D, MC, V | BP.

ST. CHARLES

▼▼▼

Founded in 1769 as Les Petites Côtes ("the little hills") on the banks of the Missouri River, St. Charles was Missouri's first capital and home to explorer Daniel Boone and his family. In spring 1804, St. Charles had about 100 buildings and 450 residents, primarily French Canadian. It was here on May 21, 1804, at 3 PM, in the midst of a spring rain shower, that the Corps of Discovery (now joined by Lewis, who was in St. Louis when the group set off from Camp Dubois) departed on the journey west. The Corps had spent five days in St. Charles finishing up preparations, including one vital last-minute purchase—all of the tobacco in all of the stores of St. Charles. Then, with a rather unceremonious handshake and some awkward splashing about, the boats moved upstream into the fierce spring current of the Missouri.

Despite serious damage during the Great Flood of 1993, Old Town St. Charles—the community's historic district—today looks much like it would have 200 or more years ago, with its gas lamps and its more than 50 original buildings. Outdoor cafés, restaurants, and specialty shops line its redbrick streets, providing a splendid, unobstructed view of the river that first brought life to the city. The Katy Trail, a 165-mi official segment of the Lewis and Clark Trail, also begins here. In May 2004, the city will host the Lewis and Clark National Bicentennial Event, which commemorates the Corps' time in St. Charles.

✦ INFORMATION
St. Charles Convention and Visitors Bureau | 230 S. Main St., 63301 | 636/946–7776 or 800/366–2427 | www.historicstcharles.com or www.lewisandclarkstcharles.com. **St. Charles County Historical Society** | 101 S. Main St., 63301 | 636/946–9828 | www.win.org/library/other/historical_society.

SITES TO SEE
Daniel Boone Home & Boonesfield Village. Lewis and Clark visited here with the famous frontiersman before they began their great trek west. The village includes Boone's spacious home, a one-room schoolhouse, a church, and a general store. The house is built of blue limestone and contains several of Boone's possessions. Period reenactors stroll the grounds providing an authentic interpretation of the period in which Lewis and Clark visited. | 1868 Rte. F, Defiance, 63341 | 636/798–2005 | $7 | Memorial Day–Labor Day, daily 9–6; Labor Day–Memorial Day, daily 11–4.

The Katy Trail

If the Corps of Discovery were to make the journey along the Missouri River today, most likely its members would spend much time hiking the Katy Trail, particularly given Lewis's propensity for walking the cliffs and landscape above the river.

The Katy Trail, which was once the Missouri-Kansas-Texas (MKT) Railroad, came to life in 1986 when the railroad ceased operation on this part of the line and the Missouri Department of Natural Resources acquired the right of way. Today, at 225 mi, it is America's longest rails-to-trails project and Missouri's most popular state park.

The trail begins in St. Charles, in Frontier Park. A 165-mi segment between St. Charles and Boonville is designated an official segment of the Lewis and Clark National Historic Trail. Whether you are a bicyclist, hiker, history buff, or nature lover, you can experience much of the local history of the Lewis and Clark Trail on a 40-mi stretch between St. Charles and Marthasville, considered the last point of civilization for the Corps. Markers along the trail designate campsites and landmarks noted in the journals.

One of the most popular trailheads and access is in Rocheport at 1st Street. About a mile west of Rocheport, travelers can view pictographs left by Native Americans and witnessed by Lewis and Clark. Other trailheads are in Columbia, Clinton, Sedalia, Hermann, and St. Charles.

In June, Lewis and Clark explorers are invited to participate in a bike ride along the designated section. In October, more than 200 artists gather along the trail and trailheads, documenting the beauty of the trail in their various mediums.

Frontier Park. This 16-acre park is the centerpiece of many activities celebrating the Corps of Discovery and is where the Corps camped in 1804. The riverfront park includes a 15-foot bronze statue of Lewis, Clark, and Lewis's dog, Seaman, as well as a historic railroad depot and picnic tables. The **Katy Trail** (Box 166, Boonville, 65233 | 660/882–8196 | Free | Daily) begins its 225-mi journey across the state from a trailhead here. A 165-mi segment of this rails-to-trails biking and hiking path is designated an official segment of the Lewis and Clark National Historic Trail. Modern-day explorers can experience much of the local history of the Lewis and Clark Trail on a 40-mi stretch between St. Charles and Marthasville, considered the last point of civilization for the Corps. | Riverside Dr., one block east of Main St. | 636/949–3372 | www.stcharlescity.com | Free | Daily.

Lewis and Clark Boat House. Set on the riverfront, this center houses three replicas of the boats used by Lewis and Clark. The museum includes maps, tools, and clothing similar to those used by the expedition and by the St. Charles townspeople. | 314 S. Main St. | 636/947–3199 | www.lewisandclark. net | $1 | Daily 10:30–4:30.

St. Charles Historic District. Covering more than 10 blocks along the Missouri River, this National Historic District of cobblestone streets is filled with restaurants, cafés, and shops. Maps for self-guided walking tours of the district are available at most businesses and the visitor center (230 S. Main St. | 636/946–7776 or 800/373–7007 | www.historicstcharles.com | Free | Daily). Of particular interest is the **First Missouri State Capitol State Historic Site** (200–216 S. Main St. | 636/940–3322 | www.dnr.state.mo.us/dsp | $2 | Daily), where Missouri's first legislators met from 1841 to 1846. The **Lewis and Clark Center** (701 Riverside Dr. | 636/947–3199 | www.nps.gov | $1 | Daily 10:30–4:30) houses displays and dioramas that portray the beginning of the Lewis and Clark expedition, including entries from their journals and exhibits on the Native Americans encountered.

✦ ON THE CALENDAR

Mar. Louisiana Territory Land Transfer Commemoration. A messenger from St. Louis arriving at Frontier Park on horseback to announce that the Louisiana Territory is now a U.S. property is the highlight of this three-day festival, which also includes music, food, and period crafts artists. | 636/946–7776.

May Lewis and Clark Heritage Days. This reenactment of the events of 1804, prior to Lewis and Clark's departure, includes a parade with fife-and-drum corps, a Sunday-morning church service, a demonstration of weapons, a skillet throw, an encampment, exhibits of boat replicas, and 19th-century crafts and food, all at Frontier Park on the third weekend of May. | 636/946–7776.

May 2004 Lewis and Clark National Signature Event. A reenactment of the Lewis and Clark encampment is the focal point of this event, which features the arrival of a keelboat, a Native American encampment, and interpreters in authentic dress. Parades, crafters, and food from the period are in the plans. | 636/946–7776.

Oct. Missouri Storytelling Festival. The history of Missouri, its rivers, and specifically the Corps of Discovery comes alive in a weekend of storytelling and historic workshops in Frontier Park. | 636/946–7776.

HISTORIC DINING AND LODGING

Bonaparte's. French. Inside an 1850s building, this upscale restaurant serves country French cooking with a Spanish influence, reflecting the region's culture in 1804. Try the sherry chicken. | 140 N. Main St. | 636/940–9463 | Reservations essential | No lunch | $15.95–$23.95 | AE, D, DC, MC, V.

Lewis and Clark's Public House. American/Casual. In a building that dates to the 1830s, the explorers for which this pub is named would enjoy the prime rib and Cajun dishes on the menu. Weather permitting, dine upstairs on the third-floor patio for views of the Missouri River. | 217 S. Main St. | 636/947–3334 | $10.50–$18.95 | AE, D, DC, MC, V.

Mother-In-Law House. American/Casual. Missouri River catfish and local produce are always on the menu, but the restaurant's reputation is for its made-from-scratch pie crusts. The restaurant is in a building built in 1866 for the owner's mother-in-law and has a great view of the Missouri River. | 500 S. Main St. | 636/946–9444 | Reservations essential | Closed Sun. | $7.50–$12 | D, MC, V.

Boone's Lick Trail Inn. This Federal-style hostelry with a galleried porch was built in the 1840s. The only inn within the historic district, it's also within walking distance of the Katy Trail, downtown shops and museums, and the Missouri. Owner Venetia McEntire is the chairperson of the St. Charles Lewis and Clark Bicentennial Commission and can answer any questions you have about Lewis and Clark in her city. Rooms are furnished with period antiques and some reproductions. Fresh flowers are placed in every room before a guest checks in. No smoking. | 1000 S. Main St., 63301 | 636/947–7000 or 888/940–0002 | fax 636/946–2637 | www.booneslick.com | 6 rooms | $125–$175 | AE, D, DC, MC, V | BP.

Geery's Bed & Breakfast. If you ever wanted to talk with Lewis and Clark about their experience, you may well consider a conversation with Peter Geery the next best thing. Geery plays Corps member John Ordway in an expedition reeanactment team that has traveled the entire route of Lewis and Clark by river. When not organizing trips along the Missouri, Geery and his wife, Marilyn, operate this Victorian inn with three porches and lots of Scottish antiques. No smoking. | 720 S. 5th St., 63301 | 636/916–5344 | fax 636/916–4702 | www.geerys.com | 3 rooms | $65–$125 | MC, V | BP.

AUGUSTA

▼▼

When Augusta was founded in 1836 as the town of Mount Pleasant, it was built right along the Missouri River. But the river changed course in the 1870s, leaving several hundred acres of fertile farmland between Augusta and the river. Situated high on a bluff, the town provides a view of the river for some distance.

One of the more defining moments of the journey happened near here on May 23, 1804, as Meriwether Lewis was exploring the cliffs around Tavern Cave. He slipped and fell more than 20 feet before he caught himself by digging his knife into the cliffside. Today the cave includes the names and drawings of several explorers over the years, including Lewis's.

◆ INFORMATION
Greater Augusta Chamber of Commerce | Box 31, 63332 | 636/228–4005 | www.augusta-missouri.com.

SITES TO SEE
Tavern Cave. On the south side of the river is a cave measuring about 40 feet by 20 feet that is mentioned in the journals of Lewis and Clark, as well as in the diaries of other explorers. The names of those who traveled the river in the early 19th century are carved inside. | Park at St. Albans and walk 2 mi north along the railroad tracks | Free | Daily.

Fort Charrette. A local historian has relocated three log cabins from the 1820s to this area to re-create the image of the Fort Charrette trading post. The buildings are furnished with period antiques, and even the fences and gates of the village date from the late 1700s. | 2 mi east of Washington on Rte. 100 | 636/239–4202 | Free | Variable hrs.

MARTHASVILLE
▼▼▼

The first settlement here, which dates back to 1763, was known as LaCharrette to the French fur traders and trappers. Lewis and Clark had intended to spend the winter of 1803 at LaCharrette in order to organize their expedition. However, the official transfer of the territory had not yet taken place and Spanish authorities would not allow the expedition members into the region. When the Corps eventually arrived in LaCharrette in May 1804, the town consisted of seven houses, lean-tos, and shanties. The families shared eggs and milk with the Corps members. Some of the journals refer to LaCharrette as St. John's, a Spanish name.

On the return trip in September 1806, the journals record "a shout . . . raised for joy" when the members of the Corps saw cows grazing near the river. This was a sign they were getting close to civilization and to home. After several adventures in the West, Corps member John Colter returned to this area to live and is buried south of the Missouri River somewhere between New Haven and Washington. The Katy Trail now passes through the town, which was renamed Marthasville in 1817 for the wife of the man who platted the area.

✦ INFORMATION
Marthasville Area Chamber of Commerce | Box 95, 63357 | 636/433–5242.

SITES TO SEE
Interpretive Marker and Kiosk. This marker includes journal entries from May 25, 1804, including meeting with a French trapper who had just returned from Sioux country. | Adjacent to City Park | Free | Daily.

HERMANN
▼▼▼

The Corps camped on the east side of Loutre Island across from what is now Hermann. During their time here, the men organized themselves into crews for each boat and assigned duties to each person. The journals mention grapes growing wild on the banks here, a fact that attracted the German Settlement Society of Philadelphia into the area. In 1836, the group intended Hermann to be a self-supporting refuge for people of German heritage and traditions. Like the Rhine River region of Germany, the area the Society chose for its town was teeming with grapevines, and for many years wine production was the area's main industry. Today, the village comes alive in October with the celebration of Oktoberfest.

✦ INFORMATION
Gasconade County Historical Society | 315 Schiller St., 65041 | 573/486–3200.
Hermann Visitors Bureau | 312 Schiller St., 65401 | 573/486–2744 or 800/932–8687 | www.hermannmo.com.

✦ ON THE CALENDAR
May **Maifest.** This typically German festival includes a storytelling festival in the streets of downtown Hermann and a family reunion of descendants of John Colter, the Corps member who later settled near Hermann. | 573/486–2744 or 800/932–8687.

HISTORIC LODGING
White House Hotel. Near the old train station, this four-story, 32-room hotel dating from 1868 is now partially restored as a B&B and museum. Owner Bob Plummer is a member of the Corps of Discovery reenactment team based in St. Charles and is an area authority on Lewis and Clark. One of the third-floor rooms is devoted to the expedition and includes many of Plummer's costumes and his equipment. Guest rooms are furnished with period

antiques. The bridal suite overlooks the Missouri. No room phones, no smoking, no kids. | 232 Wharf St., 65041 | 573/486–3200 or 573/676–5951 | 5 rooms | $75–$85 | Closed Jan.–Mar. | No credit cards | BP.

JEFFERSON CITY

▼▼

On June 3, 1804, the expedition reached the area of Jefferson City, where Clark wrote in his journal that he was tormented by mosquitoes and ticks. Not established until 1821, the town was named for the president who sent Lewis and Clark forward. Thomas Jefferson was apparently pleased by this honor, and many new citizens who settled here were his friends and associates from Virginia.

Although the first state capitol building was completed in 1826, several mid-Missouri towns squabbled over which would become the seat of state government until 1911, when Jefferson City was named the capital. Today, the capitol building sits high above the banks of the Missouri, and its lighted dome is visible from the river for miles.

✦ INFORMATION

Jefferson City Convention and Visitors Bureau | 213 Adams St., 65102 | 573/632–2820 or 800/769–4183 | www.visitjeffersoncity.org. **Missouri Lewis and Clark Bicentennial Commission** | 100 Jefferson St., 65102 | 573/522–9019 | www.lewisandclark.state.mo.us.

SITES TO SEE

Clark's Hill/Norton State Historic Site. William Clark first climbed this hill on June 1, 1804, noting that the rocks afforded "a delightful prospect" of both the Missouri and Osage rivers. A number of the Corps members joined him and carved their initials on the rocks, which are still visible today. In June 2002, 13 acres surrounding this site and nearby Native American burial grounds were donated to the state of Missouri by the William Norton family, fifth-generation Missourians, to become Missouri's 83rd state park. | Rte. J, 3 mi east of Jefferson City | 573/751–6510 | www.mostateparks.com | Free | Daily.

Jefferson Landing State Historic Site. This is one of the few remaining 19th-century river landings on the Missouri. Two buildings tell of the time when this was a busy river port with original loading equipment, barrels, and other goods. A small theater shows videos on the history of the city as well as one entitled "Lewis & Clark: Corps of Discovery in Missouri." | 100 Jefferson St. | 573/751–3475 | www.mostateparks.com | Free | Mon.–Sat. 10–4.

Missouri Information Center. The focal point of the lobby is a series of commissioned works by Missouri artist L. Edward Fisher of the Corps of Discovery in the Jefferson City area. The center also houses numerous records and archives as well as the state library. | 600 W. Main St. | 573/751–2000 | www.sos.state.mo.us | Free | Daily 8–5.

Museum of Military History. The Lewis and Clark exhibit here highlights the military aspects of the expedition such as discipline, teamwork, and uniforms. Other exhibits include a hands-on activity for children and displays on local Native American history. A deck overlooks the Missouri and has interpretive panels citing journal entries from the days the Corps passed through this area. | 2007 Retention Dr. | 573/638–9603 | www.moguard.com/museum/mong/museum | Free | Weekdays 8–3.

State Capitol Building. A 13-foot-tall bronze statue of Thomas Jefferson welcomes visitors at the center of the great stairway at this building's main entrance. Opposite the capitol, a riverfront park provides a vantage point from which you can survey Missouri River country. A second statue of Jefferson in the park commemorates the signing of the Louisiana Purchase. Inside the capitol stand statues of Meriwether Lewis, William Clark, and Sacagawea. In the senate chamber is a four-panel mural by Richard E. Miller entitled *President Jefferson Greets Lewis and Clark*. Tours are conducted hourly. | High St. | 573/751–4127 | www.visitjeffersoncity.org/capitol | Free | Daily 8–5.

✦ ON THE CALENDAR
Apr. 2004 **Signing of the Louisiana Purchase.** This ceremony at the capitol building reenacts the signing of the Louisiana Purchase. | 573/751–4127.

HISTORIC LODGING
Huber's Ferry Bed & Breakfast. As Lewis and Clark explored the mouth of the Osage River in late May 1804, it is likely they traveled past the bluff that is now home to Barbara and David Plummer's B&B. Built in 1881 as a home to one of the area's German settlers, the house is now on the National Register of Historic Places. Barbara and David are members of several local historical societies and often host guests traveling the Lewis and Clark Trail. The home is filled with family heirlooms and period antiques. Guest rooms are bright and spacious, some have fireplaces, and all have a view of the rivers or garden. No room phones, no smoking. | Box 159, Rte. 501, at the junction of U.S. 50 and Rte. 635, 65101 | 573/455–2979 or 877/454–2979 | fax 573/455–9806 | www.bbim.org/huber | 4 rooms | $65–$95 | D, MC, V | BP.

COLUMBIA

Founded in 1819, Columbia is home to the University of Missouri–Columbia, the first land-grant university in the Louisiana Purchase, and university activities and events dominate the town. However, it is also home to the State Historical Society of Missouri and is an access point to the Katy Trail. Because of its central location and easy access to Interstate 70, most state conventions and conferences are held in the area and it makes a good base for exploring Lewis and Clark sites within the state.

✦ INFORMATION

Columbia Chamber of Commerce | 300 S. Providence Rd., 65203 | 573/874–1132 | www.visitcolumbiamo.com. **State Historical Society of Missouri** | 1020 Lowery St., 65201 | 573/882–7083 | www.system.missouri.edu/shs.

SITES TO SEE

Midway Expo Center Tipi. This conference and exhibition center includes an authentic Cheyenne tepee that is available for private events. Activities include bonfires, hayrides, archery, and buffalo-stew dinners. | 6401 U.S. 40 | 573/445–8338 | Variable hrs.

University of Missouri. Founded in 1839 as the first public land-grant university in the Louisiana Purchase, "Mizzou" is recognized internationally for its journalism and veterinary science programs. Visually, the university is recognized by the four quad columns in the center of campus, the major gathering spot for students and campus visitors. The Mizzou Quad is modeled after the University of Virginia, which Thomas Jefferson founded. On the campus Quad is **Thomas Jefferson's Original Grave Marker** (Free | Daily), which came to Missouri on July 4, 1885, from Monticello. Interpretive panels near the grave marker detail Jefferson's commitment to education. The **Museum of Art and Archaeology** (Pickard Hall, corner of 9th St. and University Ave. | 573/882–3591 | Free | Wed.–Sat. 10–4) houses more than 13,000 works from five millennia and six continents. An outfitted fur trader's canoe, Pacific Northwest cultural artifacts, a replica pioneer cabin, and Native American artifacts are of interest to Lewis and Clark historians. | S. 6th St. between Stewart Rd. and Elm St. | 573/882–6333 or 573/882–2121 | www.missouri.edu | Free | Daily.

ROCHEPORT

The Corps passed through this area first on June 7, 1804, and again on September 19, 1806. Clark noted seeing a number of rattlesnakes on the limestone bluffs and finding curious paintings and carvings on the rocks. The

The Journey Continues

In reading the journals and studying the efforts of the Corps members, one can easily wonder, "Does the modern-day adventurer have the character, the stamina, the courage, and the vision to do what was accomplished 200 years ago?" The answer is yes.

In 1984, Glen Bishop, a St. Charles native, began building a full-size keelboat according to William Clark's original expedition notes and naval drawings. For 14 years, Bishop labored over the boat, which eventually won first-place awards in the 1992 Washington, D.C., Independence Day parade. It was considered the most authentic reproduction of the Lewis and Clark keelboat ever built.

Not satisfied with that accomplishment, Bishop and a crew of other river enthusiasts took the keelboat on a 450-mi journey from Wood River, Illinois, to St. Joseph, following the journal notes to the degree that a modern river would allow. That 1996 journey was the first in a series of reenactments that have now received national recognition as the official Corps of Discovery reenactment. Since that time, volunteers have built the two pirogues, taking five months to construct the white one and eight months to produce the red one. The expedition has twice retraced all portions of the Missouri rivers traveled by the original Corps of Discovery.

The 21st-century team is a little larger than that of 200 years ago for reasons of simple economics. Because the modern-day Corps is made up of volunteers and not paid by the United States government, few can afford to leave jobs and families for more than a few weeks at a time. About 260 men, mostly of retirement age, regularly reenact the journey on various portions of the river. The average age of the original Corps was 29; the average age of the modern Corps is 49.

A few other changes include those imposed by the Coast Guard for water safety. Both pirogues and the keelboat have life jackets as required by law. Other additions include a radio and motors. The keelboat has a 115-horsepower motor; the pirogues each have a 50-horsepower motor. The modern Corps was successful in persuading the Coast Guard not to require running lights and navigation lights because the original Corps did not travel at night or in foggy weather.

Despite these modern accommodations, today's Corps members often paddle or pole the boats in many parts of the river. In the more shallow water, they actually pull the boats upstream by rope as the original Corps often did. Members are assigned duties as hunters and gatherers, as with the original team. Although some of that gathering takes place at local supermarkets on the route, a good deal is actually hunted by rifle. The Corps members dry their own meats and regularly consume buffalo, elk, venison, and goose. Other allowances for the 21st century include sleeping bags, modern latrines, and necessary medications.

The authenticity, however, is carried out through clothing, language, and equipment. Perhaps the most authentic element of the modern voyage is the reenactor who plays William Clark. His name is Charles Clark, the sixth-generation grandson of the team's co-leader. The crew also travels with a black Newfoundland dog, although today he responds to the name Meriwether rather than Seaman.

Glen Bishop, the founder of the modern Corps of Discovery, died in October 2001, but his spirit, and the spirit of the original Corps of Discovery, lives on in educational programs and study of American history brought to towns along the great rivers of America by the modern Corps of Discovery.

town of Rocheport was not founded for another 30 years after the Corps returned. The ferry crossing here made the little town a thriving river port until the 1880s when the railroad came through.

Today, the entire town is listed on the National Register of Historic Places. In addition to being an access point for the Katy Trail, Rocheport is a haven for antiques shops and art galleries and provides views of the Missouri River. The carvings noted in Clark's journal, as well as the rattlesnakes, are still visible.

◆ INFORMATION
Columbia Convention and Visitors Bureau | 300 S. Providence Rd., Columbia, 65203 | 573/875–1231 or 800/652–0987 | www.visitcolumbiamo.com.

SITES TO SEE
Katy Trail State Park. A 165-mi segment of this 225-mi-long rails-to-trails biking and hiking path is designated an official segment of the Lewis and Clark National Historic Trail. The Katy Trail is perhaps the best way to experience the natural beauty of the river that Lewis and Clark experienced, whether you are a bicyclist, hiker, history buff, or nature lover. Here, you can touch

A Musical Journey

". . . they spent the evening with much hilarity, singing and dancing," wrote Meriwether Lewis on April 26, 1805. The journals of the Lewis and Clark expedition contain references to some 30 occasions when the men turned to song and dance for their own recreation or to entertain and impress the Indian people they met. One of those events was New Year's Day 1805 at Fort Mandan.

The Native Americans also incorporated music to communicate with the Corps. According to the journal of Patrick Gass on August 30, 1804, ". . . the Indians came over the river. Four of them, who were musicians, went backwards and forwards, through and round our camp, singing and making a noise."

Music continues as a part of the journey today with the nation's first musical drama about the Lewis and Clark expedition. The University of Missouri, the first public land-grant college in the former Louisiana Territory, commissioned a three-act work entitled *Corps of Discovery* to commemorate the Bicentennial. In three acts, the opera depicts the journey at the personal level of the Corps, from the youngest corporal to the tragic death of Meriwether Lewis. A star that surfaces in the play is the route itself in the form of the Missouri River. Highlighting the cultural diversity of the Corps members and the Native Americans encountered along the journey, "Corps of Discovery" celebrates the lasting gifts of friendship and understanding that Lewis and Clark brought to this country. To ensure the historical and cultural accuracy, the creative team of Michael Ching and Hugh Moffatt consulted with historians and Native American advisers.

The world premiere performance of *Corps of Discovery* was at the University of Missouri. It is now on tour at cities along the trail and across the United States.

the limestone bluffs, hear the rustle of the cottonwood trees, and take in the long, scenic stretches of the Missouri River. You'll find one of the most popular trailheads and access in Rocheport at 1st Street, which is right in the middle of the National Historic Trail. You can also access the trail in Columbia, Clinton, Sedalia, Hermann, and St. Charles. At mile marker 174, between Rocheport and Huntsdale, the **Lewis and Clark Cave** (573/751–8459 | Free | Daily) appears where Torbett Springs runs off of a bluff. It's one of the most scenic sites on the trail because of its height above the river, but no evidence exists to indicate that Lewis and Clark actually explored this cave, although they did explore many caves along the river. The cave is gated off to explorers shortly after the mouth to protect breeding bats inside. Of greater interest to many are the Native American pictographs about 50 feet above the cave. | Box 166, Boonville, 65233 | 660/882–8196 | www.mostateparks.com | Free | Daily.

✦ ON THE CALENDAR
June **Katy Trail Bike Ride.** This five-day, guide-led ride covers 160 mi on the Historic Trail. | 660/882–8196.

BOONVILLE
▼▼

Just four years after the Corps returned along the Missouri River, European settlers had made a home in the fertile farming community that is now Boonville. Named for frontiersman Daniel Boone, Boonville remains a small but active river community.

✦ INFORMATION
Boonville Chamber of Commerce | 320 1st St., 65233 | 660/882–2721 | www. c-magic.com/boonvill. **Friends of Historic Boonville** | Box 1776, 65233 | 660/ 882–7977 or 888/588–1477.

✦ ON THE CALENDAR
June **Heritage Days.** As the Corps of Discovery Reenactment crew camps on the riverbank, downtown is filled with a Lewis and Clark art show, crafts demonstrations, and music. | 660/882–7977.

SITES TO SEE
Harley Park Overlook. You can have a picnic lunch and see down the river for miles from this park. Two interpretive panels here detail the exploits of the Corps of Discovery in June 1804. | W. Spring St. | 660/882–2721 | Free | Daily.

HISTORIC DINING AND LODGING
Settler's Inn. American/Casual. Buffalo brisket and fried chicken are among the many family-style dishes served on tin campware in this log-cabin-like structure. The inn serves dinner on Friday and Saturday nights only, at 7:30. | 16920 Rte. 135 | 660/882–3125 | Reservations essential | $15 | No credit cards.

Rivercene Bed & Breakfast. This Victorian mansion, built in 1864, is across the Missouri from Boonville and provides a great view of the river for several miles. Owner Ron Lenz is president of Friends of Historic Boonville and is quite knowledgeable about river lore and about Lewis and Clark history. Some rooms have fireplaces and all are spacious, with period antiques and some reproduction furniture. The gas lamps and hardwood floors are all original. Some in-room hot tubs; no room phones, no smoking. | 127 Rte. 463, New Franklin, 65274 | 660/848–2497 or 800/531–0862 | fax 660/848–2142 | www. rivercene.com | 9 rooms | $90–$150 | D, MC, V | BP.

ARROW ROCK

▼▼

The name Arrow Rock comes from the flint rocks on this bluff above the Missouri River, where Native Americans gathered stone for arrowheads. Lewis and Clark noted the bluff and nearby salt licks in their journals, as well as its panoramic view of the waterway.

Arrow Rock continued as an important stop for those traveling the river throughout the 19th century. The town was founded in 1829 and remnants of its early history still exist: a working blacksmith shop, a gunsmith shop that has operated continuously since 1840, and century-old buildings and businesses. The entire town is on the National Register of Historic Places, and many authentic cabins operate as inns.

✦ INFORMATION
Historic Arrow Rock Council | Box 15, Arrow Rock, 65320 | 660/837–3335 | www.arrowrock.org.

SITES TO SEE
Arrow Rock State Historic Site Visitor Center. Displays here are arranged in chronological order from the days of the earliest Native American presence in the Missouri Valley to the present. "The Waterway West" details the Louisiana Purchase, the Lewis and Clark adventure, and its impact on the Missouri River system. | 4th St. and Van Buren St. | 660/837–3330 | www. mostateparks.com | Free | June–Aug., daily 10–5; Sept.–Nov. and Mar.–May, daily 10–4; Dec.–Feb., weekends 10–4.

Van Meter State Park. Black-walnut trees and wildflowers surround an Indian village site from 10,000 BC. Of special interest is the "old fort," a 6-acre Missouri Indian earthwork of unknown purpose. Interpretive markers detail the expedition's visit to the area in June 1804 and September 1806. To reach the park take Route 41 north to Route 122 and head west 5 mi until you see signs for the park. | Rte. 122, Miami, 65334 | 660/886–7537 | www.mostateparks. com | Free | Daily 7–10. Visitor center: Oct.–Apr., Wed.–Mon. 10–4; May–Sept., daily 10–4.

Oct. Arrow Rock Heritage Crafts Festival. On the second weekend of the month, costumed artisans demonstrate their prowess in such 19th-century skills as basketmaking, wood carving, and quilting in several historic buildings along Main Street. | 660/837–3231.

HISTORIC DINING AND LODGING

Historic Arrow Rock Tavern. American/Casual. Built in 1834 by Joseph Huston, one of the first settlers in the region, the Tavern is the oldest continuously operating restaurant west of the Mississippi River. Elk here comes in burgers and steaks. But the Tavern is equally popular for fried chicken and ham dinners served family-style. Candlelight dinners during the holidays require reservations. | 302 Main St. | 660/837–3200 | Closed Mon. May–Sept. and weekdays Oct.–Apr. | $12–$16 | AE, D, MC, V.

Borgman's Bed & Breakfast. Built in the 1850s by a relative of Missouri artist George Caleb Bingham, this simple clapboard farmhouse has original plank floors and woodwork throughout. Many family heirlooms, antiques, and quilts fill the spacious, cheery rooms. One guest room on the first floor and three on the second floor share three bathrooms. Kathy Borgman works for the Friends of Arrow Rock and knows just about all there is to know about this community. No room phones, no smoking. | 706 Van Buren | 660/837–3350 | 4 rooms | $55–$60 | No credit cards | BP.

Down Over Bed & Breakfast. This blue-painted 1912 bungalow in the center of town has a wraparound porch complete with swing. The sprawling main house is called a "Stick-style," an unusual construction style for mid-Missouri. One room, named the Lewis and Clark Room, has a bay window and private deck with king-size brass bed and handmade quilts. Most rooms are decorated in bright pastels and antiques. The cottage has its own kitchen. No room phones, no smoking. | 602 Main St. | 660/837–3268 | 5 rooms, 1 cottage | $55–$95 | AE, D, MC, V | BP.

GLASGOW

▼▼

French fur trappers had already settled at this bend in the river, where the Chariton River flows into the Missouri, by June 1804. The Corps spent the night with French traders in this area and noted that the land was good and well timbered; a hunting party traveled up the Chariton a few miles and killed a bear here. It is believed that the trading post was named for John Chariton, a leader of the trading party that was headquartered there. Today, the county bears his name. The town of Glasgow was founded in 1836 by James Glasgow and is home to the oldest library west of the Mississippi.

The Construction of Fort Clark

". . . a high commanding position, more than 70 feet above high-water mark, and overlooking the river, which is here but of little depth" is how William Clark described the site in 1804 that would become the second U.S. outpost in the Louisiana Purchase. On September 4, 1808, Clark returned to this point on the river near Independence with a unit of nearly 80 dragoons to begin building Fort Osage. In all, more than 160 men worked on the fort, including Nathan Boone, youngest son of Daniel Boone, and Reuben Lewis, Meriwether's youngest brother.

Clark's first task was to determine the placement of the blockhouse and other structures that would eventually total 17 in a triangular shape. Men began felling trees and moving them into position with horses and wagons. Heavy rain, however, slowed work, but by September 15, the fort had become a reality. A blacksmith shop was complete, the blockhouse was nearly completed, and a roof covered two buildings for trade goods.

During this time, 75 Osage chiefs and warriors arrived at the site. On September 13, Clark met with the Osage leaders and agreed to a treaty wherein the Osage would relinquish their lands between the Missouri and Arkansas rivers. The treaty was later rejected and replaced by one written by Meriwether Lewis, who was serving as governor of the Louisiana Territory.

On September 16 Clark departed back downriver via keelboat. He was accompanied by two chiefs who had signed the treaty. When the treaty began to unravel, one of the attempts to save relations was to rename the fort in honor of the Native Americans. On November 10, Fort Clark became Fort Osage, which it remains today. As exploration expanded the western frontier, the fort was abandoned in 1827.

The purpose of Fort Clark was to house soldiers to guard the new territory, to protect trade, and to help the U.S. government in befriending the Native Americans. It also provided early settlers along the Missouri River a stopping point for supplies and rest. Today Fort Osage is a National Historic Landmark. The replica, built according to War Department record and on the original footings unearthed in an archaeological dig, now contains 12 buildings. Its purpose is to educate and entertain visitors with reenactments, festivals, and heritage workshops. Its commanding view of the Missouri River remains as it did when William Clark first climbed this bluff in June 1804.

Glasgow Chamber of Commerce | 100 Market St., 65254 | 660/338–2377 | www.historicglasgowmo.com.

SITES TO SEE
Missouri River Overlook. From this overlook, you can see the mouth of the Chariton River as it joins the Missouri and Stump Island, which was mentioned in a June 10, 1804, journal entry. Picnic tables and running water are available. | One block west of Main St. | 660/338–2377 | www.historicglasgowmo.com | Free | Daily.

✦ ON THE CALENDAR
May **Stump Island Encampment.** Reenactors and period-dressed artisans celebrate the river history of Chariton County. | 660/338–2377.

LEXINGTON
▼▼

Sergeant Ordway's journal noted the abundance of gooseberries and raspberries along the Missouri River banks in the area of what is today Lexington; these are still in evidence today. Fruit farms and orchards contribute to tourism and the local economy. Much of Lexington's history centers on a Civil War battle fought here in 1863—a battle in which William Clark's grandson Captain Churchill Clark participated.

✦ INFORMATION
Lexington Tourism Bureau | Box 132, 64067 | 660/259–4711 | www.historiclexington.com.

SITES TO SEE
Lexington Heritage Tours. Riverfront tours exploring the days when Lexington was a busy river port and Lewis and Clark history of the region are among the specialized programs arranged by this company. | 608 Highland Ave. | 660/259–2094 | Variable hrs.

INDEPENDENCE
▼▼

During the Corps time here, Clark went ashore to hunt and became separated from the party. In his journal, he writes about getting mired in mud and being tormented by mosquitoes. Exactly where in this part of Jackson County he wandered is uncertain, but by signaling with a shot of his rifle he realized he was about 6 mi from the Corps.

Today's Independence is synonymous with westward expansion. The first settlers arrived in what would become Independence in 1827, and the area became a starting point for those heading to the American West via the Santa Fe, California, and Oregon trails. In the 1920s the town proved itself to be a different sort of starting point, when a country lawyer by the name of Harry S. Truman opened a law office here. Today you can stop in at the Harry S. Truman Library and Museum, as well as numerous other historic spots.

✦ INFORMATION

Independence Chamber of Commerce | 210 W. Truman Rd., 64050 | 816/252–4745 | www.independencechamber.com. **Jackson County Historical Society** | 129 W. Lexington Ave., 64050 | 816/461–1897 | www.jchs.org.

SITES TO SEE

Fort Osage. Overlooking the bends of the Missouri River, this site was noted in Clark's journal entry as "a high commanding position, more than 70 feet above high-water mark, and overlooking the river, which is here but of little depth." Erected in 1808 under the direction of Clark, Fort Osage was the second U.S. outpost built in the Louisiana Purchase. In 1941, the fort was reconstructed, including the Factory building and the remaining four blockhouses, officers' quarters, soldiers' barracks, and surrounding log stockade. Fort Osage was recognized as a National Historic Landmark in 1961 and today provides tours and history programs. You can reach the fort, which is about 14 mi northeast of Independence, by taking U.S. 24 to Buckner, then heading north to Sibley. From Sibley there are signs. | 105 Osage St., Sibley | 816/795–8200 or 816/249–5737 | www.historicfortosage.com | $5 | Apr.–Nov., Wed.–Sun. 9–4:30; Dec.–Mar., weekends 9–4:30.

National Frontier Trails Center. The only national center dedicated to the study of the western trails has a section devoted to Lewis and Clark. A floor-to-ceiling map details the route taken; other exhibits include a compass, mapping equipment, combs, and clothing authentic to the period of the expedition. An interactive computer game tests your knowledge of the trail. The Merrill J. Mattes Research Library is recognized as the largest collection of books, documents, and manuscripts on the westward expansion. The gift shop has additional books, videos, and maps available for purchase. | 318 W. Pacific | 816/325–7575 | www.frontiertrailscenter.com | $4 | Mon.–Sat. 9–4:30, Sun. 12:30–4:30.

✦ ON THE CALENDAR

Sept. **Santa-Cali-Gon Days.** The history of the wagon trains that started west from here is celebrated on Truman Square with period crafts, authentic food, reenactors, and more. | 816/252–4745.

KANSAS CITY

▼▼▼

One of William Clark's strengths was identifying points along the river that had all of the assets for becoming permanent settlements or forts. Kansas City, at the junction of the Kansas (Kaw) and the Missouri rivers, was one of those locations. Today Kansas City is the largest metropolitan area along the Lewis and Clark Trail. The Corps spent several days in this area in late June 1804 and passed through again in early September 1806. It was a short 15 years later, in 1821, that French fur trader François Choteau established the fur trading post that would become Kansas City. The town quickly became a significant river port and played a major role in American history as a gateway for pioneers heading west along the Oregon, California, and Santa Fe trails. In the mid-1800s, settlers, missionaries, and traders began their overland journeys here or from nearby Independence and Westport. Several Civil War battles were fought here, and the 33rd president of the United States, Harry S. Truman, began his political career here.

✦ INFORMATION

Convention and Visitors Bureau of Greater Kansas City | 1100 Main St., 64105 | 816/221–5242 | www.visitkc.org.

SITES TO SEE

Arabia Steamboat Museum. In 1856, the steamboat *Arabia,* loaded with goods for frontier towns along the Missouri, sank with a full load near Parkville. In 1988, the boat was found buried in the river, its goods fully preserved. A video tells a dramatic story of river exploration from the days of Lewis and Clark until the time the wrecked steamboat was uncovered. Exhibits change on a monthly basis as new items are restored. Among those are glass beads, buttons, a full set of china, food items, and period clothing. | 400 Grand Blvd., in the River Market | 816/471–1856 | www.1856.com | $9.75 | Mon.–Sat. 10–6, Sun. noon–5.

City Market. As the city of Kansas City grew, this area adjacent to the Missouri River was filled with warehouses and loading docks for the many steamboats making their way with people and supplies along the water. The expedition came ashore nearby in 1804 and 1806. Today, the market is a central location with a variety of vendors and restaurants and a lively roster of riverfront events. **Berkley Riverfront Park,** a mile-long esplanade named after a long-time mayor of Kansas City, provides a paved walking path atop the levee overlooking the Missouri. Interpretive panels and artwork detail river history, including events connected with the Lewis and Clark expedition. The park is the beginning of the **Riverfront Heritage Trail,** a 9-mi walking-biking trail along the Missouri, which links historical and cultural sites on both sides of the state line. | Main and 5th Sts. | 816/842–1271 | www.kc-citymarket.com | Free | Daily.

Clark's Point. At this point, overlooking the confluence of the Missouri and Kansas rivers, a bronze plaque designates the spot as being the one Lewis and Clark visited on September 15, 1806. A statue of the explorers together with Sacagawea, York, and Seaman is also in the small park. | Between 8th and 10th Sts. on Jefferson | Free | Daily.

Discovery Center. This Missouri Department of Conservation Center, named in honor of the Corps of Discovery, explores the flora and fauna of Missouri, one of the Corps' objectives. Hands-on activities for children include plant identification, water management, and cooking natural foods. Programming throughout the year focuses on the expedition and the natural elements of the state. | 4750 Troost Blvd. | 816/759–7300 | www.kcconservation.com | Free; additional fee for classes | Mon.–Wed. and Sat. 8–5, Thurs. 8–8.

Kansas City Museum. Originally an ornate 70-room mansion, the museum displays exhibits on frontier life and early regional history. The Lewis and Clark area includes a replica of the keelboat they used. Other exhibits include an Osage Indian lodge, and native animal and plant life. | 3218 Gladstone Blvd. | 816/483–8300 | www.kcmuseum.com | $3 | Tues.–Sat. 9:30–4:30, Sun. noon–4:30.

Pioneer Park. Many wagons departed from here for the Santa Fe Trail. A large map in the ground of this small park in the historic Westport district shows the routes of westward expansion. | Westport Rd. and Broadway | Free | Daily.

✦ ON THE CALENDAR

July **A Journey Fourth.** Held in conjunction with activities in nearby Atchison and Leavenworth, Kansas, this Independence Day event includes a reenactment of the Corps' first Fourth of July, riverboat cruises, an air show, and fireworks. | 816/691–3846.

HISTORIC DINING

Stroud's. American/Casual. The two front rooms of this sprawling farmstead restaurant date back to 1827 and once served as a stagecoach stop on the route to St. Joseph. Stroud's is best known for its fried chicken dinner and homemade biscuits. The rooms remain rustic with low ceilings, uneven wood floors, and wooden tables. | 5410 N.E. Oak Ridge Dr. | 816/454–9600 | Closed Mon.–Thurs. No lunch | $10.95–$15.95 | AE, D, DC, MC, V.

PARKVILLE AND WESTON

▼▼▼

The journal entries made by Clark as the Corps moved through what is now Platte County describe the area as "the most butifull Plains I ever Saw, open and butifully diversified with hills and vallies all presenting themselves to the river covered with grass and a few scattering trees." Today, Platte County is the most affluent county in the state, with top-rated schools and a diverse economy that includes the Kansas City International Airport. However, when locals think of Platte County, they usually think of the historic, well-preserved river communities of Parkville and Weston.

Parkville was founded in 1844 and for several years was a busier river port than Kansas City. Although the river channel has moved south by several hundred yards since the days of Lewis and Clark, the water still dominates life in Parkville, whose downtown was devastated by the Great Flood of 1993.

Nearby Weston was founded in 1837 and its role as a 19th-century river port has earned the entire town a designation as a National Historic District. During flooding on the Missouri River in 1858, the channel moved west, but a marker at the end of Main Street in Weston designates where the channel was and where Lewis and Clark would have camped. Today, Weston is popular among antiques lovers and crafts hunters.

✦ INFORMATION

Parkville City Hall | 1201 East St., 64152 | 816/741–7676 | www.parkvillemo. com. **Platte County Convention and Visitors Bureau** | 415 3rd St., Platte City, 64079 | 816/858–3349 | www.co.platte.mo.us. **Weston Development Company** | 502 Main St., 64098 | 816/640–2909 | www.ci.weston.mo.us.

SITES TO SEE

Bear Medison Island Marker. In downtown Weston, an interpretive marker describes the changes in the Missouri River channel and the location of Bear Medison Island, where the Corps stopped for a four-hour rest on July 2, 1804, to install a new mast on the keelboat. | North Bluff Rd. | 816/640–2909 | Free | Daily.

Cow Island Marker. Now the site of a major electrical power plant for Kansas City, this area was so named by the French trappers who kept cows on the island. An interpretive marker includes Clark's journal entries of passing the area, noting large beaver and nut trees, as well as his other find—a horse. | 5 mi north of Weston on Rte. 45 at Iatan | 816/858–3349 | www.co.platte. mo.us | Free | Daily.

English Landing Park. An interpretive marker in this riverfront park describes the changes in the river channel, the abundant wildlife noted in the journals, and details of the keelboat's operation on the river. The 3-mi walking trail on the river's edge affords a waterfront perspective of the fierce current and driftwood obstacles the Corps members battled every day. | South end of Main St., Parkville | 816/741–7676 | www.parkvillemo.com | Free | Daily.

Lewis and Clark State Park. Lewis and Clark found the banks of Sugar Lake to be an ideal spot for bird-watching when they first explored here in July 1804. Clark wrote that "the great quantity of those fowl in this lake induced me to call it the Gosling Lake." Today, the former Gosling Lake is popular with bird-watchers and campers. An interpretive display details the Corps' activities on July 3–4, 1804. The park has a 121-acre campground and a 365-acre lake and provides modern camping facilities and opportunities for fishing, swimming, and boating. The park is about 20 mi northwest of Weston. | Rte. 138, Rushville, 64484 | 816/579–5564 | Free | Daily.

Weston Bend State Park. A scenic overlook provides a view of the Missouri River, Fort Leavenworth, and beyond. The interpretive sign at the overlook describes how and why the river has changed over the years and identifies locations referenced in the explorers' journals. A hiking trail meanders through the woods and along the edge of the bluff, providing still other great vistas. | 16600 Rte. 45 N | 816/640–5443 | www.mostateparks.com | Free | Oct., Nov., Mar., and Apr., daily 7 AM–8 PM; Dec.–Feb., daily 8–5; May–Sept., daily 7 AM–10 PM.

◆ ON THE CALENDAR

June **Lewis and Clark Tradin' Days.** This two-day festival held the third weekend in June along Main Street brings together Native American tribes of the region in a cultural celebration with dances, food, and crafts. | 816/640–2909.

Ongoing **Park University Lecture Series.** A number of nationally recognized scholars on Lewis and Clark and western exploration present public lectures at Park University in Parkville. | 816/741–2000.

HISTORIC DINING AND LODGING

American Bowman. American/Casual. Portions of this building, Weston's oldest restaurant, date back to 1842. Kerosene lighting and hand-hewn log tables make the place feel especially authentic. Owner Pat O'Malley is an area history buff and will be glad to join you at your table to answer any questions. Irish and other imported beers are on the menu, which also includes prime rib, chicken, and quail. | 500 Welt St. | 816/640–5235 | Closed Mon. | $8–$15 | D, MC, V.

Hatchery House. This Federal-style home within walking distance of downtown historic attractions was built in 1845 by Weston's first mayor, but it got its name during the period it was a boardinghouse for newlyweds. All four guest rooms have private baths, queen-size beds, and views of the river. Two rooms have balconies. Some in-room hot tubs; no room phones, no smoking. | 618 Short St., Weston | 816/640–5700 | www.bbim.org/hatchery | 4 rooms | $100–$130 | MC, V | BP.

The Porch Swing Bed & Breakfast. Built in the 1890s as a home for a Park College professor, this stately three-story home with a wraparound porch overlooks Route 9, which is the Lewis and Clark Trail through Parkville. Each room is named for and themed around western characters, including Jesse James, Calamity Jane, Molly Brown, and then Colonel Park, who founded Parkville. Outdoor hot tub, Internet; no room phones, no smoking. | 702 East St. | 816/587–6282 | www.theporchswinginn.com | 4 rooms | $80–$100 | D, MC, V | BP.

ST. JOSEPH
▼▼▼

In 1804, the Corps of Discovery spent about three days in the area that is now St. Joseph and visited again in September 1806. They documented a great deal of wildlife, encountered a strong river current, and suffered from the heat. The river continues to dominate life in this town, affectionately known to locals as St. Jo. Founded in 1826, St. Jo is best known as the home of the Pony Express, the place where Jesse James was killed, and the former site of stockyards filled with hogs and cattle.

✦ INFORMATION
Missouri/Kansas River Bend Chapter of the Lewis and Clark Society | Box 128, 64502-0128 | 816/232–8471. **St. Joseph Convention and Visitors Bureau** | 109 S. 4th St., 64502 | 800/785–0360 | www.stjomo.com.

SITES TO SEE
Glore Psychiatric Museum. Lewis spent four months studying medicine, including psychiatry, in preparation for the care of his men during the journey. Of the many exhibits at the unusual museum is one on the medical aspects of the Lewis and Clark expedition. For that reason, it is a designated site on the Lewis and Clark National Historic Trail. | 3406 Frederick Ave. | 816/837–2310 or 877/837–2310 | www.gloremuseum.org | Free | Mon.–Sat. 9–5, Sun. 1–5.

Jentell Brees Conservation Area. Named for a description in William Clark's journal, this river access is the approximate location of the July 6, 1804, campsite. An interpretive marker includes excerpts from Clark's journal from this area. | South on U.S. 59, 7 mi west on Rte. U, then right on the gravel road at Contrary Creek | 816/271–3100 | www.conservation.state.mo.us | Free | Daily.

St. Joseph Museum. An internationally famous Native American collection, St. Joseph history, and Midwest natural history are featured exhibits here. Also displayed is a detailed Lewis and Clark exhibit, with Clark's journal entries from July 7, 1804, describing St. Michael's Prairie, the site of present-day St. Joseph. A large sculpture of Lewis, Clark, Sacagawea, York, and Seaman stands outside. | 1100 Charles St. | 816/232–8471 | www.stjosephmuseum.org | $2 | Mon.–Sat. 9–5, Sun. 1–5.

✦ ON THE CALENDAR

Aug. Trails West! This arts festival held the third weekend of August in Civic Center Park celebrates the city's heritage of westward migration. Juried fine-arts competitions, displays by artists and crafters, food vendors, and a hands-on children's art area keep things lively. | 816/233–0231 or 800/216–7080.

HISTORIC DINING AND LODGING

Sunset Grill. American/Casual. An interpretive sign here tells of the men's first encounter with the papaw fruit. The modern menu includes catfish, seafood, and steaks, and the dining room has a great view of the river to the west. | 1412 River Rd. | 816/364–6500 | $10.95–$20.95 | AE, D, DC, MC, V.

River Towne Resort. The cabins of this modern resort are on a documented Lewis and Clark campsite in a valley that was sacred to the Native Americans who inhabited this land. The current in the river is more gentle here than in much of Missouri, allowing for swimming from the banks. Restaurant, in-room data ports, some kitchenettes, cable TV, fishing. | 4012 River Rd., 64505 | 816/364–6500 | fax 816/279–7020 | www.rivertowneresort.com | 7 cabins | $110–$165 | AE, D, DC, MC, V.

Kansas

Lewis and Clark spent perhaps less time in what is now Kansas than in any other state along the trail. Nonetheless, the Corps of Discovery encountered significant events that would greatly influence the coming months of the journey. The official Lewis and Clark Trail follows about 123 mi of the Missouri River abutting the northeast corner of Kansas between Kansas City and the Nebraska border. The Corps camped in about eight places in Kansas in 1804 and again in 1806.

For three days in 1804, the Corps camped at Kaw Point, the confluence of the Kansas River, also known as the Kaw, and the Missouri River. They took numerous celestial readings and mapped the area thoroughly. It was this place that both Lewis and Clark noted would be good for development. Metropolitan

Kansas City was born. From the perspective of the Native Americans, the entrance into Kanza territory may well have been the beginning of the end. The Corps of Discovery reports encouraged settlement of the area, and within a few years French trappers and their families would come to live in this very spot. Decades later, the Kanza Indians would be forced from the state that bears their name to the land of Oklahoma.

The journals also noted the abundance of wildlife and berries in the region. The Native Americans gave them squash to eat. Clark's journal notes that on June 28, they killed nine deer in one day and "tracks are as plentiful as hogs about a farm." Clark frequently wrote that the water from the Missouri River was "very disagreeable." Yet the land of Kansas was quite agreeable, as Clark eloquently expressed time and again. "Nature appears to have exerted herself to beautify the scenery by the variety of flowers, delicately and highly flavored above the grass, which strikes and perfumes the sensation and amuses the mind."

Two significant events occurred during their brief stay in Kansas. First was the much-acclaimed court-martial of Hugh Hall and John Collins, the first court-martial west of the Mississippi River. Although harsh in its punishment, it established a tone of respect for rules and order that carried the Corps through the two years and four months of its journey.

Another important event in Kansas was the snakebite of Private Joseph Field. Although the type of snake is unknown and it may not even have been poisonous, the experience brings to light the time and energy Meriwether Lewis devoted to learning the practical application of medicine on the trail. That Fields recovered from his snakebite underscores the monumental accomplishment that only one man died on this journey, despite the thousands of risks and unknown obstacles.

Two years later, the banks of the Missouri River in Kansas certainly felt like familiar territory as the Corps neared home. It was with a sense of accomplishment and pride that the group sailed the keelboat at record speeds through this part of the river.

Traversing Kanza Territory

A DRIVING TOUR FROM KANSAS CITY TO ATCHISON

▼▼

Distance: 123 mi   **Time:** 2 days
Breaks: Stay for dinner and the night in Leavenworth.

Lewis and Clark in Kansas is a whirlwind tour of 123 mi up to the northeastern edge of the state. This journey follows the trail on the Kansas side with views of Missouri to the east.

The Corps of Discovery spent three days in late June 1803 at the mouth of the Kaw River at what is now **Kansas City, Kansas.** Kaw Point, the exact spot

Discipline on the Expedition

Military discipline was crucial to the success of the mission and the functioning of the Corps as a team. The first major test of the discipline expected by Captains Lewis and Clark came on June 29, 1804, in what is today Kansas City, Kansas. Privates John Collins and Hugh Hall, while on overnight watch, tapped into the whiskey barrel. The charge, according to Sergeant Floyd, was "with getting drunk on his post this morning out of whiskey put under his charge as sentinel and for suffering Hugh Hall to draw whiskey out of the said barrel intended for the party."

Sergeant Nathaniel Pryor served as judge, and the jury consisted of John Colter, John Newman, Patrick Gass, and John Thompson. Whiskey was carefully rationed for all members of the party throughout the journey and any undue abuses were in violation of military order. Being found guilty, John Collins received 100 lashes on his bare back and Hugh Hall received 50 lashes. It is believed the lashing was with a willow cane rather than a leather whip, which would have resulted in slightly less bodily harm. The sentence was carried out at 3:30 in the afternoon, and the next day the whole crew continued rowing upriver.

Such behavior on Collins' and Hall's part should not have been a great surprise to Clark. In his notes from the winter at Camp Dubois, he described Collins as "a blackguard" and wrote that Hall "drank quite heavily and was quite adventuresome." Although the punishment was carried out by others, Lewis and Clark, as commanding officers, approved of the sentence. Other court-martials were held throughout the journey, some for falling asleep while on watch, for fighting, or for desertion. The recorded punishment for those offenses included running a gauntlet where members of the Corps whipped with canes, rifles, and whips.

The punishment was quite brutal by today's standards but was typical of military procedures of the period. Historians agree that much of the success of the journey can be attributed to the limited disciplinary problems and the high standards of fairness in punishment. Even those who were the recipients of such tough judgments spoke highly in later years of their commanding officers and the procedures that ensured the success of an otherwise very difficult mission.

where the Corps is believed to have landed, provides an intimate view of the river as it swirls and merges with the Missouri. This is also where the first western court-martial was held. Although not present at the time of the expedition, both the Huron Indian Cemetery and the Wyandotte County Historical Society Museum provide valuable insight into the changes that took place in this region as a result of the European settlement that followed Lewis and Clark.

Begin your drive by traveling north from Kansas City along Route 7 until you reach **Leavenworth,** a town historically known for its federal penitentiary and military outpost. This is where Lewis and Clark spent July 4, 1804. The Frontier Army Museum at Fort Leavenworth is a worthwhile stop for understanding the demanding role of the military at this point in history. Plan on spending the night at the Prairie Queen Bed & Breakfast.

On day two, continue your drive north along Route 7 to the river-bluff community of **Atchison.** Stop at the Atchison County Historical Society Museum to see its displays on the natural surroundings encountered and documented by the Corps. A walk or picnic in Riverfront Park is an enjoyable way to appreciate the river's grandeur.

After lunch, continue to Doniphan County and the communities of **Highland** and **White Cloud.** A view of four states (Iowa, Kansas, Missouri, Nebraska) from atop the White Cloud Main Street and a tour of the Ma Hush Kah Museum complete your tour.

KANSAS CITY

▼▼

The Corps camped for three nights at the mouth of the Kansas River on the north side of the river. They spent much of their time hunting bear, deer, and wolves, drying out supplies, and resting for another leg of the journey. They hiked to Diamond Island, which is now under present-day Interstate 435.

In 1869, Kansas City sprang to life in the bottomlands along the Kansas-Missouri state line. It developed simultaneously with the Missouri city of the same name, and little more than the Kansas River separates the history and activities of the people of each state. Stockyards and other agricultural enterprises took advantage of the railroads on the Kansas side of the river, which has witnessed immigration on overland trails, steamship commerce, and bitter struggles surrounding the Civil War. In celebrating the passage of the Corps of Discovery through this area, the many municipalities are working together to create hiking, biking, and commemorative trails.

✦ INFORMATION
Kansas City/Wyandotte County Convention and Visitors Bureau | 727 Minnesota Ave., 66117 | 913/321–5800 or 800/264–1563 | www.kckcvb.org or www.lewisandclarkwyco.org.

SITES TO SEE

Huran Indian Cemetery. This cemetery was established in 1843 after the forced migration of the Wyandot nation from their homes in Ohio. Set at a high point overlooking the Missouri and Kaw rivers, the cemetery has an interpretive panel on 7th Street, which tells of the number of Native Americans who died of cholera and other illnesses brought by Euro-American exploration. | 7th and Ann Sts. | 913/596–7077 | Free | Daily.

Kaw Point. For three days in late June 1804, the expedition camped here, made repairs to its boats, and eventually court-martialed Privates John Collins and Hugh Hall for dereliction of duties. At the confluence of the Kansas and Missouri rivers, the Kaw Point boat ramp allows modern-day explorers to access the river. An interpretive kiosk tells about the Corps' activities in the area. | Fairfax exit at I–70 westbound, take first right and go straight to the end of the parking lot; follow signs | 913/321–5800 | www.lewisandclarkwyco.org | Free | Daily.

Wyandotte County Historical Museum. A model Kanza village and a 300-year-old black-walnut dugout canoe are among the displays here. Another exhibit highlights details of the court-martial of Privates John Collins and Hugh Hall that took place on June 29, 1804. The museum also tells the story of fur trappers who came to the region after Lewis and Clark. | 631 N. 126th St., Bonner Springs, 66012 | 913/721–1078 | Free | Mon.–Sat. 10–4.

✦ ON THE CALENDAR

June Kaw Point Commemoration. The arrival of a full-scale keelboat, as well as music, food, and Native American dance, is among the activities the last weekend in June. | 913/321–5800.

June Trial at Kaw Point. In 2004, a local theatrical group will re-create the June 1804 Kansas City court-martial. | 913/321–5800.

July A Journey Fourth. Held jointly with activities in nearby Atchison and Leavenworth, this event includes a reenactment of the Corps' first Fourth of July, riverboat cruises, an air show, and fireworks at numerous locations around the metropolitan area. | 913/321–5800.

LEAVENWORTH

▼▼▼

The Corps made a great find on the banks of the Missouri here—an abandoned horse in need of food and attention. Once healthy, the horse became an important part of the expedition for many months. On the Missouri River bluffs where Kansa, Delaware, and Osage tribes once lived, the U.S. government established a fort in 1827 to regulate relations between traders and Native Americans. This locale boomed after Kansas Territory opened, and the new city become a major jumping-off point for travelers on the Santa Fe and Oregon trails.

Established in 1854, Leavenworth, the "First City in Kansas," is most notable today as home to the United States Federal Penitentiary. Fort Leavenworth creates a military culture in much of the city. The fort itself, open to the public, displays numerous attractions and artifacts. Among these are the Frontier Army Museum, the Buffalo Soldier Monument, and a national cemetery.

✦ INFORMATION
Leavenworth/Lansing Convention and Visitors Bureau | 518 Shawnee St., Box 44, 66048 | 913/682–4113 or 800/844–4114 | www.lvarea.com/chamber.

SITES TO SEE
Fort Leavenworth. Established in 1827, this is the oldest army fort in continuous operation west of the Mississippi River. Branches of the Oregon and Santa Fe trails traverse the fort. Some of the highlights include the National Cemetery, Command and General Staff College, Memorial Chapel, Main Post Chapel, and the Buffalo Soldiers Memorial, which honors black cavalrymen. The Frontier Army Museum has exhibits on the Lewis and Clark expedition and artifacts from the military, pioneers, and Indians. | 600 Thomas Ave. | 913/684–5604 | leav-www.army.mil | Free | Daily 10–4.

Leavenworth Landing. A riverfront marker commemorates Lewis and Clark's passage through the area in July 1804 and again in September 1806. | North of 2nd and Dakota Sts. | 913/682–4113 | Free | Daily.

✦ ON THE CALENDAR
July 2004 **Riverfest.** Held the first weekend in July in Riverfront Park in conjunction with the arrival of the Lewis and Clark reenactment group, this three-day event celebrates the heritage of the river, the military, and the Native Americans of this region. | 913/682–4113.

HISTORIC DINING AND LODGING
High Noon Saloon and Brewery. Steak. Rustic wooden floors and a bar constructed in 1894 set the mood for a hearty western meal in the historic Great Western Manufacturing Building. The High Noon serves juicy burgers, Kansas beef, smoked barbecue, home cooking, and lighter fare—you won't go wrong on anything you order. Ask about the seasonal beers, and don't forget the made-from-scratch chocolate stout cake. | 206 Choctaw | 913/682–4876 | $6–$15 | MC, V.

Celebrating Independence Day

It was just the 28th time Independence Day had been celebrated by the United States. On July 4, 1804, the military expedition found itself on the banks of the Missouri River at what is now Atchison. Corps members began the day by firing the swivel cannon on their keelboat. Clark wrote in his journal that they "ussered in the day by a discharge of one shot from our Bow piece."

But the holiday didn't stop the crew from its appointed task of moving forward up the river. It is estimated that they progressed about 10 mi and at the end of the day camped at the mouth of what they named, and remains today, Independence Creek. As a final tribute to the nation's birthday, the cannon was fired again and the men received an extra ration of alcohol. Clark wrote: "We closed the day by a Descharge from our bow piece, an extra Gill of whiskey."

Meriwether Lewis had spent the previous year with his friend Thomas Jefferson at Monticello, the next day departing for the beginning of his journey west. The 27th birthday of the country was opened with an 18-gun salute, a military parade, and readings of the Declaration of Independence. At that time, the Fourth of July was more of a political event, with speeches and toasts to the young nation. Jefferson, who wrote the Declaration of Independence, died on July 4, 1826, at the age of 87. The Fourth of July was not declared an official holiday until 1941.

Prairie Queen Bed & Breakfast. Built in 1868, this stately B&B takes its name from a Missouri River riverboat once docked at Leavenworth. All rooms have a king-size bed and private bath; two have a porch. You may eat in the dining room or outdoors under the pergola overlooking the garden and pond. Owner Bob Topping is an area history buff and the expedition is among his favorite subjects. Dining room, hot tub; no room phones, no room TVs, no smoking. | 221 Arch St., 66048 | 913/758–1959 | fax 913/758–1959 | www.prairiequeen.com | 3 rooms | $125–$140 | MC, V | BP.

ATCHISON

▼▼

On a bend in the Missouri River known as the Great Detour, this town of 11,000 is Kansas's easternmost city and was a major starting point for overland wagon trains heading west. Kanza, and later Kickapoo, Indians once occupied the Independence Creek valley. When the Corps camped here in 1804, Private Joseph Field was bitten by a snake and received medical care from Captain Lewis. They celebrated the Fourth of July in the area, which, according to Clark's journals, reminded him of his home in central Virginia.

✦ INFORMATION
Atchison Area Chamber of Commerce | 200 S. 10th St., 66002 | 913/367–2427 or 800/234–1854 | www.atchisonkansas.net.

SITES TO SEE
Atchison County Historical Society Museum. This museum provides one of the most comprehensive looks at the natural world encountered by the Corps, including a huge exhibit on the mosquitoes that so badly plagued the crew. On the scale-model of Kansas City's Lewis and Clark statue look at the dog's tail for an interesting twist on the story. Other exhibits highlight Atchison's railroad history and the life of aviator Amelia Earhardt, who was born and raised here. | 200 S. 10th St. | 913/367–6238 | www.atchisonhistory.org | $2 | Mon.–Sat. 8–5, Sun. noon–4.

Independence Creek Site. This 10-acre site includes a biking path and bridge across Independence Creek, as well as a replica of a Kanza village authorized by the Kanza nation. This is where the Corps camped on the Fourth of July. | Rte. 314 at the Doniphan-Atchison county line | 913/367–6238 | Free | Daily.

Independence Park. This riverfront park commemorates the landing of Lewis and Clark on July 4, 1804. An interpretive kiosk links this site to others in the region. | Parallel and River Rds. | 800/234–1854 | Free | Daily.

✦ ON THE CALENDAR
July **A Journey Fourth.** Atchison joins several other metropolitan communities for a weeklong July 4 celebration that includes the arrival of the Corps reenactment team from St. Charles, a reading of the Declaration of Independence, fireworks, and 19th-century entertainment. | 913/367–2427.

HISTORIC DINING AND LODGING
The Riverhouse Restaurant. American/Casual. At the base of a bluff believed to have been climbed by Lewis and Clark on July 4, 1804, this plain white structure has perched on the Missouri River's edge since the riverboat era, and the staff enjoys telling of the building's colorful past. The restaurant fare is flavorful and creatively presented. Start with hot artichoke and garlic dip, and then try a cut of Kansas City beef or the always tasty salmon of the day. | 101 Commercial St. | 913/367–1010 | Closed Sun. | $11.95–$24.95 | AE, D, MC, V.

Medical Care on the Trail

It could have been a rattlesnake, cottonmouth, water moccasin, or copperhead. They are all native to the eastern Kansas prairie where, in the morning of July 4, 1804, the Corps stopped to rest along the western bluffs of the Missouri River near Atchison. Private Joseph Field, maybe taking a walk, maybe resting, was bitten on the foot by a snake. The journals read that Field's foot "swelled much," although there is no documentation that the snake was even poisonous.

Fortunately, in preparation for the journey, Captain Lewis had taken four months of medical training from Dr. Benjamin Rush in Philadelphia. Rush signed the Declaration of Independence and was Thomas Jefferson's personal physician. Packed among the cargo on the three boats were bottles of crude, foul-tasting medicine to treat a variety of complaints. The journals noted that through Kansas several men complained of headaches. It could have been a result of the extra rations of alcohol on July 4, but more likely it was a result of the severe heat and humidity in which they toiled. Either way, the cure for the headache was a dose of niter. For the snakebite, however, Lewis treated the wound with a poultice of gunpowder and tree bark, possibly the bark of the slippery elm but more likely Peruvian bark or cinchona. The incident didn't slow the group down. They traveled yet another 6 mi to the base of what is today Atchison. Three days later, the journals noted that Fields had much improved.

Considering the absence of medical training, the uncertain elements encountered, and the rudimentary practices used, it is amazing that only one member of the team died on the journey. Nearly six weeks after the snakebite incident, Sergeant Charles Floyd died near Sioux City, Iowa, of what is believed to have been a ruptured appendix.

The Majestic House. In 1890 the brothers of St. Benedict's Abbey built this three-story native stone farmhouse on their 600-acre dairy farm. The abbey abandoned the property in the mid-1900s and it stood unused for years, but hard work brought back the high ceilings and rich pine woodwork. Cable TV, outdoor hot tub, fishing, hiking, Internet; no kids, no smoking. | 18936 262nd Rd., 66002 | 913/367–3696 | www.themajestichouse.com | 5 rooms | $90–$130 | D, MC, V | BP.

HIGHLAND/WHITE CLOUD

▼▼

The Highland/White Cloud area was the last stop for the Corps as it traveled through present-day Kansas. The region was dominated by wildlife and abundant fruits and grains, but the Corps was beginning to encounter Native Americans. Overnight watches were increased and the men stayed alert. A high hill in White Cloud provides a spectacular view of the four-state region and is believed to have been climbed by Meriwether Lewis on one of his many forays along the riverbanks.

✦ INFORMATION

Doniphan County Chamber of Commerce | Box 325, Elwood, 66024 | 913/365–2604 | www.dpcountyks.com.

SITES TO SEE

DAR Historical Marker. This riverfront marker, erected by the Daughters of the American Revolution, commemorates the passage of the Corps through this area in 1804 and in 1806. | Riverfront, White Cloud | 913/365–2604 | Free | Daily.

Four State Lookout. Climb the hill at the north end of Main Street and enjoy a view of Kansas, Missouri, Iowa, and Nebraska. Lewis often left the men below as he climbed these various overlooks and noted them in the journals; it is believed that he climbed this point as well. | Main St., White Cloud | 913/365–2604 | Free | Daily.

Ma Hush Kah Museum. A former schoolhouse, the building now houses Native American artifacts and attempts to interpret the changes taking place in these tribes as a result of European settlement in the region. | Main St., White Cloud | 913/365–2604 | Variable hrs.

Native American Heritage Museum. About 30 mi north of town, near Highland, this cultural center uses ancient artifacts and modern-day art to share the moving stories of tribes of present-day Kansas: the Iowa, Kickapoo, Potawatomi, and Sac and Fox. | 1727 Elgin Rd., 3 mi east of Highland | 785/442–3304 | www.kshs.org/places/sites.htm | $3 | Wed.–Sat. 10–5, Sun. 1–5.

Nebraska and Iowa

The midwestern summer's heat and humidity dogged the Corps of Discovery as they passed through Nebraska and Iowa during the summer of 1804. It was here that the men saw the boundless prairie that is the Great Plains. The state introductions that follow detail the history of their time in the area. Today's route passes through towns and cities, many of which include sites that provide a sense of the land and river the Corps of Discovery experienced as well as museums, monuments, and scenic overlooks. Driving tours for each state show you the way.

Nebraska

The earliest documented explorations of Nebraska by Europeans took place by the Spanish in 1714 and 1720 in central Nebraska near the Sandhills community of Columbus. Their encounters with the Pawnee resulted in bloodshed, and the Spanish retreated into New Mexico. By the mid-1790s French explorers and fur traders made the earliest claims to the region, setting up trading posts on the Missouri River. The citizens of Nebraska at that time included the Pawnee, Omaha, Osage, Ponca, Otoe, Missouria, Arapaho, Cheyenne, Comanche, and Lakota (also called Nebraska) nations.

The United States acquired Nebraska as part of the 1803 Louisiana Purchase, with little consequence to the Native Americans in the first few years of the 19th century.

When the Corps reached what is now Nebraska in July 1804, it had been coping for weeks with the oppressive heat and humidity of a midwestern summer and the challenges of a debris-ridden river swollen in a late-spring flood. The men were tired, occasionally suffering from heatstroke and irritated by swarms of mosquitoes. Their wool uniforms contributed to the discomfort; the wool got wet in the river, rubbed against their skin, and caused blisters. But as the three little boats came into what is now Nebraska, the physical challenges of the river lessened ever so slightly. (Here the river begins to widen and slow; if you had been poling a pirogue for two months, the break would be a blessing.) More and more, the Corps was entering uncharted territory. Clark wrote of an open and boundless prairie, "because I could not see the extent of the plain in any derection . . . covered with grass about 18 inches high."

Amid this scenic backdrop the Corps also had hopes of encountering chiefs of the tribes who lived along the Missouri, primarily the Otoe and Missouria. A council took place on August 3, 1804, after interpreter George Drewyer encountered Missouria while hunting on the prairie. In full military dress, Lewis and Clark presented gifts that included whiskey, cloth, medals, and other items from the storage bins. Lewis fired his air rifle and made speeches regarding the wishes of the United States government to interact freely and peaceably with the Native Americans. The chiefs acknowledged the speeches favorably and the Corps continued up the river by 3 PM that day.

The significance of this meeting, which took place at present-day Fort Atkinson, cannot be overlooked. Had the chiefs not found Lewis and Clark's presentation favorable, word would have spread throughout the plains and up the Missouri River valley, warning other tribes that the white man was not to be trusted. But the Corps was welcomed and traveled in peace throughout the Nebraska Territory, later meeting the Yankton Sioux on a bluff north of present-day Crofton, Nebraska.

As the Corps returned along this stretch of the river in 1806, word had already spread of the riches they had encountered. The crew met boatload after boatload of trappers and explorers heading west with confidence in their safety along the path opened by the expedition. Zebulon Pike was already crossing southeast Nebraska en route to Santa Fe, New Mexico, meeting with the Pawnee near Guide Rock.

Pioneers did not wait for the Nebraska Territory to be formed in 1854 before exploring the land themselves. By the 1840s millions were dreaming of prosperity and freedom in the American West, and Nebraska was their first hurdle en route to the Pacific. Three great trails—the Oregon, the California, and the Mormon—all cross this state. The Homestead Act of 1862 encouraged many of the travelers to put down roots in Nebraska, which became a state in 1889.

Much of the eastern Nebraska Clark wrote about is now tree-covered, thanks in part to pioneering politician J. Sterling Morton, a lover of trees, who moved to Nebraska City in 1854. Within a few years Morton had planted an orchard of 300 apple trees. In 1902 President Teddy Roosevelt created the Nebraska National Forest, a 1-million-acre, completely man-made preserve in central and western Nebraska.

"The air is healthy and pure," wrote Captain Lewis on August 3, 1804, and so it remains today. Although much of the landscape has changed, parts of the river in northeast Nebraska look the same as they did in 1804 and 1806, when the Corps of Discovery passed through and opened the doors to the West.

Nebraska Journey

A DRIVING TOUR FROM BROWNVILLE TO CROFTON

▼▼

Distance: 404 mi   **Time:** 3 days
Breaks: Stay in Nebraska City or Omaha.

This tour takes you along the Missouri River, closely following the route of the Corps of Discovery in 1804. You visit small river towns, agricultural communities, and Omaha, the state's largest metropolitan area. The Nebraska Division of Travel and Tourism, in conjunction with the Iowa Division of Tourism, has published a brochure that outlines this journey in greater detail.

Begin in **Brownville,** one of the first towns established in the Nebraska Territory. Spend the morning walking through the historic district to see the many homes dating to the 1860s and 1870s and visiting the *Meriwether Lewis,* a Missouri River dredge boat on which guides describe the history of river exploration. Leave Brownville around noon, and head west on U.S. 136 to Auburn. At Auburn, turn north on U.S. 75 toward Nebraska City, home of Arbor Day founder J. Sterling Morton. Spend the afternoon at the Missouri River Basin Lewis and Clark Interpretive Center, where you can row or pole a boat up the Missouri River and explore a keelboat's lockers and sleeping quarters.

On your second day, drive north on U.S. 75 to **Bellevue,** the site of a fur-trading post established in the early 1800s. Today several nature centers and wildlife parks allow you to experience the Nebraska Lewis and Clark documented in 1804. The Sarpy County Historical Society has items from the fur-trading post first established here by Peter Sarpy in 1803. From Bellevue head north on U.S. 75 to **Omaha.** After visiting exhibits at the Great Plains Black Museum and the Durham Western Heritage Center, spend the afternoon walking along the riverfront at Lewis and Clark Landing, where numerous pieces of sculp-

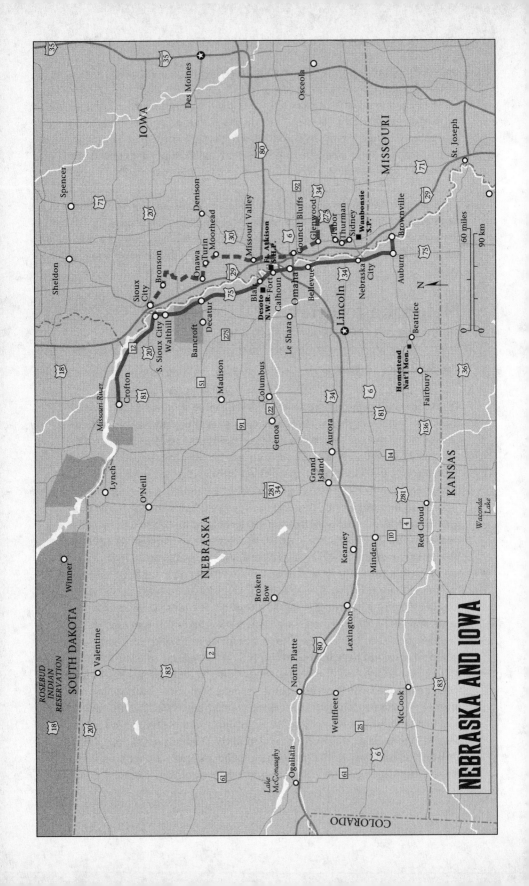

NEBRASKA AND IOWA

ture and artwork as well as interpretive panels tell of the time Lewis and Clark camped here. The landing has restaurants and refreshment stands where you can enjoy a view of the river and Council Bluffs beyond. A walking or driving tour with the Douglas County Historical Society will enhance your understanding of the Omaha area in the overall Lewis and Clark experience.

On day three drive north from Omaha on U.S. 75, also known here as the Lewis and Clark Scenic Byway, for a visit to Fort Calhoun in Fort Atkinson State Historical Park. This is where, after 2½ months on the trail, Lewis and Clark held their first council with Native Americans, on August 3, 1804. An interpretive trail and observation deck overlooking the Missouri River, along with artwork and panels, help you understand the significance of this meeting of the Missouria and Otoe to the success of the mission. As you leave the park, continue north on U.S. 75 to **Blair**; then turn east on U.S. 91 and continue for 3 mi to the DeSoto National Wildlife Refuge. The cargo from a steamboat that sank here in 1865 is on display at the visitor center. Return to U.S. 75 and head north to **Decatur,** where you should climb Blackbird Hill, as did Lewis and 10 other men. Or take time to visit the Omaha and Winnebago people on their reservations west and north of town.

Continue on the Lewis and Clark Scenic Byway until you reach U.S. 20. Go west 5 mi, and then turn north on Route 12. As you drive, check out the view of the Missouri River; of all the areas that the Corps passed through in Nebraska, this looks most like what Lewis and Clark experienced. Route 12 turns west toward **Crofton,** where Lewis and Clark eventually crossed the Missouri River into South Dakota. A historical marker 3 mi west of Newcastle marks the location. At the Lewis and Clark Lake Visitor Center, exhibits illustrate the progress of the expedition through this region. Five miles farther, the Corps of Discovery Welcome Center dispenses additional information and hosts numerous reenactments of the period. You can pick up pamphlets here with driving directions for the community-organized George Shannon Trail.

BROWNVILLE
▼▼▼

When the expedition entered what is now Nebraska around July 10, 1804, the men wrote in their journals of beautiful plains as far as the eye could see, broken only by cherry and plum trees and berry thickets. Clark and five others explored about 3 mi up the Nehama River and discovered numerous Native American burial mounds. A storm on July 14 nearly swamped the boats when the riverbanks caved in. Although they were tired and ill with boils and sunstroke, they still progressed at about 20 mi a day along this part of the river.

A Journey of Freedom

At one point, William Clark described this member of the Expedition team as "an extension of himself." It wasn't his good friend Lewis but instead his slave, York.

Born near the York River in Caroline County, Virginia, in the early 1770s, York became the property of William Clark when he was about 15. It is believed that York was a year or two younger than Clark. York accompanied the Clark family when they moved to Kentucky in 1780, and while there he developed skills as a woodsman that would prove vital years later.

York served in a variety of capacities during the expedition. Records from December 26, 1803, tell how he labored with a whipsaw. Other references describe how he swam to a sandbar to collect greens for dinner. Another time he strained himself carrying meat and wood. He attended to Sacagawea during the last months of her pregnancy. He developed into a strong hunter and was responsible for bringing at least three elk, one deer, and five buffalo to the camp for food. A tributary of the Yellowstone River, now called Custer's Creek, was named as York's Dry River on the maps created by Lewis and Clark.

The Native Americans the Corps encountered along the way were fascinated with York more than with any of the weapons, gadgets, and gifts delivered to the chiefs. His color and strength represented to them a special spiritual power. York was often examined from head to toe. A Hidatsu chief spitting on his hand to rub the black from York is now the subject of a Charles Russell painting entitled *Big Medicine*.

York was in his early twenties at the time of the expedition, and especially for a man who had never known freedom, it was the journey of a lifetime. During this trip he was treated as an equal, appreciated for his contributions and accomplishments, and even allowed to vote when the group voted on matters of campsites and other issues. For all intents and purposes he was a free man during those two years. So as the journey concluded and others received their pay and land grant for service, York simply asked for his freedom. At first Clark denied the request, and a rift developed between the captain and the man Clark had called "an extension of himself." But 10 years after the expedition, Clark granted York his freedom. He started a freighting business in Tennessee and Kentucky and died there of cholera sometime before 1832. He would have been about 60 years old.

In 1856 Brownville was incorporated and soon became an important river town and a jumping-off point for travelers headed west. Thirty-two of the original buildings remain and are part of a National Historic District.

✦ INFORMATION

Brownville Historical Society | Box 1, 68321 | 402/825–4131 or 800/305–7990 | www.ci.brownville.ne.us.

SITES TO SEE

Brownville State Recreation Area. On the eastern edge of town below the U.S. 136 bridge, these 22 acres are popular for family picnicking and boating. A dredge boat called the *Meriwether Lewis,* built in the 1930s by the Army Corps of Engineers, is filled out with displays about river travel and has panels on the Corps as it passed this way. | 2402 Clay St. | 402/825–3341 | $3 | Memorial Day–Labor Day, daily 1–4.

Indian Cave State Park. History enthusiasts find much to enjoy at this 3,000-acre park named for a cave with etchings of ancient Native American picture writings. These pictographs are the only example of their kind in Nebraska. The undisturbed woodlands here evoke images of what the Corps encountered in the region. Within park boundaries are the ongoing excavation and reconstruction of St. DeRoin, a trading post possibly referred to in the journals in July 1804. | 9 mi south of Brownville on Rte. 64 | 402/883–2575 | www.ngpc.state.ne.us/parks | Nebraska Parks Permit | Daily.

Missouri River Basin Lewis and Clark Interpretive Center. At this center built for the Bicentennial, you can row or pole a boat up the Missouri, and you can open lockers filled with Native American trade goods, barrels of salt pork, and canisters of gunpowder. In a cutaway model of the keelboat used by the Corps you can see the cabin where the captains slept and the desk where they kept their journals. Built on 79 acres overlooking the Missouri River, the center includes walking trails and Native American and indigenous wildlife exhibits. At the time of writing, the center was scheduled to open in July 2004. Call for more information. | 806 1st Ave., 25 mi north of Brownville, Nebraska City, 68410 | 402/873–4293 | www.mrb-lewisandclarkcenter.org.

Spirit of Brownville. See the river as the Corps did most of the time—from the middle of it. Although the *Spirit of Brownville* is a paddle wheeler—and paddle wheelers did not debut on the river until about 50 years after the Corps traveled this way—the boat provides a wonderful experience on the river. Dinner, sightseeing, and historical cruises are available. | 402/825–6441 | Dinner cruises $6 and up | Weekends only.

Oct. **Old Time Autumn.** Broom makers, blacksmiths, and fiddlers fill the downtown streets demonstrating life in Brownville in its heyday. | 402/825–4131 or 800/305–7990.

HISTORIC DINING

Camp Rulo River Club. American/Casual. On the banks of the Missouri River, this restaurant serves catfish, carp, and walleye, the exact items the Corps members caught for their dinner. The steaks and hamburgers are great, and portions of whiskey are generously sized. | U.S. 156, 12 mi south of Brownville, Rulo | 402/245–4096 | Closed Mon. | $9.50 | MC, V.

BELLEVUE

▼▼

The region where the Platte flows into the Missouri was the domain of the Otoe and Pawnee tribes at the time the Corps traveled through present-day Bellevue. A small fur-trading post was established here in 1795 by James Mackay, who was working for Spain. When Meriwether Lewis and William Clark hoisted an American flag in the vicinity on July 23, 1804, it was likely the first time the United States banner had ever flown over Nebraska. Bellevue has some of the state's oldest buildings, which you can see on a guided or self-guided tour.

✦ INFORMATION

Bellevue Chamber of Commerce | 204 W. Mission Ave., 68005 | 402/898–3000 | www.bellevuenebraska.com. **Sarpy County Historical Society** | 2402 Clay St., 68005 | 402/292–1880. **Sarpy County Tourism** | 1210 Golden Gate Dr., No. 1129, Papillion, 68046 | 402/593–4354 or 800/467–2779 | www.gosarpy.com.

SITES TO SEE

Fontenelle Forest Nature Center. More than 25 mi of trails crisscross these more than 1,300 acres of hilly woodlands, wetlands, and land fronting the Missouri River on the northern edge of town; a 1-mi boardwalk is accessible to wheelchair users. The Nature Center has exhibits on ecology and history as well as a variety of programs, including guided hikes. Throughout the Bicentennial, interpretive signs at many exhibits will include Lewis's journal entries describing the trees and flowers on the grounds. | 1111 Bellevue Blvd. N | 402/731–3140 | $7.50 | Weekdays 8–5, weekends 8–6.

Lee G. Simmons Wildlife Safari Park. For weeks the Corps of Discovery could see buffalo in the distance throughout this region but never got close enough to actually shoot one. In this drive-through park, buffalo, elk, and antelope are among the many forms of wildlife that the Corps would have encountered on the plains 200 years ago. | 16406 N. 292nd St., Exit 426 off I–80, Ashland | 402/944–9453 or 402/733–8401 | $10 per vehicle | Apr.–Oct., weekdays 9:30–5, weekends 9:30–6; Nov.–Mar., weekends 9:30–5.

Sarpy County Historical Museum. Peter Sarpy was active in the fur-trade business of the 1830s, which the Lewis and Clark expedition helped open up throughout the region. Many of Sarpy's original possessions are on display, including old traps, knives, buffalo-hide clothing, and other artifacts. | 2402 Clay St. | 402/292–1880 | $2 | Tues.–Sun. 9–4.

Schilling Wildlife Management Area. This 1,800-acre reserve, 6 mi south of Bellevue, provides an outstanding view of the convergence of the Platte and Missouri rivers. An interpretive panel at the viewing area describes the river conditions that made the voyage through the area so challenging for Lewis and Clark. | 17614 Refuge Rd., Plattsmouth | 402/296–0041 | www.ngpc. state.ne.us/wildlife/schill | Free | Apr.–Oct. 15, daily 7 AM–9 PM.

✦ ON THE CALENDAR
May **Native American Festival.** Native American performers and musicians stage concerts at the Fontenelle Forest Learning Center the first or second weekend of the month. | 402/731–3140.

OMAHA
▼▼▼

The Omaha area was originally the homeland of the Omaha and Otoe tribes. Lewis and Clark wrote about their burial mounds when they entered what is now downtown Omaha on July 27, 1804, but were unsure as to what they were. The first fur traders established posts on the western bank of the Missouri River in the early 1800s. In 1846 the Mormons built a city called Winter Quarters, which housed 4,000. Omaha grew quickly after the Nebraska Territory was created in 1854. It expanded farther in 1863 when it became the terminus of the Union Pacific Railroad. Omaha was also the site of the trial of Standing Bear, during which a Native American was given the legal rights of a U.S. citizen for the first time.

✦ INFORMATION
Douglas County Historical Society | 30th and Fort Sts., Bldg. 11A, 68111 | 402/ 455–9990 or 402/451–1013 | www.omahahistory.org. **Greater Omaha Convention and Visitors Bureau** | 10001 Farnham St., Suite 200, 68102 | 402/444–4660 or 866/937–6624 | www.visitomaha.com.

SITES TO SEE
Botanical Gardens. Much of Lewis's work documenting the flora and fauna of the region could be completed with one visit here. Divided into several

Gifts of Peace

It was a tough shopping list by any standards—hundreds of gifts for complete strangers whose tastes and dislikes were completely unknown. But Meriwether Lewis approached the task with the same discipline and solemnity with which he carried out the entire expedition. While William Clark was beginning to recruit men, Lewis went shopping in Philadelphia. Congress had authorized $2,500 for the expedition and much of that went for supplies, scientific equipment, and additional food and clothing for the men.

Lewis, however, set aside $669.50 for presents to bring to the Native Americans the Corps surely would encounter along the journey. For them, Lewis chose 12 dozen pocket mirrors, 4,600 sewing needles, 130 rolls of tobacco, silk ribbons, ivory combs, handkerchiefs, tomahawks, pipes, brass kettles, vermilion face paint, and 33 pounds of colorful beads. The Corps carried with them 87 silver peace medals, minted in 1801, with a profile of the president on one side and two hands clasped in friendship on the opposite side. Lewis also invested his own money in a long-barreled rifle that fired bullets of compressed air rather than flint and powder. Demonstrations of its technology were meant to impress the Native American chiefs and often did.

At each council, the men were paraded in full military dress, guns were fired, and the scientific equipment demonstrated. Then each chief would receive a peace medal. Lesser chiefs received paper certificates signed by President Jefferson explaining that the United States now owned the land and everyone was to live in peace. At many ceremonies, it was recorded that the chiefs appeared more interested in the military clothing and Lewis's dog, Seaman, than in any of the gifts.

different specialty areas, the 75-acre gardens overlooking the Missouri River include large rose gardens, herb gardens, children's gardens, and spring flowering gardens. | 5th and Cedar Sts. | 402/346–4002 | Free | Apr.–Oct., Tues.–Sun. 9–4.

Durham Western Heritage Museum. This museum in Omaha's restored Union Station details the facets of Omaha's history, among them the Lewis and Clark encampment here. Other exhibits include railroad cars, a steam engine, and the Byron Reed Coin and Document Collection. | 801 S. 10th St. | 402/444–5071 | www.dwhm.org | $5 | Tues.–Sat. 10–5, Sun. 1–5.

Father Flanagan's Boys and Girls Town. At the large campus of this children's home in west Omaha, you can tour Father Flanagan's House, the rose and Biblical gardens, the chapel, and other facilities. Special exhibits in the visitor center through 2006 focus on Lewis's and Clark's letters to President Jefferson, family members, and others. There will be reproduction letters, information on how mail traveled in the early 19th century, and commemorative postage stamps of the expedition. | 13628 Flanagan Blvd. | 402/498–1140 | Free | May–Aug., daily 8–5:30; Sept.–Apr., daily 8–4:30.

Great Plains Black Museum. In this museum in a former telephone exchange building now listed on the National Register of Historic Places, photographs, documents, paintings, and rare books depict the history of African-Americans on the Great Plains. York, the only African-American on the expedition, is represented in paintings and is the subject of special lectures throughout the year. | 2213 Lake St. | 402/345–6817 | Donations requested | Weekdays 10–2.

Joslyn Art Museum. The Karl Bodmer oil painting collection here, which dates from the 1830s, captures early explorations of the Missouri River. Connected to a concert hall via an atrium and restaurant, the museum also displays art of the American West and many other examples from 19th- and 20th-century America. | 2200 Dodge St. | 402/342–3300 | www.joslyn.org | $6; free Sat. 10–noon | Tues.–Sat. 10–4, Sun. noon–4.

Lewis and Clark Landing. Numerous historical markers and interpretive panels tell of the Corps' explorations of the mounds found near this 23-acre site on the Missouri River, adjacent to Heartland of America Park. A walking trail incorporates sculptures and other art forms as well as signage that brings the Corps' journey to life. | 6th St., at the riverfront | 402/444–5900 | www.livelyomaha.com | Free | Daily.

Omaha History Tours. The Douglas County Historical Society provides a number of one - to five-hour walking, driving, and river tours that tell you about the Corps of Discovery presence in this area. | 5730 N. 30th St. | 402/455–9990 | www.omahahistory.org | Varies | Variable hrs.

Opera Omaha. Based in Omaha's Rose Theatre, this local company is one of seven opera companies that commissioned the writing of *Dream of the Pacific*, a musical journey along the Missouri. Children's performances are also scheduled throughout the Bicentennial. | 1625 Farnham, Suite 100 | 402/346–7372 or 877/346–7372 | www.operaomaha.org | Varies | Variable hrs.

Platte River State Park. Frenchmen Paul and Pierre Mallet were probably the first explorers to visit this area, in 1739, when they left St. Louis with their six comrades in search of a route through the wilderness to open French trade. Lewis explored up the Platte River, where, nowadays, you can see herds of buffalo and camp in a tepee. Horseback trail rides, buffalo-stew cookouts, and hikes enrich your experience. | 14421 346th St., Louisville | 402/234–2217 | www.ngpc.state.ne.us/parks/prsp.html | Nebraska Parks Permit | Daily.

River City Star. Narrated history tours aboard this three-deck paddle wheeler last one or two hours. Dinner cruises are also available. | 1515 Abbott Dr. | 402/342–7827 or 866/227–2827 | www.rivercitystar.com | $12 and up | Apr.–Oct., daily 10 AM–1 AM.

✦ ON THE CALENDAR
Sept. **Fort Omaha Intertribal Powwow.** This traditional powwow includes participants from members of Nebraska's Omaha, Ponca, Winnebago, Santee Sioux, and other tribes. There are regional foods, crafts, dances, and discussions on topics relevant to the Native American tribes. | 402/457–2253.

BLAIR
▼▼

It was near here that Private Fields killed the first badger ever documented by an American. Lewis skinned and stuffed it to send back to President Jefferson. Also in this area, on August 8, 1804, the journals record that Lewis was summoned above deck to see what appeared to be a white sheet spread across the river. As they drew near, the men realized it was a layer of feathers from molting pelicans on a sandbar upriver. Lewis killed one and wrote extensively of its details in the journal, adhering to the assignment given him by President Jefferson to document the plants and animals of the West. Today many of those same animals can be seen at the DeSoto National Wildlife Refuge, which spans Iowa and Nebraska.

Fort Atkinson, where Lewis and Clark had their first council with Native Americans, later became the first American military fort in present-day Nebraska. Oglala Sioux holy man Black Elk, immortalized by the poet John Neihardt, was an important figure in the area.

✦ INFORMATION
Blair Area Chamber of Commerce | 1526 Washington St., 68008 | 402/533–4455 | www.blairchamber.org.

SITES TO SEE
Boyer Chute National Wildlife Refuge. This restored river channel alongside the Missouri River is surrounded by 3,300 acres of grassland, woodland, and wetlands. On two short nature trails and a 4-mi hiking loop, you can see how much the river looked as it did when the Corps traveled its route between

1804 and 1806. | 3720 Riversway Way, 10 mi southeast of Blair on Rte. 34, Fort Calhoun | 402/468–4313 | Free | Daily dawn–dusk.

DeSoto National Wildlife Refuge. The almost 8,000 acres of protected land in Nebraska and Iowa are home to hundreds of species of wildlife, including migrating waterfowl and especially snow geese, many of which Lewis documented. The visitor center, 5 mi east of Blair, houses more than 200,000 well-preserved items recovered from the steamboat *Bertrand,* which sank in the region in 1865. | Off U.S. 30, 5 mi east of Blair | 712/642–4121 | www.midwest. fws.gov/desoto | $3 per vehicle | Daily.

Fort Atkinson State Historical Park. One of President Jefferson's four directives to Lewis and Clark was to meet with Native Americans and establish peace and goodwill on behalf of the United States government. That first council with Otoe and Missouria chiefs took place near present-day Fort Atkinson on August 3, 1804. The fort was built in 1820, 10 mi south of Blair. Today, a re-created fort with barracks and log walls illustrates what life was like for the 1,000 men billeted there.

The **Lewis and Clark Council Bluff Interpretive Monument** (www.firstcouncil. org) was added in 2003 for the Bicentennial. Six life-size figures are arranged as they might have been during the meeting nearly 200 years ago—Lewis, Clark, two Native Americans representing the Otoe and Missouria tribes, a French interpreter, and Lewis's dog, Seaman. An interpretive trail and observation deck overlooking the Missouri River, along with artwork and panels, explain the significance of this meeting with the Missouria and Otoe to the success of the mission. | 7th and Madison, Fort Calhoun | 402/468–5611 | www.ngpc.state.ne.us/parks | $2.50 | Grounds daily 8–7; visitor center late May–early Sept., daily 9–5.

Pelican Point State Recreation Area. On August 8, 1804, Lewis saw feathers of "the breadth of the river" floating down the Missouri River here. Soon the Corps came across hundreds of pelicans. One of the birds was killed and examined; it was reported that its pouch held 5 gallons of water. The cottonwoods in today's pristine 36-acre forest tower more than 200 feet; there's also river access. | 640 Rte. 19, 12 mi north of Blair, Craig | 402/374–1727 | www.ngpc. state.ne.us/parks | Nebraska Parks Permit | Daily.

Washington County Historical Museum. Displayed among artifacts dating from the days of the Woodland Indian tribes that inhabited this land as far back as 450 BC is a diorama that details the Lewis and Clark expedition in this area. | 102 N. 14th St., Fort Calhoun | 402/468–5740 | www.newashcohist. org | Free | Mar.–Dec., weekends 1:30–4:30; Jan. and Feb., Wed.–Fri. 9–12:30 PM; also by appointment.

May–Oct. Living History Days. The first weekend of each month, costumed infantrymen, tradespeople, laundresses, and cooks re-create life at Fort Atkinson during the 1820s. | 402/468–5611.

June Gateway to the West Parade. Just for the fun of it, anyone named Lewis and anyone named Clark are invited to participate in Blair's annual community celebration the second weekend of June. The families of all Lewises and all Clarks eat for free and become celebrities for the day. The parade also has a Seaman entry for owners of black Newfoundlands in honor of the dog that accompanied the Corps on its journey. | 402/533–4455.

July 31–Aug. 3, 2004 First Tribal Council. This National Signature Event of the Bicentennial at Fort Atkinson State Park commemorates the first council that Lewis and Clark held with the Otoe and Missouria tribes. | 402/468–5611.

Aug. William Clark's Birthday Party. On the weekend nearest Clark's August 3 birth date, the Washington County Museum holds this annual celebration. The main feature is watermelon, one of the captain's favorite foods. Reenactors and historical presentations are additional highlights of the party. | 402/468–5740.

DECATUR
▼▼▼

The Corps was moving slowly north along this part of the river in late July and early August 1804 for two reasons. Two men, Private Moses Reed and a French engagé, had disappeared and were presumed to have deserted. A party was dispatched to find them, and did. The men were forced to run a gauntlet four times for their transgression, and Reed lost his status as a permanent member of the party. This was the last mention of discipline noted in the journals. More important to the mission was the dispatch of two groups of men to visit the camps of the Omaha and Ponca to arrange a meeting with Lewis and Clark. That meeting took place in this vicinity on August 17.

Founded in 1854, Decatur is the second-oldest settlement in Nebraska and named for Stephen Decatur, a clerk in a trading company. Today, this community on the Lewis and Clark Scenic Byway has a population of 700, and agriculture and manufacturing are the primary industries.

✦ INFORMATION
City of Decatur | 913 S. Broadway, 68020 | 402/349–5360 | www.ci.decatur. ne.us.

SITES TO SEE

Blackbird Hill. At this scenic overlook of the Missouri River, interpretive signs tell of the Omaha chief named Blackbird, who died of smallpox and was buried here two years before the expedition. Lewis and Clark, along with 10 other men, visited the grave site on August 11, 1804, and fixed a red, white, and blue flag over the grave as a mark of respect for the great chief. | Milepost 152, 6 mi north of Decatur on U.S. 75 | 402/837–5301 | Free | Daily.

John G. Neihardt Center. Exhibits here relate to both the life and literature of Nebraska's famous poet laureate, whose best-known individual work is *Black Elk Speaks*. You can visit a small library for researchers, a prayer garden, and the little cabin Neihardt used as his study. Neihardt was devoted to Native Americans and their plight, which is reflected in many of his works. | Washington St. at Elm St., 5 mi west of Decatur on Rte. 51, Bancroft | 888/777–4667 or 402/648–3388 | Free | Mon.–Sat. 9–5, Sun. 1:30–5.

Lewis and Clark Scenic Byway. From Walthill to South Sioux City along U.S. 75, this 86-mi drive meanders along the riverfront and through 10 small towns, each with tidbits of history related to the Lewis and Clark expedition and the Native American tribes of the region. Maps of the area are available at businesses along the drive. | 376 Rte. 34, Tekamah, 68061 | 402/685–5175 | www.lewisandclarkscenicbyway.com | Free | Daily.

Omaha Reservation. The 3,000 residents of the Omaha reservation welcome the public. Tribal council leaders will answer questions about their heritage and culture. | 100 Main St., 2 mi north on U.S. 75, Macy, 68039 | 402/837–5391 | Free | Variable hrs.

Picotte Center. Susan LaFlesche Picotte, an Omaha and sister of activist Suzette LaFlesche, was the first Native American female physician. The former Picotte Memorial Hospital serves as a museum devoted to Dr. Picotte's life, her family history, and her work. Exhibits include medical equipment from the late 19th and early 20th centuries and information about changes in laws impacting the lives of Native Americans, for whom the Picotte family lobbied. It was the ancestors of Dr. Picotte who met with Lewis and Clark on their voyage. | 503 Mathewson St., Walthill, 68067 | 402/846–5109 or 402/846–5428 | Free | Variable hrs.

Winnebago Buffalo Herd and Monument. This herd of 60 bison grazes on land adjacent to U.S. 75, north of Winnebago, and represents a traditional food source and the cultural heritage of the tribe. | Box 687, Winnebago, 68071 | 402/878–2626 | www.winnebagotribe.com | Free | Daily.

Winnebago Cultural Learning Center and Museum. On the grounds of Little Priest Tribal College, this center highlights the Winnebago culture and its connection to the Maya culture. Exhibits include portraits of tribal elders and traditional craftworks such as baskets and dolls. Lecture programs are scheduled throughout the year. | 601 E. College Dr., Winnebago | 402/878–2380 | www.winnebagotribe.com | Free | Weekdays 8:30–4:30.

✦ ON THE CALENDAR
July **Winnebago Tribal Powwow.** This three-day celebration, held on the grounds of Little Priest Tribal College the third weekend in July, includes singing, dancing, and other cultural activities. | 402/878–2272.

Aug. **Omaha Tribal Harvest Celebration.** Held in conjunction with the first full moon, this event stages traditional tribal dances and other ceremonies of the Omaha people. | 402/837–5391.

SOUTH SIOUX CITY
▼▼▼

On August 18, 1804, just south of the town known in frontier times as the "wildest little town on the Missouri," Meriwether Lewis celebrated his 30th birthday. The men were issued an extra gill of whiskey (about 4 ounces), and there was fiddle playing and dancing until 11 PM. From the water's edge, you can see Iowa's Sergeant Floyd Monument across the river, dedicated to the only man to perish during the journey. Many of the celebrations and recognitions of the Corps of Discovery in this area link Sioux City, Iowa, and South Sioux City, Nebraska.

✦ INFORMATION
South Sioux City Chamber of Commerce | 3900 Dakota Ave., 68776 | 402/494–1626 or 800/793–6327. **South Sioux City Convention and Visitor's Bureau** | 3900 Dakota Ave., 68776 | 402/494–1307 or 800/793–6327 | www.southsiouxcity.org.

SITES TO SEE
Cottonwood Cove. This Dakota City park on the Lewis and Clark Scenic Byway has a riverfront walkway with interpretive signs about the expedition in this area. The overlook provides a view of the Sioux City skyline and the Sergeant Floyd Monument. | 13th and Hickory Sts., Dakota City | 402/987–3448 | Free | Daily.

Ionia Volcano. On August 24, 1804, Clark wrote of passing bluffs that looked as if they had been recently scorched by fire. Although these cliffs may have looked like a volcano, the effect was likely the result of a chemical reaction between the iron pyrite in the soil and its contact with water. The land is privately owned, but you can tour with permission of the landowner. An interpretive sign is in Newcastle's City Park. | 402/355–2675 (landowner) or 402/355–2370 (village of Newcastle) | Free | Daily.

Ponca State Park. Overlooking an untamed stretch of the Missouri, this 1,200-acre park has a lake and recreational facilities, including a modern pool. However, its 17 mi of hiking trails are especially prized for the bird-watching opportunities—be on the lookout for the lovely ruby-throated hummingbirds. The **Missouri National Recreation Scenic River Resource and Education Center** opened in 2003 to interpret the river in this area. Interactive displays explore the fur trade opened up by the Corps of Discovery and the steamboat traffic that followed. | 2 mi north of Ponca on Rte. 26 E off Rte. 12 | 402/755–2284 | www.ngpc.state.ne.us/parks/ponca.html | Nebraska Parks Permit; camping $8–$13 (2-night minimum) | Daily dawn–dusk.

✦ ON THE CALENDAR

Aug. **Dakota/Thurston County Fair.** Coinciding with Lewis's birthday on August 18, this four-day event includes a birthday celebration on the fairgrounds south of town. | 402/987–2140.

HISTORIC DINING

Kahill's. Steak. A panorama of rippling water unfolds at night at this restaurant. Ensconced among its rich mahogany furnishings, you can dine on steak, fish, chicken, duck, or the specialty, catfish. | 4th and B Sts. | 402/494–5025 | $10–$50 | AE, D, DC, MC, V.

CROFTON
▼▼

European trappers began trade with the Ponca as early as 1789. Then in 1804 the Corps of Discovery spent a week in this area during its council with the Yankton Sioux. Several journal entries note that wildlife was exceedingly abundant in this region. The Fort Laramie Treaty of 1868 gave Ponca land to the Sioux Indians in Knox County. The area where Crofton now sits remained unsettled until railroad workers pitched their tents here in 1892 while they constructed a route linking Norfolk, Nebraska, and Yankton, South Dakota. Railroad promoter J. T. M. Pearce liked the spot, established a town, and named it for Crofton Courts, his home in England.

✦ INFORMATION

Crofton Chamber of Commerce | Box 81, 68730 | 402/388–4385 | www.crofton-ne.com.

SITES TO SEE

Corps of Discovery Welcome Center. At the intersection of the Lewis and Clark Trail and the Pan-American Highway, this center hosts weekly historical programs and dispenses tourist information about the area. Large maps detail the Corps' progress through the region. An art gallery and gift shop sell items authorized by the Bicentennial Commission as authentically made. | 89705 U.S. 81, 3 mi east of Crofton | 402/667–6557 | www.crofton-ne. com/discover.htm | Free | Late May–early Sept., daily 9–6; early Sept.–late May, daily 10–4.

George Shannon Trail. You'll need to pick up a pamphlet with a special driving map from the Welcome Center to participate in this scavenger hunt spanning 12 northeastern Nebraska towns. While in search of lost packhorses, Private George Shannon—the Corps' youngest member—got separated from the party. He survived for 16 days on his own, and when he was finally discovered, he was in the vicinity of the statue you'll find in this town. Local artist Joe Serres carved wooden statues of the unfortunate Shannon, and each is "lost" for you to rescue in this scavenger-hunt activity. The **George Shannon Statue** is a depiction of Shannon leading a packhorse. Another statue can be found somewhere in the city park, north of town. | Crofton | 402/667–6557 | shannontrail.cjb.net | Free | Daily.

Kreycik Elk and Bison Ranch. Covered wagons convey you out to see, close up, the animals that the men of the Corps of Discovery hunted and fed upon throughout the journey. | 88971 517th Ave., Niobrara, 68760; 2 mi west of Niobrara on Rte. 12 to Niobrara State Park; turn left on oiled road and go 8 mi to a cemetery; turn left and drive ½ mi. | 402/857–3850 | www.bloomnet. com/elktours | $5.50 | Mid-May–mid-Sept., weekends 10, 2, and 4.

Lewis and Clark Lake Visitor Center. Maintained by the U.S. Army Corps of Engineers, this center sits on Calumet Bluff overlooking the Missouri River and Lewis and Clark Lake. Interior and exterior exhibits, a 30-minute film, and a comprehensive bookstore provide detailed information about the Corps of Discovery's trek through the region and councils with the Yankton Sioux. | 10 mi north of Crofton on Rte. 121 | 402/667–2546 | www.nwo.usace. army.mil | Free | Late May–early Sept., Sun.–Thurs. 8–6, Fri. and Sat. 8 AM–9 PM; early Sept.–late May, weekdays 8–4:30, weekends 10–6.

Niobrara State Park. The course of the Missouri has changed since the Corps camped here in September 1804, so the exact spot, marked by an American flag and bronze plaque, is now closer to the water. This park protects the least-disturbed stretch of the Missouri River in Nebraska. From late May through early fall, take a three-hour float trip with park rangers providing a history of the river, the Lewis and Clark expedition, and the Ponca nation, who once lived in this area. The trip costs $12 and is aboard a 20-foot, 11-person rubber raft. Buffalo-stew cookouts are a part of the park's Saturday-night activities in summer. | 28 mi west of Crofton on Rte. 12, Niobrara, 68760 | 402/857–3373 | fax 402/857–3420 | Free | Daily.

Ponca Tribe Museum. This tribal museum displays vintage photos as well as artwork and artifacts once housed at the Smithsonian, which date back to the 16th century. Photo and wax displays depict Lewis and Clark among the tribe. | 258–4 Park Ave., Niobrara, 68760 | 402/857–3519 | Free | Weekdays 8–4, Sat. 10–4.

✦ ON THE CALENDAR
June **Santee Sioux Tribal Powwow.** Intertribal dancing, traditional foods, and Native American crafts demonstrations are a part of this three-day festival, held the third weekend in June on the reservation north of Crofton. | 402/857–2302.

Aug. **Lewis and Clark Festival.** On the second weekend of the month, the Lewis and Clark Lake Visitor Center hosts this annual festival commemorating the famous expedition with reenactments, speakers, and demonstrations. | 402/667–2546.

Aug. **Ponca Tribal Powwow.** This three-day celebration of Ponca traditions, held on the powwow grounds south of Niobrara on the third weekend in August, includes dancing, Native American foods, and crafts. | 402/857–3519.

Sept.–Oct. **Lewis and Clark Motor Coach Tours.** Daylong motor coach tours from Crofton stop at several locations where Lewis and Clark traveled. | 402/582–4866.

LYNCH
▼▼

Set just before the Missouri River takes a sharp turn to the north, Lynch is the last community in Nebraska visited by the Corps of Discovery. Two items of significance occurred in this region. Private George Shannon, lost for more than two weeks after having been dispatched to find stray packhorses, almost starved near present-day Lynch before he was reunited with the group. The area is also where the Corps documented the first prairie-dog town. The group spent the better part of the day here, pouring water into a hole in an attempt to capture a live prairie dog (or "barking squirrels" in Lewis's words) to send back to Thomas Jefferson.

Barking Squirrels

One of the four directives Thomas Jefferson gave Lewis and Clark was to document the wildlife, flora, and fauna they found along their journey. On September 7, 1804, on a hill in what is now Boyd County, Nebraska, the Corps of Discovery first encountered "barking squirrels," or prairie dogs. Clark wrote in his journal: "The hill contains great numbers of holes on top of which those little animals sit erect and make a whistling noise and when alarmed step into their hole." He also wrote that his team spent the better part of a day pouring water down a hole just to capture the black-tailed prairie dog that was later sent to President Jefferson.

The prairie dog was sent sailing down the Missouri to New Orleans, then around Florida to the Chesapeake Bay, and finally to Baltimore Harbor. President Jefferson was quite impressed and created a living space for him in Independence Hall in Philadelphia, where the president lived. A stuffed prairie dog is on display at the Smithsonian, although it is not certain that this is the actual prairie dog the Corps sent to Jefferson.

Today, most ranchers and farmers in the West struggle with problems caused by prairie dogs. Prairie-dog holes can trap water and flood cropland. On ranches, cattle and horses sometimes step into the holes and break their legs. Prairie dogs are also primary carriers of many diseases that infect livestock. However, in Lynch, the town closest to where the prairie dogs were captured, the Community Club has copyrighted what they believe is the only pattern for a prairie dog. Twice a week, a volunteer group meets in the high school home economics room to make fuzzy, little "Lynch Dawgs" similar to the ancestors encountered by Lewis and Clark. Proceeds from the sale of the Lynch Prairie Dog, sold in gift stores throughout the area, help support a scenic overlook of the Missouri River near the area where Lewis and Clark traveled.

◆ INFORMATION
Lynch Community Association | Box 122, 68746 | 402/569–3202 | www.ci.lynch. ne.us.com.

SITES TO SEE
Old Baldy. One of the most notable landmarks along this part of the Missouri River—which looks much as it did when the Corps traveled this way—is this

300-foot geological formation made of chalk rock, formed when this area was a shallow inland sea. Clark's journal entry for September 7, 1804, tells of climbing its domelike knob, void of vegetation. An 1834 painting of Old Baldy by Swiss artist Karl Bodmer hangs at the Joslyn Art Museum in Omaha. | 7 mi north on County Rd. | 402/569–2706 | Free | Daily.

HISTORIC DINING AND LODGING

Two Rivers Saloon and Hotel. American/Casual. Buffalo, elk, and catfish are among the dishes you can order in this western-style restaurant and bar. Three mounted elk heads and a mural of the river as it would have appeared in the 1800s hang in the dining room. | 254-11 Park Ave., Niobrara | 402/857–3340 | Closed Mon. | $9.50 | D, MC, V.

Cross J Ranch Bed and Breakfast. This bed-and-breakfast 13 mi south of Lynch, surrounded by natural prairie, has been a working cattle ranch since the 1800s; the ranch house dates from 1916. You can use the living and dining rooms, kitchen, screened-in porch, and fireplace. Tours and hunting trips are available. Dining room. | Box HC 85, 68763 | 402/336–2007 or 877/427–6775 | fax 402/336–2007 | 2 rooms, 1 suite | $65–$75 | MC, V | BP.

Frontier Return to Nature Cabins. This is a true "roughing it" experience in two authentic early 1800s log cabins with an outhouse and no electricity. Owner Dean Wavrunek, a lifelong resident of Knox County, leads hunting trips for turkey and deer in the area, as well as buffalo hunts on the nearby Santee Reservations. | 88037 523rd Ave., Verdigre, 68783 | 402/668–2868 | 2 cabins | $25 per person, per night | No credit cards | BP.

Iowa

On Wednesday, July 18, 1804, Patrick Gass wrote, "This is the most open country I ever beheld, almost one continued prairie." The Corps of Discovery had entered southwest Iowa, and the group was exploring what is now Fremont County, a part of the rich, fertile prairie that would quickly attract settlers from the eastern shores. Iowa takes its name from a Native American word meaning "beautiful land," and the soil here, among the most fertile, most wisely managed, and most lucrative on the planet, is the greatest of many riches in the state.

The Corps members were the first Euro-Americans to document exploration of the state's western reaches. However, nearly 125 years earlier, French-Canadian explorers Louis Joliet and Father James Marquette had traveled Iowa's eastern shore via the Mississippi. The Ioway, a Native American tribe originally from the Great Lakes, were living along many of the tributaries to the Mississippi. Iowa was claimed for France by explorer Robert Cavelier sieur de La Salle in 1682, and it became part of the terrain in the Louisiana Purchase in 1803.

The century that passed between de La Salle's claims and the land's exploration by the Corps saw the arrival of Sauk and Fox Indians, who had been pushed out of Wisconsin and Illinois by settlers. The Ioway chose not to resist the settlers, and in 1838, they abandoned their land here and moved west; by the end of the next decade most of the Sauk and Fox Indians had followed.

Between 1846 and 1848 more than 70,000 Mormons crossed Iowa on their way from Illinois to Utah. You can still see their campfire rocks and the ruts of their wagons in parts of southern Iowa, where they battled the elements at the beginning of their journey. The Corps also battled the elements, writing of blistering heat, snakes, mosquitoes, and horrid squalls that nearly capsized the boats. They also described pleasant days and evenings, when the breezes helped move the craft along the river and kept insects at bay. Wildlife was plentiful and berries abundant, and at one point Clark wrote that fish could be caught by simply dropping a line.

The Corps' explorers were also among the first Euro-Americans to see and document one of Iowa's greatest geological marvels—the Loess Hills. Pronounced *luss,* these hills were formed thousands of years ago by harsh winter winds that blew the loose Missouri River silt into windswept dunes or hills. The Loess Hills run from the Missouri border to Sioux City, and at the time of the Corps' exploration little vegetation covered them, unlike the trees and plant life that cover them today.

The greatest loss of the journey took place on the banks of the Missouri in what is now Sioux City with the death of Sergeant Charles Floyd, apparently of a burst appendix. With great care and full military honors, the Corps buried Floyd on a bluff overlooking the Missouri and placed a cedar cross above his grave. Patrick Gass was then promoted to the rank of sergeant and continued to make great contributions. When the Corps members returned to the grave nearly two years later, they saw it had been disturbed and once again paid honors to their friend.

Sergeant Floyd's grave has been moved three times in the 200 years since he was interred, primarily because the powerful river has cut away at the bluffs and banks at this southerly turn in the river's course. Nowadays six dams on the upper Missouri control the levels and river channel and contain erosion.

The Corps would find navigating the river much different than in the early years of the 19th century. There were times, notably August 5, 1804, when the Corps traveled 20 mi of a winding curving channel, only to loop around on themselves and camp just a few hundred yards from where they had been the previous night. The Missouri was wider and shallower then; dredging, levees, and wing dams have cut nearly 127 mi from the route the Corps traveled.

The Loess Hills

A DRIVING TOUR FROM SIDNEY TO SIOUX CITY

▼▼▼

Distance: 220 mi   **Time:** 2 days
Breaks: Turin is a good choice for a night's stay.

Western Iowa's Loess Hills were created thousands of years ago, when wind swept silt deposits from the Missouri River's floodplain into huge clouds of dust, which were then deposited a few miles away. The range of loess, the most extensive outside China, extends along the Missouri River from the Missouri border to north of Sioux City.

Note: The Loess Hills Scenic Byway has 16 excursion loops along its main route and not all of them are paved. Each loop is marked with a byway sign.

Begin in southern Iowa, where the Corps of Discovery first encountered these distinctive dunes and bluffs. **Sidney,** a typically friendly Iowa farm town, borders Waubonsie State Park, which provides a good view of the river from scenic overlooks. Stop by any of the orchards and stands that line the road to sample some of the fruit the Corps enjoyed as it explored the Nishnabotna River valley.

Leave Sidney heading north into the hills on Route J34, which goes through the small towns of Thurman and Tabor. You'll pass Forney Lake, known as a nesting ground for bald eagles; keep your eyes open for the nests, on high branches, and for the eagles, which occasionally swoop down over the lake in search of fish. From Tabor, you'll come across the Waubonsie Loop, the first of 16 byways. The road is partially gravel; the yellowish soil is the loess. Driving down this road makes your car dusty.

If you forgo the byway (or after you emerge from the byway), continue north on U.S. 275 to **Glenwood.** A must-see in Glenwood is the earthen Indian lodge outside the Mills County Historical Museum, which houses Native American tools, arrowheads, and other artifacts. Glenwood is a suburb of **Council Bluffs,** where you'll find the Western Historic Trails Center. The center has numerous walking trails and interpretive programs relating to Lewis and Clark.

After your visit, continue on U.S. 275 until it becomes Route 183. Remember the roadway is clearly marked with signs indicating you are on the Loess Hills Scenic Byway. Route 183 passes through Crescent and Honey Creek on its way into **Missouri Valley.** This community has several attractions of interest, including the Harrison County Historical Village, which doubles as an Iowa Welcome Center. Lots of information and driving maps of the Loess Hills are available here. Missouri Valley is also in the center of the DeSoto National Wildlife Area, a preserve that straddles the river and extends into Nebraska; it is home to thousands of waterfowl, such as those documented by the Lewis and Clark expedition.

The Men's Best Friend

Some historians say he was the most valuable member on the journey, yet he was never rewarded monetarily or recognized publicly. He was Seaman, a black Newfoundland who belonged to Lewis. As the captain was gathering supplies, materials, and education along the East Coast in spring 1803, he spent $20 of his own money for this fun-loving animal, who proved to befriend all the men at one point or another.

As Lewis made his way down the Ohio River, his journals noted that Seaman was making himself useful in catching squirrels. Later, farther along the Missouri, Seaman caught geese, ran down deer and antelope, and rousted beaver out of their lodges at the banks of the river. Journals note that he warned sleeping men of a charging buffalo bull on May 29, 1805, and patrolled through the night in watch for grizzly bear.

Seaman probably walked the shoreline most of the way with his master. He was certainly a great comfort to Lewis, given the captain's propensity toward depression and moodiness. When his dog disappeared, stolen by Indians, Lewis threatened to burn the village until the animal was returned, and he was.

The journals often note that the Indian tribes were quite impressed with Seaman's strength and intelligence. On November 16, 1803, near the confluence of the Ohio and Mississippi rivers, Lewis mentioned that they encountered an encampment of Shawnee and Delaware Indians. "[O]ne of the Shawnees a respectable looking Indian offered me three beaver skins for my dog with which he appeared much pleased . . . I prised much for his docility and qualifications generally for my journey and of course there was no bargain."

Newfoundlands are known as the gentle giant of the dog world, with a gentle temperament. Bred in the maritime province for which it is named, the Newfoundland is a great swimmer with a heavy coat to protect him from the frigid elements.

Seaman suffered the same hardships, illnesses, and risk to life that the men of the Corps did. He was once bitten by a beaver in the left hind leg so badly that Lewis feared for the dog's life. The pads of his feet were tortured by prickly pear cactus, rocks, and other debris. Mosquitoes swarmed the dog's nose and eyes until he howled in pain, the heat was oppressive under his heavy coat, and surely he was as close to starvation as any of the men during those dismal weeks in the Bitterroot Mountains.

No one knows for sure what happened to Seaman. A final journal entry in July 1806 complains that the mosquitoes were bad and even the dog was tormented. Historians, however, believe that Seaman completed the journey with his admiring masters and was with Lewis at his death in 1809.

For his faithful companionship, Lewis named a creek for him in Montana. Although that stream has since been renamed and is now Monture Creek, Seaman continues to be recognized and appreciated well into the 21st century. Hundreds of sculptures, murals, paintings, and crafts items associated with the expedition include Seaman front and center, as surely he was in the hearts of the men he accompanied for two years, four months, six days, and beyond.

Route 183 remains the primary route of the scenic byway as you continue north through the villages of Magnolia, Pisgah, and Moorhead. Numerous loops shoot off of the main route here, and depending on how you are progressing in your journey, you may want to explore a few. Take time to look for yucca plants, a desert species found nowhere else in Iowa. You can also see more than 350 species of prairie flowers along this roadway. Take Route 37 east to **Turin** and spend the night at the Country Homestead Bed & Breakfast, which has spectacular views of the Loess Hills at sunset and sunrise.

On day two, leave Turin via U.S. 175 east to visit **Onawa,** home to Lewis and Clark State Park and the keelboat replica, which sits ready to go on the lake. Return to the scenic byway via Route L12, which leads through the communities of Smithland, Climbing Hill, and Bronson to your final destination, **Sioux City.** Here you'll want to explore the numerous Lewis and Clark sites, including the Sergeant Floyd Monument, the Sergeant Floyd Welcome Center and Museum, and the Lewis and Clark Interpretive Center.

SIDNEY
▼▼▼

Native Americans did not call this part of southwest Iowa home until long after the Corps of Discovery came through and the federal government began relocating tribes. The Pottawattamie were the first to arrive. The Corps of Discovery reached this area on July 18, 1804, and explored about 10 mi up the Nishnabotna River, noting the heavy growth of cottonwood and mulberry trees. They shot turkey and geese and enjoyed fruit from the trees.

✦ INFORMATION
Sidney City Hall | 604 Clay St., 51652 | 712/374–2223.

SITES TO SEE

Fremont County Historical Museum. This museum on the courthouse square houses Native American artifacts and displays on the Loess Hills and the fur-trading business, which developed in this area after the Corps returned home. Perhaps the most impressive exhibit is of the mastodon tusks, discovered in a quarry in the Loess Hills. | 801 Indiana Ave. | 712/374–2335 or 712/374–3248 | Free | Memorial Day–Labor Day, Sun. 1–4 or by appointment.

Waubonsie State Park. Named for Pottawattamie chief Waubonsie, this 1,200-acre park has some 7 mi of hiking trails and 8 mi of equestrian trails winding through the Loess Hills. You can view the Missouri River valley from the scenic overlook, which has interpretive kiosks that describe the Corps' trip this way in 1804 and 1806. Interpretive programs are conducted in summer. | 2559 U.S. 239, 4 mi south of Sydney, Hamburg | 712/382–2786 | www.iowadnr. com | Free | Daily dawn–dusk.

GLENWOOD
▼▼

Migrating westward in 1846, the Mormons found Pottawattamie and Omaha Indians, who had moved here from the Great Lakes in 1833. Though most of the Mormon group went on to Utah, a few remained and called the community Rushville, later renamed Coonville, after a local doctor; it acquired its present name in 1851, when the town incorporated.

✦ INFORMATION

Glenwood Chamber of Commerce | 32½ N. Walnut, 51534 | 712/527–3298 | www. glenwoodnet.com.

SITES TO SEE

Mills County Historical Museum. Early Native American life predating Lewis and Clark is interpreted here; displays include earthen lodges, arrowheads, spear points, pottery, and other artifacts collected in the area. Historical buildings include a schoolhouse, barn, and jail. | 89 Sharp St., in Glenwood Lake Park | 712/527–5038 | www.glenwood.net | Free | May–Sept., weekends 1:30–4, or by appointment.

COUNCIL BLUFFS
▼▼

Many people assume that the city of Council Bluffs was built on the land where Lewis and Clark had their first council with the Otoe and Missouria tribes. Historians, however, have determined that the council actually took place on the Nebraska side of the river, about 20 mi north of present-day Council Bluffs.

Certainly Lewis and Clark explored these banks of the river, but they found no Native Americans on the eastern shore. The first settlement here was known as Kanesville, in honor of Thomas Kane, who was sympathetic to the plight of the Mormons, who spent the winter of 1846–47 here. In 1853, the residents elected to incorporate and rename their community Council Bluffs.

✦ INFORMATION
Council Bluffs Chamber of Commerce | 7 N. 6th St., 51502 | 712/325–6171 or 800/228–6878 | www.councilbluffsiowa.com. **Western Iowa Tourism Region** | 103 N. 3rd St., Red Oak, 51566 | 712/623–4232 or 888/623–4232 | www.traveliowa.org.

SITES TO SEE
Lake Manawa State Park. Manawa is a Native American word meaning "peace and comfort," which is appropriate for this area, where the Corps camped for six days in late July 1804. It was the Corps' first rest since the start of the journey two months earlier. Catfish were plentiful, so the explorers called the site White Catfish Camp. The lake wasn't here at that time but was created in 1881 by excessive flooding of the Missouri River. Today the 1,500-acre park is popular for camping and boating and has a walking-biking trail that connects to the Western Historic Trails Center. | 1100 S. Shore Dr., Exit 3 off I–80 | 712/366–0220 | www.state.ia.us/dnr/organiza/ppd/manawa | Free | Daily.

Lewis and Clark Monument Park. The monument and park atop a bluff north of Council Bluffs honor the Corps of Discovery. The area provides vistas of the Council Bluffs–Omaha metro area and the Missouri River valley. Hiking trails and picnic facilities are available. | A962 Monument Rd., Exit 55 off I–29 to N. 25th St. | 712/328–4650 | Free | Daily.

Western Historic Trails Center. Inside this museum, multimedia exhibits use photos, film, interactive maps, and sculpture to document the Lewis and Clark, Mormon, Oregon, and California trails. You can also participate in activities designed to re-create the everyday life of experiences for early settlers. | 3434 Richard Downing Ave. | 712/366–4900 | www.iowahistory.org/sites | Free | Apr.–Sept., daily 9–6; Oct.–Mar., daily 9–5.

✦ ON THE CALENDAR
July **White Catfish Encampment.** Annually on the third weekend in July, the Western Historic Trails Center hosts this three-day festival with historic music, lecturers, artists, and reenactors. | 712/366–4900.

HISTORIC DINING

Riverside Grill. American/Casual. Walleye, salmon, and catfish are served at this eatery with a river-level view of the Missouri with the Omaha skyline beyond. Breakfast is also available. | 2 Harrahs Blvd. | 712/328–7079 | Closed Sun.–Tues. No dinner | $13–$20 | AE, MC, V.

MISSOURI VALLEY

▼▼▼

The Corps camped near here on August 3, 1804, just before the council with the Otoe and Missouria. The day before, one of the hunters had killed a white heron, which excited Lewis a great deal. Today, this species and 240 others continue to make the Missouri Valley area their home. The DeSoto National Wildlife Refuge, created in 1958, encompasses nearly 8,000 acres on both the Nebraska and Iowa sides of the river. After the Corps of Discovery opened the area to explorers and traders, emigrants from Tennessee founded the town of Missouri Valley in the 1850s. A few miles on up the river, on August 6, is when it was first noticed that Private Moses Reed and the boatman La Liberté were missing and assumed deserted. A search party was sent for them with orders to shoot if they did not return peacefully. The two were court-martialed on August 18, near Sioux City.

✦ **INFORMATION**

Missouri Valley Chamber of Commerce | 100 S. 4th St., 51555 | 712/642–2553 | www.missourivalley.com.

SITES TO SEE

DeSoto National Wildlife Refuge. The 8,000 acres of protected land that make up this park in Nebraska and Iowa are home to hundreds of species of wildlife, including migrating waterfowl. Lewis documented many of them in various forms to show to the president. Half a million snow geese rest here during annual migrations and forage on the refuge's grasses, corn, and soybeans. | Exit 75 off U.S. 30 | 712/642–4121 | $3 per vehicle | Daily.

Harrison County Historical Village. More than 10,000 items from the 19th century, including household items and farm equipment, are on display in five vintage buildings, among them a log cabin and a schoolhouse 3 mi northeast of town on U.S. 30. You'll find the Iowa Welcome Center here; it has many informational items on the Lewis and Clark Trail in this area. | 2931 Monroe Ave. | 712/642–2114 | www.harrisoncountyia.org/welcome | $2 | Mon.–Sat. 9–5, Sun. noon–5.

ONAWA

▼▼

Onawa sits in the heart of the Loess Hills, which Clark described as "a bald-pated prairie." The word Onawa means "wide awake" and comes from an old Ojibway love song that was incorporated into Henry Wadsworth Longfellow's poem "Song of Hiawatha." Whether by coincidence or design, this town is known for its wide streets and alert citizenry. The town is in Monona County, which means "beautiful valley." The Ojibway were not living in the area at the time of Lewis and Clark but were forced from their homes in Wisconsin and Minnesota with the coming of settlers there.

✦ INFORMATION

Onawa Chamber of Commerce | 140 W. Hawthorne St., 62048 | 712/423–1801 | www.onawa.com.

SITES TO SEE

Lewis and Clark State Park. On August 10, 1804, the expedition passed this site and spent time exploring the flora and fauna of the area. Today, the area is a 280-acre park and incorporates Blue Lake, a popular camping and fishing destination. A key attraction is a keelboat, like the one used by the Corps, built by volunteers in 1986 and refurbished in 2000. White and red pirogues are brought out on the water for demonstrations each June during the Lewis and Clark Festival. | 21914 Park Loop | 712/423–2829 | www.state.ia.us/parks | Free | Daily dawn–dusk.

Loess Hills Scenic Byway. More than 220 mi of roads create the Loess Hills Scenic Byway, which runs from Iowa's southern border to north of Sioux City. The byway's main route is paved, although some loops use gravel roads as they pass cities and towns; wind through farmland, woods, prairies, and orchards; and take in historic sites, overlooks, and state parks. Corps journals noted exploring the Loess Hills all along the Iowa border. | Box 180, Oakland, 51560 | 712/482–3029 | www.goldenhillsrcd.org/byway | Free | Daily.

Monona County Arboretum. On the east side of town, this 300-tree arboretum displays native grasses, plants, and trees that were documented by Lewis in the early 1800s. Exhibits in a small natural history museum and conservation center tell how Lewis recorded the flora he observed. | 318 E. Iowa Ave. | 712/423–2400 | Free | Weekdays 7:30–4.

Monona County Historical Museum. A native-flower prairie garden highlights this museum, which also includes exhibits of Native American stone tools and arrowheads and a scale model of the Corps of Discovery keelboat. The

Sergeant Charles Floyd

"A young man of much merit" is how Meriwether Lewis characterized 22-year-old Charles Floyd, a member of the permanent party. Sergeant Floyd is famous for his singularity—the only man to die on the expedition and the first U.S. soldier to die west of the Mississippi.

Little is known about Floyd. He was born in Kentucky in 1782 to Mary and Charles Stuart Floyd and may have been a distant relative of William Clark. He had one younger brother, Robert C. Floyd, who inherited his brother's land grant at the conclusion of the expedition. Forensic evidence indicates that he was between 5 feet 6 inches and 5 feet 8 inches tall, which was good sized for the period. Like all the others, according to Lewis, he was "stout, healthy, unmarried . . . accustomed to the woods and capable of bearing bodily fatigue."

Floyd was a leader and quite literate. He kept good journals throughout the first three months and often mentioned the physical condition of the other men. That diary is now the property of the Wisconsin Historical Society. July 31, 1804, was his last journal entry, which in part read: "I am verrry sick and has been for sometime, but have recovered my helth again."

The entire entry describes what is believed to be an infected appendix, which became acute and perforated. The others on the journey described his complaint as somewhat like "bilious cholic." Although Lewis had studied medicine in Philadelphia before beginning the journey, he wasn't equipped to help Sergeant Floyd—appendectomies were uncommon at this time.

For days the journals reflected the great concern by all of the men, yet the mission moved forward with a fair wind until 2 PM on August 20. At that time, "he died with a great deal of composure," according to Clark. "This Man at all times gave us proofs of his firmness and Determined resolution to doe Service to his country and honor himself."

He was buried with the Honors of War on a hill that is now known as Floyd's Bluff near Sioux City at the mouth of Floyd's River, so named in his honor. Private Patrick Gass was promoted to sergeant in his place and became a key leader in the expedition. August 20, 1804, was a beautiful evening, the journals noted.

Eskimo Pie ice cream sandwich machine, invented in Onawa, is also here. | 212 N. 12th St. | 712/423–2776 | Free | Memorial Day–Labor Day, weekends 1–4:30.

Snyder Bend County Park. On August 13, 1804, the expedition passed this site, where James McKay had operated a trading post from 1795 to 1796. The explorers caught fish weighing more than 100 pounds and, across the river, found the shambled remains of an Omaha village, whose residents had been wiped out by smallpox four years earlier. The park has camping sites and river access, as well as an interpretive panel that explains the Corps' activities in this area. | Exit 134 off I–29 | 712/423–2829 | Free | Daily.

✦ ON THE CALENDAR
June **Lewis and Clark Festival.** Although the Corps camped here in August 1804, this three-day festival is held the second week in June to accommodate the schedules of reenactors and schoolchildren and to avoid the late-summer heat of August. Authentic lodges and encampments, 19th-century costumes, and 19th-century homemade root beer and buffalo burgers enrich the experience. | 712/423–1801.

HISTORIC LODGING
The Country Homestead Bed & Breakfast. Owner David Zahrt's great-grand-father homesteaded this land in the Loess Hills in 1865 and built the original wing of this sprawling one-story farmhouse. A picture taken in 1885 shows the property exactly as barren and treeless as the journals described the area in 1804. The Zahrts are restoring and protecting much of the native prairie that surrounds their antiques-filled home. Cable TV; no smoking. | 2213 Larpenteur Memorial Rd., 6 mi east of Onawa on Rte. 175, Turin, 51509 | 712/353–6772 | fax 928/832–8463 | www.country-homestead.com | 3 rooms | $75–$85 | No credit cards | BP.

SIOUX CITY
▼▼▼

Although this part of western Iowa is known as Siouxland, it was once also inhabited by the Omaha and Ponca tribes. It was in the stifling heat of August 20–21, 1804, that the Corps traveled through what is now Sioux City. It was also here that Sergeant Charles Floyd died of apparent appendicitis, the only casualty of the expedition. At the time, his companions placed a cedar cross above his grave, and in 1806, on their return journey, they repaired damage to the grave site. The Missouri River eventually tore away much of the bluff, and Sergeant Floyd was later reburied up to three times to protect his remains from the forces of the current. His grave is on a hill overlooking the water. In 1900 local leaders commissioned a 100-foot Egyptian obelisk for the site, and it remains a significant marker for those who travel the river and interstate highway through Siouxland.

Modern-day Sioux City is known as the home of the Sioux Bee honey company and as the birthplace of twin sisters and columnists Ann Landers and Dear Abby (Pauline and Esther Friedman).

✦ INFORMATION

Sioux City Convention and Visitors Bureau | 801 4th St., 51101 | 712/279–4800 or 800/593–2228 | www.siouxland.com/ccat. **Tri State Chapter, Lewis and Clark Trail Heritage Foundation** | 3121 Grandview Blvd., 51104 | 712/252–2364 | www.lewisandclarksiouxcity.com.

SITES TO SEE

Chief War Eagle Monument. This steel sculpture atop a bluff honors the Yankton Sioux chief, who was friendly and supportive to traders and explorers. He was the last Sioux chief to live in the Iowa Territory. The bluff provides a breathtaking view of the Missouri River. | North on Riverside Blvd., east on W. 4th St. to War Eagle Dr. | 712/279–4800 or 800/593–2228 | www.siouxland. com | Free | Daily.

Lewis and Clark: An American Adventure. Inside the unlikely setting of a suburban shopping mall, this 269-foot mural composed of 37 individual paintings depicts the entire expedition from beginning to end. From the first meeting Lewis had with Thomas Jefferson to the expedition's return past the grave of Sergeant Floyd, the mural's level of detail on each panel provides a visual image rarely found at other expedition sites. | 4400 Sergeant Rd. | 712/274–0109 | www.southernhillsmall.com | Free | Daily.

Lewis and Clark Interpretive Center. A 15-star, 15-stripe flag flies above this center, opened in 2002, which explores some of the everyday aspects of the expedition. The responsibilities of lesser-known Corps members, including the laborers and the hunters, are detailed in interactive exhibits; at these you can listen to campfire discussions and the prayers over Sergeant Floyd's grave. Each visitor to the center receives a journal, similar to those kept by the leaders of the expedition. The center also displays an enlarged copy of Sergeant Floyd's journal in his own writing. | 900 Larsen Park Rd. | 712/224–5242 | www.siouxcitylcic.com | Free | Memorial Day–Labor Day, daily 9–6; Labor Day–Memorial Day, Tues.–Sat. 9–5, Sun. noon–5.

Sergeant Floyd Monument. On the east bank of the Missouri River, this monument is dedicated to the only man to die on the Lewis and Clark expedition. A plaque at the base of the monument tells the story of Sergeant Floyd. Picnic tables and a view of the river valley make this a pleasant place to take a break. | Glen Ave. at U.S. 75 | 800/593–2228 | www.lewisandclarksiouxcity.com/history | Free | Daily.

Sergeant Floyd Welcome Center and Museum. A life-size model of Sergeant Floyd welcomes you to this U.S. Army Corps of Engineers diesel inspection ship turned river transportation museum, which houses artifacts dating from the Lewis and Clark expedition, scale models of Missouri River steamboats, and Iowa's only professional model-shipbuilding shop. | 1000 Larsen Park Rd. | 712/279–0198 | www.sioux-city.org/museum | Free | May–Sept., daily 8–6; Oct.–Apr., daily 9–5.

Sioux City Art Center. Displays scheduled throughout the Bicentennial include art and crafts used as gifts from President Jefferson, the works of Karl Bodmer, and contemporary photos of the Lewis and Clark Trail. In the summer of 2004, more than 40 statues of the Newfoundland that accompanied the Corps of Discovery will be displayed throughout the city. | 225 Nebraska St. | 712/279–6272 | www.sc-artcenter.com | Free | Tues., Wed., Fri., and Sat. 10–5; Thurs. noon–9; Sun. 1–5.

Sioux City Public Museum. As the Corps passed the mouth of the Big Sioux River on August 21, 1804, an interpreter told Clark that the river originated far to the north, where one of its creeks passed through red cliffs where Indians made peace pipes. That area is today known as Pipestone, Minnesota, a sacred Native American ceremonial land. The third floor of this 23-room Romanesque mansion displays artifacts of the Plains and Woodland Indians; elsewhere you can see pioneer and Civil War artifacts and natural-history displays. | 2901 Jackson St. | 712/279–6174 | www.sioux-city.org/museum | Free | Tues.–Sat. 9–5, Sun. 1–5.

Stone State Park. On August 21, 1804, Clark and Patrick Gass both noted in their journals of passing the pale-color bluffs that reach about 170 feet high at the mouth of the Big Sioux River. This is now Stone State Park, an area once inhabited by the Dakota Sioux. Although little is known specifically about their activities in Stone Park, the area probably was used for hunting, migration, and encampments. An interpretive marker at Elk Point Overlook tells of the Corps' exploration of the river valley below. The park is a good spot for birding and camping. The **Dorothy Pecaut Nature Center** (4500 Sioux River Rd. | 712/258–0838 | www.woodburyparks.com | Free | Tues.–Sat. 9–5, Sun. 1–5) showcases the Loess Hills and indigenous plants and animals, many of which Lewis and Clark discovered. Hiking trails, hands-on exhibits, and educational programs are available. | 5001 Talbot Rd. | 712/255–4698 | www.state.ia.us/parks | Free; camping $11–$16 | Daily 4 AM–10:30 PM.

✦ ON THE CALENDAR
Aug. Sergeant Floyd Memorial Encampment. An 1804 living-history encamp-ment on the grounds of the Sergeant Floyd Welcome Center displays authen-tic tents, camp equipment, uniforms, and firearms. Activities during the two-day event include an 1804 reveille and flag-raising ceremony, musters, and inspections and arms drills. | 712/279–0198.

South Dakota

hen Lewis and Clark passed through South Dakota in the summer of 1804, they discovered a land with waist-high prairie grasses and enormous buffalo herds. The explorers found the prairies teeming with game and inviting further exploration. But, because of strong head winds, nagging sandbars, and strong currents, the crew was often forced to use towropes and manhandle their boats and supplies in an upriver struggle through South Dakota.

On good days, the expedition made 15 to 20 mi. The Corps often stopped to explore, hunt, collect berries, and take measurements of wind, water, and temperature. On the rivers of southeastern South Dakota—the Big Sioux, Vermillion, James, Choteau, and Missouri—Arikara and later Sioux Indians fished and gathered food. It was here, between the Vermillion and Yankton rivers, where the explorers first met Native Americans. In late August 1804, during a council with the Yankton Sioux, Lewis named an infant boy, Struck by the Ree, the first Sioux citizen of the United States.

On September 15, 1804, the expedition passed the mouth of the White River, just south of Chamberlain, and paused the following day to let the crew rest and to let the baggage dry out after three days of heavy rains. Along the Missouri River bluffs, the explorers' hunters killed bison, elk, deer, and pelicans. On September 17, Lewis set out on foot to explore the countryside along the river. The short, rich prairie grasses reminded him of a "beautiful bowling green," and he spotted wolves, polecats, and, circling above on the air currents, a number of hawks. He was also pleased by the scenery and impressed by a nearby bison herd, which he estimated at 3,000 animals. Three days later the expedition reached the Big Bend of the Missouri. One of the party walked the distance across land and found it was only 2,000 yards, or about a mile. By water, the loop was 30 mi.

Although the Corps passed fairly peaceably through South Dakota, there was one standoff with the Teton Sioux, a belligerent tribe also known as Titonwan Lakota, which by this time had pushed most of the Arikara into western South Dakota. Warned that the Teton Sioux were known to rob traders, Lewis and Clark ordered the Corps to be armed and ready to fight. As a result, the men spent several sleepless nights as they proceeded through lands occupied by the powerful Teton Sioux. Journal entries from September 23 to 30 note that the soldiers were on high alert as they passed the vicinity of present-day Fort Pierre and Pierre.

The explorers held a council with the Teton Sioux on September 25, 1804, at the mouth of the Bad River, south of South Dakota's present-day capital of Pierre. Lacking a competent interpreter, and with suspicion firmly entrenched on both sides, the council quickly came to the brink of violence with weapons drawn and sighted on both sides. Teton chief Black Buffalo managed to defuse the situation, earning the respect of both his people and the Corps. Although the underlying tension never eased, Lewis and Clark talked to, lectured, feasted with, and observed the Teton Sioux people for the next few days. On the final day of their council with the Teton, violence was once again narrowly averted when a group of Chief Black Buffalo's followers took control of the rope tethering the keelboat to the riverbank and refused to let go without further consideration—namely more tobacco. When Lewis would not comply, tempers flared, and Clark prepared to fire the port swivel gun. Lewis, insisting that the Corps would proceed, called the chief's leadership into question and goaded him into persuading his warriors to accept a lesser amount of tobacco than they had originally demanded. That done, Lewis disdainfully tossed a few twists of tobacco to the men holding the rope, then watched as Black Buffalo jerked the rope from their hands and handed it to a member of the Corps. The expedition continued without threat of further violent incident.

The next month the Corps passed an abandoned village of about 80 Arikara lodges. Then, just upstream, they met the Arikara, who welcomed the explorers. Clark noted that the villagers grew corn, tobacco, and beans and traveled along the river in a bowl-shaped vessel made of bison hide.

Farther up the Missouri, the party was joined by French trader Toussaint Charbonneau and his 15-year-old wife, Sacagawea, a Shoshone who had been captured by the Blackfeet, sold as a slave to the Hidatsa Sioux, and won by the Frenchman in a gambling match. Sacagawea would accompany the expedition all the way to the Pacific.

Traversing South Dakota

A DRIVING TOUR FROM ELK POINT TO MOBRIDGE

▼▼▼

Distance: 400 mi   **Time:** 3 days
Breaks: Stay in Chamberlain and Pierre, both Missouri River towns with historical and recreational opportunities as well as numerous lodging options.

This driving tour follows the Corps' 1804 trek along the Missouri north and west through the state.

The Corps entered present-day South Dakota soon after the loss of Sergeant Charles Floyd, who died near the mouth of the Big Sioux River in August 1804. Begin your tour in **Elk Point,** the site of the election of Patrick Gass as Sergeant Floyd's replacement. Elk Point is 15 mi north of Sioux City, Iowa, on Interstate 29. If you are traveling from North Sioux City, you'll pass the Adams Homestead and Nature Preserve, which has nature trails and one of the last free-flowing segments of the Missouri River. Continue north on Interstate 29 for 8 mi, west on Route 50 for 7 mi, and again north on Route 19 for 7 mi past **Vermillion** for a hike to the top of the legendary Spirit Mound, the hill Lewis and Clark dared to climb after disregarding numerous reports from local tribes of the small but murderous devils who inhabited the place.

After your hike drive 26 mi west on Route 50 to the town of **Yankton** for a picnic lunch at Terrace Park or any number of other lakeside areas at the Lewis and Clark Recreation Area. In the afternoon you can either continue west along Route 50 to **Pickstown,** near the Fort Randall Dam, or stay closer to the Missouri River along smaller South Dakota highways, which take you past Struck by the Ree's Grave and enable you to see the bison herd maintained by the Yankton Sioux near Greenwood. From Pickstown follow Routes 50 and 45 north for 100 mi and Interstate 90 west for 26 mi to **Chamberlain** and stay the night. While you're here, visit the Akta Lakota Museum and the modern Lewis and Clark Interpretive Center, with its replica of the keelboat that carried the explorers up the river.

On your second day, take the Native American Scenic Byway from Chamberlain to **Pierre,** South Dakota's state capital. This 100-mi drive takes you through both the Crow Creek and Lower Brule Indian Reservations, which surround the Big Bend of the Missouri River with great scenery—the surrounding prairie, and the bison herds roaming the countryside. The byway begins by heading via Route 50 north from Chamberlain; follow signs along Routes 4, 47, 10, and 1806 to Pierre. You'll cross from the east side of the river to the west over the Big Bend Dam. Have a steak at the Cattleman's Club, and stay the night in Pierre.

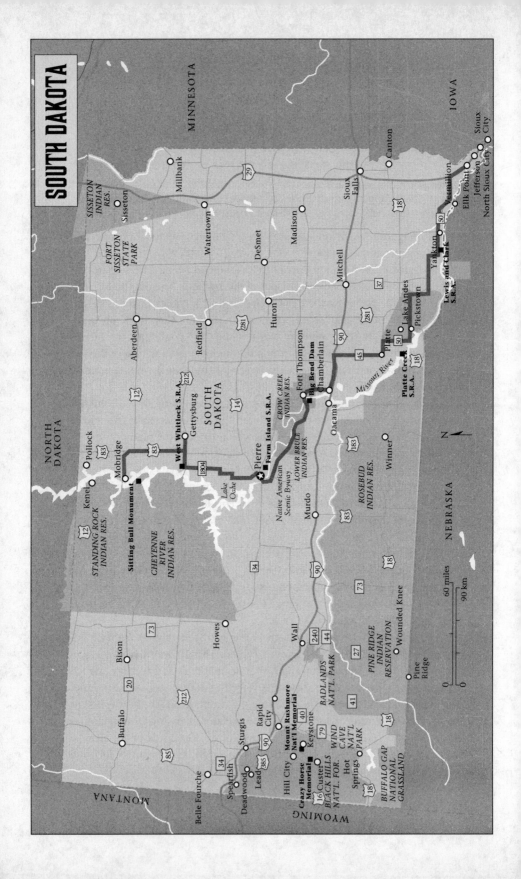

Begin day three with stops at Farm Island State Recreation Area and LaFramboise Island, both important Lewis and Clark historical sites. Near Pierre the group spent many tense days in council with the Teton Sioux. Much of the negotiation concerned a suitable toll for river passage through Teton Sioux land. The state capitol has an impressive dome and intricate tile floor. Children love to search for the approximately 50 blue tiles set in the floor, one for each of the artists who laid the flooring.

Traversing the prairie north along Route 1804 for 45 mi will take you to West Whitlock Recreation Area, west of **Gettysburg.** In this stretch of the river, the explorers met with the Arikara, who had built villages and farms along the water. At West Whitlock Recreation Area, you can walk inside a replica of an Arikara earthen lodge. Next, continue north on U.S. 83 for 47 mi and west on U.S. 12 for 17 mi to **Mobridge.** While in Mobridge, stop to see the Oscar Howe Indian Murals, immense works that portray Sioux history in the artist's early style. The Sitting Bull Monument, sculpted by Crazy Horse Memorial artist Korczak Ziolkowski, is a cultural icon that stands on a windswept bluff and marks the location of the legendary leader's grave. Nearby is the Monument to Sacagawea, the only woman to travel both to and from the Pacific with Lewis and Clark.

ELK POINT
▼▼

After the unfortunate death of Sergeant Charles Floyd, the Corps continued upriver to Elk Point, which became the site of the first election west of the Mississippi River, held to determine who would replace Floyd as one of the group's three sergeants. On August 22, 1804, Patrick Gass, a former army sergeant who had accepted a demotion to join the Corps, won, with 19 votes.

In his journal, Meriwether Lewis wrote, "Vast herds of buffalo, deer, elk, and antelopes were seen feeding in every direction as far as the eye of the observer could reach." Long before the explorers arrived, Native Americans knew the area as one where elk were sure to be found.

✦ INFORMATION
Elk Point Commercial Club | Box 872, 57025 | 605/356–2152 | www.elkpoint. org. **Union County Historical Society** | Box 552, 57025.

SITES TO SEE
Adams Homestead and Nature Preserve. When the Corps of Discovery navigated the Missouri, it was a shallow and unpredictable waterway. Since then, dams have tamed the waters. This preserve—a gift to the state of South Dakota from the Adams family, who first homesteaded the area more than 100 years ago—has one of the last free-flowing segments of the Missouri. |

A Changing River

The 2,500-mi Missouri River traveled by Lewis and Clark on their journey nearly 200 years ago was a different waterway than it is today. Before man made his mark, the river was known for its changing course, its high turbidity, and its periodic flooding. Its diverse ecosystem included riparian and floodplain habitats full of twisting channels, sandbars, and islands, as well as backwater areas rich with fish and fowl. In their journals, Lewis and Clark recorded species previously unknown to science. From prairie dog, elk, buffalo, and antelope to pelicans, black-billed magpies, grouse, terns, and Carolina parakeets, most of these then-unknown animals found their food and made homes along the river.

For man, taming the river has been an ongoing project. The first river explorers simply removed the snags that hindered their passage. Later, landowners and farmers built small levees, dams, and breaks to make new land and prevent flooding. Since 1944, the U. S. Army Corps of Engineers has built a string of earthen dams and channels in an effort to make the river navigable to barge traffic south of Sioux City, Iowa. Today one-third of the entire river is channelized, another third has been dammed, and a final third is free flowing (including a 45-mi stretch below Fort Randall Dam and a 58-mi stretch below Gavins Point Dam known as the Adams Homestead and Nature Preserve). The river is more than 100 mi shorter and two-thirds narrower than it once was.

The dams created to make the river navigable, provide water for farmers, prevent flooding, and generate power have created lakes in many areas. The Missouri River reservoir system is the largest in the nation; four of the six Missouri River dams are in South Dakota. Oahe Dam, completed in 1958 near Pierre, is the second-largest earthen dam in the world, surpassed only by Egypt's Aswan Dam. Oahe Dam was authorized by the Flood Control Act of 1944, and construction began four years later. President John F. Kennedy officially dedicated the dam and lake on August 17, 1962, and the dam began generating hydroelectric power that same year. Lake Oahe—230 mi long, backing water up into North Dakota—is the fourth-largest man-made reservoir in the United States and has a storage capacity of 23½ million acre-feet.

Big Bend Dam to the south, built in 1963 near Fort Thompson, was the last impoundment of the mighty waterway. Fort Randall Dam created Lake Francis Case near Pickstown in 1952. The smallest impoundment is Gavins Point Dam, finished in 1955 near Yankton.

Recreational use of the Missouri River has been on the upswing since the dams were constructed. Boating, camping, swimming, and especially fishing have made the Great Lakes of South Dakota a haven for outdoor enthusiasts. Species such as walleye, white bass, and smallmouth bass flourish in the clear lake waters, and anglers come from all states for tournaments and weekends aboard a boat.

272 Westshore Dr., North Sioux City | 605/232–0873 | $3 per person, $5 per vehicle | Visitor center weekdays 8–4:30; trails daily dawn–dusk.

Gass Election Monument. In what has been called the first election by U.S. citizens west of the Mississippi River, Patrick Gass was voted in to replace Charles Floyd as sergeant. A plaque in downtown Elk Point commemorates the event, as do markers in front of the courthouse and at Heritage Park. | Union County Courthouse, 200 E. Main St. | Free | Daily.

Union County Museum. The museum houses pioneer and Native American artifacts depicting the history of the county and the surrounding area. Family history books provide genealogical information. One curiosity is the Horn chair, dated 1886, Deadwood, Dakota Territory. It is made of deer and elk antlers. Don't miss the Lewis and Clark campsite exhibit and the diorama of the prairie and river near Elk Point at the time of Lewis and Clark. | 124 E. Main St. | Donations welcome | Weekends 1–4.

✦ ON THE CALENDAR

Aug. **Elk Point Heritage Days.** Held at Elk Point Heritage Park, this annual event celebrates the election of Patrick Gass to the rank of sergeant. A reenactment, an encampment, living-history demonstrations, and musical entertainment are on the activities roster. | 605/356–3336.

VERMILLION
▼▼▼

When Lewis and Clark passed by the Missouri's confluence with the Vermillion River, they saw an abundance of white stone and red clay. Native Americans extracted white and red pigments from the clay and called the Vermillion "White Stone River"; today, the river takes its name from the red colorations. The time spent hunting in the area provided four deer, an elk, a goose, and the expedition's first bison.

On a hot and gusty day, Lewis, Clark, York, and a group of men from the party set out to hike to the top of Spirit Mound, a hill said to be inhabited by 18-inch-tall warriors. Clark noted that the only remarkable characteristic was its separation from any other hill. Although the men found no warriors, they saw from the top a "handsome prairie" and in it many birds and bison.

Fort Vermillion, established by the American Fur Company in 1835, was the area's earliest settlement. The town of Vermillion was founded in 1859 on the banks of the Missouri and Vermillion rivers 1 mi south of the fort, but a major flood in 1881 swept away most of its structures. Following the flood, most homes were built higher up on the bluffs and farther from the river. Vermillion's history is interwoven with both the pioneer heritage and Native American culture.

✦ INFORMATION
Vermillion Chamber of Commerce | 906 E. Cherry St., 57069-1602 | 605/624–5571 or 800/809–2071 | www.vermillionchamber.com.

SITES TO SEE
Spirit Mound. On a hot August day in 1804, Lewis and Clark and other members of the Corps of Discovery walked to the top of this hill, which was rumored to be inhabited by 18-inch-tall warriors. The explorers noted no warriors—only a flock of swallows feeding on the mound and a splendid view of the surrounding prairie. Today you can hike to the top to enjoy the same panorama. | Rte. 19, 7 mi north of Vermillion | Free.

W. H. Over State Museum. Sioux artifacts, including a canvas tepee, an authentic 1882 claim shanty, and post–Civil War–era photographs of Indians, members of the U.S. Army, and pioneers and prospectors round out the collection at this museum of South Dakota cultural and natural history. | 1110 Ratingen St. | 605/677–5228 | Free | Weekdays 9–5, Sat. 9:30–4:30, Sun. 1–4:30.

✦ ON THE CALENDAR
Aug. Lewis and Clark Festival. A commemoration of the explorers' journey through the area, this event at the W. H. Over State Museum hosts reenactments, Native Indian cultural demonstrations, an exhibit of prairie grasses, a walk to Spirit Mound, and a canoe trip up the Missouri. | 605/624–5571.

YANKTON
▼▼▼

The Corps of Discovery held council with the Yankton Sioux at Calumet Bluff in August 1804. During the days-long council at Calumet Bluff, the Yankton camped on the north side of the river while the explorers camped at Gavins

Point, in present-day Nebraska. The Yankton's "conical" lodges were new to the Corps, as they had not yet seen the tepees of the Plains Indians. In describing the Yankton Sioux camp, Clark noted that the lodges covered with buffalo hides were large enough for 10 to 15 people.

Founded in 1859 by fur trappers and traders plying the Missouri River, the original capital of the Dakota Territory stands on the banks of the Missouri River. After the passing of the Homestead Act of 1862, Yankton became a major destination for settlers, who arrived mainly by riverboat. When the Dakota Southern Railroad passed through the state in 1873, Yankton lost its importance as a port city. Shortly after South Dakota gained statehood in 1889, the more centrally located Pierre was chosen as the state capital over Yankton. Historic homes reflect a heritage of riverboats and railroads, frontier forts, and the fur trade.

✦ INFORMATION

Springfield Chamber of Commerce | 807 8th St., 57062 | 605/369–2266. **Yankton Area Chamber of Commerce** | 218 W. 4th St., 57078 | 605/665–3636 | www.yanktonsd.com.

SITES TO SEE

Cramer-Kenyon Heritage Home. This preserved Queen Anne–style structure, built in 1886, displays many furnishings original to the house, including oil paintings by Alice Bullfinch Cramer and a parlor suite. The home was built by James Teller, secretary of Dakota Territory, and later sold to attorney Nelson Cramer and his wife, Alice, who decorated the rooms during the 1890s. Heavy double doors, fine woodwork, and four fireplaces with imported tile enrich the home. | 509 Pine St. | 605/665–7470 | $2 | Memorial Day–Labor Day, Wed.–Sun. 1–5.

Dakota Territorial Museum. Sioux artifacts and steamboat displays trace the history of the region and the first settlement in the Dakota Territory. Historic buildings on the museum grounds include the Great Northern Depot, the Territorial Council building, and a working blacksmith shop, all of which date back to the late 1800s and early 1900s. | 610 Summit Ave. | 605/665–3898 | $2 | Late May–early Sept., Tues.–Sat. 10–5, Sun. noon–4; early Sept.–late May, weekdays 10–5, Sun. by appointment.

Lewis and Clark Recreation Area. This park is home to both Gavins Point Dam and Lewis and Clark Lake, which was formed when the Missouri River was dammed. One of the state's most popular recreational lakes, it is home to many species of fish, including catfish, bass, and bluegills. A hiking and biking trail affords views of the bluffs that tower above the water. Campgrounds, cabins, a restaurant, and a marina are on the grounds. | 43349 Rte. 52 | 605/668–2985 | www.lewisandclarkpark.com | $5 per vehicle.

Meeting the Yankton Sioux

30th of August, 1804

The fog was so thick that we could not see the Indian camp on the opposite side, but it cleared off about eight o'clock. We prepared a speech, and some presents, and then sent for the chiefs and warriors, whom we received, at twelve o'clock, under a large oak tree, near to which the flag of the United States was flying. Captain Lewis delivered a speech, with the usual advice and counsel for their future conduct. We then acknowledged their chiefs, by giving to the grand chief a flag, a medal, a certificate, with a string of wampum; to which we added a chief's coat; that is, a richly laced uniform of the United States artillery corps, and a cocked hat and red feather. One second chief and three inferior ones were made or recognized by medals; and a suitable present of tobacco, and articles of clothing. We then smoked the pipe of peace, and the chiefs retired to a bower, formed of bushes, by their young men, where they divided among each other the presents, and smoked and ate, and held a council on the answer which they were to make us to-morrow. The young people exercised their bows and arrows in shooting at marks for beads, which we distributed to the best marksmen; and in the evening the whole party danced until a late hour, and in the course of their amusement we threw among them some knives, tobacco, bells, tape, and binding, with which they were much pleased. Their musical instruments were the drum, and a sort of little bag made of buffalo hide, dressed white, with small shot or pebbles in it, and a bunch of hair tied to it. This produces a sort of rattling music, with which the party was annoyed by four musicians during the council this morning.

—*The Journals of the Expedition of Lewis and Clark,* 1804

Meridian Bridge. Finished in 1924, this bridge, with a 250-foot lift span to accommodate river vessels, was the first permanent highway crossing of the Missouri River in South Dakota and the last link in the Meridian Highway connecting Canada and Mexico. It was built to transport automobile traffic across the top deck and workhorse and railroad traffic below. Though the tollhouse and railings are gone and the lift is no longer operable, the bridge remains a proud city landmark. | 2nd and Walnut Sts. | Free | Daily.

Running Water. On Lewis and Clark's return voyage, the explorers met a group of Yankton Sioux here. When the parties realized they were friends, they traded stories from the two years that had passed since the Corps' first visit to the area. The town of Running Water is the southern point of a stretch of the Missouri that closely resembles the natural landscape of pre-settlement days. | Running Water; Rte. 50 west to Rte. 37 south, 10 mi south of Springfield.

Springfield Historical Society Museum. Shown in the museum's small theater, a video presentation weaves together photographs and narration to tell the uplifting story of a young nation exploring the wilderness, from the days of Lewis and Clark to the present. Other exhibits include antique horse-drawn farm machinery, a one-room school, and a reconstructed six-room pioneer home. | 709 8th St., Springfield; Rte. 50 west to Rte. 37 south | 605/369–2381 or 605/369–2622 | May–Sept., Sun. or by appointment.

Terrace Park. On a high bluff overlooking Lewis and Clark Lake, this park affords a tremendous view of the water. While picnicking, you can see some of the native flora of the region, particularly the American plum, important to the Native American diet and often noted in the explorers' journals. An informational kiosk tells about the Corps of Discovery, and signs describe the native plants. | South end of Walnut St., Springfield; Rte. 50 west to Rte. 37 south | 605/369–2266 or 605/369–2309.

✦ ON THE CALENDAR

June **Czech Days.** Tiny Tabor (20 mi east of Yankton) celebrates the old country and its Czech heritage with polka music, traditional dances featuring 130 performers in native costume, and a parade. You can also see how a popular Czech pastry, the *kolache,* is made. | 605/463–2476.

Aug. **Lewis and Clark Festival.** Held at the Gavins Point Dam on a weekend, this festival includes reenactments of frontier skills such as fire starting, hide tanning, and musket shooting, as well as period music and Native American dance and cultural activities. Tents and tepees are set up to re-create the Corps of Discovery's expedition to the area in 1804. Don't miss the buffalo feed. | 402/667–2546.

Aug. **Yankton Riverboat Days.** This three-day celebration of the town's ties to the Missouri River includes food booths, a beer tent, free live entertainment, fireworks, parades, hot-air balloon rides, car shows, antique tractor pulls, paintball and golf tourneys, and a summer arts festival with more than 100 artists. The event attracts more than 100,000 people to Riverside Park, on the banks of the Missouri. | 605/665–3636.

Sept. **Springfield Discovery Day.** In honor of the Lewis and Clark expedition, Springfield hosts a variety of educational and entertainment activities alongside the Missouri. | 605/369–2266.

HISTORIC DINING

The Quarry Steak House & Lounge. Steak. This restaurant sits west of Yankton on the site of its namesake, at the limestone quarry first exploited for cement beginning in 1887. By 1891 the chalk bluffs were mined at full scale, and the town had earned the name Cement City, sending its product as far away as the Panama Canal. The boom was over by 1910. Try the filet mignon or the rib eye. | W. Rte. 52 | 605/665–4337 | Reservations essential | Closed Mon. and Tues. | $10–$22 | AE, D, MC, V.

PICKSTOWN
▼▼

Traversing what would become South Dakota, the Corps of Discovery found an abundance of "exotic" animals previously unknown in America. Besides describing coyotes, pronghorn sheep (mistakenly known as antelope), and magpies, they wrote in detail about their encounter with "an animal the French call the prairie dog." Preferring to call the dog "barking squirrel," the men spent an entire day near present-day Pickstown trying to catch the talkative critter.

✦ INFORMATION

Platte Chamber of Commerce | 500 Main St., 57369 | 605/337–3921. **Yankton Sioux Tribe** | Box 248, Marty, 57361 | 605/384–3641.

SITES TO SEE

Fort Randall Dam. At the base of this massive earthen dam in the Missouri River, completed in 1956, is the Fort Randall Historic Site, commemorating a military outpost established in 1856. Among the fort's early visitors were William Tecumseh Sherman, George Custer, and Sioux leader Sitting Bull. You can see the post cemetery and the ruins of the chalk rock chapel, and walk along a path around the parade grounds to read about the buildings that used to stand at the fort. Marked trails lead to overlooks of the dam and Lake Francis Case, which is surrounded with recreational areas and campgrounds. A few miles downstream from the dam, one of the country's largest year-round populations of both bald and golden eagles in the country makes its home.

The well-protected **Platte Creek State Recreation Area,** a natural cove where Platte Creek flows into Lake Francis Case, has a beach, a boat launch, boat rentals, fish-cleaning stations, and campsites. Once called Fish Creek, it was renamed in the 1800s for a fur-post operator, Bernard Pratte; the spelling error has endured. | Rte. 44, 8 mi west and 10 mi south of Platte | 605/337–2587| $3 per person, $5 per vehicle | Daily.

Wooded ravines and scenic Missouri River bluffs, known since the days of Lewis and Clark as "burning bluffs," form the backdrop for the **Snake Creek State Recreation Area.** The bluffs appear to burn whenever lightning strikes or chemical reactions ignite the oil-rich shale, and it may burn for months at a time. | U.S. 281/18 | 605/487–7847 | $5 per vehicle | May–Oct., daily.

Greenwood. The town of Greenwood began as the center of the Yankton Sioux agency in 1858. Today the tribe maintains a bison herd and conducts guided tours. | Greenwood; 20 mi south and east of Pickstown on Rte. 37 | 605/384–3804 or 605/384–3641.

Lake Andes National Wildlife Refuge. Preservation of the prairie pothole landscape is one of the purposes of this refuge, where you can observe deer, beaver, muskrats, and some 240 species of birds, including bald eagles. November 1 through March 1 is the best time to see the eagles; some areas of the preserve are open to fishing and hunting. | 6 mi north of Pickstown on Rte. 50 | 605/487–7603 | Weekdays 8–4:30.

Struck by the Ree's Grave. The legend of Struck by the Ree, whose name comes from a battle with the Arika, or "Ree," tribe, begins with Lewis and Clark's first encounter with the Yankton Sioux in 1804. The infant was wrapped in an American flag by Lewis and named the United State's first Sioux citizen, a distinction Lewis never forgot. Struck By The Ree grew up to become a respected Yankton chief and died in Greenwood in 1888. | 2 mi north of Greenwood. | Free | Daily.

Treaty of 1858 Monument. This monument marks the location of the signing of the 1858 treaty between the Dakota Sioux and U.S. Government. The treaty designated land for the tribe. | 2 mi north of Greenwood. | Free | Daily.

✦ ON THE CALENDAR

Aug. **Fort Randall Powwow.** This powwow takes place annually on the first weekend in August at Lake Andes, complete with displays of Native American dress and ceremonial singing and dancing. | 605/384–3641.

CHAMBERLAIN–OACOMA

▼▼▼

After a few days of steady rain, the crew rested in the sun at a place they named both Plum Camp and Camp Pleasant, just south of present-day Chamberlain. The men feasted on the "great quantities of fine plums" and waited longer than they had planned for their gear to dry out. In the meantime, Lewis noted the presence of prairie dogs, coyotes, skunks, and magpies. The steep, irregular hills were an added challenge for hunters. Clark killed a "curious" species of deer, which he later named mule deer for its large ears. (This is one name that stuck.) On the swifter return trip, the Corps returned to this camp.

Established just across the river from each other, with Chamberlain on the east and Oacoma on the west, the two towns have thrived because of the surrounding fertile farmlands and visiting hunters and fishermen. Chamberlain got its start in 1880, named for Selah Chamberlain, the director of the Milwaukee Railroad, which helped attract settlers to the region. Oacoma, a word that is similar to the Sioux word for "a place between," was founded in 1890. Fort Hale, a U.S. Army post, was established in 1890, 20 mi north. The soldiers who manned the fort were known as "buffalo soldiers" because of the buffalo robes they wore to keep warm.

◆ INFORMATION
Chamberlain-Oacoma Area Chamber of Commerce | 115 W. Lawler St., Chamberlain, 57325 | 605/734-4416 | www.chamberlainsd.org.

SITES TO SEE
Akta Lakota Museum and Lakota Visitors Center. This place offers a moving look at Sioux life on the Great Plains prior to the arrival of European settlers. Our Lady of the Sioux Chapel has striking stained-glass windows and a tapestry of Oscar Howe's *Indian Christ*. The chapel is open to the public at all times. | St. Joseph's Indian School, N. Main St., Chamberlain | 605/734-3452 | Free | Memorial Day–Labor Day, Mon.–Sat. 8–6, Sun. 1–5; Labor Day–Memorial Day, Mon.–Sat. 8–5 or by appointment.

Great Plains Resource Center. The center includes a walking trail through prairie landscape and Roam Free Park, a wildlife loop where you might see free-ranging animals. | Rte. 50, 2 mi north of Chamberlain | Free.

Lewis and Clark Interpretive Center. The most prominent feature of this interpretive center is a 55-foot keelboat that passes through a wall of windows overlooking the Missouri River. The keelboat is a replica of the one the Corps used during the expedition. Replicas of trade goods and gear and a list of supplies are displayed throughout the building. | Chamberlain Rest Area, on I–90 between Exits 263 and 265 | 605/734-4562 | Free | May–Sept., daily 8–6.

◆ ON THE CALENDAR
Sept. **St. Joseph's Indian School Powwow.** Generations of Native American families of many tribes gather to sing and dance and welcome others at Chamberlain's annual powwow. | 605/734-3300.

Aug. 2004 **Oceti Sakowin.** In commemoration of the Bicentennial, South Dakota's Lewis and Clark signature event is the Oceti Sakowin (Lakota for "seven council fires"), an event featuring a Native American art show, powwows, and traditional arts demonstrations. The event begins in Chamberlain-Oacoma on August 27–28, 2004, and then is slated to spread across South Dakota to reservations and tribal lands, continuing throughout the month of September. | 605/473–0561 or 605/773–3301.

HISTORIC LODGING

Cable's Riverview Ridge B&B. This contemporary structure lies on 30 acres a little more than 3 mi from the town center alongside the Missouri River, surrounded by prairie, on the Lewis and Clark Trail. The story is that Lewis and Clark actually slept under the house. The view of the river from inside is stunning. Laundry service; no smoking. | 24383 Rte. 50, Chamberlain, 57325 | 605/734–6084 | 3 rooms | $70–$85 | MC, V | BP.

FORT THOMPSON

▼▼

Two of South Dakota's seven Indian reservations lie 20 mi north of Chamberlain. The Lower Brule and Crow Creek reservations are separated only by the Missouri, the former tribe's land falling on the west, the latter on the east of the natural divide. In the heart of the land, the river makes a curious turn to form the Big Bend of the Missouri River. The Big Bend Dam, completed in 1966, flooded what Lewis and Clark traversed as a shallow waterway, creating Lake Sharpe, but the loop in the river still creates the almost full circle Clark reported in his journals. "Proceeded on to the Gouge of this Great bend . . . we sent a man to Measure the Distance across the gouge, he made it 2,000 yds; The distance arround is 30 Mls."

Fort Thompson, on the northeast end of the Big Bend Dam, was first established in 1863 as the reservation headquarters for Santee Sioux and Winnebago agencies. Two years later, the site became the Yankton Sioux reservation. The original town sites of Fort Thompson and Lower Brule, across the river, were flooded in the 1950s when the Big Bend dam went in. Today Fort Thompson is the tribal headquarters for the Crow Creek and Lower Brule tribes.

✦ INFORMATION

Crow Creek Sioux Tribe | Box 50, 57339 | 605/245–2221. **Lower Brule Sioux Tribe** | Box 187, Lower Brule, 57584 | 605/473–5561.

SITES TO SEE

Big Bend Dam–Lake Sharpe. The dam, museum, and visitor center on the south end of Lake Sharpe afford spectacular views of the Missouri. Exhibits of Native American artifacts, the early fur trade, and prairie wildlife are on display in the museum. Lake Sharpe is home to walleye and other fish, and bison often graze north of Fort Thompson. | Rte. 47 | 605/245–2255.

Native American Scenic Byway. This scenic driving route passes through both the Crow Creek and Lower Brule reservations. The prairie surrounding the river valley and the river itself open up to expansive views under a dome of often cloudless skies. The route was laid out to help you feel the spirit of the land. Besides the scenery, there are historical points of interest along the way, which detail Lewis and Clark's travels through the area and acquaint you with Native American history. | 605/245–2221 or 605/473–5561.

✦ ON THE CALENDAR

Aug. Crow Creek Sioux Tribe Annual Powwow. Fort Thompson hosts this annual powwow in midmonth with music, dance, and traditional foods. | 605/245–2221 | Free | Daily.

Aug. Lower Brule Sioux Tribe Annual Fair and Powwow. This mid-August event is held at the powwow grounds in Lower Brule. Dancers and singers of all ages celebrate their Native American heritage. | 605/473–5561.

PIERRE
▼▼

Commanding the central location in the state and graced with one of the nation's prettiest capitol buildings, Pierre may well be the country's most isolated state capital. Arikara villages once lined the shores of the Missouri River in the area. Later, tribes of the Sioux nation migrated to the area. The first record of explorers dates from 1743, when Chevalier and Louis Verendrye claimed the region for their French king. Sixty-one years later, the Corps of Discovery had its first encounter with the Teton Sioux here. Lewis and Clark met with three Teton Sioux chiefs, one of whom demanded payment, including one of the group's pirogues; when the captains refused, a skirmish threatened to erupt. Clark noted in his journals, "We discover our interpreter do not Speak the language well." The Corps spent a few days with the Teton people, talking and feasting, but never relaxing, as the tensions remained high during the entire visit. The town itself was founded in 1882. Nine years later, it was named the state's first capital, chiefly because of its central location. Once a laid-back cow town, Pierre now thrives as a regional commercial and medical hub.

Just west across the river is Fort Pierre, the first permanent settlement in South Dakota, established in 1832. It wasn't long before Fort Pierre had become the largest fur-trading post on the upper Missouri, and an average of 17,000 buffalo hides valued at $3 to $4 each were traded each year. Settlement of Fort Pierre helped pave the way for major routes into the American

West. In 1855 the post was sold to the U.S. Army, which dismantled it two years later. Today the town claims 1,800 residents and a past firmly grounded in the origins of the state. One of its most admired residents was James "Scotty" Philips, largely credited with preserving bison from near-extinction in the early 1900s. He raised the herd from a few dozen to nearly 1,000.

✦ INFORMATION

Fort Pierre Chamber of Commerce | 310 Casey Tibbs St., Fort Pierre, 57532 | 605/223–2178| www.pierrechamber.com. **Pierre Area Chamber of Commerce/Pierre Convention and Visitors Bureau** | 800 W. Dakota Ave., 57501-0548 | 605/224–7361 or 800/962–2034 | www.pierrechamber.com.

SITES TO SEE

Farm Island State Recreation Area. The Corps hunted elk around Farm Island during the expedition. Later, the fur traders who built Fort Teton, which later became Fort Pierre, established gardens on the site. Today you will find a modern campground with cabins, a nature area, and boat-launching facilities. | 1301 Farm Island Rd. | 605/224–5605 | $3 per person, $5 per vehicle | Daily.

Hilger's Gulch and Governor's Grove. A 1 1/10-mi path good for walking, jogging, and bicycling meanders through this city park, which contains hundreds of new trees and 28 monuments dedicated to former South Dakota governors. The stone Gate of the Counties—two pillars built of native stone from each of the state's 50 counties—marks the entrance into Governor's Grove from Hilger's Gulch. | 500 E. Capitol Ave. | 605/224–7361 or 800/962–2034 | Free | Daily.

LaFramboise Island. Ten miles of foot trails traverse this island, which is accessible by a causeway off Dakota Avenue in Pierre. | Dakota Ave.

South Dakota Cultural Heritage Center. Early Native American cultures, the arrival of settlers, riverboats, and railroads are a few of the subjects of the exhibits in this museum; the most popular display is a walk-through sod shanty, where you can listen to stories told by a pioneer woman, visit a Lakota tepee, and explore an old-time gold-mining operation. | 900 Governor's Dr. | 605/773–3458 | Free | Weekdays 9–4:30, weekends 1–4:30.

South Dakota National Guard Museum. Civil War and vintage guns, World War I machine guns, a World War II Sherman tank, Lieutenant Colonel Custer's dress sword, and an A-7D aircraft fill this museum. | 303 E. Dakota Ave. | 605/224–9991 | Free | Mon., Wed., and Fri. 8–5; Tues., Thurs., and weekends by appointment only.

The Powwow Experience

The powwow, or *wacipi,* is a Native American gathering with religious roots that today is both a social and spiritual celebration of music, dance, and family. Many powwows now include competitions in various dance forms. You are welcome to attend powwows no matter what your background; they're good places to learn about Native American culture and tradition.

As soon as you enter the powwow grounds you'll hear a drumbeat, which represents the heartbeat of the people and their spiritual connection to one another and to the Earth. The dance area, known as the arbor, is the large circular area at the center of the grounds. The arbor is blessed before the powwow and is considered sacred. Dancers usually enter the circle from the east. Drums surround the dance area and set the pace for all the dances and songs and direct the movements of dancers in intricate, brightly colored regalia.

During the Grand Entry, when dancers first enter the arbor, all drums sing. Everyone stands to show respect. After that are the contests for particular dance styles, giveaways, honor songs, and intertribal dance. During the intertribal dance, even spectators are allowed to enter the circle.

The dance styles and regalia you see at a powwow are distinct from one another, and each reflects some aspect of the Native American tradition. Men's traditional dance was originally meant to recount an act of battle or hunting; often the regalia is more subdued in color and decorated with beads and quillwork. Spectators are often asked to stand as a sign of respect during this dance. During women's traditional dances, the dancers wear either a beaded buckskin dress or a cloth dress decorated with ribbon work, elk teeth, and shells; they carry a shawl over their arm and a feather fan, which they raise to acknowledge words of a song with special meaning to them. Men may also compete in grass dance or fancy dance, and women in fancy-shawl or jingle-dress dance. Each dancer has his or her own style of dance, and each one's outfit is unique.

Powwows sometimes coincide with rodeos, parades, and athletic tournaments; these take place nearby but outside the arbor. Traditional food such as buffalo and fry bread are available, and vendors sell traditional arts, crafts, and jewelry.

Whether events take place indoors or out, powwow grounds are considered sacred, and spectators and participants alike are expected to show respect for the event and the people involved.

State Capitol. Marble wainscoting, Ionic columns, early decorative 19th-century artwork, and a terrazzo tile floor are some of the details in this building, which was constructed between 1905 and 1910 and modeled after Montana's capitol. A copper dome and marble and bronze statues ornament the facade. | 500 E. Capitol Ave. | 605/773–3765 | Free | Weekdays 8 AM–10 PM.

Verendrye Monument. French explorers, the Verendrye brothers, claimed the land around what is now Pierre for France, in 1743, by burying an inscribed lead tablet on a bluff near present-day Fort Pierre. In 1913, the plate was found by high school students playing on a hillside and is now on display at the South Dakota Cultural Heritage Center. The monument commemorating the explorers is atop a hill overlooking the river and surrounding prairie. | Rte. 83, Fort Pierre | Free | Daily.

✦ ON THE CALENDAR

Aug. Riverfest. A rodeo and an air show are some of the highlights of this festival, which also includes a free picnic, an outdoor concert, raft races, and a carnival. It's held the first weekend in August. | 605/224–7361.

Sept. Lewis and Clark Goosefest and Bad River Gathering. This annual festival includes reenactments of Lewis and Clark's famous first meeting with the Teton Sioux and dance, music, and displays honoring Lakota culture. | 605/945–3124.

HISTORIC DINING AND LODGING

Cattleman's Club. Steak. This is an Old West steak house that you can trust to serve you a juicy T-bone without the frills. Piles of sawdust on the floor add to the cowboy flavor, and the view of the Missouri River is impressive. | 29608 Rte. 34 | 605/224–9774| $10–$19 | AE, D, MC, V.

Goodner House Bed & Breakfast Inn. The Ivan W. Goodner house, built between 1881 and 1884, is one of Pierre's oldest homes. An early-1900s remodeling created its present Colonial Revival style, with a wraparound porch and an oval stained-glass window. Most of the original fixtures, flooring, and trim remain in the house. The Gold Room is decorated in Victorian style and the Yellow Room in country style. South Dakota's capitol building is just 1½ blocks to the east. No kids. | 216 E. Prospect, 57501 | 605/224–6739 | 2 rooms | $75 | No credit cards | BP.

GETTYSBURG

▼▼

Following the anxious period spent with the Teton Sioux, the Corps of Discovery continued upriver, where it encountered the Arikara. In October

1804 the group spent many days with the tribe, studying and learning from one another. Because the Arikara villagers were primarily farmers, their settlements were more permanent and had earthen lodges and gardens of corn, beans, squash, and tobacco. The lodges were made of logs and branches and were completely blanketed, matching surrounding prairie.

The town of Gettysburg was founded by Civil War veterans who joined emigrants in scrambling for some of the last land in the United States available for homesteading. Today it is a tranquil place surrounded by rolling prairie.

✦ INFORMATION
Cheyenne River Sioux Tribe | Box 590, Eagle Butte, 57625 | 605/964–4155. **Gettysburg Chamber of Commerce** | Box 33, 57442 | 605/765–2731.

SITES TO SEE
Dakota Sunset Museum. Displaying artifacts from the numerous Mandan and Arikara villages that once dotted the nearby prairie and river bluffs, this museum also houses Medicine Rock, a large, flat boulder carved with handprints, footprints, and bird and animal tracks. The museum was built around the rock, which is sacred to the Lakota people. | 207 W. Commercial | 605/765–9480 | Free | Daily 1–5.

Timber Lake and Area Museum. This cultural and natural history museum on the Cheyenne River Sioux reservation and 2 mi south of the Standing Rock Sioux reservation houses a collection of marine fossils native to South Dakota as well as artifacts from both the Cheyenne River Sioux and the Standing Rock Sioux tribes. | 800 Main St., Timber Lake, 57656 | 605/865–3553 | Free | Weekdays 9–5.

West Whitlock Recreation Area. Once an Arikara village where the Corps spent several days with the tribe, the site later became a homestead known as Whitlock Crossing, named after a nearby ferry crossing on the Missouri. Today you can walk through a full-size replica of an Arikara earth lodge, much like the explorers would have seen during their voyage. Follow interpretive trails, camp and hike, and go boating, fishing, and swimming on the shores of the Missouri. | Rte. 1804, 15 mi west of Gettysburg | 605/765–9410 | $3 per person, $5 per vehicle | Daily.

✦ ON THE CALENDAR
Aug. **Civil War Festival.** This annual festival highlights the colorful past of Gettysburg's sister city and battlefield in Pennsylvania. Several reenactment groups reprise the historic Civil War battle. | 605/765–2731.

MOBRIDGE

▼▼▼

Mobridge sits on the eastern bank of the Missouri River, on land once farmed by the Arikara. Lewis and Clark spent many days in early October 1804 in friendly council with the tribe, visiting their earthen lodges and inviting them to the Corps' camp. In later years, the Arikara were forced to move north and west by the more powerful Sioux, who now hold large reservations of land west of Mobridge, directly across the river.

On the expedition's last night in South Dakota, Private John Newman was court-martialed for making mutinous statements against the captains and the expedition itself. He was sentenced to 75 lashes and was not allowed to ride aboard the keelboat. Newman was discharged from the party and sent downriver the following spring.

Mobridge was founded in 1906 by the remnants of the Milwaukee Railroad crew that constructed a bridge over a horseshoe bend in the Missouri River nearby. An unknown telegrapher sent word of their location as succinctly as possible, and his dots and dashes, intended to signal "Missouri Bridge," gave Mobridge its name.

✦ INFORMATION

Mobridge Chamber of Commerce | 212 Main St., 57601-2533 | 605/845–2387 or 888/614–3474 | www.mobridge.org. **Standing Rock Sioux Tribe** | Box D, Fort Yates, ND 58538 | 701/854–7207.

SITES TO SEE

Conqueror's Stones. These stones are often referred to as prayer rocks because it was believed that if you placed your hands in the handprint grooves on the rocks your spirit would be taken to the Sky World. The stones stand at the entrance to the park. | North side of City Park | Free | Daily.

Fort Manuel Site. Fort Manuel, near present-day Kenel, was the location of a Missouri Fur Company post, where Sacagawea died just six years after her journey with the Corps of Discovery. She was 21. You can stand on the river bluffs near her final resting place, but the fort no longer exists; it was destroyed by British soldiers and their Native American allies in March 1813, and only an interpretive sign south of Kenel marks its location. | 18 mi north of U.S. 12 on Rte. 1806 | Free | Daily.

Jedediah Smith Monument. Smith is credited with charting the central route across the Great Plains to the Pacific in 1826 and 1827. The monument is at the entrance of Indian Memorial Campground, or Smith's Bay, across the river from Mobridge. | 3 mi west of Mobridge on U.S. 12 | Free | Daily.

Klein Museum. The highlight of this museum is the Fool Soldier Band Monument, which commemorates the August 1862 negotiation by a group of young Teton Sioux for the return of white captives of the Santee Sioux to their homes. The Teton Sioux were called the "fool soldier band" because the odds against their success were so high; nevertheless the young men accompanied the nine women and children on a 100-mi trek south to Fort Pierre to be reunited with their families. Local pioneer clothing and tools, Sioux artifacts such as beadwork and headdresses, a restored schoolhouse from the early 1900s, and changing art exhibits round out the museum's displays. | 1820 W. Grand Crossing | 605/845–7243 | $2 | Apr.–Oct., Mon. and Wed.–Fri. 9–noon and 1–5, weekends 1–5.

Oscar Howe Indian Murals. Ten murals painted in 1942 by the celebrated Sioux artist Oscar Howe adorn the walls of the Scherr Howe Arena and are among Mobridge's most prized possessions. The murals, nearly 20 feet wide, depict Sioux ceremonies and history. | 212 Main St. | 605/845–3700 or 605/845–2387 | Free | Weekdays 9–5.

Sacagawea Monument. In 1929, to honor the Shoshone woman's work with Lewis and Clark, area schoolchildren raised money to build this concrete and bronze monument, which stands in the same park as the Sitting Bull Monument. | Rte. 1806, 4 mi west of Mobridge | 605/845–2387 | Free.

Sitting Bull Monument. Alone on a windswept bluff above a horseshoe bend of the Missouri River stands a 7-ton granite bust of Sitting Bull, the Hunkpapa Sioux leader who, with his band, defeated George Armstrong Custer at the Battle of the Little Bighorn in 1876. Sculpted by Crazy Horse Memorial artist Korczak Ziolkowski, this enduring work captures the quiet pride of the legendary warrior. It also sits atop his final resting place, where a group of South Dakotans reinterred his remains in the dead of night in 1953 after making off with the great Sioux leader's bones from a lonely, all-but-forgotten abandoned military cemetery in North Dakota. The act returned the legendary Lakota leader's bones to his place of birth—the bluffs of the Missouri River. | Rte. 1806, 4 mi west of Mobridge | 605/845–2387 | Free.

✦ ON THE CALENDAR

May **Kenel Memorial Day Wacipi.** The wacipi ("dance") is nearby Kenel's annual powwow held in late May. | 605/823–2024.

July **Sitting Bull Stampede Rodeo and Celebration.** Among the oldest rodeos in the world, this Mobridge celebration includes daily professional rodeos, two big parades on Main Street, a carnival, and fireworks. | 605/845–2387.

Aug. **Lewis and Clark Rediscovery Festival.** Mobridge remembers the famed explorers' trek each year with reenactments, homemade boat races, a triathlon, black-powder gun displays, historian-speakers, and activities for all ages. The event is held on the river at Jed's Landing the second weekend in August. | 605/845–2387.

Sept. **Threshing Bee.** The Klein Museum hosts this event, where you can see an old-fashioned harvest with horse-powered threshing machines. Steam-powered tractors, arts and crafts, a feeder calf show, rodeo, and plenty to eat and drink round out the event, held annually on the second Saturday in September. | 605/845–7243.

North Dakota

ewis and Clark entered what is now North Dakota from the south via the Missouri River in mid-October 1804 and eventually spent more time in North Dakota than anywhere else along their route. The "Mighty Mo" juts like a giant elbow into the southwestern section of the state and marks the eastern edge of the Rocky Mountain foothills. Lewis and Clark traveled north on the river for about two weeks and then wintered at Fort Mandan just east of what is now Washburn. They encountered freezing temperatures and snow. Ice began to form on the river, and on October 26 they stopped for the winter. Here the two explorers met Toussaint Charbonneau, a French-Canadian trader, and his wife, Sacagawea, a Shoshone teenager. The couple joined the Lewis and Clark expedition. Sacagawea served as a guide and interpreter, but her husband, according to expedition journals, was a man of "no peculiar merit," who was reluctant to perform camp duties while on the trail.

Lewis and Clark also spent a great amount of time at Fort Mandan with the friendly Mandan and Hidatsa, who lived nearby. These nations had a tradition of accepting people into their villages. Sheheke, or Big White, the chief of the lower Mandan village, told Lewis and Clark: "Our wish is to be at peace with you. If we eat, you shall eat; if we starve, you must starve also." The tribes prepared for the winter by harvesting and drying beans, corn, squash, and various roots, which they buried in large storage holes. They generously shared their food with the Corps, who probably would not have survived the winter without their assistance. Lewis and Clark busied themselves by traveling to Sacagawea's home, the Knife River Indian Villages, near today's Stanton, to socialize and gather information that would help them as they continued their journey west in the spring.

The 32 members of the expedition left Fort Mandan on April 7, 1805, in two large pirogues and six small canoes they had built while at the fort. Snowmelt from the mountains and northwest winds made the river rough, and the wind actually tipped a pirogue at one point, throwing one of the Corps of Discovery journals into the water. Sacagawea retrieved it. The explorers marveled at deer, antelope, buffalo, elk, prairie dogs, and beaver. The Corps even sent four magpies, a sage grouse, and a prairie dog in cages to President Jefferson. One of the magpies and the prairie dog survived to be displayed at the White House.

Strong winds and rough waters made the journey a challenge as the men camped along the river at various sites near today's Garrison and New Town. The expedition continued northwest on the Missouri River as far as the confluence of the Yellowstone River, near present-day Williston and the North Dakota border, then crossed into today's Montana, heading southwest on April 25.

On their return to North Dakota in 1806, Lewis and Clark, after separating in present-day eastern Montana, reunited at the confluence, near what is now New Town on the Fort Berthold Indian Reservation. They persuaded Mandan chief Sheheke-Shote, whom they had met in 1804 at Fort Mandan, to accompany them to St. Louis. The chief continued with them to Washington, D.C., where he met President Jefferson.

Native Americans had inhabited the region for thousands of years before Lewis and Clark arrived. Besides the Mandan and Hidatsa nations, the Corps also met Arikara, Cheyenne, Assiniboine, and Teton Sioux in North Dakota. The only tribes who were unfriendly to the expedition were the Sioux, who stole two horses and some weapons from the men. Four federally recognized Native American tribes live in North Dakota today. Two reservations—the Standing Rock Nation near Fort Yates, whose members are Lakota and Yanktonai Sioux, and the Three Affiliated Tribes, consisting of the Mandan, Hidatsa, and Arikara nations, near New Town—are on the Lewis and Clark Trail. Both nations have been active in the state's preparations for the Lewis and Clark Bicentennial and welcome travelers on the reservations.

Today, many of the places where Lewis and Clark stopped in North Dakota are underwater, on reservations, or on private property. But the State Historical Society of North Dakota has placed Lewis and Clark historical markers at 26 sites positively identified from journal entries or reliable sources. And much of North Dakota, with its wide expanses of undeveloped prairie and abundant wildlife, looks like what Lewis and Clark saw during their time here. Routes 1804, on the east bank of the river, and 1806, on the west bank, make it easy for motorists to retrace the route of the expedition.

North Dakota Journey

A DRIVING TOUR FROM BISMARCK TO WILLISTON

▼▼

Distance: 243 mi   **Time:** 3–4 days
Breaks: Overnight in Williston, Bismarck, Mandan, Beulah, or Hazen. For authentic Lewis
and Clark dining and lodging experiences visit Birdwoman Canoeing, Knife River Ranch, or
Outpost 1806.

This tour retraces Lewis and Clark's travels through North Dakota, where you
will still encounter what Meriwether Lewis termed the "beginning of the vast
unknown." Many North Dakota attractions included in this driving tour simu-
late the expedition experiences and surroundings.

Spend your first morning at Fort Abraham Lincoln State Park south of
Mandan on Route 1806. The hill above Fort Abraham Lincoln provides great
views of the Missouri River valley with blockhouses standing guard over the
fort. Within walking distance is the On-A-Slant Indian Village, composed of
lodges that were inhabited by Mandan Indians.

Return to Mandan's Main Street and visit Five Nations Art, where jewelry,
sculptures, paintings, and other art made by the region's Native Americans
are for sale. In the afternoon or evening, take Interstate 94 to Exit 157, then
North River Road to the Port of Bismarck. Here you can take an afternoon
or evening cruise on the Missouri River aboard the *Lewis and Clark,* a 150-
passenger riverboat. Overnight in **Bismarck.**

On your second morning, visit the North Dakota Heritage Center. Have
your photo taken by the Sacagawea statue at the entrance, and get a thor-
ough introduction to Lewis and Clark's time in North Dakota by viewing the
state's comprehensive Lewis and Clark interactive displays. Leave Bismarck
by midmorning and take U.S. 83 north for 34 mi to **Washburn.** Stop at the
Lewis and Clark Interpretive Center, where displays tell the story of the
winter the Corps headquartered at Fort Mandan. Then drive 2 mi west to
Fort Mandan, a fully furnished fort with interpreters and a visitor center. Have
lunch in Washburn, and then drive 24 mi west on Route 200A to **Stanton**
and ½ mi north of Stanton on Route 37 to Knife River Indian Village National
Historic Site. Here you can see the impressions in the ground from the earth
lodges and Native American travois trails. Drive to Beulah, 23 mi west on
Route 200A, for dinner at Outpost 1806 Steakhouse. Overnight at either Beulah
or Hazen, 9 mi to the east.

On your third day, return to Washburn and travel north on U.S. 83 for
53 mi, then turn left on Route 23 and drive 56 mi to **New Town.** Stop for an
early lunch at Four Bears Casino and visit the Three Affiliated Tribes Museum,
3 mi west of the casino. From New Town, drive west on Route 23 for 49 mi,
turn right on U.S. 85 and go 41 mi; then turn right on Route 1804 and drive
5 mi to **Williston.** Here you'll want to tour two historic forts, Fort Buford and

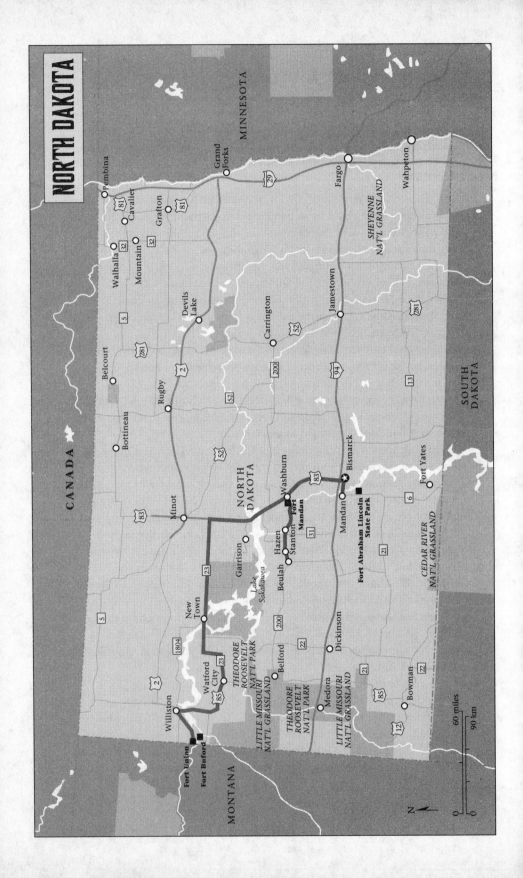

Fort Union. Begin with Fort Buford by taking U.S. 2 west out of Williston. Turn south on Route 1804 and drive 20 mi, where signs direct you into Fort Buford. To get to Fort Union, return to Route 1804, turn west, and go 1 mi, where you will see entrance signs to Fort Union. Return to Williston to stay overnight.

FORT YATES
▼▼▼

In their journals Lewis and Clark described finding an abundance of perfectly round stones along the shore of the Cannon Ball River near Fort Yates, when they came through the area in October 1804. These stones can still be found near the mouth of the river, named by fur traders who passed through in the late 1700s. The Sioux lived in the region, and Fort Yates was founded as a military post in 1875. The fort was abandoned officially in 1903, but local residents kept the name for the town that had sprung up around the fort. The town (population 183) is now the headquarters of Standing Rock Indian Reservation, home to 4,500 Sioux. The reservation itself—2,394,995 acres straddling North Dakota and South Dakota—is a tableau of huge hills dotted by occasional clumps of trees with fantastic roadside views of the Missouri River.

✦ INFORMATION
Standing Rock Sioux Tribe | Box D, 58538 | 701/854–7201 or 701/854–7226 | www.state.sd.us/tourism/sioux/srock.htm.

SITES TO SEE
Standing Rock. The large, unusual stone from which the reservation takes its name was here when Lewis and Clark traveled through, but it wasn't given an identity until many years later. In certain lighting, the stone resembles a seated woman with a shawl. Legend says that a jealous Arikara woman refused to leave with her tribe when they broke camp because her Dakota husband had taken a second wife. Two men were sent back after her; when they arrived, she had turned to stone, but the men carried the "stone woman" back with them anyway. | Standing Rock Ave. | 701/854–7202 | www.state.sd.us/tourism/sioux/srock.htm | Free | Daily dawn–dusk.

Standing Rock Agency Stockade. Throughout the 1800s following the Lewis and Clark expedition, military forts sprang up all over the West, and communities grew around them. Here the first was Fort Yates, built in 1878 and abandoned in 1903; it was the last of the forts in North Dakota to close as settlements formed. The Standing Rock Agency Stockade is the only original building that remains. | Cottonwood St. at Proposal Ave. | 701/854–7202 | www.state.sd.us/tourism/sioux/srock.htm | Free | Daily dawn–dusk.

June–Aug. **Powwows.** Just about any weekend throughout the summer, the Standing Rock Indian Reservation hosts a powwow. Most follow the traditional format with a grand entry, gift giving, dance competitions, and concessions. Among the larger ones are Cannonball Powwow in Cannonball in June and the Wild Horse Stampede and Powwow at Fort Yates in August. | 701/854–7201 or 701/854–7226.

HISTORIC LODGING

Lodge at Prairie Knights. Original art with Lewis and Clark themes, created by area Native Americans, adorns this hotel next to Prairie Knights Casino, near a marina. Buffalo, venison, and walleye pike are on the menu of the attached restaurant, the Hunters' Club. All rooms have queen- or king-size beds and Native American motifs. Restaurant, bar, in-room data ports, in-room safes, some in-room hot tubs, cable TV with video games, no-smoking rooms. | 3932 Rte. 24, 58538 | 701/854–7777 or 800/425–8277 | fax 701/854–3795 | www.prairieknights.com | 96 rooms, 4 suites, 32 RV sites | $60–$75 rooms, $85–$130 suites | AE, D, DC, MC, V.

MANDAN
▼▼

Mandan, across the Missouri River from Bismarck, was settled in 1872 when the Northern Pacific Railroad laid tracks through the area. The town had several names until 1878, when a railroad official settled on Mandan, after the Mandan tribe who lived near the river. When Lewis and Clark traveled through here, they wrote about the Mandan encampments they found in their journals and about the stories of Mandan living along the riverbanks. After the Northern Pacific Railroad completed a bridge from Bismarck across the Missouri River in 1882, Mandan's future was secured. Main Street is still lined with tall false-front stores, a few bars, and western-wear shops.

◆ INFORMATION

Convention and Visitors Bureau | 1600 Burnt Boat Dr., 58503 | 800/767–3555 or 701/222–4308 | www.bismarckmandancvb.com.

SITES TO SEE

Five Nations Art and Gift Shop. A restored Great Northern Railroad depot provides an authentic setting for Native American paintings, jewelry, sculpture, and baskets handcrafted by local artists. | 401 W. Main St. | 701/663–4663 | www.5nationsarts.com | Free | Mon.–Sat. 10–7, Sun. noon–5.

Fort Abraham Lincoln State Park. Originally occupied by Mandan natives, fur traders, and trappers who plied the Missouri River, North Dakota's oldest state park got its start when President Theodore Roosevelt deeded 75 acres to the State Historical Society in 1907. Here you'll find General George Custer's restored home and the 7th Cavalry barracks and commissary. Guides dressed in period clothing take you back to 1875, the year before the 7th Cavalry rode to its destiny at the Little Bighorn. The natural history museum and four reconstructed earth lodges in **On-A-Slant Indian Village** (Memorial Day–Labor Day, 9–7; May and Sept., 9–5; Oct.–Apr., 1–5) bring an ancient civilization to life. The restored earth homes are filled with artifacts and examples of how the agricultural-based Mandan tribe worked and played. Nearly 1,500 Mandans lived here from about 1650 to the late 1700s. Smallpox wiped out nearly the entire village in 1781. Daily guided tours are available. | Rte. 1806, 7 mi south of Mandan | 701/663–9571 | www.fortlincoln.com | Free | Late May–early Sept., daily 9–7; early May–late Sept., daily 9–5; Oct.–Apr., daily 1–5.

✦ ON THE CALENDAR

July **Lewis and Clark Wagon Train.** Four-day covered wagon and horseback trips follow Lewis and Clark's path up the Missouri River starting at Mandan. | 701/663–3085 or 701/873–4296.

Aug. **American Legacy Expo.** Relive the days of the 7th Cavalry with displays, drills, demonstrations of how the Mandans lived, and entertainment during this weekend encampment at Fort Abraham Lincoln State Park. | 701/663–9571.

BISMARCK
▼▼▼

In October 1804 the Corps of Discovery camped across the river from what is now Bismarck. Founded in 1872 as Edwinton—after Northern Pacific Railway chief engineer Edwin Stanton—the city was renamed in 1873 for the chancellor of Germany, Prince Otto von Bismarck, in hopes of attracting German investments in transcontinental railroads. By 1874, when George Armstrong Custer arrived at nearby Fort Abraham Lincoln, Bismarck was thriving as a transportation town with the Northern Pacific Railway crossing the steamboat-laden Missouri River. North Dakota became a state in 1889, and Bismarck, which now has a population of about 55,500, was named its capital.

✦ INFORMATION

Bismarck-Mandan Convention and Visitors Bureau | 1600 Burnt Boat Dr., 58503 | 800/767–3555 or 701/222–4308 | www.bismarckmandancvb.com.

The Long Winter: Fort Mandan

Lewis and Clark stayed in North Dakota for 146 nights at Fort Mandan, a log compound they built in November 1804 just below five Mandan and Hidatsa villages near what is today the city of Washburn. The expedition had intended to stop for the winter farther up the Missouri River, but the men encountered freezing rain and snow on October 21, 1804, and the river began to close with ice.

The Corps first arrived at the Mandan and Hidatsa Indian villages on October 25, 1804. They found the Mandan people hospitable and decided not to resume their journey up the river until the spring thaw. On November 3, William Clark wrote in his journal, "We commence building our cabins." These cabins formed part of an enclosure that was christened Fort Mandan in honor of their hosts.

Chief Sheheke of the Mandans befriended the Corps and helped the group survive the cold winter. Here Lewis and Clark also met Sacagawea, who gave birth to her son, Jean-Baptiste, at or near the fort on February 11, 1805, and who traveled as an interpreter in the spring. During their stay at Fort Mandan, Lewis and Clark mingled with Native Americans, studying and recording their lifestyles. Although the Mandans were familiar with white men because of the explorers who had preceded Lewis and Clark into the area, they had never seen an African-American. Chief LeBorgne, of the Hidatsa, believed that Clark's slave, York, a large black man, had been painted. LeBorgne even rubbed York's skin in an attempt to wash off his paint. Artist Charles M. Russell depicted this scene in his painting *York in the Camp of the Mandans*.

Today's Fort Mandan has been authentically reconstructed about 12 mi from the original fort site; the course of the river has changed since the early 1800s. A must-see for anyone traveling the Lewis and Clark Trail, it has guard posts, a blacksmith shop, captain's room, and recreation room typical of those Lewis and Clark would have known. A new service center was constructed from lignite coal products in 2002. Although energy development hadn't begun when the expedition traveled through, Lewis did note in his journals the existence of burning veins of lignite coal.

Fort Mandan marked the expedition's move from known country into undiscovered country. Lewis and Clark believed that white civilized men had not been west of that point and that they were the first to explore the area beyond Fort Mandan.

SITES TO SEE

Double Ditch Indian Village State Historic Site. Named for the twin-ditch fortification around it, this large earth-lodge village was inhabited by Mandan from 1675 to 1780. Lewis and Clark remarked on the deserted village in their journals. A path with interpretive signage leads through the lodge ruins. | Rte. 1804, 7½ mi north of Bismarck | 701/328–2666 | www.state.nd.us/hist | Free | Daily dawn–dusk.

Lewis and Clark Riverboat. Traveling the Missouri River on this replica paddle wheeler, you'll follow the path taken by Native Americans and trappers. A full bar and food are on board; breakfast, lunch, and dinner cruises are available. | Port of Bismarck, N. River Rd., Exit 157 off I-94 | 701/255–4233 | $15–$35 | Mid-May–early Sept., daily at 2:30, 6, and 8:30.

North Dakota Heritage Center. Peace medals distributed by Lewis and Clark as tokens of friendship, drawings by Hunkpapa Dakota No Two Horns, trade beads, pictographs of three Hidatsa villages on the Knife River, and Mandan villages near where Lewis and Clark camped are among the state's largest collection of historic artifacts housed here. A 1910 statue of Sacagawea and her infant, Jean-Baptiste, by Chicago artist Leonard Crunelle stands in front of the Heritage Center. | 612 E. Boulevard Ave. | 701/328–2666 | www.discovernd.com/hist | Free | Weekdays 8–5, Sat. 9–5, Sun. 11–5.

Spirit of the Plains Gallery. On the United Tribes Technical College campus, the gallery exhibits art by Native American students. Several pieces depict the Lewis and Clark period. | 3315 University Dr. | 701/255–3285 Ext. 426 | www.unitedtribestech.com | Free| By appointment only.

Ward Indian Village Overlook. Ward Village, which overlooks the Missouri River from atop a high hill, was occupied by Mandan natives in the 1500s. The village was protected from enemy attack by a deep ditch and log palisade. A self-guided tour takes you around earth-lodge depressions and a fortification ditch. The village may be closed in the shoulder seasons due to bad weather, so call before you visit. | Burnt Boat Dr., off I-94 at Exit 157 | 701/328–2666 | Free | Apr.–Oct., daily.

✦ ON THE CALENDAR

Sept. United Tribes Indian Art Expo and Market. Native American artists from the United States and Canada perform traditional and contemporary songs, music, dance, and storytelling. | 701/225–3285.

Sept. United Tribes International Powwow. One of the largest powwows in North America, this weekend festival features competitions in Native American dancing and singing as well as vendors selling native foods and handmade crafts. | 701/255–3285 or 701/222–4308.

Oct. National Professional Rodeo Association's Edge of the West Rodeo. Cowboys and fur traders had entered North Dakota even before Lewis and Clark came through the state. Modern cowboys compete in the grand finale of more than 20 North and South Dakota circuit rodeos in this Old West event. | 701/222–6487.

Oct. 22–31, 2004 Time of Renewal and Exchange. Commemorating the 200th anniversary of the first meeting between the United States and the Mandan, Hidatsa, and Arikara nations, this signature event presents a look at the culture of the earth-lodge peoples of the Upper Missouri in 1804. Scholarly presentations, musical performances, and a living history experience are part of the festivities, which also include visits to historic Fort Mandan, Fort Lincoln, and the North Dakota Heritage Center, plus a re-creation of an 1804 Mandan village. | 701/222–6487.

HISTORIC DINING
Peacock Alley Bar and Grill. American. Bismarck's history from the earliest days is portrayed in photos displayed throughout this landmark 1800s building, Bismarck's first hotel. Menu choices include pan-blackened prime rib, walleye, and sunflower sandwiches—an avocado and Swiss cheese sandwich served with sunflower seeds on the side. The bar has 17 beers on draft. | 422 E. Main Ave. | 701/255–7917 | $13–$17 | AE, D, DC, MC, V.

WASHBURN
▼▼

The Mandan and Hidatsa tribes lived along the Missouri River banks in this area long before the city existed. A major stopping place for fur traders and explorers following the river west in the post-Corps years, Washburn is on the Lewis and Clark National Historic Trail and now has a population of 1,500.

✦ INFORMATION
Lewis and Clark Interpretive Center | 2576 8th St. SW, 58577 | 701/462–8535 or 877/462–8535 | www.fortmandan.com.

SITES TO SEE
Bird Woman Missouri River Adventures. On these trips down the Missouri River, you travel in a replica 19th-century canoe with guides in period clothing and learn about the Lewis and Clark expedition as you experience what it was like. The guides cook meals over an open fire, and nights are spent in tepees. Half-day to multiday trips are available. | Box 59, 58577 | 701/462–3367 | www. birdwoman.com | $40–$250 | Late May–early Sept. by appointment.

Cross Ranch Centennial State Park. Towering cottonwood trees, like those Lewis and Clark felled to build their canoes at Fort Mandan the winter of 1804, fringe the last free-flowing, undeveloped stretch of the Missouri River. There are interpretive exhibits, hiking trails, campsites, and picnic shelters; a visitor center provides information on the Missouri River. Bison roamed the prairies and served as meat for meals for the Lewis and Clark expedition and their Mandan neighbors. You can see the shaggy beasts today on the 5,000-acre **Cross Ranch Nature Conservancy Preserve** (701/794–8741) on the park grounds. Walk the hiking trails and bring binoculars so you don't miss the great wildlife viewing. | 1403 River Rd., 8 mi southwest of Washburn on Rte. 1806, Center | 701/794–3731 or 800/807–4723 | www.state.nd.us/ndparks | $4 per vehicle | Visitor Center May–Sept., weekdays 9–5, weekends 9–9; park daily dawn–dusk.

Fort Mandan. Lewis and Clark set up their headquarters for the winter of 1804–05 in Fort Mandan. Some 40 members of the Corps of Discovery helped to build the fort and dig out six canoes, which were later used to continue up the Missouri River. Lewis and Clark named the fort after their hospitable Mandan neighbors, who taught expedition members how to stay alive during the bitterly cold weather. Today you can visit a perfect replica of Fort Mandan, built from rough logs like the original. Rooms contain reproduction bunks, buffalo-skin robes, tools, dried vegetables, and a blacksmith's workshop, just as when the Corps lived here. Costumed interpreters are on site from June through August daily. A new visitor center, built from lignite coal products and opened in spring 2003, carries a large selection of Lewis and Clark books and gifts. | Rte. 17, 1½ mi west of Lewis and Clark Interpretive Center at the junction of U.S. 83 and Rte. 200A | 701/462–8535 or 877/462–8535 | www.fortmandan.com | Free | Grounds daily. Buildings June–Sept., daily 9–5; Oct.–May variable hrs.

Lewis and Clark Interpretive Center. The hand-built, 36-foot canoe here is a replica of the 16 that Lewis and Clark built during the winter they spent in the area. Also on display are buffalo-skin robes, a baby cradle like the one Sacagawea used to carry her son on her back, dioramas of native life, and watercolor prints by Karl Bodmer, a Swiss artist who visited the Knife River villages with German prince Maximilian in 1833–34. Mandan flute music plays in the background. | Junction of U.S. 83 and Rte. 200A | 701/462–8535 | www.fortmandan.com | $5 | Late May–early Sept., daily 9–7; early Sept.–late May, daily 9–5.

Lewis and Clark Mural. Local artist Bill Reynolds created a mural of Lewis and Clark's stay at Fort Mandan. It covers the wall of a building adjacent to the two McLean County historical museums on Main Street. | Main St. | www.washburnnd.com | Free | Daily dawn–dusk.

McLean County Historical Society Museum. Tools, camping equipment, furs, and other items used in the Lewis and Clark era are on display. | 610 Main Ave. | 701/462–3660 or 701/462–3744 | Free | Memorial Day–Labor Day, Tues. 1–5, Sat. noon–5 or by appointment.

✦ ON THE CALENDAR

Feb. **Heritage Outbound Adventure.** At this weekend event at Fort Mandan held during North Dakota's coldest season, you camp and live as Lewis and Clark did during the winter they were at Fort Mandan. Snowshoe hikes, Native American storytelling, and a traditional pipe ceremony are among the activities. | 877/462–8535 or 701/462–8535.

Apr. **Departure from Fort Mandan.** Actors in period clothing reenact the departure of the expedition from Fort Mandan using tools and equipment similar to those used by expedition members here. | 877/462–8535 or 701/462–8535.

June **Lewis and Clark Days.** Interpreters at Fort Mandan reenact the days when Lewis and Clark wintered here, and the city of Washburn celebrates its Lewis and Clark affiliation with a parade, fur-trading demonstrations, and old-time music. | 877/462–8535 or 701/462–8535.

June–Aug. **Lewis and Clark Kayaking.** When you rent a canoe or kayak and paddle down the Missouri River, you will likely see many of the same species the expedition spotted 200 years ago. | 701/462–3368 or 701/462–8635.

STANTON

▼▼

The Hidatsa and Mandan nations built their first agricultural communities here on the confluence of the Knife and Missouri rivers. In the early and mid-1800s, the area served as a trade center. Thomas and James McGrath settled here in 1882 and named the city Stanton, their mother's maiden name. German and Swedish immigrants arrived soon afterward. Energy development has surpassed agriculture as the community's economic mainstay.

✦ INFORMATION

City of Stanton | Box 156, 58571 | 701/745–3202 | www.stanton.com. **Mercer County Visitors Bureau** | 120 Central Ave., Beulah, 58523 | 701/873–4585 or 800/441–2649 | www.beulahnd.org.

SITES TO SEE

Fort Clark State Historic Site. One of three major fur-trading posts on the Missouri River, Fort Clark was built in 1831 to continue the trade with the Mandans. Depressions of the earth-lodge villages built by the Mitutanika

Mandan in 1822 are still visible. You can pick up a card in the fort's stone building to follow a self-guided tour. | 7½ mi southeast of Stanton on Rte. 200 | 701/328–2666 | www.state.nd.us/hist | Free | Mid-May–mid-Sept., daily dawn–dusk.

Knife River Indian Villages National Historic Site. Sacagawea met Lewis and Clark here and became their guide and translator. Today's 1,758-acre site preserves the ruins of Hidatsa and Mandan villages near Fort Mandan, including a village where Sacagawea lived and historic and archaeological items reflecting Northern Plains native culture and agricultural lifestyle. The surrounding prairie is dotted with hundreds of depressions that mark where the earth lodges used to stand. Walking trails take you to the remains of these dwellings and to cache pits, fortification ditches, and travois trails. | ½ mi north of Stanton on Rte. 37 | 701/745–3309 | www.nps.gov/knri | Free | Late May–early Sept., daily 8–6; early Sept.–late May, daily 8–4:30.

✦ ON THE CALENDAR

July **Northern Plains Indian Culture Festival.** Music, dancing, and traditional native cooking are part of this festival, which is held the last weekend in July at Knife River Indian Villages National Historic Site. | 701/745–3300.

Aug. **A Fond Farewell.** At the Knife River Indian Villages National Historic site, this event commemorates the homeward departure of the Lewis and Clark expedition with educational programs and recreational events typical of that era. | 701/745–3300.

HISTORIC DINING AND LODGING

Outpost 1806 Steakhouse. American. Here a map of Lewis and Clark's journey is burned into the floor of the lounge, animals they recorded seeing in their journals add atmosphere, and each tabletop is marked with a wildlife or Lewis and Clark motif. Specials include prime rib, walleye, and the like. | Beulah Bay Rd., 12 mi west of Rte. 200 N on Rte. 1806, Beulah | 701/873–4600 | No dinner Sun. | $7.95–$24.95 | AE, D, DC, MC, V.

Knife River Ranch. At this working ranch in an isolated valley you can ride horseback across rugged land where tepee rings are still visible, canoe down the Knife River like trappers and Native Americans did, and then settle down for a deep sleep in a bunkhouse or cabins. A hanging bridge built by farmhands in the early 1900s provides passage across the river to the horse barns. Cabins have wood floors, handmade quilts, and front porches overlooking the river. There are no private baths. Packages include up to three meals daily. Dining room, refrigerators, horseback riding, horseshoes, cross-country skiing; no a/c, no room phones, no smoking. | 1700 Rte. 5, Golden Valley, 58541 | 701/983–4290 | fax 701/983–4295 | www.kniferiverranch.com | 5 cabins, 1 bunkhouse | $55 | MC, V.

Missouri River Lodge. This working ranch is on the site of a former buffalo jump on the Missouri River in a deep valley surrounded by badlands. A Turtle Turf Cut Effigy, a rare Native American spiritual site, dates to the mid-1800s and sits on the ranch's highest butte. Lewis and Clark passed over this land, too. Fishing, hiking, hunting, and riding in horse-drawn wagons are offered. In-room data ports; no smoking. | 140 42nd Ave. NW, Stanton, 58571 | 701/748–2023 | fax 701/748–2763 | www.moriverlodge.com | 6 rooms, 1 suite | $60–$85 | DC, MC, V | BP.

GARRISON

▼▼▼

Garrison, population 1,300, sits on the north shore of Lake Sakakawea, which was named after the young Shoshone woman who accompanied Lewis and Clark. The original town site was established when a regiment of about 200 soldiers set up a camp near Fort Stevenson. Incorporated in 1903, the city was moved 5 mi to its present site two years later, because the Soo Line Railroad planned to build a depot in the new location.

✦ INFORMATION
Garrison Area Improvement Association | Box 445, 58540 | 800/799–4242 | www.garrisonnd.com.

SITES TO SEE
Audubon National Wildlife Refuge. In their journals, Lewis and Clark recorded several bird species they had never seen before. More than 200 bird species, including some that are endangered, such as the piping plover, make this 14,300-acre refuge their home. On a 7-mi driving tour you can see Canada geese and other waterfowl, as well as indigenous wildlife. Stop by the visitor center to check out the exhibits and collect information. | 3275 11th St. NW, 12 mi south of Garrison, Coleharbor | 701/442–5474 | Free | Daily dawn–dusk.

Fort Stevenson State Park. The expedition camped here on its return trip on August 13, 1806, and in the late 1800s a frontier fort was built to serve as a supply depot for military posts. This state park has a full-service marina with 70 slips and hosts numerous summer events, from frontier reenactments to fishing tournaments. | Rte. 83 | 701/337–5576 | www.state.nd.us/ndparks | $4 per vehicle | Daily.

Garrison Dam Overlook Historical Site. The river Lewis and Clark were following when they stopped here on their return trip in August 1806 was much less immense. Garrison Dam, the fifth-largest earthen dam structure in the

United States, controls flooding on the Missouri River and generates electricity. It backs up the third-largest reservoir in the nation, Lake Sakakawea, which measures 178 mi in length, has 1,530 mi of shoreline, and covers 382,000 acres. | Rte. 200, 23 mi from Garrison, Riverdale | 701/654–7441 | Free | Daily dawn–dusk.

Lake Sakakawea State Park. Along this stretch of undeveloped land that Lewis and Clark traveled when they returned to the state in 1806, wildlife—such as the deer, prairie dogs, and birds that Lewis described in his journal—lived here in abundance as it does today. This park next to the Garrison Dam has a full-service marina with 80 slips, two large boat ramps, and campsites. | Rte. 200, 23 mi south of Garrison, Riverdale | 701/487–3315 | www.state.nd.us/ndparks | $4 per vehicle | Mid-May–early Oct., daily.

✦ ON THE CALENDAR
June **Fort Stevenson Military Days.** Military life in the 1800s is depicted at Fort Stevenson State Park through such activities as military weapons demonstrations, fur trading reenactments, and daily life in a military encampment. | 701/337–5576.

HISTORIC LODGING
Indian Hills Resort. Lewis mentioned the existence of tepee rings in the part of his journal describing this site on April 11–12, 1805. Sitting on the point of Good Bear Bay on Lake Sakakawea, this fishing resort promises some of the best walleye fishing on the Missouri. The rustic cabins share bathrooms and have twin or double beds. A bathhouse is available for cabins without plumbing. Cafeteria, some kitchenettes, lake, fishing, hiking, no-smoking rooms; no room TVs. | 202 Frontage Rd., 31 mi west of Garrison on Rte. 37, 58540 | 701/743–4122 | 6 cabins, tent and RV sites | $25–$60 | Closed Nov.–Apr. | MC, V.

NEW TOWN
▼▼▼

Lewis and Clark reunited west of what is now New Town on their return trip in 1806, having separately explored the Missouri and Yellowstone valleys. New Town, a community of 2,000, is the seat of tribal government for the Three Affiliated Tribes, a formal association of the Mandan, Arikara, and Hidatsa nations, who live on the nearly 1-million-acre Fort Berthold Reservation. New Town was created in 1950 by developers to replace three tiny towns now at the bottom of Lake Sakakawea. Elbowoods (founded in 1889), Sanish (1914), and Van Hook (1914) were all flooded when the Garrison Dam went in.

Sacagawea and the Knife River Indian Villages

As influential and as large as Chicago, the Knife River Indian Villages served as the hub of a vast trade region for thousands of years.

On October 13, 1804, William Clark marveled in his journal at the sophistication he found in this community. "These people are . . . possessing national pride . . . live in warm houses, large and built in an octagon form, forming a cone at top which is left open for smoke to pass. Those houses are generally 30 to 40 feet in diameter . . . those people express an inclination to be at peace with all nations." Established communities date back at least 8,000 years, and it's estimated that about 4,000 Native Americans lived here when they welcomed Lewis and Clark as their guests.

The Knife River Indian Villages was also home to Sacagawea, the pregnant Shoshone teenager who joined the expedition. The Hidatsa spelling—adopted by the state of North Dakota, where the Hidatsa tribe lives—is Sakakawea, for Bird Woman ("Sakaka" means "bird" and "wea" is "woman"). Other common spellings for her name are Shoshone spellings—Sacajawea or Sacagawea.

Sacagawea is believed to have been taken captive by a Hidatsa war party. The French-Canadian trader Toussaint Charbonneau later took her as his wife. Both Charbonneau and Sacagawea joined the Lewis and Clark expedition at Fort Mandan and continued with the expedition westward. Their first child, Jean-Baptiste Charbonneau, was born at Fort Mandan on February 11, 1805.

When the expedition left Fort Mandan in the spring, Sacagawea carried on her back a child less than two months old. The only member of the expedition who had traveled beyond the area of Fort Mandan, she acted as an interpreter. She was also valuable because of her ability to find food, identify landmarks, and communicate with the Shoshone, her native people, on the Montana-Idaho border.

Sacagawea's value increased when the expedition learned her brother was one of the head men of the Shoshone tribe. Lewis and Clark needed horses from the Shoshones to cross the Rockies. Some reports say Sacagawea guided Lewis and Clark to the Pacific, but she actually acted as a guide on only a couple of occasions, both near her homeland in Montana. Although her contributions have been debated by historians, William Clark clearly saw her as an asset. Following their return home, he wrote Charbonneau and said, "Your woman who accompanied you that long dangerous and fatiguing rout to the Pacific Ocian and back diserved a greater reward for her attention and services on that rout than we had in our power to give her."

Sacagawea also seemed to be more valued than Charbonneau. For example, both captains were on shore near today's New Town when a squall struck. Charbonneau, who was at the helm, panicked but Sacagawea stayed calm and salvaged valuable items such as the captains' journals.

When the expedition traveled back through North Dakota in 1806, Sacagawea and Charbonneau remained in the state. In 1809, they traveled down the Missouri River to St. Louis, where they entrusted their son, Jean-Baptiste Charbonneau, to Clark before returning north. Sacagawea lived at the Hidatsa villages and died in her early twenties from a fever. Historians have not been able to establish where she was buried.

Today the 1,758-acre Knife River Indian Villages Historic Site has a visitor center with exhibits, research facilities, an audiovisual program, books, and Indian crafts depicting the culture and agricultural lifestyle of Northern Plains Indians. The ruins of the villages have been preserved, including Sacagawea's home village. A reconstructed earth lodge provides an insider's look at how Native Americans lived in Sacagawea's lifetime. Thirteen miles of hiking paths afford opportunities to view wildlife and walk the paths where Native Americans lived. Their travois paths—the trails made as they moved camp—are still visible to the naked eye.

✦ INFORMATION
New Town Chamber of Commerce | 100 Soo Pl., 58763 | 701/627–3500 | www. newtownnd.com.

SITES TO SEE
Crow Flies High Butte Historical Site. The bluffs and buttes of North Dakota's Badlands, which Lewis and Clark noted in their journals but never explored, are visible from this high site overlooking Lake Sakakawea. The expedition passed through here in 1805 and again the following year. | Rte. 23 | 701/ 627–4477 | May–Sept., daily dawn–dusk.

Paul Broste Rock Museum. Many of the rocks and formations the Corps saw in North Dakota were unfamiliar. This museum houses a private collection of 5,000 rocks, agates, minerals, and crystals, which include not only rocks found in North Dakota but also examples from around the world—all cut, ground, and polished to show off their beauty. | N. Main St., Parshall | 701/ 862–3264 | $4 | May–Oct., Tues.–Sun. 10–5.

Three Affiliated Tribes Museum. Here you can learn about Mandan, Arikara, and Hidatsa tribal history and see traditional Native American art-and-crafts items such as handmade leather clothing decorated with elk teeth. | Rte. 23, 4 mi west of New Town | 701/627–4477 | $3 | Late May–early Sept., daily 10–6.

✦ ON THE CALENDAR

May, Aug., and Dec. **Little Shell Powwow and Four Bears Celebration.** The Native American dancing and regalia are dazzling during this celebration held in New Town the last weekend in May, the second weekend in August, and the last weekend in December. | 701/627–2870.

June **Twin Buttes Celebration.** Dance competitions for all ages and other traditional cultural observations are among activities at this event, held 15 mi north of Halliday, on the third weekend of June. | 701/627–2870.

July **Mandaree Powwow.** Singing, dancing, and honoring ceremonies are among the traditional activities at this festival held north of Scenic Byway 12 near Mandaree. | 701/627–2870.

Aug. **Nux-Bah-Ga Powwow.** Parshall, a small community on the Fort Berthold Indian Reservation 18 mi east of New Town, hosts this powwow, where you'll find dance and costume competitions. | 701/627–2870.

Aug. 17–20, 2006 **Return to the Home of Sakakawea.** This signature event on Fort Berthold Reservation was still in the planning stages at press time. | 701/627–2870.

HISTORIC LODGING

Four Bears Casino and Lodge. Statues of Sacagawea, framed prints chronicling her journey with Lewis and Clark, and other information detailing her involvement with the expedition highlight the Three Affiliated Tribes' pride in this Native American woman. Named for a Mandan chief, Four Bears is a gaming and recreational establishment on Fort Berthold Reservation. In the modern rooms, Native American artwork hangs on the walls, and beds are double, queen-, or king-size. The attached restaurant serves buffalo entrées—the buffalo are raised on a nearby ranch owned by the Three Affiliated Tribes. Restaurant, indoor pool, exercise room, video game room, some pets allowed. | 202 Frontage Rd., 58763 | 800/294–5454 | fax 701/627–4018 | www.4bearscasino. com | 96 rooms, 3 suites | $55–$99 | AE, D, MC, V.

WILLISTON

▼▼▼

In 1887 the Great Northern Railroad built a station at the confluence of the Missouri and Yellowstone rivers, where Lewis and Clark camped, and called it Little Muddy. Visiting a year later, the president of the company renamed it in honor of a friend. Agricultural settlers found the soil to their liking and turned from ranching to wheat farming.

✦ INFORMATION

McKenzie County Tourism Bureau | 201 5th St. SW, Watford City, 58854 | 800/701–2804 or 701/444–2526 | www.4eyes.net. **Williston Convention and Visitors Bureau** | 10 Main St., 58801 | 701/774–9041 or 800/615–9041 | www.willistonnd.tourism.com.

SITES TO SEE

Confluence Interpretive Center. Opened in 2003, this center and a reconstructed 1870s infantry barrack mark the site where Lewis and Clark reunited after they split up to take separate paths on their return trip in 1806. A 3½-mi hiking and biking trail leads to Fort Union Trading Post along the Missouri River. | Rte. 1804, 20 mi east of Williston | No phone number at time of printing | www.state.nd.us/hist | Admission not determined at time of printing | Year-round, daily, hrs not set at time of printing.

Fort Buford State Historic Site. This site at the Missouri-Yellowstone confluence attracted the Corps, who camped here before leaving the state and again when members entered the state two years later. Chief Joseph and Sitting Bull were once detained at this fort. Now you can walk among the original buildings, including the officers' quarters, where an educational center provides information on the rivers and about the flora and fauna of the region. | Rte. 1804, 21 mi southwest of Williston | 701/572–9034 | $4 | Mid-May–mid-Sept., daily 10–6.

Fort Union Trading Post National Historic Site. Lewis noted in his journal that this was an ideal spot for a fort, and from 1828 to 1867, Fort Union was one of the largest trading posts on the upper Missouri River, with walls 18 feet high and cornerstone towers. Today the partly reconstructed white-clapboard fort contains a bookstore and a museum that showcases clothing and accessories from the fur-trading era. Replicas of trade goods like buffalo hides and beaver furs are sold in the Indian Trade House. | Rte. 1804, 24 mi southwest of Williston | 701/572–9083 | www.nps.gov/fous | Free | May–Sept., daily 8–8; Oct.–Apr., daily 9–5:30.

Lewis and Clark State Park. When Clark walked on shore near what is now Lewis and Clark State Park, he found the remains of Assiniboine encampments. Today, towering buttes surround Lake Sakakawea, and white-tailed deer, mule deer, ring-necked pheasant, porcupine, sharp-tailed grouse, and chipmunks abound. This park has a marina and boat ramp, campgrounds, and a self-guided nature trail. | 19 mi southeast of Williston on Rte. 1804 | 701/859–3071 | $4 | Daily; marina, boat ramp, and nature trail mid-May–mid-Sept.

✦ ON THE CALENDAR

May–Sept. Little Knife Outfitters. Experienced guides lead horseback rides through forest and prairie, where you're likely to see white-tailed and mule deer, American bison, bighorn sheep, antelope, prairie dogs, and wild longhorn cattle. A variety of rides are arranged; longer rides include sleeping under the stars and eating meals cooked at a campfire. Experienced guides match your riding ability to an appropriate horse and provide instruction and practice before the ride begins. | 701/842–2631.

July Fort Union Trading Post Rendezvous. Antique weapons and tools are on display, and there are reenactments of all kinds of activities related to the fur trade, all to the sound of bagpipes and fiddles. It's held at Fort Union. | 701/572–9083.

July Fort Buford 6th Infantry Encampment. Military ceremonies, drills, and black-powder firing demonstrations evoke Fort Buford's most spirited years, 1866–95. | 701/572–9034 or 701/328–2666.

HISTORIC DINING AND LODGING

Trapper's Kettle. American. Animal traps from the 1800s and stuffed animals give this place a western touch. A canoe holds the salad bar, and food is served in iron skillets. The menu includes steak, chicken, sandwiches, and soups. | 3901 2nd Ave. W | 701/774–2831 | $9–$15 | AE, D, MC, V.

Tobacco Garden Resort and Marina. Surrounded by some of the state's most rugged and isolated territory, this resort draws adventuresome souls who want to experience life in a primitive setting. Campsites and tent sites are available, and a separate bathhouse serves all guests. Boating, fishing, shop. | Rte. 1806, 28 mi north of Watford City, 58854 | 701/842–6931 | www.4eyes.net | 2 cabins | $35 per cabin | Closed Oct.–Apr. | MC, V.

Montana

pril 25, 1805, was a day of rest and celebration for the Corps of Discovery. They had finally arrived at the confluence of the Missouri and Yellowstone rivers—their first day in the area that would become the state of Montana. It was a high point for Lewis and Clark, who hoped they were only weeks away from the Pacific by water. However, in the months ahead, confrontations with grizzly bears, the Blackfeet, mosquitoes, the Great Falls of the Missouri, extreme weather conditions, the changing nature of the river, and the Rocky Mountains would shake the Corps' confidence and enthusiasm.

The Corps spent more time crossing Montana than any other state. Today, many of the dramatic landscapes described in the Lewis and Clark journals remain unchanged. From solitary sandstone monuments, through river canyons to mountain meadows, Montana's rivers flow past scores of landmarks related to the expedition. One bears the signature of William Clark in clear, round letters—the clearest piece of physical evidence of the Corps' passage along the entire route. Some of this landscape is preserved as state parks, and many highway markers provide information about Montana's past.

The state nickname, "Big Sky Country," reveals its full meaning in eastern Montana, a vast land of prairies, coulees, and sun-washed sandstone ridges beneath spacious skies. Here the sun sets in flaming glory and huge Vs of honking Canada geese can be seen silhouetted against crimson clouds. At night, the moon rising over the land seems so close you can touch it, and the dancing aurora borealis is captivating, if you're lucky enough to see it.

As you drive, the Montana landscape is ever-changing. Turning south from U.S. 2 at Malta you see the first mountains—the Little Rockies. This is a lonely landscape of sage-covered foothills, where cattle, sheep, and wildlife graze—the transition from flat open land to the pine-forested coulees of the Missouri River Breaks.

On the trip west, it took the Corps two weeks to cover the land along the beautiful Missouri River bottomlands, now contained by the Charles M. Russell National Wildlife Refuge. The refuge land has changed little since those days except for the U.S. 191, which allows visitors to make the trip in a couple of hours. Wildlife was abundant in 1805, and all the species noted in the expedition journals can still be seen across Montana.

After exploring the wild and scenic Missouri through "seens of visionary inchantment" in the White Cliffs area (even today accessible only by boat), the Corps arrived at the Marias River—an unexpected junction near Fort Benton. They spent nine days exploring this area before deciding to follow the south fork, which led to the "sublimely grand spectacle" of the Great Falls of the Missouri. It took a month of backbreaking work to complete the 18-mi portage around the falls over the uneven, rocky, cactus-strewn terrain.

On July 15, the Corps once again took to the river and continued southwest past the towering limestone cliffs that create the optical illusion known as Gates of the Mountains and from there to the headwaters of the Missouri at Three Forks. (It was here, five years earlier, that Sacagawea had been kidnapped by the Hidatsa.) The view is spectacular from the cliff that Lewis climbed to view the Headwaters Valley, where three rivers—the Madison, the Jefferson, and the Gallatin—converge in a huge bowl, nearly 100 mi in diameter, ringed by mountains. After a two-day rest the Corps began its trek to the southwest along the Jefferson, passing through an area that is now rolling ranchland, south of Whitehall. When they came to Beaverhead Rock, a monolith that resembles a swimming beaver, Sacagawea assured Lewis and Clark that her people would be found nearby—if not on this river then on the one immediately to the west.

On August 12 Lewis and three men climbed to the top of Lemhi Pass and were disheartened to discover "immence ranges of high mountains still to the West." Along with the scenery from the Missouri River between Fort Peck Lake and Fort Benton, the view from Lemhi Pass looks more like what Lewis saw in 1805 than any other scene in Montana. The first meeting with the Shoshone went better than Lewis and Clark had even hoped. Sacagawea recognized the chief as her brother, Cameahwait, and they spent six days at Camp Fortunate (the area that is now Clark Canyon Dam). Having acquired horses from the Shoshone, the expedition began the arduous trek across the Continental Divide over Lost Trail Pass into the beautiful Bitterroot Valley. As they traveled down the valley, the craggy, snow-covered, heavily forested Bitter-root Mountains impressed Sergeant Patrick Gass as "the most turrible mountains I've ever beheld." On September 9 they arrived at Travelers' Rest on Lolo Creek, 12 mi south of present-day Missoula.

The Corps camped at Travelers' Rest once again on June 30, 1806, on their return trip. Then, after a three-day rest, Lewis and Clark separated. Lewis and nine others traveled through the heavily timbered country of high and rocky mountains along the Blackfoot River, which the Nez Percé called "River of the Road to Buffalo." The party explored the Marias, but their quest to anchor the northern boundary of the Louisiana Territory at the 49th parallel ended at Camp Disappointment near what is now Glacier National Park. Returning to the Great Falls, after a run-in with some Blackfeet warriors, they proceeded down the Missouri, following the route they had used in 1805.

Meanwhile, Clark returned across Lost Trail Pass to Camp Fortunate to retrieve the dugouts and supplies cached there earlier, then proceeded down the Jefferson River to the Three Forks. From there he and his party traveled east through the fertile Gallatin Valley, which Native Americans of the area knew as the "Valley of the Flowers." Sacagawea directed Clark to a gap in the mountains—Bozeman Pass—and the party arrived on the banks of the Yellowstone River just south of Livingston. The Yellowstone remains the longest free-flowing river in the Lower 48 States, and Clark's trip along it held pleasant surprises and visual wonders—as it does today. It is easy to miss the more subtle beauty that surrounds you while driving through the Lower Yellowstone region of Montana, past Billings and Pompeys Pillar, where Clark engraved his name on July 25, 1806. Unlike the spectacle of the mountains of western Montana, with their majestic vistas, the beauty of the plains and prairies here is gentler with its nuanced palette and rugged badlands.

Uncertain at their parting of ever seeing each other again, Lewis and Clark reunited on August 12, 1806, just beyond the confluence of the Yellowstone and Missouri.

Tracing the Trail through Montana
A DRIVING TOUR FROM SIDNEY TO MISSOULA

▼▼

Distance: 1,069 mi　　**Time:** 5 days
Breaks: Lewistown, Great Falls, Dillon, and Missoula have a variety of dining and lodging options.

This trip leads you along the route taken by Lewis and Clark during their journey through Montana between April 25 and September 11, 1805. Many areas along the route, some of the most scenic and spectacular country in the United States, have not changed since the Corps of Discovery first saw them.

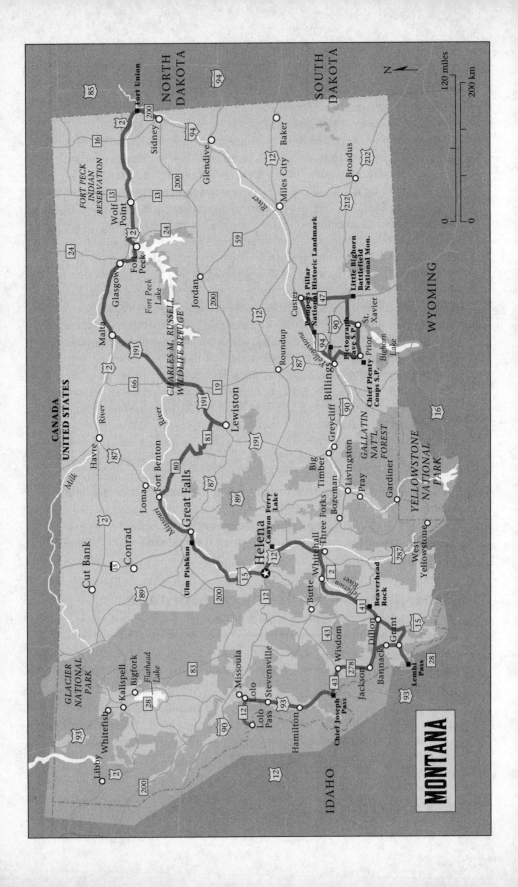

Plan to start day one early, because the mileage is the longest of any day on the tour. Leave from **Sidney,** amid the subtle beauty of plains and badlands, and drive 20 mi north on Route 200 and Route 58, crossing the Missouri River, to the junction with North Dakota Route 1804; turn west 2 mi to Fort Union. Here, at the confluence of the Missouri and Yellowstone rivers, the Corps of Discovery celebrated its long-anticipated arrival on April 25, 1805. The fort has been reconstructed to appear as it did in 1851, when it was a trading head-quarters for the American Fur Company. Between Fort Union and Fort Buford, travel north on Route 5, then west along U.S. 2 through the Fort Peck Indian Reservation, home of the Sioux and Assiniboine nations. Stop here to visit the Fort Peck Assiniboine and Sioux Culture Center and Museum. West of Wolf Point, turn south on Route 117 and drive 18 mi to **Fort Peck.** The 4-mi-long dam here, completed in 1940, is the largest earth-filled dam in the world and creates Fort Peck Lake, one of Montana's recreational and scenic gems.

Returning to U.S. 2 via Route 24, you travel through high plains country, where huge herds of buffalo once roamed. At Malta, turn south on U.S. 191. The Little Rockies, considered sacred by generations of Native Americans, are the first mountains you see as you make the transition between the prairie and the rugged, pine-covered coulees of the Missouri River Breaks. It took Lewis and Clark two weeks to travel through this spectacular area, which is now encompassed in the 1,100,000-acre Charles M. Russell National Wildlife Refuge. The Missouri Breaks National Back Country Byway, an 81-mi loop, parallels the lower 50 mi of the Upper Missouri Wild and Scenic River, with some unforgettable scenery (allow two to three hours). The 20-mi Charles M. Russell National Wildlife Tour (one to two hours) puts you amid scenic grandeur nearly like that the Corps experienced. This is a rugged, remote area, and in wet weather, the bentonite gumbo soil becomes slick and the gravel roads impassable, even for four-wheel-drive vehicles. End your day in **Lewistown,** taking time to stroll through its historic downtown.

On day two, leave Lewistown via U.S. 191, head north to Route 81, and then go west to Route 80 and north to **Fort Benton,** the birthplace of Montana. Today the trip takes you past cattle ranches and grain farms in the area known as the Golden Triangle, where amber waves of grain ripple in the late-summer breeze. The Corps camped here on June 4, 1805, and spent nine days exploring the area trying to decide which major river would take the group to the Pacific. Stretch your legs with a walk along the Fort Benton Levee, where the first steamboat arrived in 1850, and then visit the Museum of the Upper Missouri. An 11-mi drive north on U.S. 87 brings you to Loma and the Decision Point Overlook. There is an interpretive display here, and you can walk to the top of the cliff where Lewis stood to get a better view of the land at the confluence of the Marias and Missouri rivers. If you have extra time, plan to take a one- to five-day guided keelboat or canoe trip through the area on the Missouri where Lewis remarked on "seens of visionary inchantment." The Wild and Scenic section of the Missouri is accessible only by boat, so this is definitely worth the time and effort. Before leaving Fort Benton, relax along the riverside over a meal of Rocky Mountain cuisine at the 1882 Grand Union Hotel; spend the night in Fort Benton or travel 42 mi south on Interstate 15 to overnight in **Great Falls,** where there is a large choice of lodging accommodations.

Begin day three in Great Falls. On June 13, 1805, Lewis arrived at the first of five falls and wrote of a "truly magnificent and sublimely grand object." Making the portage around the series of falls took a backbreaking month. Here, stop at the Lewis and Clark National Historic Trail Interpretive Center to see the exhibits of tools, canoes, furs, leather clothing, and other materials used by travelers and Native Americans of the era. The River's Edge Trail takes you to Giant Springs Heritage State Park, a great place for a picnic lunch with overlooks for Black Eagle and Rainbow Falls. At this point you may want to take a three-day side trip to Glacier National Park to learn more about Native American heritage and see some of the most beautiful scenery in the country.

If you continue along the Lewis and Clark Trail, follow the Missouri River south from Great Falls on Interstate 15. Along the way are Ulm Pishkun and scenic pull-outs that overlook the river. On July 19, 1805, Lewis and Clark were paddling upstream in between towering cliffs that seemed "ready to tumble," Lewis wrote. "I shall call them Gates of the Mountains," he said. Today, a 105-minute boat cruise from the marina at Gates of the Mountains takes you past the 1,200-foot limestone cliffs, where you can spot ancient Native American pictographs and wildlife species that the Corps of Discovery may have seen. Return to Interstate 15 and drive 17 mi to **Helena,** the state's capital, where you'll find a variety of hotels and restaurants—some dating to the late 1800s.

On day four, spend the morning in Helena with a visit to the Montana Historical Society Museum and the state capitol building, where you can see western artist Charles M. Russell's largest mural—a 12- by 25-foot scene of Lewis and Clark meeting a group of Native Americans at Ross' Hole. A ride on the Last Chance Tour Train gives you a quick look at historic Helena and a chance to hear the stories of this city. Traveling south from Helena on U.S. 12/287 you pass by Canyon Ferry Lake and recreation area, a great place to fish, boat, sail, camp, and look for wildlife. At the junction of U.S. 287 and Interstate 90, get onto Interstate 90 and go 3 mi east to **Three Forks.** After traveling 2,500 mi from its mouth, Lewis and Clark found the headwaters of the Missouri River here at the confluence of the Jefferson, Gallatin, and Madison rivers, where Headwaters State Park has interpretive exhibits and a grand view from the hilltop. It was here five years earlier that Sacagawea had been kidnapped by the Hidatsa. The Headwaters Heritage Museum on Main Street has several fine exhibits on Lewis and Clark, Sacagawea, and trapping days.

Continue west through town to U.S. 2, which follows the Jefferson River west. Stop at the Lewis and Clark Caverns along the way to **Whitehall,** where several murals on buildings around town depict Lewis and Clark's trip through this region. Turn south on Routes 55 and 41 to follow the Jefferson River through cattle country. Along the way look for Beaverhead Rock, a huge monolith that resembles a swimming beaver. When Sacagawea saw the rock, she knew she would find her people either on this river or the one to the west. Spend the night in **Dillon,** a town with a diverse mix of culture, history, and recreation. The town's visitor center has a diorama of the Lewis and Clark expedition at Beaverhead Rock. For a dusk view of Beaverhead Valley, stop at Clark's Lookout State Park.

On day five, take Interstate 15 south from Dillon. Here the Corps camped for a week at Camp Fortunate, now flooded by Clark Canyon Reservoir, and acquired horses from the Shoshone for the trek over the mountains. On August 12, 1805, Lewis and three others climbed to the top of Lemhi Pass and were disheartened to see the high mountains ahead of them—they had hoped to see the ocean. A gravel Forest Service road (not suitable for large trailers and motor homes) leads to the summit of Lemhi Pass, where there is a small campground and memorial to Sacagawea. Backtrack to Grant and take the gravel county road north past Bannack, Montana's first capital and site of Montana's first major gold strike, in 1862, or return to Interstate 15 and head north to Route 278, a paved shortcut to Montana's westernmost Lewis and Clark Trail sites. Route 278 closely follows the route Clark took on his return journey eastward in 1806. Chief Joseph and his band of Nez Percé went this way on their 1,500-mi odyssey in 1877 and were attacked at the Big Hole Battlefield.

Continue west on Route 43 over Chief Joseph Pass into the beautiful Bitterroot Valley, whose craggy, heavily forested mountains impressed Sergeant Patrick Gass as "the most turrible mountains I've ever beheld." On September 9, the Corps arrived at Travelers' Rest on Lolo Creek, 12 mi south of present-day **Missoula,** Montana's Garden City and one of America's most sophisticated small cities. Stop here for dinner and a night's rest before following the trail over Lolo Pass into Idaho.

Through Native American History
A DRIVING TOUR STARTING AND ENDING IN BILLINGS
▼▼

Distance: 205 mi (226 mi)   **Time:** 1 day
Breaks: Eat lunch in the Hardin/Crow Agency area, where several restaurants serve homemade soups, pies, Indian tacos, and fry bread.

This tour takes you to see Native American pictographs, Pompeys Pillar, the Little Bighorn Battlefield, and Garryowen at the home of Chief Plenty Coups, the last traditional Crow chief.

Begin by driving 7 mi east of Billings via Interstate 90; follow the signs from the Lockwood exit to **Pictograph Cave State Park,** a complex of three caves that was home to generations of prehistoric hunters 10,000 years ago. Ocher and black-and-white drawings of figures, tepees, and wildlife can be seen on the walls of Pictograph Cave, accessed by a short trail, and on the rock outcroppings nearby. Return to Interstate 94, travel to Exit 23, and then drive 28 mi east to **Pompeys Pillar National Monument,** an immense sandstone outcropping that Clark named after the nickname given to Sacagawea's infant son. On July 25, 1806, Clark carved his name and the date on the rock; these inscriptions are the clearest physical evidence left anywhere on the trail by the expedition.

Next head for the **Little Bighorn Battlefield National Monument**: take a mostly gravel county road from Pompeys Pillar south for 22 mi, or continue east on Interstate 94 for 28 mi to Custer and then south on Route 47 and Interstate 90 for 46 mi. The preserved battlefield, monument, and cemetery are lasting symbols of the battle now variously known as Custer's Last Stand, Sitting Bull's War, and the Sioux War of 1876. In this famous battle, Lieutenant Colonel George Armstrong Custer and 225 other soldiers clashed with Crazy Horse and more than 3,000 Sioux and Cheyenne warriors. An interpretive museum, living-history programs, ranger talks, and guided and self-guiding tours tell the story.

From here travel 24 mi west and south on Route 313 to St. Xavier, then west 41 mi to Pryor and **Chief Plenty Coups State Park.** The last traditional chief of the Crow Nation, Plenty Coups led his people into the 20th century. The park includes Plenty Coups' two-story log home, medicine spring, and grave site, as well as a museum interpreting Crow culture and Plenty Coups' life. End the day by returning to Billings—35 mi via U.S. 416.

SIDNEY
▼▼

This rural ranching community of 5,200 on the banks of the Yellowstone River is just a few miles west of the North Dakota border. Sometimes called the Sunrise City, Sidney is the largest town in northeast Montana. Stay and explore some of the badlands and breaks along the Yellowstone River just south of town. The colors and play of light on the rugged landscape are at their best in the evening. On April 27, 1805, Lewis and Clark and the Corps of Discovery first entered what would become Montana, 20 mi to the northeast of the present-day city. Clark passed through here in 1806 to rejoin Lewis.

◆ INFORMATION
Missouri River Country | 202 1st Ave. E, Plentywood, 59624 | 800/653–1319 | www.missouririver.visitmt.com. **Sidney Chamber of Commerce** | 909 S. Central Ave., 59270 | 406/482–1916 | www.sidneymt.com.

Montana's Native Americans

The heritage of Montana's 11 Native American tribes contributes to the distinct flavor of the state. Before trappers and settlers came west, tribes roamed freely, following the huge buffalo herds that once covered the plains. Although Montana's Native Americans, who now make up 6% of the population, have worked to adapt to the changing world around them, each tribe has kept its own customs and traditions.

Dance, songs, games, language, and religious ceremonies performed in traditional dress on sacred lands just as they have been for hundreds of years celebrate each tribe's culture. Beautiful arts and crafts reflect the groups' special connection with nature. Tribal powwows, hand games, rodeos, and shinny games (similar to soccer) are social events usually open to the public. Some cultural and religious ceremonies require a special invitation or are not open to the public. All tribes hold their religions and traditions in high regard, and showing respect and courtesy is mandatory. Always ask before you take a photograph, and always use the tribe's name, such as Crow or Gros Ventre, rather than the word "Indians."

Each tribe has its share of interesting places to visit as well. In Browning, there's the Museum of the Plains Indian. Pryor has the Chief Plenty Coups State Park Museum. Lame Deer is the site of the Northern Cheyenne Tribal Museum. Poplar claims the Fort Peck Assiniboine and Sioux Culture Center and Museum. Gros Ventre and Assiniboine tribal members on the Fort Belknap Reservation explain the sacred relationship between native peoples, the buffalo, and the prairie during tours of the buffalo preserve near Harlem. At the National Bison Range on the Flathead Reservation, buffalo roam across 20,000 acres. The Little Bighorn Battlefield National Monument on the Crow Reservation honors the site of the Native American victory over Custer's 7th Calvary. The Assiniboine Village in Wolf Point, a re-creation of a traditional village, gives you the opportunity to experience the Assiniboine culture firsthand.

The largest Native American celebration in Montana is the Crow Fair and Rodeo at the Crow Agency, but there are other events, among them the Arlee Fourth of July Celebration, Fort Belknap's Milk River Indian Days, and Rocky Boy's Annual Powwow. For more information on additional celebrations around the state, contact Travel Montana (800/847–4868, visitmt.com).

SITES TO SEE

Fort Union Trading Post Historic Site. On April 25, 1805, the Corps of Discovery camped at the confluence of the Missouri and Yellowstone rivers, and Lewis and Clark recognized the area for its strategic location and potential wealth. Built in 1829 by John Jacob Astor's American Fur Company, Fort Union became the headquarters for trade with the Assiniboine, Crow, and Blackfeet. Today's structure looks like the fort did in 1851. Bourgeois House, once the setting for elegant dinners with distinguished guests, is now a visitor center. In summer you can take guided tours and see living-history programs and exhibits. | 15550 Rte. 1804, between U.S. 2 and Rte. 200 between Williston, ND, and Sidney, MT | 701/572–9083 | www.nps.gov/fous/index.htm | Free | Daily 9–5:30.

✦ ON THE CALENDAR

Apr. **Lewis and Clark at the Confluence.** At this event, you can celebrate the April 1805 arrival of the Corps of Discovery at the Missouri-Yellowstone confluence on the weekend closest to April 25—the date the Corps arrived in the area. The event, held at Fort Union, involves Lewis and Clark reenactors, demonstrations, and lectures. | 701/572–9093.

June **Fort Union Rendezvous.** Traders sell crafts and period products, and artisans demonstrate pottery making, candle making, fire starting, beaver skinning, black-powder weapons use, flint knapping, and more. Presentations and talks on fur-trade history, Native American culture, clothing of the fur-trade era, and other topics round out the schedule. | 701/572–9083.

July **Fort Buford Encampment.** The second weekend of July 2½ mi east of Fort Union, at this encampment—a frontier military post—actors stage a reenactment of 1870s garrison life. Infantry and cavalry soldiers in period costume drill with small arms and fire rifles and 10-pound Mountain Howitzers. | 701/572–9083.

Aug. **Indian Arts Showcase.** Usually held the third weekend of August at Fort Union, this event celebrates the tradition of the Northern Plains tribes with arts, crafts, storytelling, stone-pipe making, doll making, weapon crafting, bead- and quillwork, flint knapping, and flute playing. | 701/572–9083.

Sept. **Fort Union Living History.** Every Labor Day weekend, staff and volunteers dress, live, work, and eat as employees of the American Fur Company would have in the mid-19th century. Last Bell Tours, a first-person living-history tour telling an actual story from Fort Union's past, is part of the program. | 701/572–9083.

FORT PECK

▼▼▼

The expedition found this region teeming with wildlife. It was here they began to confront grizzly bears. On May 8, 1805, Lewis named the Milk River for its cloudy appearance, noting its "peculiar whiteness, being about the color of a cup of tea with the admixture of a tablespoonful of milk." The river would become an important means of travel for fur trappers in the 1850s. The original Fort Peck, constructed in 1867, stood at the mouth of the Milk River and served as a trading post. When the area became reservation land for the Assiniboine, it served as agency headquarters. Fort Peck is a rare treasure, and many early buildings are still in use today.

The fastest way to get to the next major interpretive site, Fort Benton, is to take U.S. 2 across to Havre and then south on U.S. 87. However, if you prefer to stick more closely to the expedition route and see more back-country views along the Missouri River, take U.S. 191 south at Malta to Lewistown.

SITES TO SEE

Fort Peck Assiniboine and Sioux Culture Center and Museum. This is a perma-nent exhibit of the Assiniboine heritage, with artifacts, traditional cloth-ing, beadwork, and arts and crafts. | U.S. 2, Poplar | 406/768–5155 | Free | Daily 8–4:30.

Valley County Pioneer Museum. Lewis and Clark exhibits fill this museum. Dioramas, Plains tepees, and a reconstructed town depict frontier life. Other displays showcase fossils, Native American artifacts, and collections on the railroad, early business, aviation, and wildlife. | 816 U.S. 2, Glasgow | 406/228–8692 | Free | Memorial Day–Labor Day, daily 9–5.

HISTORIC DINING AND LODGING

Fort Peck Hotel Restaurant. American/Casual. Here chef John Johnson prepares the area's best barbecued ribs as well as homemade Indian tacos, prime rib, walleyed pike, and seafood. Breakfast, lunch, and dinner are all served, and you can eat either in the dining room or on the front porch. | 135 S. Missouri Ave. | 406/526–3266 | Closed Dec.–May 1 | $7–$17 | AE, D, MC, V.

Fort Peck Hotel. The rustic lobby and comfortable lounge of this hotel built in the 1930s invite relaxation. Furniture is of the period, and most rooms have showers. During theater season, the hotel offers special packages that include dinner for two, play tickets, room, and breakfast. Restaurant, lounge, free parking, no-smoking rooms; no room phones, no room TVs. | 135 S. Missouri Ave., 59223 | 406/526–3266 or 800/560–4931 | 37 rooms, 10 with shared bath | $58 | Closed Dec.–May 1 | AE, D, MC, V.

LEWISTOWN

▼▼

When Lewis and Clark passed through central Montana, they continued up the part of the Missouri River that lies in the area now bounded by U.S. 2 and Route 81. Lewistown began as a small trading post and evolved into a town of 6,000 residents in the shadow of the low-lying Moccasin Mountains.

◆ INFORMATION
Lewistown Chamber of Commerce | 408 N.E. Main St., 59457 | 406/538–5436 or 800/216–5436 | www.lewistownchamber.com.

SITES TO SEE
Charles M. Russell National Wildlife Refuge. With more than a million acres of range sprawling around 245,000-acre Fort Peck Reservoir, this refuge is the second largest in the continental United States and preserves the still-dwindling prairie habitat that once covered most of the country. A sanctuary for at least 200 species of birds as well as 45 different types of mammals and many kinds of reptiles, it shelters bighorn sheep, pronghorn antelope, and deer as well as one of the nation's largest prairie herds of elk and one of the world's last free-roaming populations of black-footed ferrets, one of North America's rarest mammals. The prairie dog has also made a comeback here. You'll also find dinosaur bones, buffalo kill sites, abandoned homesteaders' shacks, and wagon-wheel ruts. The lake, with a 1,520-mi shoreline, is best known for its walleye fishing but contains many other game fish, including northern pike, perch, and salmon. Campgrounds and recreation areas ring the lake, and you can swim, fish, boat, and go horseback riding. A 20-mi-long self-guided tour with marked stops starts 55 mi south of Malta off U.S. 191 and exits back onto 191 a ½ mi north of the Missouri; plan on at least two hours. | Box 110, Airport Rd., Lewistown, 59457 | 406/538–8706 | cmr.fws.gov | Free | Daily dawn–dusk.

Charlie Russell Chew-Choo. You can discover the landscapes that inspired western artist Charles M. Russell on 3½-hour Saturday-night dinner tours aboard this 1950s vintage train. The fare is prime rib, and there's entertainment; surprise visitors make the trip memorable. | 211 E. Main St. | 406/538–5436 | www.lewistownchamber.com | $85 | June–Sept.

Missouri Breaks National Back Country Byway. The 81-mi loop parallels the lower 50 mi of the Wild and Scenic section of the upper Missouri, much of it unchanged since the Corps passed through. Four side trips along the road lead to scenic views of the Upper Missouri National Wild and Scenic River, the Lewis and Clark National Historic Trail, and the Nez Percé National Historic Trail. Interpretive signs describe scenery, geology, and wildlife.

Although it's a nationally designated road, 40 mi of it is gravel and becomes impassable even for four-wheel-drive vehicles when wet; large RVs are not advisable on the Lower Two Calf Road because of steep terrain. From April to October, a short side trip across the Missouri is available on the McClelland Ferry. | Bureau of Land Management Visitor Center, 80 Airport Rd., Lewistown | 406/538–7461 or 406/622–5185.

✦ ON THE CALENDAR

June **Missouri River Breaks Lewis and Clark Encampment.** At this two-day event, held the first weekend of June, the focus is life in camp, with demonstrations of cooking and tanning, songs, dances, storytelling, and a traditional buffalo meal. The venue is off U.S. 191, 70 mi south of Malta. | 406/538–5436.

FORT BENTON

▼▼

On June 4, 1805, the Corps of Discovery set up camp here at the confluence of the Missouri and the Marias rivers, then spent nine days trying to decide which of the two streams was the Missouri. Expedition journals identified this area as "a judicious position for the purpose of trade." The original fort on the site, built in 1846, has come to be known as the birthplace of Montana, because the state's oldest town developed around it. Fort Benton eventually became a major landing point for fur traders, gold miners, and homesteaders arriving from St. Louis on steamships via the Missouri River; the city was Montana's most important until the railroad went through in 1887. Nowadays, tepee rings from Plains tribes such as the Blackfeet, which Lewis and Clark passed both en route to the Pacific and back, are still visible on the bench lands along the river. The town has a population of 1,600 and is known as the gateway to the Wild and Scenic Upper Missouri River.

✦ INFORMATION

Fort Benton Chamber of Commerce | Box 12, 59442 | 406/622–3864 | www.fortbenton.com.

SITES TO SEE

Decision Point Overlook. During the nine days the expedition camped here, Lewis climbed to Decision Point Overlook for a better view of the surrounding land and reasoned that the Marias River traveled too much to the north to be the Missouri. He cached supplies at the mouth of the Marias for later use. Today, a ¼-mi trail with interpretive signs evokes Lewis's hike. | U.S. 87, 11 mi north of Fort Benton.

Fort Benton Levee. A self-guided walking tour along the four-block-long levee along the Missouri takes in museums, the ruins of the old fort, and other historical buildings. One of the highlights is the Grand Union Hotel, erected in 1882, which reveals the graceful style of living once enjoyed by travelers to the frontier. You'll also see the 15th Street Bridge, constructed in 1888, and the *Explorers at the Marias* statue, Montana's official state memorial to Lewis, Clark, and Sacagawea. The sculpture includes the figure of the Shoshone woman's infant son, Jean-Baptiste, and was created by famed western artist Bob Scriver. Also along the levee is Old Fort Park, which contains the remaining traces of the original square adobe fort and a replica of the keelboat *Mandan,* built for the 1952 Howard Hawks film starring Kirk Douglas, *The Big Sky.*

Museum of the Upper Missouri and Old Fort Benton. At these two sites in Old Fort Park, you can find out more about the town during the 19th century and its roles as a military complex and fur-trading post and later as a center for steamboat travel along the river. The museum displays exhibits relating to the people and events of the town. Next door, Old Fort Benton is considered the birthplace of Montana and is a National Historic Landmark. Its blockhouse, the oldest standing structure in the state, was created in 1846 by dismantling Fort Lewis, one of a number of fur-trading outposts farther upstream, and rafting them down to the new site; beginning in 1848, the fort was rebuilt of adobe bricks as protection against the area's extreme weather. The name honors Senator Thomas Hart Benton. When the fur trade died out around 1865, the company sold the fort to the military and by 1881 the structure was abandoned and deteriorating. In 1908, the Daughters of the American Revolution restored the last remaining bastion; additional restoration is now ongoing and the structure is open during limited hours. | Old Fort Park, Main and 21st Sts. | 406/622–5316 | www.fortbenton.com/museums | $4 | May, daily 11:30–4:30; June–Sept., daily 10–5; Oct.–Apr. by appointment only.

Upper Missouri National Wild and Scenic River. In 1805–06 Lewis and Clark explored the Missouri River and camped on its banks. Today the stream remains free-flowing for 149 mi down from Fort Benton. Highlights include the scenic White Cliffs area, Citadel Rock, the Hole in the Wall, the Lewis and Clark camp at Slaughter River, abandoned homesteads, and abundant wildlife. Commercial boat tours, shuttle service, and rentals of rowboats, power boats, and canoes are offered at Fort Benton and Virgelle. | Visitor center, 1718 Front St. | 406/622–5185 or 406/538–7461 | www.mt.blm.gov/ldo/umnwsr. html | Free | Visitor center May–Oct., daily 9–5.

Upper Missouri River Keelboat Co. During one- to four-day expeditions aboard the *Gen. Wm. Ashley,* a 38-foot replica of the keelboats that plied the fur trade on the upper Missouri before the days of steamboats, you travel through countryside that is virtually unchanged since Lewis and Clark passed this way. Camping is in comfort at places where the Corps camped, and there are living-history presentations as well. One- to five-day guided canoe trips are also available. | Box 201, Lom, 59460 | 888/721–7133 or 406/739–4333 | www.mrkeelboat.com | Reservations essential | $125–$225.

Virgelle Merc and Missouri River Canoe Company. This canoe outfitter, on the Missouri River 27 mi northeast of Fort Benton and 8 mi off U.S. 87 at milepost 66, leads guided canoe and kayak tours that follow Lewis and Clark's path down the river and last between 1 and 10 days. You'll float sections of the river from almost-a-ghost-town Virgelle, where one of the state's last river-crossing cable ferries operates. The Virgelle Merc itself is a restored homestead-era settlement with accommodations. Built in 1912 by Virgil Blankenbaker and his wife, it operated until 1970, mostly on a shoestring; since 1975, when it reopened under the stewardship of a local pharmacist, it has been selling antiques and outdoor experiences and renting rooms and cabins. | 7485 Virgelle Ferry Rd. N, Loma, 59460 | 800/426–2926 | www.canoemontana.com | AE, DC, MC, V.

✦ ON THE CALENDAR

June **Fort Benton Summer Celebration.** Fort Benton celebrates its role as Montana's first community with a parade, arts, crafts, antiques, a street dance, fireworks, Missouri River boat rides, and historical tours of Old Fort Benton. | 406/622–3351.

June **Touch the Trail of Lewis and Clark.** The era of buckskins and linen, muskets, and knives returns during this event via readings from expedition journals, demonstrations of primitive tools and weapons, and more. A western-style steak supper completes the day. The event, conducted with the Missouri River Canoe Company, takes place on the Missouri River at the Virgelle Mercantile. | 406/378–3110 or 800/426–2926.

HISTORIC DINING AND LODGING

Grand Union Grille. American. In this upscale western restaurant, you'll find sophisticated Rocky Mountain cuisine based on seafood, meat, game, pastas, and vegetables. The irresistible desserts and bread are made on the premises. Sunday brunch is a weekly event between November and mid-May, and meals are served on the riverside deck, weather permitting. | 1 Grand Union Sq. | 406/622–1882 | Closed Mon. and Tues. Nov.–Mar. and Mon. Apr.–Oct. | $21–$28 | AE, D, MC, V.

Grand Union Hotel. This imposing redbrick hotel on the shaded banks of the Missouri River is the centerpiece of town. Opened in 1882, it's the state's oldest hostelry and is on the National Register of Historic Places. Large, elegantly appointed rooms look out over either downtown or the shores of the Missouri, which are lush with grasses, willows, and cottonwood trees. Restaurant, in-room data ports, cable TV, boating, fishing, bar; no smoking. | 1 Grand

Union Sq., 59442 | 404/622–1882 or 888/838–1882 | fax 404/622–5985 | www.grandunionhotel.com | 27 rooms | $109–$159 | AE, D, MC, V | CP.

Pioneer Lodge Motel. Built in 1882 by T. C. Power as a general mercantile store, this lodge overlooking the Missouri was once a focal point of the town until 1985. Now remodeled as a motel, it retains some historic flavor, and the comfortable, spacious rooms are themed around colorful parts of the state's history. No room phones, no smoking. | 1700 Front St., 59442 | 406/622–5441 or 800/622–6088 | 8 rooms | $40–$65 | MC, V | BP.

Virgelle Mercantile. Virgil Blankenbaker built this structure in 1912 as a general store and boardinghouse for railroad workers. The boom he expected never happened but he held on until 1970. Five years later, the place was transformed into the bed-and-breakfast you see today. Accommodations—all filled with homestead-era furnishings—are in cabins (without electricity) and in the main building. You can have a hearty, homemade breakfast at the Merc or cook your own on the wood-burning cookstove in your cabin. No room phones, no TVs. | 7485 Virgelle Ferry Rd. N, on the Missouri River 27 mi NE of Fort Benton and 8 mi off U.S. 87 at milepost 66, Loma, 59460 | 800/426–2926 | www.PaddleMontana.com | 4 rooms, 4 cabins | $60–$120 | AE, DC, MC, V | BP.

GREAT FALLS
▼▼

On the afternoon of June 13, 1805, Lewis arrived at the first of the five Great Falls and pronounced the landmark, which had a combined drop of more than 400 feet, "a truly magnificent and sublimely grand object." The 18-mi portage around the falls was one of the greatest obstacles that faced the expedition and took the group a month to accomplish. The city that grew near the site, formally established in the 1880s, has become a vital part of Montana culture and industry and with 56,690 residents is the state's third-largest city. Four dams, the first built in 1890, now control the Missouri River and stem the falls, although much of the waterway below Great Falls heading north and east remains unaltered. Looking down from the sheer cliffs surrounding Ryan Dam, you can get a sense of the spectacle that so impressed Lewis. Since much of the original portage is on private land, the best place to view it is from the Giant Springs side of the river. Bikers, walkers, and cross-country skiers take advantage of the popular 24-mi River's Edge Trail, a half-paved, half-gravel pathway that links various Great Falls green spaces.

Great Falls also makes a good jumping-off point for a trip to the Blackfeet headquarters in Browning, the overlook at Camp Disappointment, Glacier National Park, St. Ignatius on the Flathead Reservation, the National Bison Range, and finally to Missoula. On this trip you follow Lewis's route along the Big Blackfoot River—called "Road to the Buffalo" by the Nez Percé.

Lewis's Return Trip

After parting from Clark, Lewis followed the Nez Percé route to the Great Falls of the Missouri to pick up supplies cached there the year before and then explore the Marias River as a possible route into the fur country of Canada.

Five miles east of what is now Missoula, Lewis, accompanied by 9 other men, 17 horses, and his Newfoundland dog, Seaman, came to the Blackfoot River, which the Nez Percé called Cokalahjshkjt ("river of the road to the buffalo")—a blue-ribbon trout stream that starred in the Robert Redford movie *A River Runs Through It.* On July 5, 1806, the explorers camped at the confluence of the Blackfoot and a creek that Lewis named for his dog, Seaman; today it is known as Monture Creek for George Monture, an early U.S. Army scout. Lewis described this part of the valley as "prarie of the knobs" because of the mounds along the trail, some of which can be seen today. Glaciers caused these knobs by dumping rocks down icy holes and cracks within the glacier; when the glaciers melted some 10,000 to 12,000 years ago, the knobs remained.

Lewis encountered no Native Americans, although he did spot fresh tracks along the trail and was concerned. "They have a large pasel of horses," he wrote. He expected to meet with either the Hidatsa or another hunting party at any time, so he and the men were "much on our guard both day and night."

Lewis's 1806 return trip took him on an extended exploration of the Marias River northwest of Fort Benton. Jefferson had requested that the expedition look for a natural boundary for a land treaty with the British. Lewis hoped the Marias would end near the 49th Parallel. However, on July 22, his journey ended within sight of the Continental Divide in what is now Glacier National Park, where he could see a creek coming out of the mountains to the southwest. Given the dreary, wet weather and his disappointment over this finding, it's not surprising that he named the place Camp Disappointment. He stayed for three days, until an unfortunate encounter with eight Blackfeet left two of the warriors dead and the party packed up and beat a path to the Missouri, where they had cached supplies near the Great Falls during the previous year. Joined by Sergeant John Ordway and his party of nine, who had come downriver from Three Forks, the group continued to the confluence of the Missouri and Yellowstone rivers, where they reunited with Clark on August 12, 1806.

✦ INFORMATION

Great Falls Chamber of Commerce | 710 1st Ave. N, 59403 | 406/761–4434 | www.greatfallsonline.net. **Upper Missouri Lewis & Clark Bicentennial Commission** | Box 5021, 59403-5021 | 406/455–8520.

SITES TO SEE

Giant Springs State Park and Trout Hatchery. Lewis and Clark passed through this area while portaging around the Great Falls, discovering along the way a large "fountain or spring" mentioned in Clark's journal. Today the cold-water springs here feed a state trout hatchery. The springs qualify as the shortest river in the world, the Roe River. There's a visitor center, picnic area, and river drive. | 4600 Giant Springs Rd., 1 mi east of U.S. 87 | 406/454–5840 | www.state.mt.us/parks | $1 | Daily dawn–dusk.

Great Falls Historic Trolley. The ride aboard these 21-seat, climate-controlled trolleys takes you through historic neighborhoods and to Rainbow Falls and other sites where Lewis and Clark stopped, including the spot where a grizzly bear chased Lewis into the river. Guides describe the history along the way. Special Lewis and Clark–themed tours and other history-related trips are also available, and luminary tours are conducted after dark during mid-December. All trips start at the visitor center at Broadwater Overlook Park, off 10th Avenue South on the west end of town, or at the High Plains Heritage Center, off 2nd Street South. | 315 5th St. S | 406/771–1100 or 888/707–1100 | www.greatfallshistorictrolley.com | $20 | June–Sept., daily; Oct.–May by appointment only.

Lewis and Clark National Historic Trail Interpretive Center. This premier Lewis and Clark Trail information center, overlooking the Missouri River, exhibits tools, canoes, furs, leather clothing, and other materials used by travelers and Native Americans of the era. Films, tours, and costumed interpreters tell the stories of the expedition's members and their struggles and successes. | 4201 Giant Springs Rd. | 406/727–8733 | www.fs.fed.us/r1/lewisclark/lcic.htm | $5 | Late May–Sept., daily 9–6; Oct.–late May, Tues.–Sat. 9–5, Sun. noon–5.

River's Edge Trail. This 24-mi path, about half of which is paved, skirts the Missouri's banks and passes the waterfalls that so awed the Corps of Discovery. Five dams control the river here, diminishing or obscuring some of the famous falls, but you can still see Black Eagle and Rainbow falls. Free maps are available at the four parking areas and trailheads along River Drive. | River Dr. | 406/771–1265 | Donations accepted | Daily dawn–dusk.

Ulm Pishkun State Park. This prehistoric bison kill site, believed to be the longest in North America, consists of a mile-long cliff with a 30-foot drop. A visitor center houses a gallery, bookstore, and storytelling area. You can drive to the top and walk in, or hike up from the visitor center, to see where the bison were driven off the edge. There's a gorgeous view of the meadows below. | Take the Ulm exit off I–15, 10 mi south of Great Falls | 406/866–2217 | www.fwp.state.mt.us | $2 | Visitor center June–Aug., daily 10–6.

✦ ON THE CALENDAR

June **Lewis and Clark Festival.** During the "week of rediscovery," from Wednesday through Saturday during the third week in June, Great Falls celebrates the Corps of Discovery's adventures with presentations, ceremonies, and tours. Reenactors are on hand in period dress, and food booths serve samplings of some of the fare members of the expedition ate. | 406/452–5661.

June 2005 **Explore the Big Sky.** For 34 days beginning June 1, a series of activities at sites between Fort Benton and Great Falls brings to life Lewis and Clark's stay at the fork of the Marias and Missouri River, their discovery of the Great Falls, the portage, and other events in the area. Reenactments, lectures, exhibits, concerts, traditional Native American villages, tribal games, scenic tours, and river tours enrich the experience. | 406/455–8451 | www.explorethebigsky.com.

HISTORIC LODGING

Charlie Russell Manor. This B&B in a brick home built by prominent local citizen W. K. Floweree in 1916 stands on the original Great Falls town site. Guest quarters have themes—you'll find a Sacagawea/Charbonneau room and a Lewis and Clark room, among others. The Missouri River is only blocks away. Dining room, in-room data ports, meeting rooms, some pets allowed; no smoking. | 825 4th Ave. N, 59401 | 877/207–6131 or 406/455–1400 | fax 406/727–3771 | www.charlie-russell.com | 6 rooms | $80–$145 | AE, MC, V | BP.

Collins Mansion B&B. With its ornate Victorian interior, the Collins Mansion is on the National Register of Historic Places, and with its spacious rooms and private baths is a premier local lodging place. The house was built in 1891 by banker T. C. Collins, who emigrated from Ireland when he was 8 and went on to found the local bank and waterworks and to serve as a state senator. The luxurious master suite has a fireplace. In-room data ports, laundry facilities; no room TVs, no kids under 12, no smoking. | 1003 2nd Ave. NW, Great Falls, 59401 | 406/452–6798 or 877/452–6798 | fax 406/452–6787 | www.collinsmansion.com | 4 rooms, 1 suite | $85–$100 | AE, MC, V | BP.

HELENA

▼▼▼

The expedition passed through this region on its way to the headwaters of the Missouri in late July 1805, and the men were cheered by the fact that

Sacagawea recognized the land and their anticipated arrival at the headwaters of the Missouri. Helena is a city of Victorian mansions and abandoned gold mines, tucked into the foothills of the Rockies and surrounded by wilderness. Last Chance Gulch, the town's main street, was named for the landform that yielded more than $15 million in gold between 1864 and 1893. Helena was one of the seats of the territorial government and became the state's permanent capital after a bribe-marred election in 1894.

✦ INFORMATION

Downtown Helena | 121 N. Last Chance Gulch, 59601 | 406/442–9869 | www.downtownhelena.com. **Helena Chamber of Commerce** | 225 Cruse Ave., Suite A, 59601 | 406/442–4120 or 800/743–5362 | www.helenachamber.com. **Montana Historical Society** | 225 N. Roberts St., 59620 | 406/444–2694 or 800/243–9900 | www.montanahistoricalsociety.org. **Montana Lewis & Clark Bicentennial Commission** | Box 201203, 59610-1203 | 406/443–2109.

SITES TO SEE

Canyon Ferry Recreation Area. Surrounded by public lands, Canyon Ferry Lake, the impoundment of the Missouri created by Canyon Ferry Dam in 1954, affords abundant opportunities for boating, sailing, camping, and wildlife viewing; rainbow, brook, brown, bull, cutthroat, and Dolly Varden trout are typical catches. Signs around the dam detail the expedition's journey through the area; the explorers spotted bighorn sheep just below. If you're here in mid-November, look for bald eagles. Canyon Ferry Lake and Dam lie between Townsend and Gates of the Mountains along U.S. 12. | Rte. 284 | 406/475–3310 | Free | Daily dawn–dusk.

Gates of the Mountains Boat Tours. On July 19, 1805, Lewis and Clark were paddling upstream in between towering rocks that really did seem "ready to tumble," as Lewis wrote. "I shall call them Gates of the Mountains." Today, you can take a 105-minute boat cruise to see these 1,200-foot limestone cliffs, plus ancient Native American pictographs, and wildlife that the Corps of Discovery may have seen, including bighorn sheep and mountain goats, otters, deer, beaver, black bears, ospreys, bald and golden eagles, peregrine and prairie falcons, and more. | Off I–15 at Exit 209, 17 mi north of Helena | 406/458–5241 | www.gatesofthemountains.com | $9.50 | June–Sept., weekends at 10, noon, 2, and 4; weekdays at 11 and 2. Additional cruises July and Aug.

Last Chance Train Tour. Hour-long tours begin in front of the Historical Society Museum and thread through the west side of town, Helena's historic neighborhood, which is filled with miners' mansions. You pass by the Governor's Mansions old and new and a rustic fire tower and take in the Last Chance Gulch, where four miners made the first gold discovery in Helena. | 6th and

Roberts Sts. | 406/442–1023 or 888/432–1023 | www.lctours.com | $5 | May, June, and Sept., daily at 10, 1, 3; July and Aug., daily 10–6 on the hr.

Montana Historical Society Museum. One of the most important collections of western artist Charles M. Russell's work is on display here in the MacKay Gallery along with beautiful black-and-white photographs of Yellowstone National Park taken by Frank Jay Haynes in the 1880s. Additionally, nearly 2,000 artifacts and documents as well as still other photographs tell the story of Montana from the time of the first settlers to the present. Special family-friendly summer programs cover folk music, Native American culture, and cowboys. | 225 N. Roberts St. | 406/444–2694 or 800/243–9900 | www. montanahistoricalsociety.org | Donations accepted | Late May–early Sept., weekdays 8–6, weekends 9–5; early Sept.–late May, weekdays 8–5, Sat. 9–5.

Montana State Capitol. With its copper dome, the Greek Renaissance–style state capitol, built 1899–1902 and expanded in 1912, is hard to miss. Inside, the detailed woodwork and other architectural features have been beautifully restored, and the spaces are filled with ornate woodwork and original paintings and murals, including Charles M. Russell's largest painting, a 12- by 25-foot *Lewis and Clark Meeting Indians at Ross' Hole,* which shows the explorers in 1805 near Missoula with members of the Salish tribe, also known as the Flatheads. Guided tours are conducted on the hour in summer from 9 to 4. | 6th and Montana Sts. | 406/444–2511 or 800/243–9900 | www.montanacapitol. com | Free | Daily 8–5.

Reeder's Alley. Carefully restored, this part of old Helena has some distinctive shops, restaurants, a pioneer cabin, and a visitor center. Miners' quarters from the late 1800s line the narrow, winding street, and brick mortar reveals fingerprints from gold-rush days. | Near the south end of Last Chance Gulch and S. Park Ave. | Free | Daily.

HISTORIC DINING AND LODGING

Stonehouse Restaurant. Contemporary. In this spot in venerable Reeder's Alley, fresh seafood is on the menu, and the preparations are nontraditional but elegant. | 120 Reeder's Alley | 406/449–2552 | Closed Sun. No lunch. | $16–$24 | AE, D, MC, V.

Barrister. Antiques furnish the rooms of this Victorian-style house with a wrap-around porch and a large common area. Carved staircases, stained-glass windows, and five fireplaces add elegance. Complimentary wine and cheese are served in the evenings. Cable TV, business services, airport shuttle, some pets allowed; no room phones, no smoking. | 416 N. Ewing St. | 406/443–7330 or 800/823–1148 | fax 406/442–7964 | 5 rooms | $90 | MC, V | BP.

Sanders-Helena's B&B. This three-story Victorian mansion was built in 1875 by Colonel Wilbur Sanders, the prosecuting attorney at some of the summary trials hosted by the Montana Vigilantes, the gang of armed horsemen who, in 1864, while the eastern states were preoccupied by the Civil War, seized 21 of their countrymen they deemed lawless and lynched them in an episode of violence that is discussed and disputed among Montana history lovers to this day. As a hobby, the colonel collected rocks, and his collection is still in the house, along with some original furnishings. Most rooms overlook the mountain-ringed downtown area. Breakfasts are a work of art, with Grand Marnier French toast, orange soufflés, and gingerbread waffles. Cable TV, in-room VCRs; no smoking. | 328 N. Ewing St., 59601 | 406/442–3309 | fax 406/443–2361 | www.sandersbb.com. | 7 rooms | $95–$115 | AE, D, DC, MC, V | BP.

THREE FORKS

▼▼▼

It was in this area that Sacagawea was kidnapped from her people's camp around 1800 by Hidatsa braves. Traveling with Lewis and Clark, she returned here from July 25 to 30, 1805, as they searched for a river that would take them through to the Continental Divide. In the process, they explored the Jefferson, Gallatin, and Madison rivers, which come together to form the Missouri.

Three Forks history does not end here, however. A couple of years after the expedition, in 1808, Corps of Discovery veteran John Colter encountered 500 Blackfeet in the area. The story goes that the Blackfeet killed Colter's partner, John Potts, then stripped Colter naked and ordered him to run for his life. What the Blackfeet didn't know was that he was fleet of foot, even barefoot; running over cactus, he had soon outdistanced all but one of his pursuers. After killing the warrior with his own spear and hiding under a logjam in the river from the rest of the angry band, Colter was able to get away; 11 days and 200 mi later, he made his way back to civilization with only the dead Blackfoot's blanket for warmth and nothing more than bark and roots to eat. Colter went on to explore around what is now Yellowstone.

Three Forks is the last surviving town of four that sprouted up at the headwaters of the Missouri River around 1862. Located in Montana's "banana belt," it enjoys more than 300 sunny days a year, with little snowfall and temperatures that are positively mild by Montana standards.

◆ INFORMATION
Three Forks Chamber of Commerce | Box 1103, 59752 | 406/285–4753 | www.threeforksmontana.com.

SITES TO SEE

Headwaters Heritage Museum. A gem off the well-traveled highway, this museum displays the largest brown trout ever caught in Montana, along with thousands of other local historical artifacts. One small anvil on view is all that remains of the trading post, Fort Three Forks, which was established in 1810. | Main and Cedar Sts. | 406/285–4778 | www.threeforksmontana.com/history | Free | June–mid-Sept., Mon.–Sat. 9–5, Sun. 1–5, or by appointment.

Lewis and Clark Caverns. Opened to the public in 1901, this is one of Montana's first tourist attractions and its oldest state park, established in 1937. Native tribes in the region had known of the cave for many years, but Lewis and Clark never came across it, the name notwithstanding. The caverns provide some of the most beautiful underground landscapes in the nation. Two-hour tours take you through narrow passages and vaulted chambers past colorful, intriguingly varied limestone formations. The temperature in the cave stays in the 50s year-round; jackets and rubber-sole shoes are recommended, along with a flashlight. Be aware that the hike to the cavern entrance is mildly strenuous and that the tour itself involves lots of bending and stooping and even some crawling. | Rte. 2, 19 mi west of Three Forks | 406/287–3541 | www.fwp.state.mt.us | $8 | June–early Sept., daily 9–6:30; May and early Sept.–end of Sept., daily 9–4:30.

Madison Buffalo Jump State Park. It wasn't until the 18th century that Native Americans of the Northern Plains had horses to help them in their daily lives. Two millennia ago, at what is now a 638-acre state park about 15 mi from Three Forks, the Blackfeet, Salish, Shoshone, and other tribes would assemble around this precipice, herd a group of bison closer and closer to this cliff, and then stampede them. When the herd tumbled to the ground below, the men, women, and children would butcher the animals for food, dry the meat, and craft tepees, blankets, and tools from the skins, horns, and bones. Historians suspect the scene that Lewis described in his journal on May 29, 1805, near today's Slaughter River, was the case of a random stampede rather than an organized kill. Yet the scene must have been similar, with some 100 carcasses rotting at the base of a 120-foot precipice. Today at this park you can see tepee rings as well as the pathways worn down over centuries. Signs explain the role of bison in Plains culture. From the jump's highest point you get a stunning view over the Madison River Valley and the mountains beyond. | Buffalo Jump Rd.; about 7 mi south of I–90 at the Logan exit | 1400 S. 19th St., Bozeman, 59715 | 406/994–4042 | www.fwp.state.mt.us | $5 per vehicle | Daily dawn–dusk.

Missouri Headwaters State Park. The Madison, Jefferson, and Gallatin rivers flow together to become the mighty Missouri River at a National Historic Landmark in this 530-acre park. Lewis and Clark named the three forks after Secretary of the Treasury Albert Gallatin, Secretary of State James Madison, and President Thomas Jefferson. In the park, be sure to climb past the pioneer graves to the top of the hill above the interpretive exhibits for a view of the surrounding mountain ranges. The park has historical exhibits, interpretive signs, picnic sites, camping, and hiking trails. | Trident Rd.; 3 mi northeast of Three Forks on I–90, exit at the Three Forks off-ramp, then go east on Rte. 205 and 3 mi north via Rte. 286 | 406/994–4042 | www.fwp.state.mt.us | $5 per vehicle | Daily dawn–dusk.

✦ ON THE CALENDAR
July **Lewis and Clark Encampment.** Break out your buckskins for this late-July reenactment of the Corps of Discovery's adventures at the Three Forks of the Missouri River. A Children's Festival of Discovery includes tepees and demonstrations. | 406/285–4753.

Sept. **John Colter Run.** This race commemorates John Colter's famous 1809 escape from the Blackfeet. Today's runners wear clothes. | 406/994–6934.

HISTORIC DINING AND LODGING
Historic Headwaters Restaurant. Contemporary. This brick structure dating from 1908 originally served train travelers en route to Yellowstone National Park. Nowadays, weather permitting, diners eat on a stream-crossed patio surrounded by native plants and flowers. The buffalo chorizo enchiladas with black-bean sauce and smoked corn salsa suggest the inventiveness of the chef and owner, who is a graduate of the Culinary Institute of America. | 105 S. Main St. | 406/285–4511 | www.headwatersrestaurant.com | Closed Mon. and Tues. | $8–$22 | MC, V.

Sacajawea Hotel. The original section of this hostelry built in 1910 by the Old Milwaukee Railroad was hoisted up onto logs and rolled to higher ground, where it became a railroad hotel for travelers bound for Yellowstone National Park. Renovated twice during the 1990s, the lofty lobby and cozy rooms retain 19th-century style, and the front porch is set with gleaming white rocking chairs, where you can relax with a book or watch the sunset. Restaurant, cable TV, fishing, bar, piano, meeting rooms, free parking, some pets allowed (fee); no smoking. | 5 N. Main St., 59752 | 406/285–6515 or 888/722–2529 | fax 406/285–4210 | www.sacajaweahotel.com | 30 rooms, 1 suite | $92–$110 | AE, D, DC, MC, V | CP.

WHITEHALL
▼▼

The Jefferson Valley was a major hunting ground and wintering area for several Native American tribes. Lewis and Clark traveled up the Jefferson River on

Camp Disappointment

Lewis's return trip in 1806 took him on an extended exploration of the Marias River. Jefferson had requested that the expedition look for a natural boundary for a treaty with the British. Lewis hoped the Marias would be that boundary. However, on July 22, his journey ended within sight of the Continental Divide in what is now Glacier National Park, where he could see a creek coming out of the mountains to the southwest.

Disappointed and wet, Lewis named the site Camp Disappointment and stayed there for three days. Deep in the land of the Blackfoot Confederacy, the most powerful coalition in Montana at the time—well supplied with firearms by British traders—it was a dangerous decision; the group saw many signs of Native American activity in the area. In fact, the day after sighting the beginnings of the Marias, the explorers encountered eight Blackfeet warriors and shared a camp with them. Unfortunately, Lewis also mentioned the fact that in the future, Americans would trade with all the tribes, including enemies of the Blackfeet. The Blackfeet envisioned that American rifles in the hands of their enemies would threaten their dominance of the area and their very existence.

Early the next morning, Lewis woke to the sounds of struggle as the warriors and expedition members fought for possession of the Corps' rifles and horses. Two warriors were killed during the skirmish. As the men prepared the horses, Lewis burned four shields, two bows, quivers of arrows, and other articles left by the warriors. He took a gun and the flag he'd given them the night before but left the medal about the neck of the dead man, "that they might be informed who we were."

The incident turned the most powerful tribe in the upper Missouri into enemies of the United States and had long-lasting ramifications. George Drouillard, present at this fight, was one of three expedition members to return west after the expedition, and it was at the hands of the Blackfeet that he died.

their way west and in 1805 spent Clark's birthday not far from present-day Whitehall. Clark returned through here in 1806. Whitehall was a stopping place for stages running from Helena to Virginia City, but the community began to develop only after the railroad came through in 1889. Today the town has a population of a little over a thousand. A number of very large murals on buildings around town recall scenes from the Lewis and Clark expedition as they traversed what later became the Jefferson Valley.

✦ INFORMATION
Whitehall Chamber of Commerce | Box 72 | 15 W. Legion, 59759 | 406/287–2260.

SITES TO SEE
Whitehall Lewis and Clark Bicentennial Murals. Muralist Kit Mather took expedition journal entries and transformed them into 12 murals on buildings throughout the Whitehall business district to tell the story of Lewis and Clark's journey through the Jefferson Valley. The largest mural, 11 feet by 90 feet, depicts buffalo and beavers. The smallest, 7 feet by 18 feet, depicts a Native American observing the Corps. A brochure describing each mural is available at the Chamber of Commerce office. | 15 W. Legion | 406/287–2260 | whitehall-ledger.com/about/murals/shtm.

✦ ON THE CALENDAR
June–July **Journey of Discovery.** This outdoor theater production is performed by Jefferson Valley Presents in an amphitheater near where Lewis and Clark camped. With a majestic mountain skyline in the east, live horses, and a cast of more than 40, the production opens with a dramatic reenactment of the kidnapping of Sacagawea as a child. It also highlights the original mustering of the Corps and re-creates the explorers' encounters with Native Americans, their run-ins with grizzly bears, their frustrations while portaging around the Great Falls, and Sacagawea's reunion with her brother. Performances are Friday and Saturday at 8 PM. | 406/287–9235.

DILLON
▼▼▼

Beaverhead Rock, a massive sandstone outcrop resembling a swimming beaver about 14 mi north of Dillon, has long been an important landmark. Native American hunting parties traveling the Jefferson and Beaverhead rivers passed it on their way to buffalo country in the east. Likewise, when the Lewis and Clark expedition paddled upriver, Sacagawea recognized the rock. Her Shoshone tribe's summer camp had been nearby, and beyond lay the Corps' route to the Bitterroot Mountains. The Jefferson River begins at the confluence of the Beaverhead River and Blacktail Deer Creek, near Dillon. One mile northwest of town on Route 91, across the railroad tracks and to the right, is Clark's Lookout State Park. Clark climbed this area to get a look at the Beaverhead Valley on August 13, 1805.

Dillon began as a shipping point between Utah and the gold fields of Montana. Later, the Union Pacific Railroad shipped cattle and sheep from here to processing. Today, a diverse mix of culture, history, and recreation characterizes the town, and its population has grown to 3,752.

Twenty miles south of Dillon, at the exit for Route 324 off Interstate 15, is an overlook on the west side of the Clark Canyon Dam reservoir with a view that approximates that from Camp Fortunate, which is now underwater. It was at this point that Sacagawea recognized her brother. Clark wrote that "those Indians sung all the way to their Camp," and Lewis noted, "The meeting of those people was really affecting, particularly between Sah cah - gar-we-ah and an Indian woman, who had been taken prisoner at the same time with her, and who had afterwards escaped from the Minnetares and rejoined her nation." Sacagawea's brother, Chief Cameahwait, provided the expedition with some of the horses they needed to take them across the mountain ranges to the west—fortunate, indeed, for the men were suffering: Clark from an abscess on his ankle, Private George Drouillard from injuries sustained in a fall, and Private Joseph Whitehouse from an injury from a swamped canoe. A gravel Forest Service road leads to Lemhi Pass, where, near the summit, there is a small campground and a memorial to Sacagawea. (In summer, although most passenger cars can make this trip, the Idaho side is too steep for trailers and motor homes.) Not far from nearby Grant, a graveled county road leads past the ghost town of Bannack.

After traveling for a time in what is now Idaho, the explorers again entered Montana very near to Lost Trail Pass. An interpretive sign at the pass explains all of the historical trails in the area. If you have come across Lemhi Pass, take Route 28 to U.S. 93 north. If you have traveled Route 278, turn west on Route 43 to cross Chief Joseph Pass. The Corps of Discovery's journey eased as the group traveled into the beautiful Bitterroot Valley and came upon a village of more than 400 Salish, also called the Flathead tribe because of the way they styled their hair. The men set up camp a few miles north of Sula (Ross' Hole), 12 mi north of Lost Trail Pass on U.S. 93, and learned of the Lolo Trail going west across the Bitterroot Mountains.

✦ INFORMATION
Beaverhead Chamber of Commerce | 125 S. Montana St., 59725 | 406/683–5511 | www.beaverheadchamber.com.

SITES TO SEE
Bannack State Historic Park. Bannack was Montana's first territorial capital and the site of the state's first major gold strike, in 1862. As a frontier boomtown, known as the Toughest Town in the West, the place was terrorized by the notorious sheriff Henry Plummer, who met his own end at the hands of the Montana Vigilantes—he was one of the 21 to be summarily lynched. The gallows on which he was hanged still stands, along with some 60 historic structures. Rumors persist that Plummer's stash of stolen gold was hidden

somewhere in the mountains and never found. The town commemorates its wild days with a celebration every year on the third weekend in July. | 21 mi west of Dillon on Rte. 278 | 406/834–3413 | $5 per vehicle | Memorial Day–Labor Day, daily 10–6; Labor Day–Memorial Day, daily 8–5.

Beaverhead County Museum. Here you can see Native American artifacts, ranching and mining memorabilia, and a homesteader's cabin as well as a boardwalk imprinted with brands from all the area's ranches. | 15 S. Montana St. | 406/683–5027 | Donations accepted | Late May–early Sept., weekdays 8–8, Sat. noon–4; early Sept.–late May, weekdays 8–5.

Beaverhead Rock State Park. This 71-acre park is named for the massive rock that anchors it, which is shaped like the head of a swimming beaver; the rock is on the National Register of Historic Places. When Lewis and Clark's Shoshone guide, Sacagawea, recognized Beaverhead Rock in 1805, she sparked new hope among the men of finding a friendly tribe and a route to the Bitterroot Mountains. The best place to view the rock is from an overlook on Route 41. | Rte. 41, 14 mi north of Dillon | 406/834–3413 | Free | Daily dawn–dusk.

Big Hole National Battlefield. One of the West's greatest and most tragic stories played out on this battlefield. In 1877, a group of some 750 Nez Percé had fled Idaho rather than submit to U.S. Army pressure to move to a reservation. On August 9, having made camp one night en route to Canada, they were attacked by soldiers in their sleep. Between 60 and 90 men, women, and children lost their lives, as did 22 soldiers. Some 13 battles and skirmishes ensued, involving 10 separate U.S. commands. Only about 150 Nez Percé entered Canada. Big Hole National Battlefield is one of 38 sites in five states that are part of the Nez Percé National Historical Park. The meadows that flank the Big Hole River, which you see from the visitor center, remain as they were at the time of the battle, but with tepee poles erected by the Park Service marking the site of the Nez Percé village—haunting reminders of what transpired here. A documentary, self-guided tour of battlefield, and ranger programs help you understand the events and their meaning. | 11 mi west of Wisdom on Rte. 43 | 406/689–3155 | www.nps.gov/biho | $5 per vehicle Memorial Day–Sept.; free rest of yr | May–Labor Day, daily 9–6; Labor Day–Apr., daily 9–5.

Clark's Lookout State Park. Lewis and Clark stood atop this rock outcropping next to the Beaverhead River to get an overview of what lay ahead. Today, a short trail goes to the top. The 7-acre site, which is completely undeveloped as a park, with no facilities or interpretive signage, is accessible by car. | Off Rte. 91, 1 mi north of Dillon | 406/834–3413 | www.fwp.state.mt.us/parks | Free | Daily dawn–dusk.

Dillon Visitor Center. This visitor center in an old railroad depot provides statewide travel information and has a diorama of the Lewis and Clark expedition at Beaverhead Rock. | 125 S. Montana St. | 406/683–5511 | Free | May and Sept., daily 8–5; June–Aug., daily 8–8; Oct.–Apr., weekdays 8–5.

✦ ON THE CALENDAR

Aug. **Lemhi Shoshone Meeting Lewis and Clark Reenactment.** Meeting the Lemhi Shoshone at Camp Fortunate was a turning point for Lewis and Clark. Annually on the first Saturday in August, the West Cameahwait Campground stages this reenactment and encampment, complete with cooking, hide tanning, jerky making, Shoshone drumming, dancing, and crafts making. | 406/683–5511.

Aug. **Lewis and Clark Festival.** This weeklong, countywide festival, which begins the first Saturday of the month, features speakers, demonstrations, a buffalo barbecue, and other activities to commemorate the activities of the Corps of Discovery in the area. | 406/683–5511.

MISSOULA
▼▼▼

Lewis and Clark noted that Native Americans frequented the natural hot springs near present-day Missoula and created pools with stones. It's here that Lewis wrote, "The weather appearing settled and fair I determined to halt the next day, rest our horses and take some celestial observations. We called the creek Travelers' Rest." The Nez Percé assisted the expedition and earned the gratitude of the Corps; all this was forgotten during the summer of 1877, however, when the tribe was pursued by the U.S. Army under General Oliver Howard along what is now known as the Nez Percé National Historic Trail.

One of America's most sophisticated small cities, Missoula mixes a bit of the Wild West with independent-mindedness and an artsy, folksy feeling. At the confluence of three mighty rivers and set in the peaceful confines of five scenic valleys, Missoula serves as western Montana's commercial and cultural hub.

✦ INFORMATION

Missoula Chamber of Commerce | Box 7577, 59807 | 406/543–6623 or 800/526–3465 | www.missoulachamber.com.

SITES TO SEE
Travelers' Rest National Historic Landmark and State Park. On September 9, 1805, after Lewis and Clark found the Bitterroot Range beyond what is now Lemhi Pass impenetrable, the explorers made camp at this point along the

Bitterroot River south of present-day Lolo—a camping spot that had also been used by the Salish, Nez Percé, and Lemhi Shoshone peoples. Here at the mouth of Lolo Creek, where there was plenty of firewood for cooking and warmth, abundant grass for the horses, and a ready source of water, the group rested before setting out on the grueling trip over the Lolo Trail. From June 30 to July 3, 1806, they camped here again when returning from the Pacific. The campsite was once thought to be farther downstream; excavations in the last few years have corrected the location based on soil samplings that contained especially high concentrations of mercury. Archaeologists surmise that the sites tested were the Corps' latrines and that the mercury started out in Rush's Thunderbolts, a cure-all of the day that Lewis often prescribed. In 1999, the site was threatened by residential development, and the National Trust for Historic Preservation had added it to its Eleven Most Endangered Historic Places List for the year. Not long after, a couple visiting on a bus tour, who knew of the crisis, resolved to buy the parcel—and did, thereby rescuing it for all to enjoy. | 6550 Mormon Creek Rd., ¼ mi west of U.S. 93 | 406/273–4253 | www.travelersrest.org | Free | Weekdays 11–4, weekends 8–5.

✦ ON THE CALENDAR
June–July **Discover Travelers' Rest.** This event at Travelers' Rest State Park, held between June 30 and July 3, commemorates the anniversary of Lewis and Clark's 1806 visit to the area with a reenactment, games, and educational events. | 406/273–4253.

HISTORIC DINING AND LODGING
Goldsmith's Bed & Breakfast. Built in 1911 for the first president of the University of Montana, this hostelry hugs the Clark Fork River shore, at the end of a footbridge that leads to the campus. Inside the prairie-style turn-of-the-20th-century redbrick home with wide eaves and a huge porch, the furnishings are of the period, the carpets wool, and the flowers fresh. Some rooms have river views, and each suite has a fireplace. You can start the day with French toast or crepes in the dining room or on the deck overlooking the river. Library. | 809 E. Front St., 59801 | 406/728–1585 | fax 406/543–0045 | www.goldsmithsinn.com | 3 rooms, 4 suites | $99–$139 | D, MC, V | BP.

Lolo Hot Springs Resort. Local tribes used the mineral hot springs for centuries prior to the Corps' stop on both legs of their journey; on September 13, 1805, Clark wrote of tasting the water and finding it "hot & not bad tasted . . ." He continued, "In further examonation I found this water nearly boiling hot at the places it Spouted from the rocks . . ." Today, the springs are still popular. The water, heated to 100°F, gushes from 5,000 feet underground through cracks in the rock. Worn glacial boulders described by Clark still surround the springs. This resort and campground has grown up on the site. Restaurant, microwaves, refrigerators, indoor-outdoor pools, hiking, horseback riding, cross-country skiing, snowmobiling, bar, casino, some pets allowed, no-smoking rooms; no room phones. | 38500 W. Rte. 12, Lolo, 59847 | 800/273–2290 or 406/273–2290 | fax 406/273–3677 | www.lolohotsprings.com | 4 cabins | $67.50 | AE, D, MC, V.

CLARK'S EASTWARD JOURNEY

▼▼

In July 1806, Clark together with 20 other men, Sacagawea, her baby, and 50 horses traveled south along the Bitterroot River, following the route they had come the previous year. Accompanied by the Nez Percé guides, Lewis and his men traveled northward, down the Bitterroot River, and camped near present-day Missoula at sunset.

U.S. 93 and Routes 43 and 278 closely follow the route taken by Clark and his larger party as they returned to the Lost Trail Pass area and entered the Big Hole Valley. The party stopped to enjoy the warm waters of present-day Jackson Hot Springs, now commercially operated. They crossed Big Hole Pass, nowadays accessible via Route 278, returning to Camp Fortunate near what is now Clark Canyon Dam to retrieve dugouts and supplies cached the year before.

Back at Three Forks, Sergeant John Ordway and nine other men took the dugouts down the Missouri to the Great Falls. From Three Forks, you can follow the approximate route of Clark and the rest of his party east on Interstate 90 through the Gallatin Valley, which Blackfeet, Crow, Salish, and Shoshone called "Valley of the Flowers." They traveled past present-day **Bozeman,** then crossed Bozeman Pass to enter the watershed of the Yellowstone River (the name an anglicized version of the French La Roche Jaune, "yellow rocks"). They arrived on the bank of the Yellowstone near present-day **Livingston,** a place with a stunning mountain backdrop. The Paradise Valley south of town was once Crow territory.

Clark and his party camped along the Yellowstone on July 15 at what is now Mission Ranch, the site of Fort Parker in the 1860s and home of the original Crow tribe. From here Clark's party rode horseback on the north side of the Yellowstone River to a point near present-day Park City, 16 mi west of **Billings,** where the group camped from July 19 to 24. At Buffalo Mirage Access, the group cut, hollowed, and burned out two canoes, lashing them together for stability, and took to the river.

Pompeys Pillar, a sandstone pillar that you can see from Interstate 94 some 27 mi east of Billings, was named by Clark for Sacagawea's infant son, whom he'd nicknamed Pompy, or Little Pomp. On July 25, 1806, Clark carved his name and the date on the rock—the clearest physical evidence left by the expedition. On July 29, the party camped at Pirogue Island near the mouth of the Tongue River at **Miles City.** A few days later Clark reunited with Lewis near the confluence of the Yellowstone and Missouri rivers.

BOZEMAN
▼▼

The Blackfeet, Crow, Salish, and Shoshone called the Gallatin Valley the "Valley of the Flowers." Clark and his party traveled through the area when crossing into the Yellowstone River valley over present-day Bozeman Pass. Later, in 1864, a trader named John Bozeman led his wagon train through this valley, one of the great hunting grounds of the Teton Sioux, en route to the booming gold fields at Virginia City and southwest Montana; the fastest route for gold seekers, it was also dangerous—in 1867, wanting to put a stop to settlement, Cheyenne and Sioux effectively closed the so-called Bozeman Trail, a northern spur of the Oregon Trail that eventually became known as Bloody Bozeman. Beginning in 1868, settlers making their way west were protected by Fort Ellis, which was founded by Captain R. S. LaMotte and named for a Civil War martyr named Augustus Van Horne Ellis.

Nestled at the base of the Bridger Range, Bozeman combines a small-town pace with big-city amenities. It has become a recreation capital for everything from trout fishing to white-water river rafting to backcountry mountain biking. The town is the home of Montana State University, and the arts have also flowered here.

✦ INFORMATION
Bozeman Chamber of Commerce | Box B, 59771 | 406/586–5421 or 800/228–4224 | www.bozemanchamber.com.

SITES TO SEE
Gallatin County Pioneer Museum. This building now on the National Register of Historic Places served as the county jail for 70 years, the site for one man's hanging in 1924. The gallows and several jail cells remain. You'll also find hundreds of artifacts, automobiles, Northern Plains crafts, and a model of nearby Fort Ellis. | 317 W. Main St. | 406/522–8122 | www.pioneermuseum. org | Free | Oct.–May, Tues.–Fri. 11–4, Sat. 1–4; June–Sept., weekdays 10–4:30, Sat. 1–4.

Museum of the Rockies. Celebrating Rockies history, this contemporary museum covers an eclectic range of topics from the history of the Earth to prehistory to pioneers. You can take in demonstrations of pioneer skills such as butter churning, weaving, and blacksmithing at the Tensley Homestead and watch workers clean dinosaur fossils and see a real Tyrannosaurus rex skeleton, excavated by the museum in 1990, along with assorted other dinosaur bones and eggs. In summer, museum-sponsored dino digs are open to the public. There's even a planetarium. | 600 W. Kagy Blvd., south end of university campus | 406/994–3466 or 406/994–2251 | www.museum.montana. edu | $7 | Memorial Day–Labor Day, daily 8–8; Labor Day–Memorial Day, Mon.– Sat. 9–5, Sun. 12:30–5.

Off the Beaten Path. The naturalist-guided adventure trips this outfitter arranges include fishing, horseback riding, llama trekking, hiking, and more. | 27 E. Main St., 59715 | 406/586–1311 or 800/445–2995 | www. offthebeatenpath.com.

HISTORIC DINING AND LODGING

Gallatin Gateway Inn. Continental. Crisp white linens and candlelight set a formal tone in this wonderful restaurant. The regional cuisine is great and elegantly presented, as is the prime rib—and it all comes with a fine view of the mountains. | 76405 Gallatin Rd. (U.S. 191) | 406/763–4672 | Reservations essential | $24–$32 | AE, D, MC, V | No lunch.

John Bozeman Bistro. Eclectic. The menu at this downtown restaurant is small, but it's one of the best in the state. Fresh seafood specials are flown in every day. You'll find Pacific Rim, Asian, and classical French entrées on the menu. | 242 E. Main St. | 406/587–4100 | Reservations essential | $24–$29 | AE, D, MC, V | Closed Mon. No dinner Sun.

Gallatin Gateway Inn. Opened on June 17, 1927, by the Milwaukee Railroad as a luxurious and sophisticated stopping-off point for visitors en route to Yellowstone National Park, this inn 10 mi from town on U.S. 191 is truly sumptuous. Over time, it fell into disrepair and became a seedy bar that staged female Jell-O wrestling matches. Now restored and listed on the National Register of Historic Places, it has contemporary rooms with modern western decor and bathrooms with original tile and brass fixtures. The restaurant is formal; the Baggage Room pub serves casual fare that hits the spot after a day in the great outdoors. Restaurant, cable TV, tennis court, pool, hot tub, bicycles, bar, airport shuttle; no a/c in some rooms. | 76405 Gallatin Rd. (U.S. 191) | 406/763–4672 or 800/676–3522 | fax 406/763–4672 | www.gallatingatewayinn. com | 35 rooms | $120–$160 | AE, D, MC, V | BP.

Voss Inn. This B&B occupies an elegant 1883 Victorian house and is lavishly and stylishly furnished with antiques and knickknacks. Stop by the parlor to enjoy afternoon tea or to catch up on the news with other guests who drop in to watch TV or to chat. Huge breakfasts are served in guest rooms or in the parlor. The lovely English garden makes a great spot for a quiet conver-

sation. | 319 S. Willson Ave., 59715 | 406/587–0982 | fax 406/585–2964 | www.
bozeman-vossinn.com | 6 rooms | $90–$110 | MC, V | BP.

LIVINGSTON
▼▼

Clark reached the Yellowstone River here on July 15, 1806, and, with his party,
killed a bull bison, made "mockersons," and caught fish, probably cutthroat
trout. He and his party stood just south of Livingston, tantalizingly close to
the wonders that would compose Yellowstone National Park. It would be left
to expedition member John Colter, who stayed in the area after the Corps left,
to experience those sights, nicknamed Colter's Hell, in about 1808. The stunning mountain backdrop and the breathtaking Paradise Valley south of town
were once Crow territory. Built to serve the railroads, the city was established
in 1882 and originally christened Clark City, in honor of William Clark. The
railroad was eventually replaced by small businesses that cater to tourists, but
the town has retained much of its turn-of-the-20th-century flavor. Two Robert
Redford movies, *A River Runs Through It* and *Horse Whisperer,* were filmed here.

✦ **INFORMATION**
Livingston Area Chamber of Commerce | 303 E. Park St., 59047 | 406/222–0850 |
www.yellowstone-chamber.com.

SITES TO SEE
Yellowstone Gateway Museum of Park County. Occupying a turn-of-the-20th-
century brick school, this museum has a remarkable display on the Anzick
Site, the oldest Native American burial site in North America with the largest
cache of ice age artifacts. Other exhibits house antique furniture like a player
piano; homemaking items like washtubs; vintage clothing; arrowheads; and
early mining, farm, and railroad tools. | 118 W. Chinook St. | 406/222–4184 |
www.livingstonmuseums.org | $3 | June–early Sept., daily 10–5:30; early
Sept.–May by appointment only.

HISTORIC LODGING
Mission Creek Ranch Bed and Breakfast. Spectacular mountain scenery,
spacious rooms, seclusion, and western hospitality draw visitors to this working cattle ranch. Clark and several other members of the Corps of Discovery
camped here on July 15, 1806. Later this parcel of land became the site of
Fort Parker, the original Crow Agency; known as the Mission, this institution attempted to provide a refuge for members of the Crow tribe. Nowadays, every day begins with a hearty ranch-style breakfast, and the Yellowstone
River and a spring-fed creek yield great fishing and abundant wildlife watch-
ing. You can stay in the three-bedroom ranch house or opt for a tepee setup

Yellowstone River

The Crow called this stream Iichiilikaashaashe, or the Elk River, as did the Cheyenne. But French fur traders referred to it as La Roche Jaune ("river of the yellow rock"). British fur trader David Thompson used the words "Yellow Stone" in notes made in the winter of 1797–98. Eventually the words were written as Yellowstone River.

The "last best river," in the words of *National Geographic,* the 670-mi-long Yellowstone is marked by waterfalls, canyons, and one of the most intact cottonwood-poplar-willow riparian habitats in the West. As Clark and his party descended the Yellowstone in 1806, he described cottonwood forests filled with bison, pronghorns, elk, deer, and grizzly bears. Near Billings, he wrote, "For me to . . . give an estimate of the different species of Wild animals on this river . . . would be increditable." Bison crossing the river nearly blocked the explorers' passage, and Clark complained that his sleep was disturbed by the sound of buffalo. "The elk on the banks of the river were so abundant," he wrote, "that we have not been out of sight of them today." The Yellowstone River region is still a spectacular year-round observatory for wildlife. Bird life is particularly abundant.

The snowpack that accumulates every winter in the mountains surrounding Yellowstone National Park feeds the Yellowstone River and its tributaries; the water is then diverted for farming and municipal water supplies. Even though dams and reservoirs have been built on many of the Yellowstone's tributaries, the Yellowstone remains the longest free-flowing river in the Lower 48 States.

The ecological importance of the Yellowstone cannot be overstated. It supports cutthroat, brown, and rainbow trout fisheries; wildlife species ranging from grizzly bears to otters to bald eagles; and rare fish species such as the sauger, sicklefin, pallid sturgeon, and paddlefish. The Yellowstone has played an important economic, historic, and cultural role in the lives of many Native American tribes and was central to the explorations of Lewis and Clark. Once sustained by mining and logging, the regional economy has become increasingly dependent on recreation and tourism.

near the Corps' own campsite. Cable TV, fishing, laundry facilities; no a/c, no room phones, no smoking. | 10 Mission Creek Rd., 59047; 10 mi east of Livingston at Exit 343 off I–90 | 406/222–8290 or 800/320–5007 | fax 406/222–8292 | www.missioncreekbandb.com | 4 rooms, 1 suite, and 1 guest house | $95–$150 | MC, V | FAP.

The Murray Hotel. Even explorers love soft pillows at this turn-of-the-20th-century town institution known for attracting silver-tipped cowboy boots, fly-fishing waders, and the sparkling heels of Hollywood players. Historic photos and taxidermied game animals decorate the lobby and surround the antique elevator (circa 1905), which is still in use. Celebrities such as Buffalo Bill and Calamity Jane, the Queen of Denmark and humorist Will Rogers have all visited, and movie director Sam Peckinpah and railroad heir Walter Hill, son of tycoon James J. Hill, called the hotel home. Today, although a steady influx of celebrities may disturb the mountain town's serenity from time to time, local businesspeople don't mind their patronage and the notoriety it brings. Restaurant, in-room data ports, cable TV, gym, hot tub, fishing, bar, baby-sitting, no-smoking floor. | 201 W. Park St., 59047 | 406/222–1350 | fax 406/222–2752 | www.murrayhotel.com | 30 rooms | $69–$108 | AE, D, MC, V.

63 Ranch. This 2,000-acre dude ranch, a working cattle spread, is one of Montana's oldest and has been owned by the same family since 1929. A full range of activities is available, from horseback riding to fishing to going on pack trips. The rustic cabins are spacious, with log furniture and private bath. Three hearty meals are served each day, with home-baked bread and desserts. Dining room, pond, fishing, horseback riding, laundry facilities; no room phones, no in-room TV, no smoking. | 12 mi southeast of Livingston | Box MA979, 59047 | 406/222–0570 | fax 406/222–9446 or 406/222–6363 | www.63ranch.com | 8 cabins | $1,250 per wk | Closed mid-Sept.–mid-June | No credit cards | FAP.

BILLINGS
▼▼

Clark's party rode horseback on the north side of the Yellowstone River to a point near present-day Park City, 16 mi west of Billings, where the group camped from July 19 to July 24, 1806. Nearby, Clark's group cut, hollowed, and burned out two canoes, lashing them together for stability, and took to the river from this point.

Billings, the regional capital of the coal and oil industry, is not only the largest city in Montana but also the largest city for 500 mi in any direction. Named for railroad developer Frederick Billings, it was nicknamed the Magic City because of its rapid growth beginning in 1882. It's surrounded by six mountain ranges and flanked in the east by sandstone cliffs called rimrocks.

Yellowstone National Park

Clark missed discovering Mammoth Hot Springs in Yellowstone Park by about 40 mi on his eastward exploration of the Yellowstone River. Near Livingston, his party stopped to rest and appreciate the view south into the phenomenal Paradise Valley but moved on the next day. So it was left to expedition member John Colter to become the first Euro-American to explore the area to where he later returned, which came to be known as Colter's Hell. A series of expeditions in the early 1870s led President Ulysses S. Grant to pronounce Yellowstone the nation's first national park, with its more than 2 million acres of natural wonders and abundant wildlife. Today the Old Faithful geyser and its smaller siblings as well as its mud pots and hot pools have become famous around the world. The park is home to the largest bison herd in the nation as well as numerous other species. Boating, camping, horseback riding, backpacking, canoeing, and photography are popular. Lodging is available in vintage hotels in the park. Yellowstone is accessible through West Yellowstone via U.S. 191/287 and 20; through Gardiner on the north via U.S. 89; and through Cooke City via U.S. 212. | Box 168, Yellowstone, WY, 82190 | 307/344–7381 | www.nps/yell/htm | $20 per vehicle | May–Oct., check road opening and closing dates.

✦ **INFORMATION**
Billings Chamber of Commerce | Box 31177, 59107 | 406/245–4111 or 800/735–2635 | www.billingscvb.visitmt.com. **Bureau of Land Management** | www.mt.blm.gov/lewisandclark. **Custer Country** | Box 160, Laurel, 59044 | 406/628–1432 or 800/346–1876 | fax 406/628–1487 | www.custer.visitmt.com. **Fish, Wildlife & Parks Regional Office** | 2300 Lake Elmo Dr., 59105 | 406/247–2970 | www.fwp.state.mt.us. **Montana Tribal Tourism Alliance** | www.montanalewisandclark.com/resources/americanindians/mtta.htm. **Pompeys Pillar Historical Association** | Box 213, Worden, 59088.

SITES TO SEE
Chief Plenty Coups State Park. This was home of Chief Plenty Coups, the last traditional chief of the Crow Nation, a visionary who led his people from the days of the buffalo into the 20th century. The museum displays and programs tell the stories of the Apsaalooke (Crow) people. The park includes Plenty Coups' two-story log home, a medicine spring and grave site, a walking tour, and a

museum interpreting Crow culture and Plenty Coups' life. The first Saturday of August a Day of Honor is held, with traditional dance and drum groups, a buffalo feast, historian presentations, and a crafts fair. | 1 mi west of Pryor off Rte. 418, 40 mi south of Billings | 406/252–1289 | fax 406/252–6668 | www.plentycoups.org | $2 | May–Sept., daily 8–8; museum, daily 10–5.

Lewis and Clark Expedition Tours. Knowledgeable guides take you canoeing on the Yellowstone River or horseback riding along the route taken by Sergeant Pryor, the member of the Corps who was responsible for herding the expedition's horses. | 888/618–4386 | www.montanafunadventures.com | Apr.–Oct.

Little Bighorn Battlefield National Monument. Little Bighorn Battlefield National Monument is the site of the June 25, 1876, battle between the U.S. Army's 7th Cavalry and several bands of Lakota Sioux, Cheyenne, and Arapaho. The preserved battlefield, monument, and cemetery are lasting symbols to what's referred to as Custer's Last Stand, Sitting Bull's War, and the Sioux War of 1876. In this famous battle, Lieutenant Colonel George Armstrong Custer and some 225 soldiers were obliterated in less than an hour when they clashed with Crazy Horse and more than 3,000 Sioux and Cheyenne. Many of these warriors carried repeating rifles, far more effective than the single-shot carbine rifles used by Custer's troops. An interpretive museum, living-history programs, ranger talks, and guided and self-guiding tours tell the story. Rangers portraying characters from the past help you understand the lives of Plains Indians and soldiers alike and discuss the battle and weapons. There are also signed walking trails, exhibits explaining archaeological findings at the site, a scattering of army grave markers, and summer ranger programs. | U.S. 212, off I–90 at Exit 510 | 406/638–2621 | fax 406/638–2623 | www.nps.gov/libi | $10 per vehicle | Memorial Day–Labor Day, daily 8 AM–9 PM; Sept., daily 8–6; Oct.–May, daily 8–4:30.

Pictograph Cave State Park. Just 7 mi east of Billings, off Interstate 90 (and signed from the Lockwood exit), is this complex of three caves that was home to generations of prehistoric hunters dating back 10,000 years. Now it is a National Historic Landmark. More than 30,000 artifacts have been identified from the park. A short paved trail gives you access to the rock paintings in Pictograph Cave, the largest of the three. Montana's first professional archaeological studies and excavations took place here. | Lockwood exit off I–90 | 406/245–0227 or 406/247–2940 | www.fwp.state.mt.us, or www.pictographcave.org | $5 per vehicle | May 15–Sept., daily 8–8.

Pompeys Pillar National Monument. Clark named this 100-foot-high chunk of sandstone, visible from Interstate 94, after Sacagawea's infant son, whom he called Pompy, or Little Pomp—"Pomp" means "little chief" in the Shoshone language. On July 25, 1806, while Clark was exploring the area around the Yellowstone River near what is now Livingston, he carved his name and the date in clear, rounded script on the rock, noting the fact in his journal. "This rock I ascended and from its top had a most extensive view in every direction on the Northerly Side of the river high romantic Clifts approach & jut over the water for Some distance both above and below." Cottonwood, willow, Russian olive, and buffaloberry trees dot the landscape around the landmark, and some of the surrounding land is farmed. Erosion has worn away some of the soil at the base; it's for that reason that the signature appears to be far too high for Clark to have reached. This is one of the only pieces of physical evidence that Lewis and Clark left along their path. Before the Corps of Discovery arrived, the Crow people knew the site variously as "Where the mountain lion lies," "The mountain lion's lodge," or "Where the mountain lion preys." Ethnographic and archaeological studies suggest the pillar was a place of ritual and religious activity, and evidence of ritual burials and 19th-century sweat lodges has been found; you can still see aboriginal rock art in the stone. Designated a National Historic Landmark in 1965, the site was named a National Monument by Bill Clinton on January 17, 2001, during the final days of his presidency. There's a visitor center and a program of interpretive tours. | Off I–94 at Exit 23 | 406/896–5013 | www.mt.blm.gov/pillarmon/index.html | $5 per vehicle | Visitor center late May–Oct., daily 8–8.

Western Heritage Center. Permanent exhibits at this downtown museum include artifacts and interactive displays that trace the lives of Native Americans, ranchers, homesteaders, immigrants, and railroad workers who lived in the Yellowstone River region between 1880 and 1940. Interpretive programs and courses for all ages are available. | 2822 Montana Ave. | 406/256–6809 | www.ywhc.org | Donations accepted | Tues.–Sat. 10–5.

✦ ON THE CALENDAR

July **Clark's Yellowstone River Camps.** Demonstrations of dugout canoes and frontier skills are on the schedule of this event, held the third weekend in July at ITCH-KE-PA Park, ¼ mi south of Columbus. You'll also find displays of Native American dress, tepees, and a re-created river camp, yielding a glimpse of the expedition's daily life. | 406/322–4468.

July **Clark Bottom Rendezvous.** Celebrating the meeting of mountain men at the confluence of the Yellowstone and Clark Fork rivers from 1823 to 1840, this program includes entertainment, history presentations, a trader's row, and black-powder shooting matches. | 406/633–2497.

July **Clark Days.** The last weekend of July, you can celebrate William Clark's visit to Pompeys Pillar in 1806 with your own visit to the landmark. Admission is free during the event, and there's a buffalo-burger cookout and live music. | 406/896–5235 or 406/875–2233.

July 25, 2006 **Clark on the Yellowstone.** One of the signature events planned by the National Lewis and Clark Bicentennial Council, this event commemorates Clark's trip through the Yellowstone Valley with his party, which included Sacagawea and her son, Jean-Baptiste. Clark's signing of his name on the stone will be reenacted, and a new interpretive center will be dedicated amid history exhibits and Native American games. | 406/256–8628 or 406/245–7019 | www.clarkontheyellowstone.org.

HISTORIC DINING AND LODGING

George Henry's. American. Lunch and dinner are served in this charming home built in 1882. Steaks, seafood, and international ethnic foods are on the menu. | 404 N. 30th Street | 406/245–4570 | Closed Sun. No lunch Sat. | $5–$20 | AE, D, DC, MC, V.

Golden Belle Restaurant. American. Billings's most elegant restaurant, downtown in the Northern Hotel, serves a lavish Sunday brunch as well as a dinner menu featuring aged beef, chicken, and seafood. Breakfast and lunch are also available.| 19 N. 28th St. | 406/245–2232 | $4–$25 | AE, D, MC, V.

Rex. American. Built in 1910 by Buffalo Bill Cody's chef, this restaurant was saved from the wrecking ball and restored in 1975. Now it's a Black Angus–certified steak house with plenty of seafood specials. | 2401 Montana Ave. | 406/245–7477 | $6–$29 | AE, D, DC, MC, V.

Northern Hotel. This historic 1904 building in downtown Billings was destroyed by fire in 1940, then rebuilt. Although remodeled, it still provides some sense of the city's past. Rooms follow an American West theme, with woven rugs and a game table, and views are glorious. A massive fireplace is the centerpiece of the comfortable lobby, a common gathering place for guests and locals. The Golden Belle Restaurant serves American cuisine in an atmosphere that's fancier than is usual in Montana. Restaurant, room TVs with movies and video games, in-room VCRs, exercise equipment, hair salon, massage, lounge, casino, shops, meeting rooms, Internet, business services, airport shuttle, free parking, some pets allowed; no smoking. | 19 N. Broadway, at 28th St., 59101 | 406/245–5121 or 800/542–5121 | fax 406/259–9862 | www.northernhotel. net | 160 rooms | $79–$129 | AE, D, DC, MC, V.

MILES CITY
▼▼▼

The ranch town of Miles City sits at the confluence of the cottonwood-lined Tongue and Yellowstone rivers. On July 29, 1806, Clark camped near the mouth of the Tongue at Pirogue Island. Later, the federal Treaty of 1868 proclaimed that the area would remain "Indian country as long as the grass is green and the sky is blue." However, when gold was found in the Black Hills of South Dakota to the east, settlers streamed into this part of the world, and ranchers followed. Ranching has been a way of life ever since.

✦ INFORMATION

Eastern Montana Lewis and Clark Commissions | www.lewisandclarkeasternmt. org. **Miles City Chamber of Commerce** | 315 Main St., 59301 | 406/232–2890 or 877/632–2890 | fax 406/232–6914 | www.mcchamber.com.

SITES TO SEE

Range Riders Museum. Built on the site of Fort Keogh, which was constructed in 1846, this museum evokes the memory of pioneer stockmen, with saddles, chaps, spurs, guns, and other cowboy paraphernalia. As the region's largest western museum, it is a must-see if you're interested in western history. In the complex are the officers' quarters of the old fort; a heritage center; a gun collection; works of three early photographers; Sioux, Cheyenne, and Crow artifacts; a re-created frontier town with 11 shops; and a gallery of works by western artist Charles M. Russell. | Old Rte. 10, at Exit 135 off I–94 | 406/232–4483 or 406/232–6146 | Apr.–Oct., daily 8–6 | $5.

✦ ON THE CALENDAR

May **Bucking Horse Sale.** Rodeo stock contractors come to Miles City from all over North America to watch some very jumpy horses try to unseat some very determined cowboys. Meanwhile, both Friday and Saturday nights are the occasion for street dances. In Miles City, this is the next best thing to Mardi Gras. | 406/234–2890.

July **Heritage Weekend.** The last weekend of the month, a mountain-man rendezvous together with presentations about the medicine used by Lewis and Clark and other topics keep things lively. Also on the schedule are Northern Cheyenne dancing, displays of arts and crafts, and wagon rides. | 406/232–2890 or 877/632–2890.

Idaho

hen Lewis and Clark made their way into Idaho at Lemhi Pass they believed they had reached the headwaters of the Missouri. They figured they needed only to cross the pass and travel down the west slope of the Rockies to the Columbia River. But when they reached the top of Lemhi Pass the view stunned the explorers. Before them lay what looked like hundreds of miles of mountains.

On the Idaho side of Lemhi Pass, Lewis and a three-man advance party came upon some Shoshone women digging for wild carrots. Lewis put red paint on the face of one of them, to indicate friendship. She assured their chief, Cameahwait, that the strangers meant no harm. The chief and a few men rode back with Lewis to meet Clark and the rest of the expedition. Sacagawea recognized the chief—it was her brother, whom she had not seen since being taken captive as a youngster. For the next 13 days, the members of the Corps of Discovery enjoyed the hospitality of the Shoshone at their villages in the Lemhi Valley.

With the help of a Shoshone guide they called Old Toby, the Corps headed west to present-day Tendoy and then north along the route followed by present-day U.S. 93 to the North Fork of the Salmon River. Clark set out with 11 other men from the party to make an exploratory trip along that branch of the Salmon and found the region too rough for travel. The explorers continued north to cross Lost Trail Pass, into the Bitterroot Valley of what is now Montana.

Lewis and Clark reentered Idaho at Lolo Pass and followed the northern Nez Percé Trail along the high ridges above the Lochsa River corridor, now traversed by U.S. 12, but they found themselves struggling through snow and cold weather. Nearly out of food by September 14, 1805, they killed one of their colts at a place since known as Colt Killed Creek.

For the next five days, traveling through snow, ice, and sleet, the bedraggled party followed the trail through a nearly impenetrable maze of fallen timber and loose rocks. Clark captured the desperation of their journey. "I have been wet and as cold in every part as I ever was in my life. . . ." Clark and six hunters left the main group on the 18th of September in search of food and native people. Four days later they reached an open prairie planted with camas, bulbs from which they boiled and ate—they taste potatolike but are not as mealy, and slightly sweet.

On September 22, near present-day Weippe, Clark and an advance party of six companions met three boys of the Nez Percé tribe. The Native Americans allowed the Corps of Discovery to spend time in their camp and provided the men with food. A chief named Twisted Hair agreed to guide the strangers to the great falls of the Columbia and drew Clark a map showing the intricate river system of Nez Percé homeland.

On September 24, intent on reaching the Pacific, the Corps left the Weippe Prairie for the Clearwater River. At an area that came to be known as Canoe Camp, near the mouth of the North Fork Clearwater and a few miles west of Orofino, they fashioned canoes from a nearby stand of pine trees. By October 7, the canoes were finished. One headman agreed to take care of their horses until next spring. Then they cached surplus gear and headed down the Clearwater, soon joined by Twisted Hair. Although rapids capsized the boats and drenched the cargo, spirits soared. Within three days they reached the confluence of the Clearwater and Snake rivers at what is now Lewiston. From there on, the Corps' journey followed the Snake and Columbia rivers to the sea.

After spending the winter at coastal Fort Clatsop, in what is now Oregon, the Corps began the return trip in March 1806. Roughly retracing their steps, they reached Idaho in early May. Deep mountain snow made travel impossible on the Lolo Trail, and the group was forced to linger in the Clearwater Valley for a month before recommencing their eastward trip. During this time, they hunted and traded for food. They bought their salmon near the mouth of the Salmon River, then turned north and east, passing north of present-day Cottonwood and Grangeville. The Nez Percé warned Lewis and Clark not to resume their homeward journey until more snow had melted. But on June 10, 1806, Lewis and Clark made the decision to move on. Predictably, even before they crossed Lolo Pass on June 29, they endured conditions that were excruciatingly difficult, including snow "from 8 to 12 feet deep."

Many interpretive areas have been developed along the various routes the Corps of Discovery took across Idaho. You can follow their trail on the Lolo Motorway or the Lewis and Clark Back Country Byway, both rough, steep dirt roads.

In the Land of the Agai-dika

A DRIVING TOUR IN SHOSHONE TERRITORY FROM SALMON TO LOST TRAIL PASS

▼▼▼

Distance: 150 mi   **Time:** 3 days
Breaks: Dinner and overnights in Salmon.

On your first day, depart **Salmon** on Route 28 and drive 1 mi to the Sacagawea Interpretive, Cultural & Education Center. From here, take Route 28 past the sites of Cameahwait's two villages to Tendoy. Interpretive signs line the route. At the Tendoy intersection, turn left (east) onto the Lewis and Clark Back Country Byway to the tour kiosk at mile 3.7. Drive ⅗ mi on Alkali Flat Road to the first place where the explorers first met the Shoshone people. Continue another 25½ mi to Lemhi Pass. Keep an eye out for wildlife, especially along creek bottoms. Trails off the byway lead to Clark's August 19 campsite and to the point where Lewis first saw Lemhi Valley. From Lemhi Pass, drive ⅗ mi into Montana to Sacagawea Memorial Camp, headwaters of the Missouri. Return to Idaho and loop back to Route 28. Twelve miles east of the Lolo Motorway intersection is where Lewis unfurled the American flag for the first time west of the Rockies. Return to Salmon.

On day two, drive north from Salmon on U.S. 93 along the Salmon River until you reach the town of North Fork. Take a left and head west onto Forest Service Route 30 to the Salmon National Wild and Scenic River. Corps member Sergeant Patrick Gass called this area, where the river narrows between high cliffs on both sides, the "dreadful narrows." Drive west along the river 16½ mi. About 1 mi to the northeast you'll see the bluff where Clark looked 20 mi downriver over steep, crumbling mountainsides to see if the Salmon River was navigable. Return to Salmon.

On day three, drive north 5⅓ mi on U.S. 93 from Salmon to Wagonhammer Springs. Here, you can hike the 2-mi trail up the creek to Thompson Gulch and the trailhead of a 6-mi path unchanged since the expedition passed through. (If you decide to hike this route, arrange to be picked up at the Trail Gulch marker on U.S. 93.) Continue on U.S. 93 to Montana. The explorers followed a trail along the east side of the Salmon River to what is now Gibbonsville. Had they stayed on this trail, they would have followed the river into Montana across Gibbons Pass. Instead, they continued along the

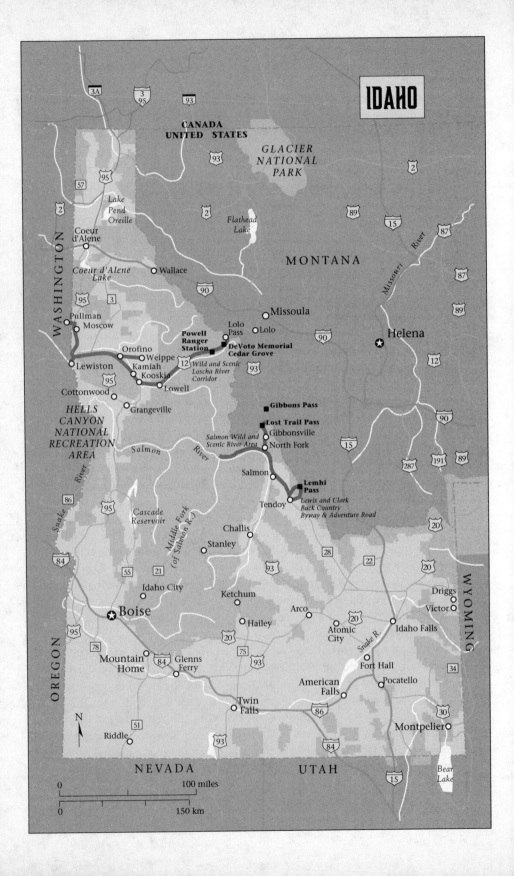

river. As you leave the valley and climb to Lost Trail Pass, look to the high peaks to the northwest. Toby, the explorers' Shoshone guide, led the expedition up a ridge and over those peaks along a divide. The group camped 2 mi to the west, near Lost Trail Pass, on September 3, and then crossed the pass out of Idaho into Montana. Spend the night in Missoula, Montana, or Hamilton, Idaho.

In the Land of the Nez Percé
FROM LOLO PASS TO LEWISTON

▼▼

Distance: 350 mi   **Time:** 3 days
Breaks: Overnights at Kamiah and Lewiston.

On day one, you'll follow the paved, winding U.S. 12 from Lolo Pass through the Wild and Scenic Lochsa River Corridor to Kamiah. Gas up in Montana; for the first 101 mi of the 108-mi drive, there are campgrounds and interpretive sites but minimal services.

Begin your tour at the Lolo Pass Visitor Center, on the Idaho-Montana border. From here, it's 10 mi west via U.S. 12 to the DeVoto Memorial Cedar Grove, where two easy loop trails, each shorter than ⅓ mi, give you a chance to stretch your legs. Another 3 mi west is the Powell Ranger Station turnoff, clearly marked to the left. Nearby, Corps members killed and ate their first horse. A level trail at the Ranger Station heads up a creek to a cedar grove. Lochsa Lodge Restaurant is nearby, a good place for lunch.

Back on U.S. 12, continue west alongside a rare stretch of the Lewis and Clark National Historic Trail that coincides with the highway. An interpretive sign on the right, at Whitehouse Pond, explains that the explorers found the route so difficult they left the river and climbed to the Lolo Trail above. Continue 35 mi to the small settlement of Lowell, at the confluence of the Lochsa and Selway rivers. Here you can find out about guide services on the two rivers. Continue 23 mi to Kooskia, at the confluence of the middle and south forks of the Clearwater River. At the intersection of U.S. 12 and Route 13 is a Lewis and Clark kiosk. Continue west on U.S. 12, just over 6 mi to the Nez Percé National Historical Park. Walk the short trail to the amphitheater, and listen to the 15-minute taped recording of the story of the origins of the Nez Percé. From here, continue another 3 mi to **Kamiah** to spend the night.

On day two, head east through town on U.S. 12 toward Kooskia. On the right, before crossing the Clearwater River Bridge, take in the exhibits at Riverfront Park. Continue across the bridge and immediately turn left onto Route 100. The sawmill that's approximately 3 mi ahead on the left is on the site of Lewis and Clark's 1806 Kamiah camp. Continue on Route 100 for about 24 mi up the hill to Clearwater National Forest Pheasant Camp interpretive sign. Midway along, the road becomes gravel but can be traveled easily by car. From here drive a short distance to where Road 100 intersects with Road 500. Take a right and drive 1 mi on this road to Route 520. When you come to Route 5132, turn right and travel the short distance. At Route 100, head right for 9½ mi to the Musselshell Meadows interpretive sign; then follow Route 100 to Brown's Creek Road, about 4½ mi.

Here, take a left, and drive 8 mi to the town of **Weippe.** At Cemetery Road on the edge of town, turn left and follow the signs to the Weippe Prairie interpretive sign. From here, take Route 11 to town and the Weippe Discovery Center. After lunch, drive west on Route 11 for just under 18 mi to the Clearwater River. Cross the river to U.S. 12, turn right, and travel for 6 mi. Take the bridge to **Orofino**; then turn left on Route 7 and head for the Dworshak Dam Fish Hatchery, where there are interpretive panels on the grounds and in a visitor center. Recross the Orofino Bridge to return to U.S. 12, and continue west. Your next stop, 2½ mi ahead, is Canoe Camp. It was here that Lewis and Clark built their canoes to take them down the Clearwater and out to the Pacific. Still on U.S. 12, continue toward **Lewiston.** The highway crosses the North Fork Clearwater near the mouth of Potlatch River, where Lewis and Clark had a serious canoe accident. Lewiston, where you will spend the night, is 13 mi ahead.

On your last day, visit sites in and around Lewiston. Plan to spend half of the day in town, visiting the LCSC Art & History Center and the Nez Percé County Museum and seeing the interpretive work and the sculpture on the levee. After lunch, visit the Nez Percé National Historical Park. To get there from Lewiston, drive 10 mi east on U.S. 12 to U.S. 95, and then head south toward Boise. On your left, 2 mi ahead, is the turnout to the park. Plan to spend an hour or so learning about the Nez Percé people before continuing to the Nez Percé Wolf Education and Research Center. To get to the center, continue south along U.S. 95 for about 30 mi. At the top of a hill, at the turnoff to the town of Winchester and Winchester Lake, turn right and follow signs to the lake and the center. Then, drive north on U.S. 95 for 35 mi to Moscow, where you can pick up Route 270 west to Pullman, Washington. The Appaloosa Museum and Heritage Center is clearly marked near the state border. Return to Lewiston for the evening.

SALMON

▼▼▼

In the valley where the Salmon and Lemhi rivers meet, surrounded by the towering Bitterroot, Lemhi, and Salmon mountain ranges, is the town of Salmon, birthplace of Sacagawea. The Corps never camped here as a group, but individually many passed by this river juncture before they all left Shoshone country.

✦ INFORMATION

Salmon Valley Chamber of Commerce | 315 Hwy. 93 N, 83467 | 208/756–1188 | www.ohwy.com/id/s/salmovcc.htm.

SITES TO SEE

Frank Church–River of No Return Wilderness. With 2,361,767 acres, this is the largest contiguous forest wilderness in the Lower 48 States. It has craggy mountains, an astonishing variety of landscapes, some 72 species of mammals, 173 species of birds, and 23 species of fish, including steelhead trout and Chinook salmon, Dolly Varden, and rainbow trout, among others. The preserve is also home to some of the nation's most powerful white water; the 104-mi Middle Fork of the Salmon and the 79-mi Main Salmon run through it, and the Selway, another celebrated white-water stream, begins here. Clark actually considered the river as a possible route to the Columbia. But before he got very far, he encountered rapids, and his Native American guides informed him that "those rapids which I had Seen . . . was Small & trifleing in comparrison to the rocks & rapids below, at no great distance & The Hills or mountains were not like those I had Seen but like the Side of a tree Streight up . . . the water runs with great violence from one rock to another on each Side foaming & roreing thro rocks in every direction, So as to render the passage of anything impossible." During the annual salmon run, the Shoshone camped along the Salmon, which they called Tom-Agit-Pah ("big fish water"), yet they, too, considered the river too dangerous for canoe travel and developed an extensive trail system around the area. The Nez Percé used the lower section of the Salmon near its confluence with the Snake River, and the Shoshone lived upstream. The Salmon has Class III to Class IV rapids, with campsites on sandy beaches along its course. River trips usually take from five to seven days. Hiking trails are found up the side canyons. | 10 mi north on U.S. 93 from Salmon | 208/756–2100 | www.fs.fed.us/r4/sc | Free.

Lemhi County Historical Museum. The Lemhi County Historical Museum, operated by the local historical society, houses the nation's largest collection of Lemhi Shoshone artifacts and displays exhibits about homesteading and ranching as well as vintage photographs connected with county history. | 210 Main St. | 208/756–3342 | $1 | Mid-Apr.–Oct., Mon.–Sat. 10–5.

Lewis and Clark National Back Country Byway & Adventure Road. Only a handful of places along Lewis and Clark's route through the West provide an opportunity to truly experience the land as it was in 1805. From Tendoy, 20 mi southeast of Salmon, this single-lane gravel road with occasional pull-outs for passing runs for 39 mi parallel to the route used by Lewis and Clark as they crossed the Continental Divide at Lemhi Pass. At the height of the road, above 8,000 feet, 18 mi into the drive, there are the spectacular vistas you'd expect—river valleys, meadows, peaks and more peaks. The byway also provides access to sections of the Lewis and Clark National Historic Trail. The road then follows the divide a few miles through fir and pine trees and high-mountain meadows before returning to Tendoy. The drive takes about half a day. Although snow usually closes the road in winter, it is groomed for snow-mobiles. | Bureau of Land Management, Salmon Field Office, Rte. 2, Box 610, 83467 | 208/756–5404 | Free | June–Oct., daily.

Sacagawea Interpretive, Cultural & Education Center. A life-size statue of Sacagawea overlooks the mountains and Lemhi River valley at this visitor center. You can take a self-guided or ranger-guided history tour and view a sweat lodge, fishing weir, and tepee encampment of the band of the Shoshone known as the Agai-Dika ("salmon eaters"). | 200 Main St. | 208/756–1188 | www.sacagaweacenter.org | $3 | Mid-May–mid-Oct., Mon.–Sun. 9–5.

✦ ON THE CALENDAR

Aug. **Sacagawea Heritage Days.** This festival celebrates the Shoshone woman who accompanied Lewis and Clark for much of the way and who was born in the Lemhi Valley, with three days of Native American dancing, food, and hot-air balloon flights. | 800/727–2540.

HISTORIC DINING AND LODGING

Bertran's Salmon Valley Brewery. American. Pub grub, homemade sodas, and home-brewed beers are served in an 1894 redbrick building with original hard-wood floors and high, pressed-tin ceilings. | 101 S. Andrews St. | 208/756–3391 | $3–$16 | AE, DC, MC, V.

North Fork Store & Cafe. American. In this miners' mercantile store, built in 1907, the menu lists elk, buffalo, and salmon and, for lunch, an array of sand-wiches. | 2046 U.S. 93, North Fork | 208/865–2412 | $4–$24 | AE, DC, MC, V.

Grey House Inn. This 1894 Victorian overlooks the Salmon River and the Bitter-root, Beaverhead, and Salmon mountains. Rooms are in the inn, where two rooms share a bath, and in two rustic log cabins and a carriage house. The owners will arrange guided float trips, fishing trips, and trail rides. | 1115 U.S. 93, opposite milepost 293, 12 mi south of Salmon | 208/756–3968 or 800/348–8097 | www.greyhouseinn.com | 4 rooms, 2 cabins, 1 house | $70–$90 | AE, DC, MC, V | BP.

Solaas Bed & Breakfast. Built in 1905 as the Baker Hotel, this bed-and-break-fast started out as a stop for stagecoaches running the Red Rock Line and later became successively a railroad depot, an apartment house, and a wilderness-trip outfitter's headquarters. Nowadays, every room has a theme—a western motif, the Amish, Americana, and the like. Shop. | 3 Red Rock Stage Rd. | 208/756–3903 or 888/425–5474 | www.salmonidaho.com/solaas | 7 rooms, 4 with bath | $40–$50 | No credit cards | BP.

Sacagawea at Home

The Lemhi Shoshone tell us that Sacagawea means "one who is carrying a great burden." When 16-year-old Sacagawea first saw her brother Chief Cameahwait, her burden was lifted. She recognized him immediately and danced for joy. At the same time she recognized another woman who had been captured with her years earlier in the Hidatsa raid. That woman had escaped and rejoined her people. Young Sacagawea's life had taken a different turn, right into the pages of history.

While exploring the Idaho side of Lemhi Pass, Lewis and a three-man advance party came upon some Shoshone women digging for wild carrots. Lewis put red paint on the face of one of them, to indicate friendship. She assured their chief, Cameahwait, that the strangers meant no harm. Lewis told Cameahwait of the expedition and their need for horses, of which the Shoshone had plenty. Lewis had promised Cameahwait they would meet Clark and the main party on the east side of the Continental Divide. The chief reluctantly rode with the strangers back across the Divide. Tensions mounted when Clark failed to appear. Then they saw a large group of strangers—and Sacagawea. Her appearance, assurances, and translating services calmed all apprehensions. Shoshone suspicions dissipated, replaced by welcoming warmth and curiosity about the strangers, their equipment, York, even Lewis's dog, Seaman. Clearly, Sacagawea's presence defused a potentially antagonistic encounter.

She was not yet home, however, until she crossed the Divide and entered the Lemhi Valley with Clark, her husband, and her son. Her descendant Rose Ann Abrahamson shares her people's remembrances of that arrival: "We saw her coming with the white men, carrying her babe on her back in a wrapped willow cradleboard. She came up over a foothill, which had loose shale rocks on one side. They were very careful to walk on the better side of the hill as they came down among us."

Sacagawea, Charbonneau, and Jean-Baptiste stayed in her brother's village while Clark led his reconnaissance party down the Salmon River. There was not much time for her to catch up on those lost five or more years.

Did Sacagawea ever return to her homeland after that fall of 1805? Her descendants say no, affirming that she joined her ancestors and loved ones beyond the Milky Way as a young woman. Most scholars believe she died at Fort Manuel, South Dakota, on December 20, 1812. However, one Nez Percé account maintains otherwise. Written in the 1930s, a piece by Chief Many Wounds tells the story of a young boy named Timothy, who was about 11 when Lewis and Clark passed through. Enthralled by Sacagawea, he never forgot her; when he became an elder of the Alpowa band of the Nez Percé, he sent his adult daughter, Jane, to the Shoshone village to meet her. As the story goes, Jane had a nice long visit with a very old Sacagawea, and when Jane returned, she brought the dress that Sacagawea wore on the expedition, as a gift for Timothy.

KAMIAH
▼▼▼

It was in spring 1806 that the Corps of Discovery arrived at Kamiah, set in a warm, sheltered valley that is one of the most beautiful in the region; ultimately the men stayed longer among the Native Americans here than at any other place, except for their winter quarters in Fort Mandan, as they watched for signs that the snow was melting in the Bitterroot Mountains. They called the campsite Long Camp because of the length of time they spent there—some 27 days. Meanwhile, they were getting to know the land and the people. They were introduced to the camas plant, which is abundant in the area; the Nez Percé boiled the bulbs and ate them. The Nez Percé had been in the area for generations, traveling to higher country and across the mountains for food and trade but always returning, and members of the tribe still claim the valley as the place where their people began. Nowadays, the town of Kamiah has a population of 1,200, and the area remains the home of an important Nez Percé community, with a small tribe-owned casino, numerous Nez Percé–owned businesses, and tribal support facilities. U.S. 12 traverses the area, also known as the Lewis and Clark Highway, and is the longest highway within any national forest in the United States. Running along the Wild and Scenic Lochsa River, it has splendid views of the pristine Selway-Bitterroot Wilderness.

✦ INFORMATION
Kamiah Chamber of Commerce | 518 Main St., 83536 | 208/935–2290 | www.kamiahchamber.com.

SITES TO SEE
Clearwater National Forest. In this 1,800,000-acre preserve, you can see herds of elk as well as black bears, mountain goats, white-tailed and mule deer, moose,

and mountain lions, and there are more than 1,700 mi of hiking trails, some of them with trailheads along U.S. 12. Interpretive signs and campgrounds line the route. It's best to visit during the summer and early fall, as the forest is snowbound from December through May. Interpretive campfire programs in the various campgrounds are planned for the Bicentennial. | 12730 U.S. 12 | 208/476–4541 | www.fs.fed.us/r1/clearwater | Free | Daily.

De Voto Memorial Cedar Grove. During the 1950s, the American writer Bernard De Voto, whose edition of the Lewis and Clark journals was published in 1953, often visited this peaceful site to meditate and write; his ashes were scattered here on his death in 1956. There are hiking trails and picnic tables. | U.S. 12, midway between the Lolo Visitor Center and Powell Ranger Station | Free | Daily.

Lochsa Historical Ranger Station. Although no longer in operation, this log ranger station built in the early 1920s and outfitted with period furnishings provides you with a glimpse of the life of a Forest Service ranger in the back-country. Especially moving is an audio presentation of rangers being trapped in the station by a deadly forest fire. Retired Forest Service employees greet visitors, answer questions, and guide tours. | Donations accepted | June–Sept., daily 10–5.

Lochsa River. This river, which parallels U.S. 12 for much of its course, orig-inates in the Bitterroot Mountains and joins the Selway and Clearwater rivers after 26 mi. Named Lochsa ("rough water") by the Nez Percé, it includes no fewer than 40 Class III to Class IV rapids. Many outfitters operate one- to three-day trips on the Lochsa, often using paddleboats to make the trip participatory. The floating season runs from mid-May to late June, and the Forest Service can provide leads on outfitters. | 12730 U.S. 12 | 208/476–4541 | www.fs.fed.us/r1/clearwater | Free | Daily.

Lolo Motorway. Narrow, rocky, and steep, with steep drop-offs and no services— and unsuited for most passenger cars and a challenge for RVs and motor homes—this single-lane road runs through 100 mi of breathtaking scenery, set in a sea of mountains along a stretch of Lewis and Clark's route that is virtu-ally as it was when the explorers passed through. Built by the Civilian Conser-vation Corps in 1934, it's also known as Forest Service Route 500. | 12730 U.S. 12 | 208/476–4541 | www.fs.fed.us/r1/clearwater/LewisClark/ LewisClark.htm | Free | Daily.

Lolo Pass Visitor Center. This new building high on the Idaho–Montana border, about 45 mi west of Missoula and 100 mi east of Kooskia, houses interpre-tive panels that tell the story of Lewis and Clark passing through the Lolo Corridor—an ancient Native American hunting trail and pathway through the wilderness—and explore the life of Nez Percé and Salish there. You can get a sense of the pristine beauty of these mountain meadows as they appeared two centuries ago along two nearby trails—among them one trail to Glade Creek Meadows, where Lewis and Clark camped in 1805, and another full of native plants, including camas—a type of lily that makes the fields as blue as a lake on a sunny day when they bloom in spring, usually at some point between April and June. The center is in the Lochsa Ranger District in the Clearwater National Forest. | U.S. 12 | 208/926–4274 | www.fs.fed.us/r1/clearwater | Daily 9–5.

Kamiah Riverfront Park. The town of Kamiah commemorates Lewis and Clark's Long Camp in this park with an interpretive kiosk, a performing arts stage, and murals. The park is landscaped with plants identified in the various Corps of Discovery journals. Throughout the Bicentennial, performances with a Lewis and Clark theme are planned. | U.S. 12, on Kamiah side of Kamiah–Kooskia bridge | 208/935–2672 | Free | Daily.

Kooskia Kiosk. At this site in the little town of Kooskia, about 10 mi from Kamiah near the intersection of U.S. 12 and Route 13, interpretive displays describe the cultural, historical, and economic heritage of the region. Although the Corps never passed this way, individual members traveled to the site from Long Camp. | U.S. 12, on Kamiah side of Kamiah–Kooskia bridge | 208/926–4362 | Free | Daily.

✦ ON THE CALENDAR
May/June **Root Feast.** Every spring in May or June, whenever the camas plants are ready to harvest, the Nez Percé celebrate with a free feast that's open to the public at the Nez Percé Tribe Wa A'Yas center in Kamiah. The event includes a root ceremony as well as traditional Nez Percé food. | 208/843–2253.

July **Frontier Music Festival.** This annual three-day event a short drive from Kamiah in Kooskia includes frontier music and dance, cowboy poetry, and western food. | 208/926–4362 or 208/756–2100.

July **Riverfest.** This annual bluegrass festival at Riverfront Park brings top-notch acts along with food and displays of arts and crafts. | 208/935–2290.

Aug. **Chief Lookingglass Powwow.** The public is welcome to this free annual Nez Percé celebration, held for three days in August. It includes dancing, drumming, and food. | 208/843–2253.

HISTORIC DINING AND LODGING
Lochsa Lodge Restaurant. American. Steak, salmon, and regionally famous hamburgers are on the menu at this log restaurant. The dining room overlooks the Lochsa River and has an immense, rustic fireplace inside and, outside, a riverfront porch where you can have your meal in good

The Lolo Trail

The Lolo Trail National Historic Landmark, designated in 1962, comprises historic and prehistoric travel routes. It extends approximately 100 mi, beginning at Lolo, Montana, to the site William Clark named Travelers' Rest, to Weippe, Idaho. Traveler's Rest was originally at the junction of Lolo Creek and the Bitterroot River. The site now named Traveler's Rest is where Highway 93 crosses Lolo Creek.

Several travel routes use the same east–west series of mountain ridges and fall within the landmark boundaries. The ancient Salish and Nez Percé Indian buffalo-to-salmon trail, sometimes called the Northern Nez Percé Trail, generally runs from the Camas Prairie in present-day Idaho to the Bitterroot Valley in Montana. Traces of that trail can still be seen in some places along the route. The Lewis and Clark National Historic Trail is managed by the National Park Service, and follows the route that the explorers followed as closely as possible, considering the changes the last 200 years have wrought. The Nez Percé National Historic Trail is the path the Nez Percé used during the Nez Percé War of 1877. The Bird-Truax Trail was constructed in 1866 to connect the gold fields of Montana to the goldfields in Orofino, Idaho.

Two routes accessible to motor vehicles provide a good idea of the kind of country the Corps of Discovery had to cross on this leg of their journey: the 120-mi-stretch of highway that runs along Lolo Creek and the Wild and Scenic Lochsa River, and the Lolo Motorway. The latter, which was built by the Civilian Conservation Corps during the 1930s, parallels the old trail that the Nez Percé used to cross the mountains to hunt buffalo. Both routes pass through the most remote and rugged mountain country that the Corps of Discovery crossed.

Before starting out, gather as much information as possible about driving conditions along the route. In some cases, the roads are single lanes and frequently have steep drops on the sides, with little or no room for turning around or passing other vehicles. Some parts of these trails will still have snow on them as late as June. Camping facilities and places to buy supplies are sometimes miles apart.

For more information, visit the Clearwater National Forest (www.fs.fed.us/r1/clearwater) and the Lolo National Forest (www.fs.fed.us/r1/lolo) Web sites.

weather. | U.S. 12, on the Powell Ranger Station turnout, 12 mi west of Lolo Pass, Lolo | 208/942–0921 | $6–$18 | AE, DC, MC, V.

Moose River Grill. American. Trees, moose images, antiques, and lanterns decorate this restaurant above the Kamiah Hotel Bar. Idaho trout tops the menu. | 501 4th St. | 208/935–0931 | Closed Sun. and Mon. No lunch | $11–$22 | AE, D, MC, V.

Hearthstone Lodge. Each room has a private balcony and a Clearwater River view at this lodge on 29 acres surrounded by more than a million acres of national forest. Furnishings are stylish, romantic, and not a bit rustic; your room may have a fireplace, a Jacuzzi, or a king-size canopy bed, and the music is classical more often than cowboy. In-room data ports, in-room hot tubs, in-room VCRs, fishing, library. Separate 3-bedroom house with a full kitchen and bathroom for groups with children 15 and under 2 mi away, $95 per night. | U.S. 12, milepost 64 | 208/935–1492 or 877/563–4348 | www.hearthstone-lodge.com | fax 208/935–2422 | 5 rooms, 2 cottages | $125 | AE, DC, MC, V.

Lewis & Clark Resort. This resort, a few miles east of Kamiah on U.S. 12, looks a little bit like a fort from the Old West. Standing tall at the entry are two 10-foot sculptures of Lewis and Clark, carved from tree trunks by well-known regional artisan Har-V. Accommodations are in the fortlike motel building and in snug log cabins; a large section of the spacious, forested grounds is given over to RV sites. There's also a fully stocked fishpond and an area nearby where you can pitch a tent. Restaurant, pool, shop, laundry facilities, meeting rooms. | Rte. 1, Box 17X, 83536 | 208/935–2556 | www.lewisclarkresort.com | 21 rooms, 7 cabins, 175 RV spaces | $40 motel room, $65 cabin, $19 RV space | AE, D, MC, V.

Reflections Inn. This country inn is on 11 forested acres overlooking the Middle Fork of the Clearwater River, 11 mi above Kooskia. The ranch is quiet and private, with accommodations both in the main house and a guest house with a full kitchen and living room. Bedrooms are simple, with flowers gathered from the property arranged in hand-thrown pottery and books lining the bookshelves. Hot tub, hiking. | U.S. 12, milepost 84 | HCR 75, Box 32, Kooskia, 83539 | 208/926–0855 or 888/926–0855 | www.reflectionsinn.com | 7 rooms | $75–$85 | MC, V.

WEIPPE

▼▼

Had William Clark and his hunting party arrived on the eastern edge of the Nez Percé root-gathering place known as Weippe Prairie in spring 1805 instead of fall, the local meadows would have been sky blue with the blooms of a member of the lily family, the camas. But they were relieved nonetheless at finally making it through the mountains. Even better was the sight of two small Nez Percé root-gathering villages in the distance, in the area of present-day Weippe (pronounced *wee*-ipe). More prominent leaders were away when the explorers rode into this area on September 20, so determining whether they were friend or foe fell to a chief named Twisted Hair, who sought advice from Wetxuuwiis, a woman who had been kidnapped by the Blackfeet, sold to French-Canadians, and helped by settlers. The Nez Percé thought that these men were strange and had their heads on upside down, because they had so much hair on their chins and so little on the tops of their heads. When the explorers returned in 1806, on their way back to St. Louis, they camped at Weippe again to prepare for crossing the Rockies. The name, written Oy-ipe and Oy-iap in the area's early days, may have meant "very old place" ("oy" means "all" in the Nez Percé language); an Irish postmaster who arrived in 1880 changed the spelling.

✦ INFORMATION
Weippe Discovery Center | 2050 Wilson Rd., 83553 | 208/435–4529 | www. weippe.com.

SITES TO SEE
Weippe Discovery Center. Covering three sides of the outside of this old former church is a painted rendition of Lewis and Clark's journey from Travelers' Rest in Montana to Canoe Camp on the Clearwater and the explorers' life among the Nez Percé; the landscape in the background is a mountain prairie full of plants listed in Corps journals. | Wood St. at Rte. 11 | Free | Daily.

✦ ON THE CALENDAR
May **Weippe Camas Festival.** Scheduled to celebrate the blooming camas meadows, this two-day festival includes a race through the meadow, speakers on Lewis and Clark, demonstrations of games and skills practiced by the Nez Percé and expedition members, music, and dramatizations of aspects of the Lewis and Clark story. | 208/435–4362 | www.weippe.com.

HISTORIC DINING AND LODGING
Timberline Café. American. Want a bison burger, a bite-size steak, or some roasted chicken? This small café, part of a cabin-and-RV-park complex on the edge of the Weippe Prairie, is just the place. | 1022 N. Main St. | 208/435–4763 | $4–$15 | AE, MC, V.

The Retreat at Someday Ranch. Overlooking the Weippe Prairie and the mountains, this ranch is designed to capture the flavor of life on the prairie in 1805. A cabin accommodates two, with cots for children, and there are tepees that sleep three or four. Sleeping bags or linens are for rent. It's rustic— the toilets are outdoors and the running water is cold. In the morning, dried fish, meat, and berries cooked in a dutch oven are served outdoors for breakfast. | 2021 Musselshell Rd. | 208/435–4362 | $35–$60 | Closed Nov.–Apr. | No credit cards | BP.

OROFINO

▼▼▼

The Corps left Weippe Prairie, traveled down Jim Ford Creek, and reached the Clearwater River a few miles east of Orofino. They camped on an island next to the island camp of Twisted Hair, a leader of the people who made their home in the Orofino-Ahsahka area. On September 26, the expedition moved downstream, crossed to the south shore near today's Orofino bridge, and continued to a fishing village opposite the North Fork Clearwater. Camping here, they built four large canoes and one smaller one—ergo the camp's namesake, Canoe Camp, the only one in Idaho that the explorers actually named. When they left on October 7, Lewis branded their 38 horses and entrusted them to a headman's care for the winter. Next spring, when they returned, all but two of the horses were retrieved.

The discovery of gold on Orofino Creek in 1860 inspired the name ("fine gold"), which another gold-rush town had previously used; the two words were joined to quash objections from the post office. Nowadays, the town—officially established in 1898—has a population of 3,314. The North Fork of the Clearwater was impounded in 1973, creating Dworshak Lake. The main river is known for its steelhead fishing and for the fall run of Chinook salmon returning from the sea—some as hefty as 25 pounds.

✦ **INFORMATION**
Orofino Chamber of Commerce | Box 2346, 83544 | 208/476–4335 | www.orofino.com.

SITES TO SEE
Canoe Camp. Here, Ponderosa pines that were barely more than seedlings two centuries ago have grown enough to be made into the same kind of dugout canoes that the explorers carved and burned at this site on the Clearwater River between September 26 and October 7, 1805. Having crossed the mountains using packhorses, they were ready to return to the river. The men were hungry, and so shortly after they arrived, the Nez Percé caught salmon and sold them some. Anticipating the return trip to Missouri, they cached their saddles and other gear and left their horses in the care of the Nez Percé. Interpretive signs in this 2½-acre park, a unit of the Nez Percé National Historical Park, describe the expedition's activities at that time. Today, the Dworshak Dam and fish hatchery dominate the view, and noise from U.S. 12 intrudes on the tranquility that Lewis and Clark would have experienced. | U.S. 12,

Hells Canyon Fish Hunt

In late May or early June, when the migrating salmon reach the inland rivers, the Nez Percé gather at the confluences of the area rivers to honor the continual cycle of life and begin their fishing season. In spring 1806, Lewis and Clark dispatched John Ordway, Robert Frazer, and Peter Weiser to the lower Salmon to purchase some of the first-run salmon. The anticipated day's ride instead was a week and covered some 100 mi.

The explorers and some Nez Percé traveled west across Camas Prairie, camping their second night at the foot of Cottonwood Butte. The luxury of easy travel then ended. Impeded by a driving thunderstorm, they "descended a bad hill" to a village where Frazer traded with a woman, exchanging an old razor for two Spanish mill dollars.

The "road" became steeper and rougher as they dropped to the Salmon River. The fish had not yet arrived. They rode down the river "some distance," then turned up a steep trail to the top of a rocky ridge and a spectacular view. To the west and straight down, Snake River chisels Hells Canyon from the base of the Blue and Wallowa mountains. Behind, Salmon River flanks the foothills of the distant Salmon River Mountains. But Ordway did not mention the view. All he described was the "steep bad hill" they crossed before descending "the worst hills we ever saw a road made down."

The first explorers to step foot in Hells Canyon reached Snake River about 3 mi below the mouth of the Salmon. There were Nez Percé men fishing on both banks and congregated in a large split timber "common house." The women were gathering couse roots along the rocky hill slopes. The next morning departing Nez Percé took most of the catch and the men had to wait to make their purchase later that day. The third morning they discovered some had been "stolen." Failure to understand Nez Percé food distribution procedure probably accounts for the word "stolen." Nevertheless, the three departed with 17 salmon.

On the way home, they followed the same impossible "road" up out of Snake Canyon and back down to Salmon River. There the natives advised a "better" road that took them over another ridge and down a zigzag trail back to Salmon River. A steep climb eventually brought them to Camas Prairie, then to the Clearwater River near Kooskia.

By June 2, Ordway, Frazer, and Weiser were at Long Camp with mostly rotten fish. Their trip became a mere footnote to the expedition journals. The few locals who have retraced their route appreciate the difficulty they encountered but are mystified by their exact route. One of the biggest mysteries is, Where, exactly, in Hells Canyon were they? Clark's journal doesn't help. He describes a "considerable rapid" near the Snake River fishery that was "nearly as great . . . as the great falls of the Columbia." Where could that have been?

4 mi west of Orofino bridge | 208/476–7530 | www.nps.gov/nepe/site18.htm | Free | Daily.

Clearwater Historical Museum. The people and history of the area drained by the Clearwater River are the focus of this small downtown museum. Artifacts in the collection relating to the Nez Percé, the Lewis and Clark expedition, and the gold rush and logging eras fill this downtown museum. There are more than 4,500 vintage photographs, as well as arrowheads, baskets, moccasins, beadwork, old newspapers, antique guns, medicinal and and barber tools, and more. | 315 College Way | 208/476–5033 | By donation | www.clearwatermuseum.org | June–Sept., Tues.–Sat. 1:30–4:30.

Dworshak Dam and Reservoir. North America's largest straight-axis dam, a dramatic, 717-foot-high structure built in 1973, has impounded the North Fork of the Clearwater to create this 54-mi-long lake. The dam visitor center, at the top of the dam, displays exhibits on area history and wildlife. Tours on top of the dam are also available. In the lake, there's good fishing for kokanee salmon and rainbow trout; hiking trails wiggle through the woods that edge the shoreline; and camping is available in state parks, among them Dworshak State Park, and in remote minicamps scattered around the lake. The dam was named for Henry Dworshak, the Republican senator for Idaho between 1946 and 1962. | Off Rte. 7, 5 mi west of Orofino | c/o U.S. Army Corps of Engineers, Box 48, Ahsahka, 83520 | 208/476–1255 or 800/321–3198 | www.cqs.washington.edu/crisp/hydro/dwr.html | Daily 10–4.

Dworshak National Fish Hatchery. Interpretive signs and exhibits on the grounds of this hatchery, the largest steelhead trout hatchery in the world, highlight the Nez Percé fishing techniques and other topics. The hatchery was built after the construction of the Dworshak Dam to make up for the loss of steelhead trout in the North Fork of the Clearwater and its tributaries; the dam blocks access of steelhead trout and spring Chinook salmon to their natural spawning grounds and is too high for a fish ladder. So the hatchery fertilizes eggs, raises the young fish, then releases them; they will then swim the 500 mi to the Pacific, through no fewer than eight dams, and return to the hatchery to spawn as adult fish. There may be as many as 27,000 steelhead and 35,000 Chinooks in the hatchery at the time of the release—the steelhead in April, when they are about a year old, and the Chinook in May, when they are about 18 months old. | Box 18, Ahsahka, 83520 | 208/476–4591 | dworshak.fws.gov | Free | Office weekdays 7:30–4, grounds daily.

✦ ON THE CALENDAR

July Festival of Discovery. This two-day event combines Orofino's annual Old-Fashioned Sunday celebration with activities commemorating the goodwill shared by the explorers and their Nez Percé hosts. Period music and costume, arts-and-crafts sales and displays, and historic and traditional food and dancing are on the schedule. | 208/476–4335 | www.orofino.com.

LEWISTON

▼▼▼

The twin cities of Lewiston, Idaho, and Clarkston, Washington, recall the visit of the captains of the Corps of Discovery to the area. But the Nez Percé thought of it as Tsceminicum, "the meeting of the rivers"—the Clearwater, which native inhabitants called the Koos-Koos-Kia for the river's transparent quality, and the murky Snake, which was known as the Kimoeenem. When the expedition members camped on the north bank in October 1805, Lewis noted, "The countrey about the forks is an open plain on either side." There was "not one Stick of timber" and only one tepee. The captains did recognize the Snake as a major tributary to the Columbia. Using a map drawn by Nez Percé chief Twisted Hair, they could tell it was the same river they had earlier decided against traveling on in Shoshone country. They were right, for the Salmon joins the Snake 45 mi to the south. Today, Lewiston has a population of 31,437. Lower Granite Dam, built in 1975, impounds the Snake, elevating it 40 feet above its natural banks and creating Lower Granite Lake. The Lewiston Levee Parkway runs along 12 mi of the 19-mi Clearwater and Snake River National Recreation Trail, paralleling Snake River Avenue in Lewiston. Specialty shops and other businesses fill the historic section of the downtown area, full of vintage buildings that have been restored. Morgan's Alley, a complex of four buildings linked by brick arches in west Lewiston, is the latest spot to be rescued from onetime blight.

✦ INFORMATION

Lewiston Chamber of Commerce | 111 Main St., Suite 120, Lewiston, 83501 | 208/743–3531 | fax 208/743–2176 | www.lewistonchamber.org.

SITES TO SEE

Appaloosa Museum and Heritage Center. This museum in Moscow, Idaho, about 32 mi from Lewiston, highlights the history of the Appaloosa horse, distinguished by its spotted markings. Regalia, saddles, and artifacts associated with the Appaloosa are on display here, including Native American items. The Nez Percé of the area practiced selective horse breeding and produced large herds of excellent Appaloosas and other horses. | 2720 W. Pullman Rd., Moscow | 208/882–5578 Ext. 279 | www.appaloosamuseum.org | By donation | Tues.– Fri. 10–5, Sat. 10–4.

Center for Arts & History. Probably the most striking exhibit in this museum a few blocks from the Lewis-Clark State College Campus is the collection of life-size wood carvings of Lewis's dog, Seaman, as he was described in different entries of the journals kept by members of the Corps. Also on display are works by nationally and internationally known artists and exhibits devoted to aspects of the Lewis and Clark expedition and Nez Percé life. A 19th-century Chinese temple recalls Lewiston's early Chinese settlers, who came largely from the Toishan district of southern China's Guangdong Province. The museum occupies a former bank building that is now on the National Register of Historic Places; it was constructed in 1884 as the Vollmer Great Bargain Store on designs by western architect Kirtland Cutter. | 415 Main St. | 208/792–2243 | www.artsandhistory.org | Donation | Weekdays 11–4, Sat. 10–3.

Hells Gate State Park. Grassy, open spaces for picnicking, a beach, a volley-ball area, boating facilities, and 93 shady campsites on 100 yards of the Snake River are the draw to this 960-acre park set 4 mi south of Lewiston. You can see upland birds such as pheasants, quail, chukar, hawks, geese, ducks, and owls, as well as eagles, pelicans, herons, and swans. Keep your eyes open for cottontail rabbits, deer, and otters. A trail from the campground runs for 2 mi along the river past basalt cliffs, and there's also a Lewis and Clark Interpretive Center. Smallmouth bass, catfish, trout, and sturgeon keep anglers busy in spring and summer, and the steelhead runs on the Snake, Salmon, and Clearwater in fall and winter are famous. Plus, there's no snow then, because the low elevation—at 713 feet, lower than that of any other Idaho park—puts the park squarely in the state's Banana Belt. | 3620-A Snake River Ave. | 208/799–5015 | www.idahoparks.org | $2 | Marina closed Dec.–Feb.

Lewis-Clark State College. On the campus's Centennial Mall, a larger-than-life bronze statue by Nez Percé sculptor Doug Hyde depicts Lewis and Clark with chief Twisted Hair, who first welcomed the explorers to his tribal lands, as well as his son and two Nez Percé women digging camas. The display includes a large waterfall and utilizes natural stone from a Nez Percé lime quarry. The two-story Fine Arts Building was designed in 1912 by the influential Northwest architect Kirtland K. Cutter. | 500 8th Ave. | 208/792–5272 | www.lcsc. edu | Free | Daily.

Lewiston Gateway. Standing in the median at the interchange of U.S. 12 and U.S. 95 in North Lewiston, this cluster of life-size sculptures shows expedition members and Nez Percé moving along the trail, walking and mounted on horses. On the south side of the Clearwater Memorial Bridge are three life-size bronze statues depicting Lewis and Clark in conversation with Sacagawea and her son. Lewiston Community Center | 1424 Main St. | 208/746–2313 | Free | Daily.

Lower Granite Lock and Dam. A visitor center at this dam constructed in 1975 has interactive displays and guided tours. The dam created 8,900-acre Lower Granite Lake, with 91 mi of shoreline. | Lower Deadman Creek Rd., off Rte. 127 | c/o U.S. Army Corps of Engineers, 100 Fair St., Clarkston, WA 99403-1943 | 509/751–0240 | www.nww.usace.army.mil/corpsoutdoors/lla/lglist. htm | Daily 8–5.

Nez Percé County Museum. Exhibits at this museum operated by the Nez Percé County Historical Society document changes in the area from the days of the Nez Percé and the arrival of Lewis and Clark through the 20th century. There are many colorful artifacts and replicas, maps, pictures, and narratives as well as hands-on activities for children. | 306 3rd St. | 208/743–2535 | By donation | Mar.–mid-Dec., Tues.–Sat. 10–4.

Nez Percé National Historical Park–Spalding Site. The peoples that Lewis and Clark knew as the Nez Percé, who called themselves the Nimiipu ("the people"), inhabited the prairies and plateaus of north-central Idaho, northeastern Oregon, and southeastern Washington for thousands of years. This site, which has 38 sites in Idaho, Montana, Oregon, and Washington, interprets the tribe's culture and history; there is plenty about interactions of the members of the tribe with Lewis and Clark and about the tragic War of 1877. At the Spalding visitor center, 11 mi east of Lewiston, you can study interpretive exhibits and audiovisual programs and attend daily ranger talks in summer. | 39063 U.S. 95, Spalding | 208/843–2261 | www.nps.gov/nepe | By donation | June–Sept., daily 8–5:30; Oct.–May, daily 8–4:30.

Nez Percé Wolf Education and Research Center. Here you can learn about gray wolves at a visitor center and on short guided tours. Lewis and Clark journals reported seeing six wolves in the area when they were here. Tours are by reservation only. | 111 Main St., Suite 150 | 208/743–9554 | www.wolfcenter. org | $3, guided tour $10 | June–Sept., daily 9–5; Oct.–May, variable hrs.

Winchester Lake State Park. Ponderosa pine and Douglas fir surround the 103-acre lake at this 480-acre park at 3,900 feet at the base of the Craig Mountains. You can camp, hike, and picnic in summer and in winter cross-country ski, ice-skate, and fish. Trails skirt the lake; keep an eye peeled for white-tailed deer, beavers, raccoons, muskrats, and painted turtles. There is a campground; it's also fun to spend the night in one of the park's domed, circular tents known as yurts, which sleep five and are sited among the pines lakeside; they come with bunk beds, futons, a table, and benches. | Off U.S. 95 near Winchester | 208/924–7563 | www.idahoparks.org | $2 | Daily.

✦ ON THE CALENDAR

June **Chief Joseph & Lawyer Pow-wow.** Past and present warriors are honored at this annual powwow, where you can see dance exhibitions, participate in group dances, socialize, and feast. | 208/843–2253 | www.nezperce.org.

June **Lewis and Clark Discovery Faire.** Costumed reenactors portraying figures in the Lewis and Clark story stroll the grounds of this event while Nez Percé storytellers, drummers, and dancers showcase the rich culture that the explorers would have encountered when they arrived in the area two centuries ago. The encampment is re-created, and there's plenty of good, hearty western food. | 208/743–3531.

June **Lewis and Clark Annual Symposium.** Scholars and Nez Percé present research findings related to the Corps of Discovery and and the tribe. Preregistration is required. | 208/792–2282 | www.lcsc.edu/cp/symposium.htm.3.

HISTORIC DINING AND LODGING

Bojack's Broiler Pit. American. At this small restaurant in Morgan's Alley, casual dining and good food are the order of the day. Prime rib and shrimp salad are house favorites. | 311 Main St. | 208/746–9532 | $9–$17 | AE, D, DC, MC, V | Closed Sun.

Jonathan's. Contemporary. Northwest-inspired dishes such as bite-size steak tips sauced with wild mushrooms and salmon with lemon-caper sauce top the menu choices here, and the artisan breads are delicious. You can sit indoors or outside on the patio. | 1516 Main St. | 208/746–3438 | $16–$30 | AE, MC, V.

Meriwether's Restaurant. Contemporary. This restaurant in the Red Lion Hotel serves local favorites such as Indian salmon and Palouse potatoes. Beers and ales, brewed by the restaurant, are named after the region's plants and produce. | 621 21st St. | 208/746–9390 | $5–$23 | AE, MC, V.

Getting Acquainted with the Nez Percé

Although Lewis and Clark often missed opportunities to observe and ask questions, thus failing to capture the depth of Nez Percé society, customs, and institutions, their journals are rich with information about the Nez Percé people and the country in which they lived. They describe daily life, hunting tactics, clothing, food preparation, customs, games, and even the practice of selectively breeding their horses. But a superficial reading of the journals fails to catch the nuances of cultural exchange shared by the Nez Percé people and expedition members during their stay at Long Camp.

The native people did not miss an opportunity to better acquaint themselves with their guests. They were especially taken by York; they liked to watch him dance and were intrigued by his stature, strength, and good looks. York is said to have fathered two children, one who died at birth and a son who grew to adulthood and has numerous descendants in the tribe today. Members of the tribe also liked to watch their other visitors dance; their style was so unlike that of traditional Nez Percé dance. The two cultures freely and joyously entertained each other with their music, dance, and games.

Clark earned the reputation as a doctor while caring for an eye ailment that plagued a number of the people the preceding fall. When word spread he was back, people came from throughout Nez Percé country for his help. Although the journals convey his feelings of inadequacy as a doctor, he nevertheless administered sulfur, cream of tartar, laudanum, and portable soup to the best of his abilities, with remarkable success. The people liked Clark's caring ways and amicable personality and remembered him fondly for generations. Clark also married into the tribe. Nez Percé tradition claims his wife traveled as far as Deer Lodge, Montana, with him when they left the country. She bore him a son, a brown-haired boy named Clark with "eyes like sky." He lived to adulthood and left many descendants. Ironically, he died as a prisoner of war in Oklahoma after the 1877 Nez Percé War.

Lewis played the role of a diplomat. Although he was not remembered as fondly as Clark, he was respected. His biggest diplomatic coup was when, as Jefferson had ordered, he negotiated with the tribes to welcome future American fur posts. He got it. The council concluded with feasting, singing, dancing, gambling, smoking, games, and gift giving. And the tribes remained true to their promise.

Sacagawea Select Inn. The proprietor's enthusiasm for regional history, especially the Lewis and Clark expedition, is apparent at this motel and at the Helm Restaurant next door. Rooms are clean and the setting quiet—you're 1½ mi from Interstate 15, close to downtown. Continental breakfast is complimentary. Restaurant, refrigerators, cable TV, pool, hot tub, exercise equipment, bar, laundry facilities, airport shuttle, some pets allowed. | 1824 Main St., 83501 | 208/746–1393 or 800/333–1393 | fax 208/746–3625 | 90 rooms | $50 | AE, D, DC, MC, V.

Washington and Oregon

The Columbia River serves as most of the border between Washington and Oregon. When the Corps of Discovery entered the river in October 1805, they encountered a violent river with rapids, chutes, waterfalls, and at its mouth, the Pacific Ocean. The state introductions that follow detail the history of their time in the area. Today's route passes through towns and cities, many of which include sites that provide a sense of the land and river the Corps of Discovery experienced as well as museums, monuments, and scenic overlooks. Driving tours for each state show you the way.

Washington

In the quiet of a fall morning as dark clouds of Canada geese rise from the Columbia River lowlands and cool fog rolls in off the Washington coast, it is not hard to imagine this place 200 years ago. The smell of sage after a summer thunderstorm rolls across the Columbia Plateau of eastern Washington's wide, open steppe country is no different now than it was when Lewis and Clark trekked across the landscape in 1805 and 1806. Take a drive following Lewis and Clark's pathway across Washington State and you will find yourself immersed in the past. Unlike the crowded "Pugetopolis" of Seattle up north, much of Lewis and Clark territory in eastern and southwestern Washington remains rural and rugged. The Columbia River divides Oregon and Washington along about two-thirds of the state's north–south borders all the way to the ocean.

Lewis and Clark entered Washington near present-day Clarkston in October 1805, paddling down the Clearwater River toward the Snake River and finally to the Columbia. The Great Columbian Plain was a sharp contrast to the densely forested mountains the party had just crossed. Thanks to their Nez Percé guides, Chief Twisted Hair and Chief Tetoharsky, the Corps passed through the extensive lands of the Nez Percé nation extending into eastern Washington without incident—and without getting lost. The chiefs accompanied the party all the way to the Columbia River Gorge. The presence of Sacagawea also served them well as they crossed into new tribal areas. As Clark wrote, "A woman with a party of men is a token of peace."

On October 16, the explorers reached the point where the Snake River joins the Columbia, set up camp, and introduced themselves to the local Native Americans. "After we had our camp fixed and fires made, a chief came up from this camp, which was about ¼ of a mile up the Columbia River, at the head of about 200 men singing and beating on their drums and keeping time to the music. They formed a half-circle around us and sang for some time. We gave them all smoke, and spoke to their chief as well as we could by signs," wrote Clark, describing the scene. At this camp, now Sacajawea State Park near present-day Pasco, the party traded metal items like thimbles and knitting needles for Indian dogs, which were preferred for meat—much more convenient than sending out a hunting party.

On October 23 Twisted Hair told Lewis and Clark they had entered Chinookan Indian territory. He also told them that the Nez Percé were at war with the Chinook and that Chinook farther downstream planned to ambush the party. They made defensive preparations, but the attack never came. Several days later, as members of the expedition rested up on the Oregon side of the river near The Dalles after navigating some of the Columbia's fiercest rapids, two Chinookian chiefs and 15 others paddled across the river from the Washington side, bringing gifts of deer meat and cakes of bread. Lewis and Clark, in turn, presented the Chinook with medals and trinkets.

Entering the present-day Columbia River Gorge National Scenic Area, the party made its way past Celilo, Oregon, and Wishram, Washington, where the Columbia turned violent, careening through the gorge in a series of enormous rapids, chutes, and huge waterfalls. Inhabited by Native Americans who had lived here continuously for more than 10,000 years, this section of the gorge was on trade routes that extended from the Pacific to the Great Plains and from Alaska to California. As they passed through the area, Lewis and Clark witnessed a rich culture that would soon be decimated by disease and relocation.

"The water passing with great velocity forming & boiling in a most horrible manner," wrote Clark near the Cascades of the Columbia at present-day Stevenson, Washington, and Cascade Locks, Oregon. In Stevenson, just across the Bridge of the Gods from Cascade Locks, is the Columbia River Gorge Interpretive Center. The museum tells the story of the gorge with interpretive exhibits on everything from natural history to Lewis and Clark and later settlements.

On November 1 and 2 the party navigated the last of the gorge rapids and emerged near a large monolith that Lewis and Clark referred to alternatively as "Beaten" and "Beacon" Rock. Today this ancient volcano looks much the same as it probably did in 1805. At Beacon Rock State Park, if you're intrepid, you can climb the rock via a steep trail for stunning views of the gorge. It was here that the captains first noticed tidal influences in the river, indicating that the Pacific Ocean was not far off.

Now past the gorge rapids, the party made swift progress down the Columbia, paddling 30 mi or more per day. Emerging out of the western edge of the gorge, the Corps discovered another world. The western gorge and lower Columbia are wet, mossy, lush, and green, filled with waterfalls, vast estuaries, and the perennially damp temperate rain forests—a jungle indeed compared with arid eastern Washington. Lewis and Clark remarked that migrating waterfowl darkened the skies, fog blanketed the now wide river each morning, and the rain had begun to fall. On November 5, 1805, "a cool, cloudy morning," the party passed the area that is now Vancouver, the state's fourth-largest city. As the Columbia River flattened out, with the rapids behind them, the explorers thought the worst was over. But the most harrowing part of the journey lay ahead. The Columbia was about to unleash its winter fury on the travelers.

It was in present-day Washington that Clark wrote his famous words, "Ocian in view. O! the joy." on November 7, 1805. This ocean was really the Columbia's large estuary. It would be days before they actually saw surf. Soon after the joyful journal entry, storm after storm rolled over the river. The entire party was pinned down, and violent waves swamped the canoes and made it impossible both to move forward and to retreat. On November 12 Clark wrote, "Our party has been wet for . . . 8 days and . . . their robes & leather Clothes are rotten from being Continually wet, and they are not in a Situation to get others, and we are not in a Situation to restore them."

The explorers continued battling storms and remained in Washington until the end of November, at which time they moved their camp inland and built Fort Clatsop near present-day Astoria, Oregon. Yet despite the misery, there was joy in camp. After two years and more than 4,000 mi of travel, Lewis and Clark had accomplished what President Jefferson had ordered. The Pacific Ocean lay at their feet.

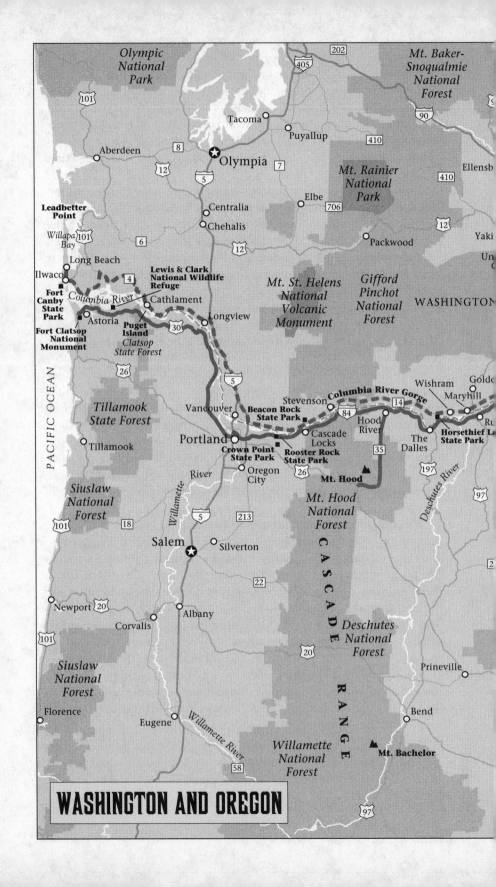

WASHINGTON AND OREGON

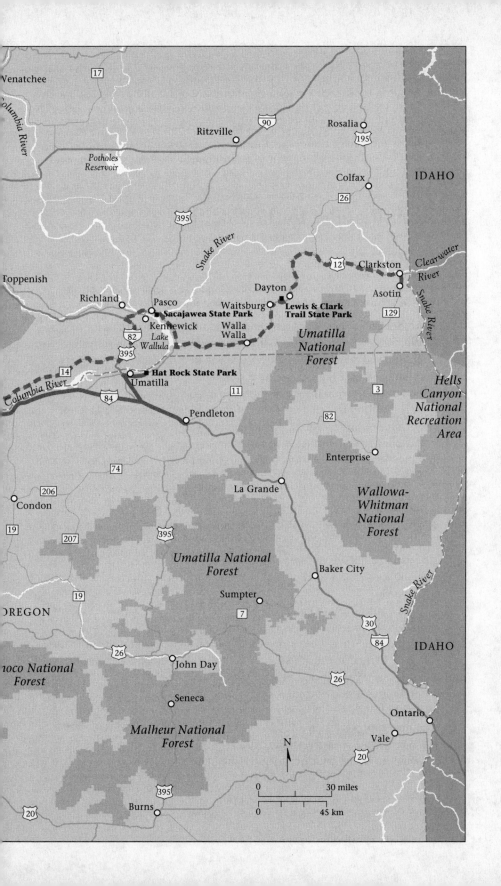

On their return trip in 1806, instead of portaging around difficult Snake River rapids, the expedition followed the advice of a Wallula chief and took an ancient overland shortcut back to the Clearwater River and the western end of the Lolo Trail along Indian paths near present-day Walla Walla. The explorers must have been eager to get home—after thousands of miles of travel, they remarked joyfully in journals that the shortcut saved them 80 precious mi.

From Plateau to the Pacific

A DRIVING TOUR FROM CLARKSTON TO ILWACO

▼▼▼

Distance: Approx. 453 mi   **Time:** 3–4 days
Breaks: Walla Walla, Stevenson, Ilwaco, and Long Beach are all good choices for dining and overnight stays. Spend some time strolling around downtown Walla Walla.

Accompanied by their Nez Percé guides and Chief Twisted Hair, the Corps of Discovery explorers pressed on from their arduous journey over the Rocky Mountains and down the Snake River, finally entering Columbia River Gorge. They had reached the great river that would take them to the sea. This tour follows the route from the shrub-steppe near the Washington–Idaho border at Clarkston through eastern Washington farm country and the Columbia River Gorge to Ilwaco, where the Columbia meets the Pacific.

Day one begins in **Clarkston,** 66 mi east of Dayton off Route 129, just across the Snake River from Lewiston, Idaho—the first place where Lewis and Clark set foot in Washington State. The town sits on the confluence of the Clearwater and Snake rivers. Before you leave, stop at the Hells Canyon Resort Marina, where a Lewis and Clark time line is etched into 200 feet of sidewalk, detailing the explorers' journey from start to finish. Drive 6 mi southwest of Clarkston on Route 129 to the Asotin County Museum, where you can tour old buildings and see pioneer artifacts. Petroglyphs estimated at more than 500 years old are on cliffs near the town at Asotin at Buffalo Rock. Return to Clarkston.

From Clarkston, take Route 129 to U.S. 12 for 66 mi to **Dayton.** The route along U.S. 12 roughly follows that of the explorers on their return trip in spring of 1806, when they skirted the Snake on an overland shortcut to the Lolo Trail. In rural, tree-shaded Dayton, 83 buildings are on the National Register of Historic Places, including Washington's oldest courthouse and railroad depot, built in 1881. Five miles west of Dayton on U.S. 12, Lewis and Clark Trail State Park has kiosks and a mile-long interpretive trail. From the park, continue southwest 31 mi on U.S. 12 to the pioneer town of **Walla Walla,** which is near the site at the mouth of the Walla Walla River where Chief Yelleppit sent the Corps on an overland shortcut in April 1806. Tour the Fort

Walla Walla Museum for a look at 14 original and re-created pioneer buildings. Spend the night in Walla Walla.

On your second day, head northeast from Walla Walla on U.S. 12 about 50 mi to the Tri-Cities area of **Kennewick, Pasco,** and **Richland.** In October 1805, the Corps rested in the area that is now Sacajawea State Park, at the confluence of the Snake and Columbia rivers, exchanging gifts with local tribes and preparing for the long journey down the Columbia. The park's interpretive center houses Lewis and Clark displays and an exhibit of Native American tools. Pick up Route 14 here and head west 114 mi to Maryhill Museum of Art, in **Goldendale.** An official site on the trail, the museum sits high above the gorge and displays an eclectic mix of exhibits, including an extensive collection of Native American basketry. From here, continue west 8 mi to Wishram. Here, Celilo Falls once dominated the river, and the ancient trading site of Wishram Village was run by natives as part of what Lewis and Clark called the "great marts of trade" on the shores of the Columbia. At Exit 85 off Route 14 is Horsethief Lake State Park and National Historic Site. The park is famous for its ancient Indian petroglyphs, still visible where Native Americans carved them into the basalt. Rangers give tours of the glyphs from April to October. Continue west about 60 mi through the Columbia River Gorge, following the river to **Stevenson** and the nearby Columbia River Interpretive Center, where exhibits illustrate the geology and history of the region. Across the river at Cascade Locks, Oregon, the sternwheeler *Columbia Gorge* leads narrated tours up the Columbia River. Overnight here.

The next morning, day three, visit Beacon Rock State Park (about 8 mi west of Stevenson on Route 14), the site of a giant monolith that is actually the core of an ancient volcano. Hiking trails lead up the rock for excellent views of the gorge. Continue west on Route 14 about 50 mi to **Vancouver,** Washington's oldest city and the site of the Fort Vancouver National Historic Reserve. Lewis and Clark passed by what is now Vancouver in early November 1805. Just 19 years later, the British Hudson's Bay Company built Fort Vancouver as a trading post. Today, the National Park Service operates the reconstructed fort.

Take Interstate 5 north toward Longview. The interstate roughly follows the Columbia River to where it turns west again at Longview, about 40 mi north of Vancouver. At Longview, take Route 4 west until it becomes U.S. 101, near **Long Beach.** An old-fashioned boardwalk town, Long Beach sits at the southern end of a beachy, 28-mi-long peninsula. Lewis and Clark found themselves stranded in the area as storms lashed the coast and the mouth of the Columbia River in November 1805. The seas are so turbulent beneath the cliffs of Cape Disappointment, where the river meets the Pacific, that several early sea captains, including James Cook and George Vancouver, mistook the river's mouth for surf breaking on a wild shore. The mouth of the Columbia became known as "the graveyard of the Pacific." Overnight in Long Beach or nearby in **Ilwaco.**

On the morning of day four, head to the cliff-top Fort Canby Lewis and Clark Interpretive Center, which has a view of the Pacific, 2 mi southwest of Ilwaco off U.S. 101. Two lighthouses on the peninsula, one at Cape Disappointment and another at North Head (the third-windiest lighthouse area in the United States), are open to visitors. Spend the rest of the day on scenic U.S. 101, north along Willapa Bay. The rocky eastern shore of the bay south of the Naselle River estuary is one of the most scenic stretches of highway in Washington and looks much as it did when Lewis and Clark found themselves at the end of the trail.

CLARKSTON

▼▼

The Snake River meets the Columbia at Clarkston and its twin border city, Lewiston, Idaho. Lewis and Clark launched their final push down the Columbia to the Pacific here. A former ferry town, surrounded by grassy hills that are green in spring and golden in summer, Clarkston was founded in 1862 as a way station for travelers heading to the Idaho goldfields. Since then, a complex series of dams along the Snake has made Clarkston and Lewiston the West's most inland seaports. Clarkston is also Washington's gateway to North America's deepest river gorge, the Hells Canyon National Recreation Area, to the south in Oregon.

✦ INFORMATION
Clarkston Chamber of Commerce | 502 Bridge St., 99403 | 800/933–2128 | www.clarkstonchamber.org. **Hells Canyon Visitor Association** | 800 Port Dr., 99403 | 509/758–7489 | www.hellscanyonvisitor.com.

SITES TO SEE
Asotin County Museum. A superb collection of branding irons is the highlight of this small museum in the Asotin county seat, Asotin. You'll also find a few late-19th-century buildings moved here from nearby communities, including a blacksmith's forge set up in a log cabin. A half-dozen horse-drawn carriages and buckboards—the station wagons of the 19th century—also hint at frontier life in the area. | 215 Filmore St., Asotin, 3 mi south of Clarkston | 509/243–4659 | Free, donations accepted | Mar.–Oct., Tues.–Sat. 1–5; Nov.–Feb., Sat. 1–5.

Petroglyphs. These petroglyphs are more than 500 years old and both difficult to find and difficult to get to. Follow Route 129 south to Asotin. At the red flashing light go straight through on Route 29 (do not turn right toward Anatone). Follow the winding two-lane road along the river's edge to where the road turns into one lane. On the left side you will see a beach and rocks next to the road. Here you can view the petroglyphs. You can see others, except

Lewis and Clark Among the Nez Percé

As the Corps of Discovery emerged from the brutal march over the Continental Divide at the Bitterroot Mountains, starving and exhausted, the men came upon a Nez Percé village at Weippe Prairie, Idaho. It was here that Twisted Hair, the local headman, was presiding while Chief Broken Arm was away fighting the Shoshone. Twisted Hair provided Lewis and Clark with food and at Clark's request drew a map on elk skin to help the party gain its bearings. They were only 5 days from the Columbia River and just 10 to the great falls of the Columbia, where they were told a great trading center was located.

But soon, after gorging themselves on buffalo, dried salmon, and camas-root bread provided by the Nez Percé, nearly everyone in the party except Captain Clark became violently ill. Historian Steven Ambrose writes that these distressful days of illness could have easily been the expedition's last. "It would have been the work of a few moments only for the Nez Percé to kill the white men and take for themselves all the expedition's goods. Had the Indians done so, they would have come into possession of by far the biggest arsenal . . . west of the Mississippi River."

The Nez Percé, according to oral tradition, discussed this option but chose to spare the party. According to the expedition journals, a tribal elder, Wetxuuwiis—who had been captured by the Blackfeet, sold to a white trader, then found her way back home—said to her people, "These are the people who helped me. Do them no hurt."

After the Corps recovered from their illness, horses were branded and left with the Nez Percé to care for until spring. Twisted Hair, along with the Nez Percé chief Tetoharsky, accompanied the party to the Columbia River and into the Columbia River Gorge. On more than one occasion the chiefs went ahead of the group to assure Native Americans living along the river that the white explorers came in peace.

Living across more than 13 million acres in aboriginal territory that encompassed north-central Idaho, northeast Washington, far western Montana, and northeast Oregon, and rich in vast herds of horses, the Nez Percé tribe was one of the most powerful in the West at the time of Lewis and Clark. They had acquired horses from the Cayuse by the 1730s and had become expert equestrians. The horse expanded their wealth and territory and had opened trade routes into the Plains and the Columbia River Gorge. Before white settlement, about 6,000 Nez Percé lived in family groups throughout their territory and were related by the Sahaptin language to the Walla Walla, Yakima, and other Northwest tribes.

In the spring of 1806, Lewis and Clark returned to the Nez Percé and retrieved most of their horses and supplies. But the snow was too deep in the mountains to continue, so the Nez Percé and the explorers spent nearly a month together. For the most part, the interaction was pleasant, filled with talk of establishing trading posts in exchange for weapons, Clark providing his unique brand of medical care, and challenges of one another's equestrian skills with races and games (the Native Americans were by far the better horsemen). Only once did tension arise. On the night of May 5, 1806, around the campfire, a Nez Percé made fun of Lewis and Clark for eating dogs, which the Nez Percé never used for food. The Indian threw a "half starved puppy nearly into the plate of Capt. Lewis." Lewis tossed the puppy back, then picked up the man's tomahawk and threatened him with it. The game went no further.

during spring floods, near the town of Asotin at Buffalo Rock, a short distance above Buffalo Rapids near water level. | 14 mi south of Clarkston | 800/933–2128 | fax 509/751–8767 | www.clarkstonchamber.org | Free | Daily.

✦ ON THE CALENDAR
Sept. **Lewis and Clark Days.** This Labor Day event involves dugout-canoe carving, demonstrations of pioneering skills, living history, and boat rides in the city's Port District. | 509/758–3126 or 800/933–2128.

DAYTON
▼▼▼

In 1806, as they headed east on the Nez Percé Trail toward the Continental Divide, Lewis and Clark walked the land that would become Dayton's main street. In 1880 Dayton claimed the first public grade school in what was then the Oregon Territory. Today in this tidy town, 117 buildings are listed on the National Register of Historic Places, including the state's oldest railroad depot and courthouse. At the 80-year-old Dingles of Dayton general store, the motto is, "If you can't find it at Dingles, you don't need it."

♦ INFORMATION
Dayton Chamber of Commerce | Box 22, 166 E. Main St., 99328 | 509/382–4825 or 800/882–6299 | www.historicdayton.com.

SITES TO SEE

Dayton Historic Depot. Built in 1881, this is Washington's oldest surviving railroad depot. Originally built a few blocks away, it was lifted onto giant logs and pulled by horses to its current location in 1899. Today it houses a museum with exhibits illustrating the history of Dayton and nearby communities. | 222 Commercial St. | 509/382–2026 | $2 | Nov.–Mar., Tues.–Sat. 11–4; Apr.–Oct., Tues.–Sat. 10–5.

Lewis and Clark Trail State Park. A rare old-growth forest and the Touchet River are the main features of this part of the Nez Percé National Historic Trail between Waitsburg and Dayton. You'll find many outdoor activities, including camping, hiking, and fishing. Lewis and Clark living-history programs are held every Saturday at 8 PM between Memorial Day and Labor Day. Topics include history, botany, animals, and astronomy. | U.S. 12, 10 mi west of Dayton | 509/337–6457 or 800/233–0321 | www.parks.wa.gov | Free | Daily.

♦ ON THE CALENDAR

Sept. Dayton's Depot Days. Held on the third Saturday in September at the Dayton Historic Depot, this celebration of railroad history includes model railroad exhibits, railroad memorabilia and artifacts, and bumper-car rides. | 509/382–2026 or 800/882–6299.

Oct. Historical Home Tours. On the second Sunday of October, the Dayton Historical Depot Society leads guided tours of a few of the more than 100 19th- and early-20th-century buildings in town on the National Register of Historic Places. Self-guided walking-tour maps of three National Historic Districts are available throughout the year at the Chamber of Commerce. | 509/382–2026 or 800/882–6299.

HISTORIC DINING AND LODGING

Weinhard Café. Contemporary. This restaurant in a former pharmacy next to the Weinhard Hotel, built in the 1890s, serves modern cuisine that relies heavily on fish, poultry, and local ingredients such as Walla Walla onions and Palouse grains. | 229 E. Main St. | 509/382–1681 | www.weinhard-cafe.com | Closed Sun. and Mon. | $17.95–$22.95 | AE, D, MC, V.

Purple House Bed and Breakfast. This Italianate-style house built by a pioneer physician in 1882 is decorated with European art and Chinese collectibles; bedrooms are individually appointed with Victorian antiques. Afternoon pastries and tea are presented in the parlor. Pool, some pets allowed; no kids under 16,

no smoking. | 415 Clay St., 99328 | 509/382–3159 or 800/486–2574 |
fax 509/382–3159 | 4 rooms | $85–$125 | MC, V.

Weinhard Hotel. Once the Weinhard Lodgehall and Saloon, this lavishly reno-
vated 1896 building is done up in full Victorian style, with plenty of red velvet,
fancy wallpaper, mahogany furniture, and glittering chandeliers. All 15 of the
smallish rooms are furnished entirely in Victorian antiques. Restaurant, in-
room data ports, cable TV. | 235 E. Main St., 99328 | 509/382–4032 |
fax 509/382–2640 | www.weinhard.com | 15 rooms | $75–$150 | DC, MC, V.

WALLA WALLA
▼▼

On the way back east, the Corps of Discovery traveled by Walla Walla when
it took a shortcut overland in an attempt to avoid the Snake River's treacherous rapids and shave a precious 80 mi off the journey. This delightful town,
founded in the 1850s on the site of a Nez Percé village, was Washington's
first metropolis. As late as the 1880s, its population was larger than that of
Seattle. Walla Walla occupies a lush green valley below the rugged Blue
Mountains. It has a beautifully maintained (and partly restored) downtown,
with many 19th- and early-20th-century residences, green parks, and the
campus of Whitman College, Washington's oldest institution of higher learning, chartered in 1859.

✦ INFORMATION
Downtown Walla Walla Foundation | 33 E. Main St., No. 213, 99362 | 509/529–
8755 | www.downtownwallawalla.com. **Walla Walla Area Chamber of Commerce** |
Box 644, 29 E. Sumach, 99362 | 509/525–0850 or 877/998–4748 | www.
wwchamber.com.

SITES TO SEE
Fort Walla Walla Park. This former U.S. Army fort was in use from 1858 to
1910. The 15-acre park on the site has picnic tables, a campground, a museum,
and an old military cemetery. | Dalles Military Rd. | 509/527–3772 | fax 509/
525–0845 | www.ci.walla-walla.wa.us | Free | Daily.

Fort Walla Walla Museum. The Fort Walla Walla Museum occupies 14 historic
or reconstructed log buildings and a new museum headquarters building.
Exhibits include a remarkable 19th-century combine drawn by a team of 33
mules, demonstrated on weekends in summer and on Sunday in April, May,
September, and October. Other living-history demonstrations are held every
Sunday and on weekends from June through August. | 755 Myra Rd., at
Dalles Military and Myra Rds., west of Walla Walla | 509/525–7703 | www.
fortwallawallamuseum.org | $6 | Apr.–Oct., daily 10–5.

Whitman Mission National Historic Site. In 1836 Dr. Marcus Whitman and his wife, Narcissa, established a Presbyterian mission for the Cayuse tribe at Waiilatpu ("place of the people of the rye grass"), 7 mi west of present-day Walla Walla. Mrs. Whitman and her fellow missionary, Eliza Spalding, were the first white women to cross the Rocky Mountains. Their trip inspired others and helped lead to the creation of the Oregon Trail a few years later. The Waiilatpu Mission became a vital station on the Oregon Trail for the sick and hungry. But tensions quickly arose between the missionaries and the Cayuse over land usage and cultural practices. In addition, a devastating measles outbreak in fall 1847 killed half of the Waiilatpu band of the Cayuse. Some of the Cayuse blamed these deaths on Dr. Whitman and retaliated by killing him, his wife, and 11 others. They also took 60 hostages, who were held at the site for about a month before the Hudson's Bay Company paid a ransom to free them. An exhibit building at the Whitman Mission National Historic Site includes a 10-minute introductory slide show, a model of what the mission looked like in 1847, life-size figures showing characters in period dress, and some of the Whitmans' belongings, including Marcus Whitman's Bible. In the surrounding park, you'll find the foundations of the mission buildings, the mass grave, and an 1897 monument to the Whitmans. | 328 Whitman Mission Rd. | 509/522–6360 or 509/529–2761 | www.nps.gov/whmi | Entrance fee varies | Daily.

✦ ON THE CALENDAR
June **Lewis and Clark Days.** Held at the Fort Walla Walla Museum, the festival includes demonstrations and reenactments of 19th-century frontier activities and events, including the Lewis and Clark expedition, 19th-century U. S. military encampments, and the battles at Steptoe Butte and Spokane Plains. | 509/525–7703.

HISTORIC DINING AND LODGING
The Marc. Contemporary. A mural of the Blue Mountains on the back wall of this restaurant in the historic Marcus Whitman Hotel makes an attractive backdrop to this serene room. Start the day with corned beef hash. For dinner, try a steak—the rib-eye Delmonico with fresh rosemary is delicious. The extensive wine list includes many local wines. | 6 W. Rose St. | 509/525–2200 | www.marcuswhitmanhotel.com | $15–$22 | AE, D, MC, V.

Whitehouse-Crawford Restaurant. Contemporary. Housed inside a historic building that was once a planing mill, this downtown eatery uses only fresh, seasonal ingredients in its Northwest cuisine. The building also houses the Seven Hills Winery production facility and a tasting room. The duck entrée is a must in season. | 55 W. Cherry St. | 509/525–2222 | Closed Mon. and Tues. | $12–$32 | AE, D, MC, V.

Green Gables Inn. One block from the Whitman campus, this 1909 Arts and Crafts–style mansion sits among flowering plants and shrubs on a quaint, tree-lined street. Rooms, named for bits from Lucy Maud Montgomery's novel *Anne of Green Gables,* are furnished with Victorian antiques. Refrigerators, in-room hot tubs, cable TV, in-room VCRs; no smoking. | 922 Bonsella St., 99362 | 509/525–5501 | www.greengablesinn.com | 4 rooms, 2 suites | $115–$145 | AE, D, MC, V.

Inn at Blackberry Creek. A restored 1912 Victorian farmhouse, the Inn at Blackberry Creek oozes with period charm. The inn is within walking distance of the city's historic Pioneer Park. Refrigerators; no smoking. | 1126 Pleasant St., 99362 | 509/522–5233 or 877/522–5233 | www.innatblackberrycreek.com | 3 rooms | $89–$126 | BP | AE, D, MC, V.

Marcus Whitman Hotel and Conference Center. This 1928 hotel within walking distance of local attractions has quickly become the crown jewel of downtown Walla Walla. Most rooms have Renaissance-style Italian furnishings, with king-size beds or two queens. Restaurant, in-room data ports, cable TV, gym, bar, shops, business services, airport shuttle. | 6 W. Rose St., 99362 | 509/525–2200 or 866/826–9422 | fax 509/524–1747 | www.marcuswhitmanhotel.com | 75 rooms, 16 suites | $119–$279 | AE, D, MC, V.

Mill Creek Inn. Twenty-two acres of gardens, a creek, and vineyards surround this turn-of-the-20th-century farm with viewful guest cottages and suites. Each cottage and suite comes with homey touches—board games, books, magazines, and hand-knit afghans. A short drive takes you to downtown Walla Walla. No smoking. | 2014 Mill Creek Rd., 99362 | 509/522–1234 | www.millcreekbb.com | 3 rooms | $155–$205 | AE, MC, V | BP.

KENNEWICK

▼▼

Yakima Indians built winter villages here, at the confluence of the Columbia and the Yakima, long before Lewis and Clark, the first explorers to visit the region, arrived in fall 1805 and spring 1806. Kennewick ("grassy place") has evolved from a railroad town to a farm-supply center, a bedroom community for workers from nearby Richland, and a food-processing capital of the Columbia Basin. The climate is more mild here than in other parts of eastern Washington.

◆ INFORMATION
Tri-Cities Visitor and Convention Bureau | 6951 W. Grandridge Blvd., 99302 | 800/254–5824 | visittri-cities.com.

SITES TO SEE

Sacajawea Heritage Trail. This 22-mi walking and biking trail loops along the Columbia River shore through Richland, Pasco, and Kennewick. There are interpretive signs through the area's shrub-steppe habitat. The trail has access points all along the route, including Marina Park in Richland, Chiawana Park in Pasco, and Columbia Park in Kennewick. Contact the Tri-Cities Visitor and Convention Bureau for a trail map. | Marina Park is off Columbia Point Dr. in Richland; Chiawana Park is off Court St. in Pasco; and Columbia Park is off Columbia Trail Park Rd. in Kennewick | 800/254–5824 | visittri-cities.com | Free | Daily.

Two Rivers Park. You'll find this park on the west bank of the Columbia. Lake Wallula, named after the tribe that helped Lewis and Clark find an overland shortcut back to the Lolo Trail, is across from the mouth of the Snake River, north of Wallula Gap. The park has a boat ramp, swimming beach, and picnic tables. | U.S. 397, left on Finley Rd. | 509/783–3118 | Free | Daily.

PASCO

▼▼

Tree-shaded Pasco, a college town and the county seat of Franklin County, is an oasis of green on the Columbia River. The Corps camped near here in 1805 and spent time trading with the area's Native Americans. The neoclassic Franklin County Courthouse (1907) is worth a visit for its fine marble interior. You can sample the bounty of local produce at the Pasco Farmers' Market, held downtown every Saturday during the growing season. The Pasco Basin, the nearby Snake River benchlands, and the Yakima Valley to the west have first-rate vineyards and wineries. The town, which started as a railroad switchyard, now has a busy container port from which barges carry wheat, fuel, hay, and other resources down the Columbia River to be shipped over the Pacific.

✦ INFORMATION

Tri-Cities Visitor and Convention Bureau | 6951 W. Grandridge Blvd., Kennewick, 99302 | 800/254–5824 | visittri-cities.com.

SITES TO SEE

Franklin County Historical Museum. Once the Pasco Carnegie Library, built in 1910 as part of Andrew Carnegie's worldwide library construction program, this museum houses Native American artifacts such as hand-carved canoes and salmon gaffs—the long poles Native Americans used to hook migrating salmon out of the Columbia. Exhibits on the railroad and on homesteading in the 19th century are also of interest. | 305 N. 4th Ave. | 509/547–3714 | Free, donations accepted | Tues.–Sat. noon–4.

Sacajawea State Park. This 284-acre park, at the confluence of the Snake and Columbia rivers, is named for the Shoshone woman who helped guide Lewis and Clark over the Rocky Mountains and down the Snake River in 1805. The park includes one of the campsites used by Lewis and Clark October 16–18, 1805. The interpretive center has information about the expedition and a large display of Native American tools. Check out the explanations about the interaction of the explorers with Native American inhabitants. | 2503 Sacajawea Park Rd. | 509/545–2361 | Free | Late Mar.–late Oct., daily dawn–dusk.

✦ ON THE CALENDAR

Oct. **Heritage Day.** Held at the Lewis and Clark campsite at Pasco's Sacajawea State Park, this event commemorates the expedition's joyful arrival at the confluence of the Snake and Columbia rivers. Living-history presentations, entertainment, Native American storytellers, skills demonstrations, and nature walks are all on the activities schedule. | 800/254–5824 | www.visittri-cities.com.

RICHLAND
▼▼

Richland, founded in the 1880s, is the gateway to the Hanford Reach National Monument, the last free-flowing stretch of the Columbia River in the United States. This is the farthest point up the river recorded by the Corps. Tourboat excursions on the Columbia leave from Richmond.

✦ INFORMATION

Tri-Cities Visitor and Convention Bureau | 6951 W. Grandridge Blvd., Kennewick, 99302 | 800/254–5824 | visittri-cities.com.

SITES TO SEE

Columbia River Exhibition of History, Science, and Technology Museum. Also know as CREHST, this museum and interactive educational exhibit explores Columbia River history and geology, science, and technology and presents the culture and history of the region, including the story of Lewis and Clark's travels here. | 95 Lee Blvd. | 509/943–9000 | fax 509/943–1770 | www.crehst.org | $3.50 | Mon.–Sat. 10–5, Sun. noon–5.

Columbia River Journeys. Narrated three-hour Lewis and Clark cruises on the Columbia River take passengers upriver into the Hanford Reach National Monument. This part of the river is one of the last free-flowing stretches and the largest remaining remnant of the shrub-steppe ecosystem that dominated the region when Lewis and Clark made their journey west. | 1229 Columbia Park Trail, Box 26, 99352 | 509/734–9941 or 888/486–9119 | www.columbiariverjourneys.com | $30–$50 | May–mid-Oct.

Pacific Northwest Cuisine: Lewis and Clark Style

Even when chefs in the Pacific Northwest decide to get back to basics with a Corps of Discovery dining event, they don't quite get it right.

At one such occasion at a restaurant near Seattle, the extensive Northwest Passage Dinner menu consisted of "juniper-grilled Washington venison with Mount Olympus huckleberry sauce, nodding onions, and root vegetable gratin" finished off with "wild sorbets of salmonberry, wild ginger, elderflower, maple blossom, and Douglas fir in hazelnut snaps." Juniper-grilled venison with huckleberry sauce would not have figured in Lewis and Clark's wildest dreams, and they most certainly would have scoffed at anything having to do with a Douglas fir in their dessert.

Pacific Northwest fare as it truly was in 1805–1806 on the Lewis and Clark Trail was simple. Very simple. In fact, to truly savor the regional victuals of 200 years ago, a chef is hardly necessary. The Corps of Discovery practiced minimalist cooking at its best. Everything except the rotten elk meat the explorers were forced to eat during the long, lean winter at Fort Clatsop was fresh. Freshly killed, that is. And complexity of preparation was never an issue with their diet. It was strictly meat and wappato (a potatolike root). There were no sauces or condiments; no need to fuss with hand-harvested morels, delicate herbs, or those tricky fiddlehead ferns. The only flavoring to speak of was fine white sea salt boiled out of ocean water near Fort Clatsop.

The rough-and-ready explorers dined heartily on dogs bought from the Indians that were butchered and immediately roasted over the open fire (and preferred over salmon, which the party had grown weary of by the time they reached the Columbia River Gorge). At the coast, they ate boiled elk—lots of boiled elk—and, of course, those sumptuous wappato roots. The occasional waterfowl was a real treat, as was whale blubber (they traded for 300 pounds of it on the Oregon coast in January 1806 and consumed it in three weeks).

Captain Meriwether Lewis expressed a tastes-like-chicken philosophy when it came to trail food. After a meal of whale blubber in January 1806, he remarked, "The want of bread I consider as trivial provided, I get fat meat, for as to the species of meat I am not very particular, the flesh of the dog the horse the wolf, having from habit become equally formiliar with any other, and I have learned to think that if the chord be sufficiently strong, which binds the soul and boddy together, it dose not so much matter about the materials which compose it."

To complement the meal, the ever-perplexing question of red or white wine was never an issue. Having run out of whiskey in July 1805, the Corps drank spring water, river water, or rainwater. Too bad. A nice Washington Syrah would have done wonders for the roasted dog.

GOLDENDALE

▼▼

North of the Columbia River off of U.S. 14, Goldendale is the county seat of Klickitat County and the commercial center for area ranchers and farmers. The Goldendale area is a good jumping-off point for activities in the Columbia gorge on the Washington side of the river. The area is also important to Native American culture. The southern portion of Klickitat County in the vicinity of Celilo Falls marked the tribal barrier between the Chinookan Columbia River tribes and the inland Sahaptin-speaking tribes. First settled in 1872, Goldendale still projects an earthy, rural appearance with its tree-lined streets and old clapboard houses.

✦ INFORMATION
Greater Goldendale Area Chamber of Commerce | 131 W. Court St., 98620 | 509/773–3400 | klickitatcounty.org.

SITES TO SEE
Horsethief Lake State Park. Lewis and Clark set up camp here, almost directly across from where they navigated the chutes of the Columbia. The Dalles Dam created Horsethief Lake on the site. The park is famous for its petroglyphs; tours are given of the glyphs from April to October, Friday and Saturday at 10 AM. You must reserve ahead. The park is also popular for rock-climbing on Horsethief Butte, fishing, and wildlife viewing. Nearby is Wishram, for thousands of years a thriving trading village run by Chinookian tribes. | Rte. 14, milepost 85, 26 mi west of Goldendale | 509/767–1159 | www.parks.wa. gov | Free | Apr.–Oct., daily 6:30–dusk.

Klickitat County Historical Museum. This is a small but delightful museum with local Indian and pioneer artifacts. | 127 W. Broadway | 509/773–4303 | $3 | Apr.–Oct., daily 9–5; Nov.–Mar., by appointment.

Maryhill Museum of Art. Here's an oddity in the wilds of the Columbia River canyon: a first-rate museum with, among other objects, an excellent collection of Rodin sculptures. Built in the 1920s by railroad magnate Sam Hill, this faux Flemish château museum is on land visited by Lewis and Clark during their travels through the Columbia River Gorge. The Osage orange trees from among these now planted on the museum's extensive grounds were among the first plant items the explorers sent back to President Thomas Jefferson after they started their journey down the Missouri. The trees, native to the Midwest, were prized for their hardwood, which the Osage used for bow making. The bronze sculpture of Maryhill Museum founder Sam Hill was created by Alonzo Lewis, a descendant of Meriwether Lewis. The museum holds ongoing Lewis and Clark programs. Three miles east of the museum, just off U.S. 14, is a replica of Stonehenge, built by the original owner of Maryhill. | 35 Maryhill Museum Dr. | 509/773–3733 | fax 509/773–6138 | www. maryhillmuseum.org | $7 | Mid-Mar.–mid-Nov., daily 9–5.

HISTORIC LODGING

Inn of the White Salmon. This quiet, cozy, two-story brick hostelry was built in 1937. Antiques and original art adorn each room and the public areas. Cable TV, hot tub, some pets allowed. | 172 W. Jewett, White Salmon, 98672 | 509/493–2335 or 800/972–5226 | www.innofthewhitesalmon.com | 16 rooms | $106–$143 | AE, D, DC, MC, V | BP.

STEVENSON
▼▼

Once a major fishing town and now the Skamania County seat, Stevenson is a hillside village on the riverfront overlooking the Columbia Gorge. It is in the Columbia River Gorge National Scenic Area and on the Lewis and Clark Trail. The Stevenson family of Missouri settled the town in 1880. The population swells in summer as windsurfers flock to the area.

✦ INFORMATION

Skamania County Chamber of Commerce | 167 N.W. 2nd St., 98648 | 800/989–9178 | www.skamania.org.

SITES TO SEE

Beacon Rock State Park. It was at Beacon Rock, the core of an ancient volcano that was named by Lewis and Clark, that the explorers first noticed tidal influences in the river. The 4,650-acre park has camping and 9,500 feet of freshwater shoreline on the river. You can climb the rock via a steep trail for amazing views of the Columbia River Gorge. | Rte. 14, 35 mi east of Vancouver | 360/902–8608 | www.parks.wa.gov | Free | Summer, daily 8 AM–10 PM; winter, daily 8–5.

Columbia Gorge Interpretive Center. Dwarfed by the dramatic basalt cliffs that rise behind it, this museum stands on the north bank of the Columbia River Gorge, 1 mi east of Bridge of the Gods on Route 14. Exhibits illustrate the geology and history of the region. Among the many artifacts are a Native American pit house, dip nets used for hunting salmon, a replica of a fish wheel, and a mechanical contraption that automatically scooped salmon from the river (they were outlawed in 1935 because they were too efficient and took too many fish). Other artifacts pertain to Lewis and Clark and other explorers as well as missionaries, pioneers, and soldiers who have passed through the gorge. | 990 S.W. Rock Creek Dr. | 509/427–8211 or 800/991–2338 | $6 | Daily 10–5.

VANCOUVER

▼▼

The site of this now-sprawling river town was discovered in 1792 by a British explorer, Lieutenant William Broughton, who named it for his commander, Captain George Vancouver. Lewis and Clark camped here in 1806, and in 1825 Vancouver became the center of fur trade for the Hudson's Bay Company and the base from which the British managed the Oregon Territory. It soon became the frontier metropolis of the Pacific Northwest, dominating the fur trade for more than two decades. The U.S. Army built a fort on the bluff above the Hudson's Bay post when Oregon Territory fell to the United States in 1846. Ulysses S. Grant, who would later become the 18th president of the United States, briefly served as quartermaster of Fort Vancouver.

✦ **INFORMATION**
Greater Vancouver Chamber of Commerce | 1101 Broadway, Suite 120, 98663 | 360/694–2588 | fax 360/693–8279 | www.vancouverusa.com. **Southwest Washington Visitor and Convention Bureau** | O. O. Howard House, 750 Anderson St., 98663 | 877/600–0800 | fax 360/693–8279 | www.southwestwashington.com.

SITES TO SEE
Clark County Historical Museum. This museum and interpretive center in the former Carnegie Library building (built in 1909) houses Chinook artifacts, reproductions of an 1890 country store and 1900 doctor's office, and a Lewis and Clark reading room. | 1511 Main St. | 360/695–4681 | Free | Tues.–Sat. 11–4.

Fort Vancouver National Historic Reserve. This splendidly reconstructed fort, with squared-log buildings, an encircling palisade, and corner bastions, was first established by the Hudson's Bay Company in 1825 and served as the western headquarters of the company's fur-trading operations. The expedition stayed here in 1805, before the fort was established, but park rangers point out the areas described in the journals. Dressed in period costume, they also demonstrate various pioneer skills ranging from carpentry to baking to sewing. | 1501 E. Evergreen Blvd. | 360/696–7655 | www.nps.gov | Free | Daily.

Officers' Row. One of Vancouver's treasures, Officers' Row is composed of 21 stately homes built between 1867 and 1906. Ulysses S. Grant lived in the 1849 log building now bearing his name when he was quartermaster of Vancouver Barracks from 1852 to 1853. Today the Grant House displays historical artifacts and hosts a folk art center. You can also tour homes that once belonged to General George C. Marshall and General O. O. Howard. | 750 Anderson St. | 360/693–3103 | fax 360/693–3192 or 360/992–1820 | Free | Daily 9–5.

Pearson Air Museum. Vintage aircraft in working order are on display at Pearson Field, the oldest continuously operating air field in the West. The museum also has hands-on children's displays and historical exhibits. | 1115 E. 5th St. | 360/694–7026 | fax 360/694–0824 | www.pearsonairmuseum.org | $5 | Tues.–Sun. 10–5.

Waterfront Renaissance Trail. You can bike, skate, jog, or stroll this 4-mi trail alongside the Columbia River. Along the way, be sure to visit the Old Apple Tree, the first of Washington's apple trees, and stop to enjoy the scenic vistas. The trail passes by the Captain Vancouver Monument and a plaza dedicated to Ilchee, a Chinook chief's daughter. | 100 Columbia Way | 360/619–1111.

HISTORIC LODGING

Vintage Inn. This 1903 Craftsman-style mansion turned B&B contains so many antiques that it almost qualifies as a small museum. It was originally owned by Alfred C. Chumasero, believed to be the first Filipino-American to live in the state of Washington. It's truly charming with comfortable and well-appointed rooms. No room phones, no room TVs, no smoking. | 310 W. 11th St., 98660 | 360/693–6635 or 888/693–6635 | www.vintage-inn.com | 4 rooms without bath | $85 | MC, V | BP.

CATHLAMET

▼▼▼

The houses of Cathlamet, the county seat of tiny Wahkiakum County, rise on a hillside above the Cathlamet Channel of the Columbia River. After Lewis and Clark passed through in 1805, the town began in 1846 as the trading post of James Birnie, a retired Hudson's Bay Company trader, just above a Chinook village in Elochoman Slough, west of town. The first salmon cannery on the lower Columbia opened here in 1866; a cannery on the Cathlamet waterfront followed in 1869. The huge riverfront sheds survive and serve as net and boat storage. Cathlamet has several houses from this early period, including one built by James Birdie in 1857. Until the last logging camp in Wahkiakum County was closed in 1859, logging also served as a mainstay of the local economy. Today Cathlamet serves as a shopping center for nearby farmers. A bridge connects Cathlamet to Puget Island in the Columbia. The only remaining Columbia River ferry connects the island to Oregon— the jaunt across the river is short but fun.

✦ INFORMATION
Long Beach Peninsula Visitor's Bureau | Box 562, Long Beach, 98631 | 800/ 451–2542 | funbeach.com. **Lower Columbia Economic Development Council** | Box 98, Steam Flough Rd., Skamakowa, 98647 | 360/795–3996.

SITES TO SEE
River Life Interpretive Center. Celebrating life on the Columbia through art and visual displays, the center is housed in Redmen Hall, a restored 1894 schoolhouse. Historic photographs and pioneer and Native American artifacts document settlement in river country from 1835 to 1930. | Rte. 4, Skamokawa | 360/795–3007 | Free | Wed.–Sat. noon–4, Sun. 1–4.

Skamokawa Paddle Center. Here you can get up close and personal with the Columbia River in a sea kayak. The Lewis and Clark tour, which follows the explorers' path along the lower Columbia, is a two-day adventure for all skill levels. Skamokawa is northwest of Cathlamet about where Meriwether Lewis first recorded seeing what he thought was the ocean but was actually the Columbia's vast estuary—impressive then as it is today. | 1391 W. Rte. 4, Skamokawa | 360/795–8300 or 888/920–2777 | www.skamokawapaddle.com | Guided Lewis and Clark tours $178—$223 | Daily.

Wahkiakum County Historical Society Museum. Pioneer history and old fishing exhibits are displayed here, along with Native American artifacts and old logging equipment. | 65 River St. | 360/795–3954 | Free | June–Sept., Tues.– Sun. 11–4; Oct., Tues.–Sun. 1–4; Nov.–May, Thurs.–Sun. 1–4.

HISTORIC LODGING
The Bradley House. Although not in the country, this bed-and-breakfast overlooks the Columbia River from atop a knoll in rustic "downtown" Cathlamet. Born as a lumber baron's mansion in 1907, with hardwood floors and fine light fixtures, this Victorian inn is furnished with period pieces. Two rooms share a bath. Dining room, no-smoking rooms. | 61 Main St., 98612 | 360/ 795–3030 | www.bradleyhousebb.com | 4 rooms | $75–$130 | MC, V.

Redfern Farm Bed and Breakfast. This Dutch-colonial farmhouse inn on Puget Island is separated from Cathlamet by a slough (spanned by a bridge) and separated from Oregon by the Columbia River (which you can cross by ferry). The 1940 home has two upstairs guest rooms. Both have a queen-size bed and private bath and are decorated in an eclectic mix of old and new furnishings. Puget Island is part of the Lewis and Clark National Wildlife Refuge. Hot tub, no-smoking rooms. | 277 Cross Dike Rd., 98612 | 360/849–4108 | www.redfernfarmbnb.com | 2 rooms | $65 | No credit cards | BP.

LONG BEACH
▼▼

Long Beach occupies part of Washington's longest sandy spit and has prospered since the 1890s as a beach resort. Pacific Highway, the main street of this elongated roadside village, consists of shops, motels, and gas stations; pretty cottages line the side streets. The 28-mi beach is the nation's longest continuous, natural strand. From November 18 to 20, 1805, Clark and 10 men made an excursion to the ocean, following the curved bay to the tip of Cape Disappointment, exploring 4 mi of the Long Beach peninsula's shore on the trek.

✦ INFORMATION
Long Beach Peninsula Visitor's Bureau | Box 562, 98631 | 800/451–2542 | funbeach.com.

SITES TO SEE
Oysterville. Founded by I. A. Clark and R. H. Espy in 1854, Oysterville was placed on the National Register of Historic Places in 1976. This charming town on the shores of Willapa Bay has a number of original buildings dating from the 1880s, including a church and a one-room schoolhouse. Take a walk through the village to get a feel for the history. Once the county seat and a bustling oyster port, it is now a sleepy village. | North on Rte. 103, on tip of Long Beach Peninsula | 360/642–2400 or 800/451–2542 | Free | Daily.

HISTORIC DINING AND LODGING
Ark Restaurant and Bakery. Contemporary. This rambling bayfront restaurant is the oldest on the Long Beach peninsula, and the views take in the oyster beds and the cord grass meadows lining the shore of Willapa Bay. Casual and relaxed, the restaurant serves innovative northwestern cooking, including seafood, vegetarian, and meat entrées. Baked goods and desserts are prepared on the premises, and a take-out bakery is out front. You can also have lighter fare (and the same great desserts and view) in the Willapa Cafe/Pub lounge. Try the lightly fried Scotch salmon—the pan is deglazed with Scotch and orange juice. | 273 Sandridge Rd., 10 mi north of Long Beach, Nahcotta | 360/665–4133 | Closed Mon. No lunch and reduced hrs in winter | $20–$30 | AE, D, MC, V.

Milton York Restaurant. American. In 1882, this establishment began producing candy and chocolate and has been a community mainstay ever since.

The dinner menu includes seafood, steaks, and chicken, and the ice cream is homemade. The candy, confected from recipes dating back to the turn of the 20th century, is a must. Breakfast is also served. | 107 S. Pacific St. | 360/642–2352 | $13.50–$17 | MC, V.

Shoalwater Restaurant. Contemporary. This restaurant in the Shelburne Inn has the most formal dining room on the peninsula. The food—fresh oysters, crab-and-shrimp cakes, oysters, salmon, and other local sea fare—is great, but the homemade breads and pastries are exceptional. You can order from the same menu or go for lighter fare at the cozy Heron and Beaver across the hallway from the front door, one of Washington's most comfortable pubs. | 4415 Pacific Hwy., Seaview, 98644 | 360/642–4142 | 11:30 AM–3 PM (pub), 5:30–9 PM (dining room) | $15–$35 | AE, D, DC, MC, V.

Boreas Bed & Breakfast. An artfully renovated 1920s vintage beach home, this bed-and-breakfast is on the site where Lewis and Clark led explorers to the Pacific. Inside, books, music, and antiques are scattered throughout the house; outside, a private path takes you through the dunes to the beach. The breakfasts are extravagant, and all the guest rooms have private baths, ocean views, and balconies. The historic Yett Beach house is also available for rent. Hot tub; no a/c, no room phones, no smoking. | 607 N. Ocean Beach Blvd., 98631 | 360/642–8069 or 888/642–8069 | fax 360/642–5353 | www.boreasinn. com | 5 rooms | $130–$140 | MC, V | BP.

Shelburne Inn. Enclosed within flower gardens and behind a white picket fence sits Washington's oldest continuously run hotel, in an 1896 Victorian structure. Antiques, original art, and fresh flowers ornament the rooms; some share private decks. The elaborate breakfasts are famous, with their homemade sausage and occasional caviar. Restaurant, bar; no a/c, no room phones, no room TVs, no smoking. | 4415 Pacific Way, 98644–0250 | 360/642–2442 or 800/466–1896 | fax 360/642–8904 | www.theshelburneinn.com | 15 rooms | $109–$179 | AE, MC, V | BP.

ILWACO

▼▼▼

At the mouth of the Columbia River, Ilwaco (pronounced il-*wah*-koh) has been a fishing port for thousands of years, first as a village of the native Chinook and since about 1840 as an American settlement. Lewis and Clark camped here in November 1805—just a few days after William Clark famously sighted "this great Pacific Ocean"—before deciding to spend the winter across the river near present-day Astoria, Oregon. Ilwaco has a colorful port where anglers gather in the early morning, a picturesque downtown of well-preserved old buildings—some of which are decorated with murals—as well as an old coastal battery, a lifesaving station, and two lighthouses atop rocky headlands.

✦ INFORMATION

Long Beach Peninsula Visitor's Bureau | Box 562, Long Beach, 98631 | 800/451–2542 | funbeach.com.

SITES TO SEE

Fort Canby State Park. Once a military installation, this 1,700-acre park still contains many of the emplacements for cannons that once guarded the mouth of the Columbia. Deer are easily spotted on the trails and eagles perch on the cliffs overhead. Fort Canby was constructed in 1863 to prevent Indian raids and was part of a buildup that saw military expenditures actually exceed the entire state budget in total cost. The most impressive structures are the Cape Disappointment Lighthouse, constructed in 1856, and the North Head Lighthouse, constructed in 1898. The lighthouses, both available for tours, were constructed to counter a growing number of shipwrecks at Cape Disappointment, and running them wasn't easy—winds at North Head sometimes reach 120 mph. The Cape Disappointment Lighthouse is the oldest lighthouse on the West Coast still in use. | Southwest of Ilwaco on U. S. 101 N | 360/902–8844 | Free; lighthouse tours $1 | Park Apr.–Oct., daily 6:30–10:30, Nov.–Mar., daily 6:30–4; call for lighthouse hrs.

On the Fort Canby grounds is the **Lewis and Clark Interpretive Center** ($2 | Daily 10–5), which examines the 8,000-mi journey of the two renowned explorers through paintings and murals. The **Colbert House Museum** (Quaker Ave. SE at Lake St. | 360/642–8002 | $1 | Late May–Sept., Fri.–Sun. 10–4) preserves an 1840s National Register of Historic Places home and its contents. The Colbert family lived here for five generations.

Ilwaco Heritage Museum. Dioramas and miniatures of Long Beach towns tell the history of this region, beginning with the Native American habitation; moving on to the influx of traders, missionaries, and settlers; and concluding with contemporary workers, fishers, and farmers. The museum also includes a permanent "Lewis and Clark in Pacific County" exhibit detailing the harrowing 18 days as the expedition neared the Pacific Ocean. Another highlight is the model of the peninsula's clamshell railroad, a narrow-gauge train that transported passengers and mail along the beach from 1888 to 1930. Ground-up clam and oyster shells formed the rail bed. | 115 S.E. Lake St., off U.S. 101 N | 360/642–3446 | $3 | May–Aug., Mon.–Sat. 9–5, Sun. noon–4; Sept.–Apr., Mon.–Sat. 10–4.

HISTORIC LODGING

China Beach Retreat. This secluded bed-and-breakfast sits between the port of Ilwaco and Fort Canby State Park, in the heart of Lewis and Clark's Long

Beach Peninsula stomping grounds. The Retreat is surrounded by wetlands and has wonderful views of Baker's Bay and the mouth of the Columbia River. A five-minute drive from the Lewis and Clark Interpretive Center at Fort Canby, the inn is just north of Cape Disappointment. Each of the three rooms has lots of natural light and is decorated with antiques and original art. In-room hot tubs; no room phones, no room TVs, no kids under 16, no smoking. | 222 Robert Gray Dr., 98624 | 360/642–5660 | www.chinabeachretreat.com | 3 rooms | $189–$229 | AE, MC, V | BP.

Oregon

From the autumn of 1805 to the spring of 1806, the Corps of Discovery paddled, walked, rode and splashed its way across the entire length of what was then the Oregon Territory, following the Columbia River from the mountains to the sea and back again. It was here, at the continent's westernmost edge, that Lewis and Clark built Fort Clatsop near present-day Astoria and settled in for the long, wet winter of 1805–06, having finally realized the expedition's goal of reaching the Pacific Ocean. Six years later, John Jacob Astor's Pacific Fur Company built Fort Astoria here, and it became the first permanent American settlement west of the Rockies.

Evidence of the Corps of Discovery is everywhere along the Columbia River in this part of the west, from prominent landmarks named by the explorers (Hat Rock, Fort Clatsop) to road signs depicting the buckskin-clad duo pointing toward the ocean, marking the Lewis and Clark National Historic Trail as it winds across the state. But what the Corps "discovered" here was not quite what the explorers had anticipated. Instead of a placid waterway that would float them on calm currents all the way to the ocean, the Columbia River consisted of some 55 mi of huge rapids and chutes. At one section the river dropped 38 feet through several channels positioned between cliffs that rose up as much as 3,000 feet on either side.

Although many of the rapids had to be portaged, the explorers ran others in their big, clumsy wooden dugout canoes. At one particularly harrowing chute, the Columbia narrowed to less than 45 yards, forming a rapid that would be Class V by today's standards—off-limits even to modern kayaks. Today, massive dams stretch all the way to the western edge of the 80-mi-long Columbia River Gorge, and many of the rapids encountered by the Corps lie deep under placid impoundments.

As they floated down the Columbia, Lewis and Clark found the region densely populated by Native American tribes with complex cultures and a well-established trading system. They were sharp traders and already familiar with European goods and trinkets. Although the area inland from the coast

O! How Horriable Is the Day

From November 7 to November 25, 1805, Lewis's and Clark's journal entries read like scenes from a Greek epic. Monster waves, thunder and lightning, rock slides, near-starvation, sheer terror, and desperation all converged on what had become a ragged group of explorers as they fought against Mother Nature to complete their journey to the Pacific Ocean.

Cheers of jubilation rose up from the party on November 7 as Captain Clark spotted what he thought was the Pacific. Waves were heard breaking on rocks. Heavy fog lifted to reveal what looked like the sea. The next morning, instead of donning their buckskin traveling clothes, they put on their official military regalia in order to greet the Pacific in style.

Indeed, the Columbia River does look like the sea near its mouth. Huge swells crash into the shore and whirlpools boil as the river's current battles with the ocean tide. There are sheer cliffs, rocky outcropping, and shifting sandbars. The weather can turn bad within minutes, with winds whipping up huge waves that can quickly cover beaches and submerge estuary islands.

On November 9 the tide swamped one poorly chosen camp. Wrote Clark, "At 2 o'clock PM the flood tide came in accompanied with emence waves and heavy winds, which floated the trees and Drift which was on the point . . . maney of the trees nearly 200 feet long and from 4 to 7 feet through, our camp entirely under water dureing the hight of the tide, every man as wet as water could make them all the last night and to day all day as the rain Continued all day."

The next day they made some progress but were driven back by wind and tide and pinned to the shoreline near Point Ellice (called Point Distress by Captain Lewis). Waves dashed their canoes, rocks tumbled from the rocky cliffs above, and there was no shelter or food. On November 11 Clark wrote, "It would be distressing to a feeling person to See our Situation at this time all wet and cold with our bedding also wet, in a Cove Scercely large enough to Contain us . . . robes and leather Clothes are rotten."

The explorers marveled at the Chinook in their coastal canoes, who easily crossed the river in the storms. The men traded with them for desperately needed food; fish and roots from the Chinook saved the wet, exhausted Corps from starvation. On November 11, Sergeant Patrick Gass summed up the situation: "We have no tents, or covering to defend us, except our blankets and some mats we got from the Indians which we put on poles to keep off the rain."

Finally, the downpour broke long enough for both Lewis and Clark to separately lead small parties of men to the ocean. Clark paid Chinook with fishhooks for a ride across the Chinook River and walked 4 mi north along what today is the sandy Long Beach peninsula. But the pleasant conditions did not last. By November 21, though the party had settled in at the temporary "Station Camp" near the site of an abandoned Chinook summer village, the weather turned nasty again. On November 22 Clark wrote of the misery, "O! how horriable is the day waves brakeing with great violence against the Shore throwing the Water into our Campt and all wet and confind to our Shelters."

Finally, on November 25, the party retreated east and crossed the river to the south side, where Native Americans reported more abundant game. But it was not until December 7 that they reached the site of Fort Clatsop. There the drama ended, but the river's legacy had not. Within 40 years, sea captains would refer to these same waters at the Columbia's mouth as "the graveyard of the Pacific."

was largely unexplored, trading vessels had established a brisk fur trade with coastal tribes years before. The few cheap trinkets that Lewis and Clark had for trading were of little use to the Native Americans of the region.

On October 18, 1805, Clark spotted Oregon's white-capped Mount Hood in the distance. The mountain, a point already on the expedition's map, gave the group hope that they were getting closer to the ocean. The next day, the expedition passed Hat Rock near Umatilla. Clark wrote, "14 miles to a rock in a Lard. Resembling a hat just below a rapid." Hat Rock kept its name and is now Hat Rock State Park in Umatilla County.

The Umatilla Reservation is near Pendleton, where the historic Pendleton Round-Up rodeo has been held each September since 1910. This arid, sparsely populated part of Oregon is still known as cattle country and is home to many large working ranches and farms. At the Tamastslikt Cultural Institute in Pendleton, operated by the Confederated Tribes of the Umatilla, the story of Lewis and Clark is told from a tribal perspective.

As Lewis and Clark followed the river west, they left the dry, rocky landscape of the high desert and entered what is now the Columbia River Gorge

National Scenic Area, beginning their final push to the ocean. They followed the river along its path directly through the Cascade Mountains, where it carved a massive gorge and connected the sides of Oregon and Washington from end to end. Today, you can drive the length of the gorge on both the Oregon and Washington sides. The changes in landscape are dramatic as you travel from the arid high plateau of eastern Oregon, following the river through the mountains to the dense Douglas fir forests and rugged basalt cliffs of the western gorge.

Near The Dalles, the party began navigating a 55-mi stretch of white water that included first the 38-foot Celilo Falls, then the Short and Long Narrows, and the Grand Rapids. Clark described the Short Narrows as "agitated gut Swelling, boiling and whorling in every direction." As they navigated giant rapids along the Columbia River between The Dalles and Cascade Locks, Lewis and Clark passed by what is now Hood River, a hot spot for windsurfers. On November 2, after spending three days carrying their canoes around rapids between Stevenson, Washington, and Cascade Locks, Oregon (site of the toll Bridge of the Gods between the states), the explorers set up camp at what is now Rooster Rock State Park.

Above Rooster Rock is Crown Point, a lookout perched high above the gorge with 30-mi views. A drive along the Historic Columbia River Highway, built in the early 1900s, is particularly splendid on a crisp autumn day. From Crown Point, with light playing off the basalt and granite cliffs, the trees ablaze in fall color and the river a silver ribbon below, it is possible to get a sense of the fine view Lewis and Clark might have enjoyed 200 years ago.

As Lewis and Clark reached the western edge of the Columbia River Gorge, Clark noted tidal influences, an Indian wearing a sailor's jacket, and seals playing on rocks. After two years of hard travel, the Pacific was within reach. At this point, the party was actually on the Washington side of the river. They would be pinned down for more than a week by violent storms, miserable in the unrelenting rain, their buckskin clothing rotting in the dampness. Finally they were rescued by Native Americans of the Clatsop tribe, who lived on the Oregon side of the estuary and paddled them across in their large coastal canoes. During the entire voyage, many different tribes came to the expedition's rescue with food, transportation, protection, and guidance. The Clatsop were no exception. After ferrying the exhausted Corps to safety, they sold the explorers the fish and roots that would save them from starvation.

On November 18, after exploring the area and getting oriented, the captains let everyone in the party vote on where to make a permanent winter camp. For the first time in American history, a black man (Clark's slave, York) and a woman (Sacagawea) were allowed to vote. With only one dissenting vote, the decision was made to spend the winter on the south side of the river, in Oregon. On December 30, 1805, Fort Clatsop was completed.

From Desert to Dunes

A DRIVING TOUR FROM UMATILLA TO ASTORIA

▼▼

Distance: 269 mi   **Time:** 2–3 days
Breaks: Hood River, a riverfront community in the heart of the Columbia Gorge National
Scenic Area, is a great place to spend the night before continuing on to the Pacific Ocean.
Spend a second night in Astoria, Lewis and Clark's final destination on the Oregon coast.

On this two- to three-day tour, you'll follow the stretch of the trail through
Oregon that took the Corps of Discovery more than a month to traverse as
they traveled west in October and November 1805. The journey begins in
the high desert where Lewis and Clark first entered Oregon and follows the
Columbia River through the Columbia Gorge National Scenic Area all the
way to the Oregon coast.

Begin at **Umatilla** (92 mi east of The Dalles off U.S. 395), part of the high
desert of the Columbia River plateau, near where Lewis and Clark first entered
Oregon. The name Umatilla is derived from the Indian word "Youmalolam"
("water rippling over sand"). Drive 9 mi west on Interstate 84 to Hat Rock
State Park, the site of a distinctive rock formation, with boat access to Lake
Wallula.

From here, drive 30 mi to **Pendleton,** home to the Pendleton Round-Up
started by Oregon farmers, ranchers, and Native Americans in the area in 1910.
Visit the Tamastslikt Cultural Institute, which documents the Lewis and
Clark expedition, from the perspective of the Cayuse, Umatilla, and Walla
Walla. Head west on Interstate 84, following the Columbia River, for 93 mi.
Get off at Exit 114, 5 mi east of Rufus, and stop at Le Page Park, where there's
boating, fishing, camping, and picnicking. The park, just off the exit, is
named after Jean-Baptiste LePage, a Frenchman who joined the expedition
at Fort Mandan. Return to Interstate 84 and drive west 22 mi to Rock Fort
at **The Dalles.** Take Exit 84, then Webber Road, then Bargeway Road to the
river to the site of Lewis and Clark's encampment. Lewis and Clark and their
party camped here twice, once as they made their way west and again on
their return trip. French traders later named the Columbia River narrows here
Les Dalles ("flagstones"). The rapids are now beneath Lake Celilo, tamed by
the dams. Interpretive displays at the 50-acre Columbia Gorge Discovery Center
tell the story of the region. Nearby at Oregon Trail Living History Park (part
of the Discovery Center complex), you can stop and hike one of the foot-
paths high above the Columbia to experience what a day on the trail might
have been like for Lewis and Clark.

Next, drive west on Interstate 84 to the former pioneer settlement of **Hood
River.** Your route takes you through the Columbia River Gorge National
Scenic Area, along the Columbia. Here, as the river cuts through the Cascades,
the landscape changes from high desert to lush temperate forests. Lewis and

The Columbia River, Then and Now

Etched in neat script on one of the hand-drawn government maps Lewis and Clark carried with them on their journey are the words, "Oragon or R. of the West." This was the river of the explorers' dreams—the Great River of the West, as the Columbia was called. This massive waterway would become a river highway, connecting East and West and ensuring the extension of American agrarian society across the continent. American sea captain Robert Gray found the Columbia's mouth in 1792. His descriptions, along with those of British and Spanish explorers, led President Thomas Jefferson to believe that the huge river must stretch east to the Rockies.

To Lewis's and Clark's disappointment, it did not. And just as the Rockies were not gentle and forgiving like the mountains of Virginia, as Jefferson had imagined them, the Columbia was not placid and smooth. Unlike the river we know today, subdued by dams, it was wild and mighty, twisting and turning north from its headwaters in Canada, then south, then sharply west through the Cascades, and finally swinging north again to the Pacific. Huge rapids dogged the expedition, beginning at its confluence with Snake River. This white water was an aftereffect of the Missoula floods—the violent breakup of a glacier ice sheet over an ice dam 12,000–14,000 years before. Some rapids took entire days to portage.

But despite the explorers' initial disappointment, the Columbia did eventually become the Great River of the West. It was at once a trade route, a great natural resource, and a regional icon. The story of this river, which quenches desert thirst and sustains miles of estuaries after it rushes headlong past the basalt and granite of the Columbia River Gorge cliffs, and through rain forests before tumbling into the surf of the Pacific, is a story of cataclysmic geologic events, complex ecosystems, and persistent human engineering.

Many rivers cross mountain ranges, but few cut their way through at near sea level as the Columbia does on its route through the Cascades. Despite the dams, the Columbia River Gorge remains one of the most scenic places on earth; some have called it the Rhine River of the Pacific Northwest. The river itself is a place where desert, forest, and sea compete and converge, shadowed by 8,000-foot basalt and granite cliffs and ancient forests. The snow-charged Columbia reaches across 1,200 mi, and its watershed drains 259,000 square mi and includes portions of seven states. Of the North American rivers to reach the Pacific Ocean, the Columbia is the third longest.

When Lewis and Clark made their way down the river, it was pristine, naturally diverse, and naturally balanced—undammed, unpolluted, and not overfished. Today, the river's rapids and falls are silent. Where the river was once narrow and fast, it is now wide and slow. According to the Portland State University Center for Columbia River History, the Columbia is, with the dams along its entire length, "the most hydroelectrically developed hydroelectric river system in the world." During the past 200 years, it has been altered by dikes, channels, locks, and dams to become a series of lakes that sustain huge agricultural economies in arid regions of the West and send electricity buzzing in all directions. At the Celilo Converter Station on a hilltop near The Dalles, the Bonneville Dam hydroelectric station transmits enough power for all of Los Angeles and Hollywood.

The Columbia may not sound or look the same as it did 200 years ago. But it is still the Great River of the West.

Clark initially named Hood River for Private François Labiche, one of their interpreters, but the name that stuck honors Samuel Hood, a British admiral. Restaurants and shops line the main street of this riverfront town. From here, take the 47-mi Mount Hood Loop Highway for a scenic tour through the Hood River valley (Route 35, off Interstate 84 Exit 64). Return to Hood River for the night.

On day two, take Interstate 84 through the gorge to Cascade Locks, about 20 mi from Hood River. Hop aboard the sternwheeler *Columbia Gorge* for a narrated tour from the true vantage point of the explorers—on the water; board at Marine Park in Cascade Locks. Next, stop by Rooster Rock State Park, where you'll find 3 mi of sandy beach plus windsurfing and hiking. Next, drive 11 mi on the Historic Columbia River Highway to Crown Point State Park. Built atop Crown Point is Vista House, a domed, octagonal monument to Oregon explorers.

Just west of the gorge is **Portland,** the state's largest city. In 1805, Lewis and Clark camped on Diamond Island, now Government and McGuire islands, just across from Portland International Airport. Here, take one of the narrated Lewis and Clark Cruise Tours down the Columbia to Astoria. After your tour, drive 12 mi north on U.S. 30 to Sauvie Island, where the Willamette River flows into the Columbia. Named Wappato Island for its abundant wappato roots, once used for food, this 24,000-acre landfall is a rural farming community and a wildlife area that shelters species ranging from bald eagles to sandhill cranes. Before tumbling into the Pacific Ocean at **Astoria,**

72 mi from Portland, the river spreads out into the estuary and marshland. Here, accessible only by boat, is the Lewis and Clark National Wildlife Refuge—35,000 acres of tidelands, mudflats, open water, and islands (called Seal Islands by Lewis and Clark). Estuary tours leave from Astoria. At Fort Clatsop National Memorial, the reconstructed fort at the site of Lewis and Clark's winter camp, National Park Service rangers dress up in buckskin, make candles and dugout canoes, and year-round present demonstrations that show what life was like during the cold, wet winter of 1805–06. At the Columbia River Maritime Museum in Astoria, you can tour the last seagoing lighthouse ship on the West Coast and learn about Lewis and Clark's river explorations and the Lower Columbia Native American culture of the area. Overnight in Astoria and spend the next day exploring the northern Oregon coast.

UMATILLA

▼▼

The Corps passed a "rock . . . resembling a hat" during a day of running the Columbia's rapids on October 19, 1805, and named it Hat Rock. It is thought that the party's camp near here may have been on an island, perhaps Blalock Island, between Irrigon and Boardman. That evening, Clark wrote, "About 100 Indians came from different Lodges, and a number of them brought wood which they gave us, we Smoked with all of them, and two of our Party Peter Crusat & Gibson played on the violin which delighted them greatly."

Umatilla was founded as Umatilla Landing in 1864 and is now a port city with a population of just over 5,000 at the confluence of the Umatilla and Columbia rivers.

✦ **INFORMATION**
Umatilla Chamber of Commerce | 1530 6th St., 97882 | 541/922–4825 | www. umatilla.org.

SITES TO SEE
Hat Rock State Park. Hat Rock, on the south shore of Lake Wallula behind McNary Dam, was the first major landmark that Lewis and Clark passed on their expedition down the Columbia and is one of the few landmarks that have not been submerged by the river's various impoundments. The rock itself cannot be climbed, but park hiking paths marked with interpretive signs detail the historical significance of the site and its place in the Lewis and Clark story. The park's tree-shaded grassy areas provide a cool respite from the heat of the eastern Oregon desert in summer, and there's waterskiing, jet skiing, swimming, boating, and fishing. | U.S. 730, 9 mi east of Umatilla | 800/551–6949 | www.oregonstateparks.org | Free | Mid-Mar.–Oct., daily.

McNary Lock and Dam. This hydroelectric dam impounds the Columbia River and creates 38,800-acre Lake Wallula, which has 242 mi of shore and extends 70 mi upstream from Umatilla to Richland, Washington; the tailwaters of the impoundment affect the lowermost parts of the Snake, Walla Walla, and Yakima rivers as well. At the dam, signage at an overlook describes the now-flooded Umatilla rapids, and there are fish viewing rooms and a gallery that explains the working of the powerhouse. Below the dam is the 318-acre McNary Wildlife Nature Area, with three short hiking trails, picnic tables, and fishing. Before planning to visit the dam, call ahead; Homeland Security may affect access. | U.S. 730 | 541/922–4388 | Free | Daily; marinas June–Sept., daily.

PENDLETON

▼▼▼

Pendleton, southeast of where Lewis and Clark entered present-day Oregon, is home to descendants of the tribes that welcomed the explorers as they started down the Columbia River and has a population of about 17,000. It also adjoins the Umatilla Reservation. Incorporated in 1800, it was named for Ohio senator George Hunt Pendleton. Historic buildings such as the Pendleton Woolen Mills, the Shamrock Card Room, Hop Sing's Chinese Laundry, and the Cozy Room bordello are now part of the city's famous Underground Tour. The town hosts the region's biggest event, the Pendleton Round-Up.

◆ INFORMATION

Pendleton Chamber of Commerce/Visitors Bureau | 501 S. Main St., 97801 | 541/276–7411 or 800/547–8911 | www.pendleton-oregon.org.

SITES TO SEE

Pendleton Underground Tours. This colorful 90-minute tour lets you experience life in 19th-century Pendleton and showcases the role of the Chinese in the West in its early days. You'll first head into a subterranean labyrinth of gambling rooms, opium dens, and cramped Chinese laborers' quarters—remnants of the days when the town had no fewer than 32 saloons and 18 brothels—then visit Madame Stella Darby's bordello. Reservations are recommended. | 37 S.W. Emigrant Ave. | 541/276–0730 or 800/226–6398 | www.pendletonundergroundtours.com | $10 | Mon.–Sat. 9–5.

Pendleton Woolen Mills. The name made famous by its classic sweaters and blankets was founded in 1889 in Salem, Oregon, by English weaver Thomas Kay; Kay's grandsons expanded the business to Pendleton in 1909. It's still a family business, and a free 20-minute tour explains the weaving process from start to finish. Bring some bucks, as there's a retail store on-site—look for blankets, sportswear, men's clothing, and bargains on factory seconds. |

1307 S.E. Court Pl. | 541/276–6911 | www.pendleton-usa.com | Mon.–Sat. 8–5; tours weekdays at 9, 11, 1:30, and 3.

Round-Up Hall of Fame Museum. The photographs, costumes, saddles, guns, and other rodeo memorabilia on display here give you a sense of the region's main event, the Pendleton Round-Up. The pictures tell some great stories—look for the Rodeo Queens and the Happy Canyon Princesses (all Native American). And don't miss War Paint, the stuffed championship bronco. | Round-Up Grounds, 1205 S.W. Court Ave., near S.W. 12th St. | 541/278–0815 | Free | May–Oct., daily 10–5; Nov.–Apr., by appointment.

Tamastslikt Cultural Institute. At this interpretive center in the Wildhorse Casino Resort, the history of the Cayuse, Umatilla, and Walla Walla is depicted. An art gallery showcases the work of tribal artists, and a theater hosts lectures, dance, and music performances. | 72789 Rte. 331 | 541/966–9748 | fax 541/966–9927 | www.tamastslikt.com | $6 | Daily 9–5.

Umatilla County Historical Society Museum. In this 1909 railway depot, photos, publications, and other memorabilia showcase the lives and times of farmers, loggers, ranchers, missionaries, explorers, and others who made the town their home. | 108 S.W. Frazer Ave. | 541/276–0012 | $2 | Tues.–Sat. 10–4.

✦ ON THE CALENDAR

Sept. **Pendleton Round-Up.** More than 50,000 rodeo performers and fans take over town for four days during the second week of the month for this event, which was launched in 1910 by a group of eastern Oregon farmers and has been held ever since. The slogan is "Let 'er buck!" You can watch wild-horse races, sample local barbecues, cheer for parades, listen to country bands, and participate in milking contests. Budget for the souvenirs you'll inevitably buy as you stroll between the beadwork and crafts stands along Main Street and Court Avenue. If you'd like to stay in town, make reservations well in advance—along with Cheyenne Frontier Days in Wyoming, the Pendleton Round-Up is one of the top two rodeos in the United States. | 800/457–6336.

HISTORIC DINING AND LODGING

Foley Station. American/Casual. The Foley Building in La Grande, part of a structure that dates from Oregon Trail days, houses this popular restaurant. The casual, busy dining room, with its booths, brick walls, and high ceilings, can be noisy, but in summer you can sit outdoors, where it's quieter. The cuisine is Northwest style with an international flair. You might find frittata with scallops, bacon, asparagus, and smoked Gouda; sides like cheddar scallion biscuits; or entrées like Alaskan sockeye salmon encrusted with southwestern spices. | 1011 Adams Ave., La Grande | 541/963–7473 | Closed Mon. and Tues. No lunch Wed. | $18–$23 | MC, V.

Great Pacific Wine and Coffee Company. Café. This 1887 Masonic temple with a restored facade is the place for a casual meal downtown—it's around the corner from Pendleton Underground Tours. Coffee, bagels, muffins, and deli sandwiches are menu mainstays for breakfast, lunch, and dinner along with Greek salads, nachos, and the turkey, avocado, and Monterey Jack sandwich. Dozens of exotic beers and wines are available as well. | 403 S. Main St. | 541/276–1350 | fax 541/966–8362 | Closed Sun. | $6–$8 | AE, MC, V.

Raphael's. Contemporary. Locals come to this restaurant in a restored 1876 Queen Anne house for the prime rib, hickory-smoked on the premises. But you can also get traditional steaks and seafood, all with a Northwest accent, and seasonal fare such as venison, elk, and rattlesnake. Seating is inside in three dining rooms and in a garden out back. For an aperitif, try the huckleberry daiquiri. | 233 S.E. 4th St. | 541/276–8500 or 888/944–2433 | fax 541/276–8333 | Closed Sun. and Mon. No lunch | $11–$35 | AE, D, DC, MC, V.

Parker House. This three-story pink stucco home, a blend of French neoclassical and Italianate styles, is unchanged since it was built in the North Hill area in 1917. It still has its original Chinese wallpaper, custom fittings, and woodwork. The comfortable rooms have eclectic furniture and beautiful rugs, and three have French doors and balconies. The three-story house also has an elevator. Picnic area, some in-room safes, library; no room TVs, no kids under 12, no smoking. | 311 N. Main St., 97801 | 541/276–8581 or 800/700–8581 | www.parkerhousebnb.com | 4 rooms, 1 suite | $75–$135 | AE, MC, V | BP.

Working Girls Hotel. This 1890s hotel was once a bordello and a boardinghouse. Antiques fill the rooms, which have 18-foot ceilings and polished wood floors. The staff is helpful and extremely knowledgeable about historic things to do and see around town. Dining room, recreation room, laundry service, free parking. | 17 S.W. Emigrant Ave., 97801 | 541/276–0730 or 800/226–6398 | fax 541/276–0665 | 5 rooms without bath | $40–$60 | Closed Nov.–May | D, MC, V | BP.

THE DALLES

▼▼

A stop for the Corps of Discovery in 1805 and 1806, The Dalles lies at the eastern edge of the 80-mi Columbia River Gorge National Scenic Area. French explorers christened this area *dalle*, or flagstone, for its place along a crescent bend of the Columbia River where the waters once narrowed and spilled over a series of rapids, creating a flagstone effect. Celilo Falls near The Dalles was once one of the region's most important Indian dip-net salmon fisheries. When the Corps passed through the area, Clark noted 10,000 pounds of salmon drying in one village. Founded in 1838, The Dalles is now the seat of Wasco County and the trading center of north-central Oregon, with a population of around 12,000 within the city limits and another 25,000 living within 25 mi. Since 1957, when the Dalles Dam raised the level of the Columbia River above the falls, the area has become a center for white-water floating, sailboarding, and fishing.

✦ INFORMATION
The Dalles Chamber of Commerce | 404 W. 2nd St., 97058 | 541/296–2231 or 800/255–3385 | www.thedalleschamber.com.

SITES TO SEE
Celilo Park. Lewis and Clark had to portage around Celilo Falls, which Native American tribes of the region knew as Wyam ("water echoes over rocks"). The site, continuously inhabited for longer than almost any other in North America, was flooded when the Dalles Dam was completed in 1957. This park on Lake Celilo, near the site of the former falls, is a favorite spot for windsurfing, swimming, sailboarding, and fishing. Interpretive signage details the portage. | I–84 at Exit 99, 7 mi east of The Dalles | 541/296–1181 | Free | Daily.

Columbia Gorge Discovery Center. Exhibits in this 50-acre complex, the official interpretive center for the Columbia River Gorge National Scenic Area, explore the lore of the Lewis and Clark expedition, Native American culture, and the geological history of the Columbia River Gorge, beginning 40 million years ago, when volcanoes, landslides, and floods carved out the area. The complex has several components. At the Oregon Trail Living History Park, high above the Columbia River, living-history performances are held Friday through Monday, Memorial Day through Labor Day. The **Wasco County Historical Museum** (541/296–8600 | www.gorgediscovery.org) focuses on 10,000 years of Native American life and exploration of the region by settlers through displays and interpretive exhibits of area artifacts. Exhibits are displayed in the museum's 17,200-square-foot exhibit wing within the Columbia Gorge Discovery Center, telling the stories of the people of Wasco County past and present. | 5000 Discovery Dr. | 541/296–8600 | www. gorgediscovery.org | $6.50 | Mid-Mar.–Dec., daily 10–6; Jan.–mid-Mar., Tues.– Sun. 10–4.

The Dalles Dam and Lake Celilo. At this hydroelectric dam just east of the Bonneville Dam, you can ride the free Dalles Dam Tour Train to the powerhouse and the fish ladder; you can watch fish using the fish ladders on closed-circuit TVs, and see petroglyphs rescued from a now-inundated canyon nearby. At the visitor center, on the site of an old fish cannery, you can see live sturgeon as well as exhibits describing the natural life of the area pond. Before planning to visit the dam, call ahead; security may affect access. | I–84 Exit 87 in summer or Exit 88 other times | 541/298–7650 | Free | www.cqs.washington.edu/crisp/hydro/hydrotda.html | Daily. Tour train second weekend Apr.–Sept., Wed.–Sun. 8–4; Labor Day–Memorial Day, daily 8–5.

Fort Dalles Museum. Housed in Fort Dalles's surgeon's quarters, a Carpenter Gothic structure dating from 1856 that's the last surviving structure of Fort Dalles, Oregon's oldest museum exhibits the clothing, furniture, and household items of the region's early settlers as well as antique vehicles. Be sure to visit the **Anderson House Museum,** an old wooden homestead across the street, which also displays pioneer artifacts. The entry fee admits you to both sites. | 500 W. 15th St. | 541/296–4547 | $3 | Daily 10–5.

Lewis and Clark Rock Fort Site. Originally named "Fort Rock" by Lewis and Clark because its geography created a natural fortification, the area is now known as Rock Fort. Lewis and Clark reported seeing near here the first wooden houses built by Native Americans since they left Illinois. The Corps camped here October 25–28, 1805, and again in the spring on the return trip. It is now planted with plants native to the area. | Northeast of Webber and 2nd St. | 541/296–2231 | www.thedalleschamber.com | Free | Daily.

HISTORIC DINING

Bailey's Place. Contemporary. Prime rib is the specialty in this bistro in an 1865 house with 10-foot ceilings and period chandeliers. But it's also worth trying the fresh seafood or the chicken Ole, in a brandy, cream, and mushroom sauce. Desserts include a huckleberry sundae, Cappuccino Decadence, and caramel custard. | 515 Liberty St. | 541/296–6708 | Closed Sun.–Mon. | $6.95–$15.95 | AE, D, MC, V.

Baldwin Saloon Historic Restaurant and Bar. Contemporary. A mural near the back bar painted by Wilbur Hayes in 1899 won first place at the Lewis and Clark Centennial Exposition held in Portland in 1905–06. The restaurant building dates from 1876. Seafood and oyster dishes top the menu. | 205 Court St. | 541/296–5666 | Closed Sun. | $9.95–$19.95 | MC, V.

HOOD RIVER
▼▼

As they passed the mouth of the Hood River in late October 1805, Lewis and Clark named it for one of their interpreters, Private François Labiche. However, it was later renamed to honor Samuel Hood, a British admiral under Lord Nelson in the Napoleonic Wars. Hood River, the headquarters of the Columbia River Gorge National Scenic Area, is now home to world-class windsurfing and is the gateway to Mount Hood, known as sacred Wy'east to area Native American tribes. Wy'east, according to the Warm Springs tribe legend, is the warrior Mount Hood, who fought Patu (Mount Adams) over Looitlatkal (Mount St. Helens).

✦ INFORMATION
Columbia River Gorge National Scenic Area. | 902 Wasco Ave., Suite 200, 97031 | 541/386–2333. **Columbia River Gorge Visitor's Association** | 2149 W. Cascade, No. 106A, 97031 | 800/984–6743. **Hood River County Chamber of Commerce** | 405 Portway Ave., 97031 | 541/386–2000 or 800/366–3530 | www.hoodriver.org.

SITES TO SEE
Bonneville Lock and Dam. Columbia River water passing through the power-house of this structure, authorized in 1933, and completed in 1938, produces 1 million kilowatts of hydroelectricity annually, enough to supply more than 200,000 single-family homes. The dam's fish hatchery teems with fingerling salmon, fat rainbow trout and 6-foot-long sturgeon. You can tour the fish ladders yourself or take a 30- to 60-minute interpretive tour. Call ahead before visiting; Homeland Security measures may affect visitor access to the dam. | I–84 at Exit 40, 23 mi west of Hood River | 541/374–8820 | Free | Visitor center and tours daily 9–5.

Crown Point State Scenic Corridor and Vista House. The 30-mi views of the Columbia River Gorge you can see from the overlook here are spectacular. The viewpoint is adjacent to Vista House, a two-tier octagonal structure built in 1916, which is home to a museum and exhibits that interpret gorge history and geology. | I–84 at Exit 22, 45 mi west of Hood River, left onto N.E. Corbett Hill Rd., slight left onto Historic Columbia River Hwy. | 503/695–2261 or 800/551–6949 | www.oregonstateparks.org | Free | Park daily; Vista House Mar.–Oct., daily (may be closed due to restoration; call ahead).

Historic Columbia River Highway. Built between 1913 and 1922, this serpentine highway high above the Columbia River—the first paved road in the gorge—was built expressly for automotive sightseers. You can drive it for about 40 mi from Mosier to The Dalles on the east end of the gorge and from Troutdale to Dodson on the west end of the gorge. Several sections of the original (totaling about 11 mi) are closed to automobiles—they've been reserved for nonmotorized recreation only and compose the Historic Columbia River Highway National Trail. The Crown Point State Park viewpoint and Vista House Interpretive Center are along the highway near Corbett, 16 mi east of Troutdale. | I–84 at Exit 17, 46 mi west of Hood River | 503/986–4334 | www.odot. state.or.us/hcrh | Free | Daily.

Lewis and Clark State Park. When they camped here, at the mouth of the Sandy River at its confluence with the Columbia, on what is now the Historic

Columbia River Highway, in November 1805, Lewis and Clark called the area Quicksand River. At that time, this was the farthest point up the Columbia that any European or American explorers had reached. The peaceful park now has a beach, a boat launch, and a trail up the cliffs to Broughton's Bluff, a geologic boundary between the foothills of the Cascade mountain range and the Willamette Valley to the west. | I–84 at Exit 18, 46 mi west of Hood River; from exit, follow signs to Lewis and Clark State Park/Oxbow County Park, stay straight to go onto Crown Point Hwy. for about 5 mi | 503/695–2261 or 800/551–6949 | www.oregonstateparks.org | Free | Daily.

Mount Hood Scenic Railroad and Dinner Train. This 1906 freight and passenger train still runs from April to October, paralleling the Hood River for stunning views of the Mount Hood foothills and plains. Morning, brunch, and dinner trips thread through forested canyons and endless fruit orchards—a relaxing way to explore this side of Oregon. | Depot at 110 Railroad Ave. | 800/872–4661 | www.mthoodrr.com | $23–$70 | Late Mar.–Dec., train schedules vary | AE, D, MC, V.

Multnomah Falls. Lewis and Clark remarked at the beauty of the "Cascades of the Columbia" on their return trip. "We passed several beautifull cascades which fell from a great hight over the stupendious rocks . . . the hills have now become mountains high on each side are rocky steep covered generally with fir and white cedar," wrote Clark in April 1806. The second-highest year-round cascade in the United States, Multnomah Falls plunges 620 feet down the side of a cliff. You have traditionally been able to hike up the falls on a steep trail; landslides may limit access, however. Numerous other trails fan out around the falls in the surrounding Multnomah Falls National Scenic Area. | I–84 at Exit 31 about 32 mi west of Hood River | 503/695–2372 | Free | Daily.

Rooster Rock State Park. Named by Lewis and Clark and used as a campsite twice, Rooster Rock is now a popular park and swimming hole with 3 mi of sandy beaches. It is also home to one of only two nude sunbathing areas in the state (not visible from the clothing-required area). | I–84 at Exit 25 about 44 mi west of Hood River | 503/695–2261 | www.oregonstateparks. org | Free | Daily.

Sternwheeler *Columbia Gorge*. As close as you can get to following Lewis and Clark's exact path in the gorge is to float down the Columbia River on two-hour narrated excursions aboard this 600-passenger ship. The scenery is some of the best. | Port of Cascade Locks, I–84 Exit 44, 17 mi west of Hood River | 541/374–8427 | www.sternwheeler.com | 2-hr cruises (no meal) $15, brunch and dinner cruises $35–$45 | Narrated cruises Memorial Day–Labor Day, daily; brunch and dinner cruises Mar.–Dec., daily.

Columbia River Tribal Culture

It is October 1805 in the Columbia River Gorge. The "First Salmon" ceremony has already taken place, signaling the start of the fall fishing and trading season. More than 3,000 people from many different native tribes are gathered near The Dalles, about 200 mi upriver from the mouth of the Columbia. Tens of thousands of pounds of dried salmon fill wooden houses along the banks. The warm east wind blows steadily through the Columbia River Gorge as the waterway roils and crashes over massive, crescent-shape Celilo Falls, known to the Indians as Wyam ("water echoes over rocks").

Such a gathering has taken place here every spring and fall for thousands of years during the salmon runs. Celilo has something for everyone. Chinookan brokers, men and women working side by side, run the trading market. Inland tribes bring berries, roots, and game harvested from the Cascade Mountains. Nez Percé, with access to the Plains, proffer buffalo meat and horses. Slaves are traded. After the hard work of salmon fishing and preserving come laughing, feasting, merrymaking, socializing, and storytelling. Goods traded at the site will make their way from here along age-old trading routes to Alaska, southern California, New Mexico, and Missouri.

This area, which was the center of the river salmon fishery, in the heart of the great Chinookan Nation (river tribes of the Chinookan linguistic family), extended from Canada to the mouth of the Columbia. Tribes of the Sahaptian-speaking people such as the Nez Percé, Umatilla, and Walla Walla lived nearby and traded here, too, but Chinookans controlled the market and even developed a language, "Chinook jargon," specifically for trade communication.

When Lewis and Clark arrived in the Columbia River Gorge, they found themselves not at the edge of a lonely frontier but in the middle of what Clark called "great marts of trade." The salmon culture was entirely different from anything the explorers had ever seen. And they certainly hadn't expected that the Indians would be expert traders, scoffing at their cheap trinkets and driving such a hard bargain that the explorers often found themselves at the losing end of the deal.

Columbia River tribes had occupied the region continuously for at least 10,000 years. Their societal structure was based on a complex hierarchy of royal families, commoners, and slaves. The Chinookans lived in permanent and seasonal settlements of earth-pit dwellings, wooden homes, and huge cedar-plank longhouses, which were often home to multiple families.

The Chinookan people were superb at crafting canoes, and the Corps marveled at the seamanship of the coastal tribes. In their large coastal canoes, Native Americans navigated with ease around the turbulent Columbia River Bar, the point where the Columbia meets the ocean, whose treacherous waters prompted early sea captains to call the area "the graveyard of the Pacific."

✦ ON THE CALENDAR

Apr. Hood River Valley Blossom Festival. The orchards are in bloom during this arts-and-crafts fair centered on the towns of Odell and Parkdale. Held the third weekend in April, the event coincides with the seasonal opening of the Mount Hood Scenic Railroad, which travels through the apple and pear orchards in the area. The annual festival is held the third weekend in April. | 541/386–2000 or 800/366–3530.

June **Return of the Sternwheeler Days.** The last full weekend in June, when the sternwheeler *Columbia Gorge* returns to its summer port, the town celebrates in Marine Park with a parade, bingo, an arts-and-crafts fair, live music, and a salmon dinner. | 541/374–8427.

HISTORIC LODGING

Columbia Gorge Hotel. Oregon pioneer Bobby Rand originally developed this site in 1904 and called it Waw Gwin Gwin Hotel, a Native American term meaning "rushing water." Steamers chugging down the river would sound the boat's whistle once for each passenger on board, sending staff scurrying to prepare rooms. Situated next to the top of a waterfall overlooking the Columbia River Gorge, the property was sold in 1920 to Simon Benson, a developer of the Historic Columbia River Highway who turned the site into an opulent estate. Presidents Roosevelt and Coolidge stayed in the hotel. Restaurant, cable TV, bar, business services, some pets allowed. | 4000 Westcliff Dr., 97031 | 541/386–5566 or 800/345–1921 | fax 541/386–9141 | www.columbiagorgehotel.com | 40 rooms | $179–$279 | AE, D, DC, MC, V.

Hood River Hotel. This 1913 gem embodies the luxury of pioneers who grew rich on the ranch and moved into town. Opulent touches include beveled glass, pine floors, and thick Oriental carpets. Four-poster beds, skylights, and antiques provide the rooms with comfort and light, and each suite has a kitchen. The restaurant serves meals with European and Mediterranean flavors. Restaurant, café, kitchens, refrigerators, hot tub, sauna, gym, lobby lounge, recreation room, laundry service, travel services, free parking. | 102 Oak St., 97031 | 541/386–1900 | fax 541/386–6090 | www.hoodriverhotel.com | 33 rooms, 9 suites | $145–$175 | AE, D, DC, MC, V | BP.

PORTLAND

▼▼

The Corps of Discovery camped near Portland on the way to the Pacific near where Portland International Airport is now located. In their hurry to reach the ocean, the explorers didn't do much exploring here in 1805, but Clark went with a party up the Willamette River in the spring and camped at present-day Cathedral Park in northeast Portland. Portland (population 1.9 million) is the state's largest city and was the site of the 1905 Lewis and Clark Centennial Exposition. The Portland Art Museum, the first art museum in the Pacific Northwest, opened in Portland in 1892 and the city has been recognized as a regional cultural center ever since.

✦ INFORMATION

Oregon Historical Society | 1200 S.W. Park Ave., 97204 | 503/222–1741 | www.ohs.org. **Portland Oregon Visitors Association** | 26 S.W. Salmon, 97204 | 503/222–2223 or 877/678–5263 | www.pova.com.

SITES TO SEE

Cathedral Park. This park figures in Portland history several times over. Clark and the eight men who explored the Willamette River on the expedition's return trip camped on the site on April 2, 1806. In 1847, pioneer James Johns settled the area and began operating a ferry across the Willamette. Today the area is the Portland neighborhood known as St. Johns. The St. John suspension bridge here, built in 1931, is the only steel suspension bridge in the city. | N. Edison and Pittsburgh Sts. | 503/823–7529 | Free | Daily.

Howell Territorial Park. Oregon's pioneer days are preserved at this historic park on Sauvie Island, where Lewis and Clark camped for several days in spring 1806; they called the place "wappato island" after the potatolike roots they harvested here. During their stay, they found several Native American villages and plentiful game and waterfowl and used the time to make preparations for the difficult journey back through the Columbia River Gorge. Pioneers who followed the explorers found the area ideal for agriculture. Today's park, operated by the Metropolitan Service District and the Oregon Historical Society, includes an agricultural museum displaying a chuck wagon among other vintage farm and ranch equipment, and the Bybee Home, one of the state's oldest examples of Greek Revival architecture, built by pioneer James Francis Bybee for his family in 1858. | U.S. 30 to Howell Park Rd. off N.W. Sauvie Island Rd. | 503/222–1741 | www.ohs.org/education_public/bybeehouse.htm | $3 (suggested) | Bybee House and museum June–Sept., weekends noon–5; park daily.

Lewis and Clark Columbia River Tours. Half-day, full-day, or multiday cruises are available. Catamarans take you down the Columbia Gorge or along the gentle Willamette River following the routes used by early explorers and Oregon pioneers. Tour leaders are informed and insightful and armed with an enthusiasm for history that makes even well-read history buffs feel as if they've learned something. Reservations are required, and departure times and dates as well as tour-launch locations vary. | 2719 N. Hayden Island Rd. | 888/464–1805 | www.lewisandclarkcruisetours.com | $44–$1,199.

Oregon Historical Society. Impressive eight-story-high trompe l'oeil murals of Lewis and Clark and the Oregon Trail cover two sides of this downtown museum, which follows the state's story from prehistoric times to the present. In July 2004 "Oregon Country," a comprehensive exhibit detailing the state's history, will open. The Lewis and Clark National Bicentennial Exhibition, which has traveled the nation, will open here from November 2005 through March 2006. The society has a research library and a bookstore, a good source for maps and publications on Pacific Northwest history. | 1200 S.W. Park Ave. | 503/222–1741 | www.ohs.org | $6.

Oregon Maritime Center and Museum. For a solid review of Northwest maritime history, starting with early trader vessels, don't miss this museum. The sternwheel tugboat *Portland* on exhibit, built in 1947, represents the bygone era of pioneer river travel before the railroads came along—sternwheelers first appeared on the American landscape as early as 1810. You'll also see ships in bottles, models of military ships such as the *Constitution* and the battleship *Oregon,* early equipment, and more. The collection's largest artifacts include the *Portland* as well as a gill net boat and a barge; all are docked nearby. | 113 S.W. Naito Pkwy. | 503/224–7724 | www.oregonmaritimemuseum.org | $4 | Memorial Day–Labor Day, Fri.–Sun. 11–4; Labor Day–Memorial Day, Thurs.–Sun. 11–4.

Portland Art Museum. The 33,000 treasures in the collection of this institution founded in 1892, at the Northwest's oldest visual- and media-arts facility—which span 35 centuries of Asian, European, and American art—include one of the region's most comprehensive collections of Native American art and artifacts. | 1219 S.W. Park Ave. | 503/226–2811 | www.pam.org | $10 | Tues.–Sat. 10–5, Sun. noon–5.

ASTORIA

▼▼

Astoria is the oldest city west of the Rockies. Lewis and Clark built Fort Clatsop on the site and spent the winter of 1805–06 near here. Five years later, New York businessman John Jacob Astor, for whom the town is named, sent two expeditions to the region to establish the American Fur Company. Since that time, it has been a seaport, a cannery town, and a logging and fishing community. Many of today's 10,000 residents have Scandinavian heritage, evidenced in the town's shops and festivals. Scores of Victorian houses perching on the hillsides flank its downtown.

✦ INFORMATION

Astoria-Warrenton Area Chamber of Commerce | 111 W. Marine Dr., Astoria 97103-0176 | 503/325–6311.

SITES TO SEE

Columbia River Estuary Tours. Lewis and Clark called the vast Columbia River Estuary the Seal Islands. Today the site is protected as the Lewis and Clark National Wildlife Refuge, with 200 named islands and 35,000 acres of mudflats, tidelands, and estuary, much of it accessible only by boat. These cruises leave from Astoria's west mooring basin. | 503/325–6311 | $15–$90 | Daily, weather permitting.

Columbia River Maritime Museum. In this fascinating museum, you will see, hear, and feel why they call the Columbia River the "graveyard of the Pacific." Thousands of personal belongings of the ill-fated passengers of the 2,000 ships that have foundered here since 1811 are on display. Other exhibits are devoted to navigation, fishing, and naval history. | 1792 Marine Dr., at 17th St. | 503/325–2323 | www.crmm.org | $8 | Daily 9:30–5.

Ecola State Park. In his journal, Clark details a coastal excursion south of Astoria near the present-day resort town of Cannon Beach, when he and party arrived here to locate a whale they'd heard had washed ashore. He named the site of his find Ecola ("whale creek"). A winding road along nearby Tillamook Head, the summit of which was named Clark's Mountain in 2002 by the U.S. Board of Geographic Names, leads to an extraordinary view of the Pacific. A 13-mi stretch of the Oregon-coast trail, a hiking trail, connects two prominent headlands within today's 2,500-acre state park, which stretches inland from 9 mi of spectacular coastline. Beach access, trails, rest rooms, and picnic shelters are all available. Tent campers have access to 30 walk-in tent sites hidden in the old-growth forest; you can load your gear in wheelbarrows provided at the parking lot and cart your belongings down a trail to the campsites. | U.S. 101 | 503/436–2844 or 800/551–6949 | www. oregonstateparks.org | $3 | Daily.

Flavel House. This prim and proper mansion built between 1884 and 1886 has six fireplaces and a fine library. Furnished in the Victorian style, the house reflects the tastes of shipping tycoon Captain George Flavel, a well-respected Columbia river pilot and entrepreneur. It it said that Flavel would get his river traffic reports by standing at the windows in the fourth-floor cupola. | 441 8th St., at Duane St. | 503/325–2203 | www.clatsophistoricalsociety.org | $5 | May–Sept., daily 10–5; Oct.–Apr., daily 11–4.

Fort Clatsop National Memorial. "Ocian in view! O! the joy." recorded William Clark, standing on a spit of land south of present-day Astoria in the fall of 1805. Fort Clatsop is a faithful replica of the log stockade depicted in Clark's journal and utilized by the 33-member Corps as a winter encampment. Rooms are furnished with period handmade artifacts, and park rangers dress in period garb in summer and perform such early-19th-century tasks as making fire with flint and steel, smoking meat, and building canoes. The fort has a damp and lonely mood that lends an air of authenticity. | Fort Clatsop Loop Rd. (5 mi south of Astoria; from U.S. 101 cross Youngs Bay Bridge, turn east on Alt. U.S. 101, and follow signs) | 503/861–2471 | www.nps.gov.focl | $5 per vehicle | Mid-June–early Sept., daily 8–6; early Sept.–mid-June, daily 8–5.

Fort Stevens State Park. The site of this 3,700-acre park 6 mi southwest of Astoria was once the site of a Clatsop settlement, according to Clark. Today you will find a museum of U.S. military history, a blacksmith shop, a replica of an Indian longhouse, Civil War–era cannon and rifle demonstrations, and guided tours. The corroded skeleton of the *Peter Iredale,* a turn-of-the-20th-century English four-masted ship, protrudes from the sand west of the Fort Stevens campground, a stark testament to the tempestuous nature of the Pacific. | 1675 N.W. Peter Iredale Rd. | 503/861–1671 or 800/551–6949 | www. prd.state.or.us | $3 per vehicle | May–Oct., daily 10–6; Nov.–Apr., daily 10–4.

Neahkahnie Mountain. The coastal U.S. 101 takes hair-raising curves as it climbs to 700 feet above the Pacific the flank of this 1,661-foot mountain south of Cannon Beach. The views are dramatic. Carvings on nearby beach rocks and old Native American legends gave rise to a tale that a fortune in gold doubloons from a sunken Spanish galleon is buried somewhere on the mountainside. | U.S. 101, 91 mi northwest of Portland.

Salt Works. This stone cam, part of Fort Clatsop National Memorial, is a memorial to the exhausting labors of five members of the Corps of Discovery from December 28, 1805, to February 21, 1806, as they continuously hauled ocean water up to their campfires to boil it down for salt. Some 1,400 gallons of ocean

Astoria's Colorful Past

Winter at Fort Clatsop near present-day Astoria was not the most enjoyable experience for Lewis and Clark. Meat rotted, even as it was being smoked over the fire. The explorers' buckskin clothing fell apart in the wet weather. The men suffered from colds, dysentery, rheumatism, and unbearable infestations of fleas. The winter was one of the wettest on record—only six days without rain from December to March.

Even Christmas, the day the Corps moved into the unfinished fort, was miserable. "We should have Spent this day the nativity of Christ in feasting, had we any thing either to raise our Sperits or even gratify our appetites," wrote Clark. "Our Diner concisted of pore Elk, So much Spoiled that we eate it thro' mear necessity."

Miserable as they were, President Jefferson's men knew a valuable piece of real estate when they saw one. When they returned to the East and told Jefferson that the area now known as Astoria had potential as an important fur-trading post, a wealthy New York businessman took notice. Just five years after Lewis and Clark packed up and eagerly returned home, Lewis and Clark's dot on the map became Fort Astoria. In 1811, John Jacob Astor, a wealthy German-born fur and real estate magnate from New York who once owned the land that today is Times Square, sent members of his Pacific Fur Company to build Fort Astoria and stake America's claim to the western shore.

The establishment of Fort Astoria was the first permanent American settlement west of the Rockies. But it would not remain in American hands for long. At war with America, the British sent troops and warships to Astoria to demand the surrender of the fort in 1813, only to find that the British Hudson's Bay Company had already bought it. In 1818, just five years after the British took over, Astoria became American again.

However, it wasn't until 1846 that the official boundaries of the United States were finally drawn at the 49th Parallel. Until then, British and American citizens alike were allowed to settle in Oregon Country. As it turned out, mostly people of Scandinavian descent settled the town.

In 1840, the first U.S. Customs Office opened in Astoria. And by 1860, almost 500 pioneers called the city home. Twenty years later, it was a bawdy port town of 7,000. Stories of shanghaied sailors, brothels, and gambling dens color the city's now celebrated past.

For nearly two decades, a local theater group has produced "Shanghaied in Astoria," a musical melodrama based on the city's history.

Today, Astoria is a rural community of 10,000—so rural, in fact, that a small LearJet hit an elk while taking off from the local airport not long ago. Yet Astoria is far from isolated. It's a working port and a popular tourist destination, and its position at the mouth of the Columbia makes it the point of entry for oceangoing ships from all around the world.

water yielded 3½ bushels of fine white salt for the return trip. | U.S. 101 to Seaside, turn west on Ave. G and follow green signs to South Beach Dr. and Lewis and Clark Way | 503/861–2471 Ext. 214 | www.nps.gov/focl/salt.htm.

✦ ON THE CALENDAR

Aug. **Astoria Regatta Festival.** This maritime festival, first held in 1894, is the oldest of its kind in the Northwest. Watch for the "Shanghaied in Astoria" melodrama and for the historic ships, which sometimes include replicas from the 17th and 18th centuries. It's held the second weekend in August along the Astoria waterfront, with related events at other locations. | 503/325–6311.

HISTORIC DINING AND LODGING

Gunderson's Cannery Cafe. Seafood. At this former cannery built in the 1880s, overlooking the Columbia River on Pier 6, Gunderson's serves specials such as lime prawns, halibut burgers, and crab and shrimp cakes. Homemade soups, focaccia pizza, breads, and desserts are also available, and the place is open for hearty home-style breakfasts every morning. | One 6th St. | 503/325–8642 | $12–$25 | AE, D, MC, V.

Home Spirit Café and Restaurant. Contemporary. Inside the 1891 Queen Anne house with a river view, everything is handmade, from the croissants to the dishes (created by potter-owner Emily Henderson). Prix-fixe dinners give you a choice of four entrées: seafood, chicken, red meat, and vegetarian. And everything is made using such fresh, organic, local ingredients such as the organic beef from Oregon's River Run Farms. | 1585 Exchange St. | 503/325–6846 | www.home-spirit.com | Reservations essential | Closed Sun. and Mon. No dinner Tues. in summer, Wed. in winter | $5–$21 | No credit cards.

Astoria Inn. This Queen Anne farmhouse with gingerbread trim, built by Norwegian settler Olie Haren, sits in a quiet residential area atop a hill high above the Columbia River. The views are inspiring, especially from the appropriately named Cape Lookout guest room. The rooms and a library are filled with antiques and wingback chairs. No kids, no smoking. | 3391 Irving Ave., 97103 | 503/325–8153 or 800/718–8153 | www.astoriainnbb.com | 4 rooms | $70–$85 | D, MC, V | BP.

Benjamin Young Inn. Gardens surround this handsome Queen Anne inn, and many of the trees are original to the property, including a large Monkey Puzzle tree planted around 1888. Inside, many details are original as well, including the faux graining on the frames and moldings, the shutter-blinds in the windows, and the Povey stained glass. The spacious guest rooms mix antiques with contemporary pieces and have views of the Columbia River from their tall windows. The city tennis courts are next door. A two-night minimum stay is required on holidays and weekends from July to September. Some in-room hot tubs; no a/c, no TVs in some rooms, no smoking. | 3652 Duane St., 97103 | 503/325–6172 or 800/201–1286 | www.benjaminyounginn.com | 4 rooms, 1 suite | $85–$145 | AE, D, MC, V | BP.

Columbia River Inn Bed and Breakfast. In this blue, pink, yellow, and white "painted lady" dating from 1870, some of the tastefully decorated rooms have river views, and all are filled with antiques. It's a short walk to the Columbia River Maritime Museum and downtown. Some in-room hot tubs, some refrigerators, airport shuttle; no room phones, no kids under 12. | 1681 Franklin Ave., 97103 | 503/325–5044 or 800/953–5044 | 4 rooms | $80–$130 | AE, D, MC, V | BP.

RESOURCES

The Lewis and Clark Trail

HISTORICAL AND TOURISM ORGANIZATIONS

Lewis and Clark Heritage Trail Foundation | Box 3434, Great Falls, MT 59403 | 406/454–1234 or 888/701–3434 | fax 406/771–9237 | www.lewisandclark.org.

Lewis and Clark National Historic Tail |1709 Jackson St., Omaha, NE 68102 | 402/514–9311 | fax 402/827–9108 | www.nps.gov/lecl.

LewisandClarkTrail.com | 119 W. 3rd St., Yankton, SD 57078 | 605/664–5920 | fax 605/260–1060 | www.lewisandclarktrail.com.

TOUR COMPANIES

History America Tours. This company runs five-day to two-week tours of Historic Texas, Lewis and Clark, War on the Central Plains, and Trail of Tears, among others. | Box 797687, Dallas, TX 75379 | 972/713–7171 or 800/628–8542 | fax 972/713–7173 | www.historyamerica.com.

River Barge Excursions. Four- to ten-day cruises up the Missouri River. | 201 Opelousas Ave., New Orleans, LA 70114 | 888/456–2206 | www.riverbarge.com.

Shebby Lee Tours. The operator specializes in Vanishing Trails expeditions, including a 15-night Lewis and Clark Trail tour that thoroughly covers the entire historic route. | Box 1032, Rapid City, SD 57709 | 800/888–8306 | fax 605/343–7558 | www.shebbyleetours.com.

FURTHER READING

Ambrose, Stephen E. *Undaunted Courage.* New York: Touchstone, 1997. A biography of Meriwether Lewis that relies heavily on the journals of both Lewis and Clark, this book also details the author's personal travels along Lewis and Clark's route to the Pacific.

Beckham, Steven Dow. *Lewis and Clark in Oregon Country: From the Rockies to the Pacific.* Traces the western portion of the famous duo's trail. Portland: Graphic Arts Center, 2002.

Burroughs, Raymond D., ed. *The Natural History of the Lewis and Clark Expedition.* This classic work describes the explorations of wildlife populations encountered by Lewis and Clark. East Lansing: Michigan State University Press, 1961.

Cutright, Paul R. *Lewis and Clark: Pioneering Naturalists.* The explorers found and described in detail more than 200 new plant and animal species during their expedition in the American West. Lincoln: University of Nebraska Press, 1969.

DeVoto, Bernard, ed. *The Journals of Lewis and Clark.* Mariner Books, 1953/revised 1997. A one-volume edition; the narrative remains essentially intact and includes nearly every important event of interest.

Duncan, Dayton, Ken Burns, William Least Heat Moon, Stephen Ambrose, and Erica Funkhouser. *Lewis & Clark: The Journey of the Corps of Discovery: An Illustrated History.* New York: Alfred A. Knopf, 1999.

Duncan, Dayton. *Lewis and Clark: An Illustrated History.* New York, Knopf, 1997. A companion to the PBS television series with introduction by Ken Burns.

Fifer, Barbara. *Going Along with Lewis and Clark.* This kids' guide to the Lewis and Clark Trail offers lively discussions of harrowing adventures and is illustrated with historic photos and spirited art. Helena, MT: Farcountry Press, 2000.

Fifer, Barbara and Vicky Soderberg. *Along the Trail with Lewis and Clark.* Historical highlights of the Corps of Discovery expedition's encounters include listings for current parks, campgrounds, and recreational opportunities. Helena, MT: Farcountry Press, 2001.

Gass, Patrick and Carol Lynn MacGregor, eds. *The Journals of Patrick Gass: Member of the Lewis and Clark Expedition.* Mountain Press Publishing, 1997. Sergeant Gass kept a consistent log of the journey that is very readable, and the log of daily activities shows the optimistic spirit of the Corps.

Gilman, Carolyn I. *Lewis and Clark: Across the Divide.* Washington, D.C.: Smithsonian Institution Press, 2003.

Holmberg, James, ed. *Dear Brother—Letters from William Clark to Jonathon Clark.* New Haven: Yale University Press, 2002.

Hunsaker, Joyce Badgley. *Sacagawea Speaks: Beyond the Shining Mountains with Lewis and Clark.* Falcon Publishing Co., 2001. Meet Sacagawea face-to-face in this well-researched, first-person account filled with professional, dramatic storytelling and user-friendly history that leaps off the page and into the imagination.

Jackson, Donald, ed. Letters of the Lewis and Clark Expedition, with Related Documents: 1783–1854. 2nd edition. Urbana: University of Illinois Press, 1978.

MacGregor, Carol, ed. *The Journals of Patrick Gass.* Missoula, MT: Mountain Press Publishing Company, 1997. Sergeant Gass's record of the journey focuses on the daily activities of the Corps of Discovery.

Moulton, Gary E., ed. *The Lewis and Clark Journals: An American Epic of Discovery.* Lincoln: University of Nebraska Press, 2002. Thirteen volumes:
Volume 1: Atlas of the Lewis and Clark Expedition
Volume 2: August 30, 1803–August 24, 1804
Volume 3: August 25, 1804–April 6, 1805

Volume 4: April 7–July 27, 1805
Volume 5: July 28–November 1, 1805
Volume 6: November 2, 1805–March 22, 1806
Volume 7: March 23–June 9, 1806
Volume 8: June 10–September 26, 1806
Volume 9: John Ordway and Charles Floyd
Volume 10: Patrick Gass
Volume 11: Joseph Whitehouse
Volume 12: Herbarium of the Lewis and Clark Expedition
Volume 13: Comprehensive Index

Ronda, James P. *Lewis and Clark: Among the Indians.* Drawing on the journals of Lewis and Clark, this book details the interactions between the Corps of Discovery and the Native American cultures throughout the expedition. Lincoln: University of Nebraska Press, 1984.

Illinois

HISTORICAL AND TOURISM ORGANIZATIONS

Illinois Historic Preservation Agency | One Lewis and Clark Trail, Hartford, 62048 | 618/251–5811 | www. state.il.us/hpa.

TOUR COMPANIES

Bluff City Tours. A complete package of Lewis and Clark programs and tours. | 3002 Godfrey Rd., Godfrey, 62035 | 618/466–8693 | www. bluffcitytours.com.

FURTHER READING

Hartley, Robert. *Lewis and Clark in the Illinois Country:* The Little-Told Story. Sniktau Publications, 2002.

Missouri

HISTORICAL AND TOURISM ORGANIZATIONS

State Historical Society of Missouri | 1020 Lowery St., Columbia, 65201 | 573/882–7083 | www.system.missouri.edu/shs.

TOUR COMPANIES

Discovery Expedition. This company has reconstructed the three Corps of Discovery boats and takes excursions of up to a week along parts of the rivers traveled by Lewis and Clark. | 314 S. Main St., St. Charles, 63301 | 636/916–5344 | www.lewisandclark.net.

FURTHER READING

Denny, James M. *Lewis and Clark in the Boonslick.* Boone's Lick Heritage, Vol. 8, no. 2–3 (June–September 2000): 3–26. Boonslick Historical Society, 2000.

Kenny, Tom. *Lewis and Clark in Missouri.* Brunswick, MO: self-published, 1992.

Moulton, Gary E., ed. *The Journals of the Lewis and Clark Expedition.* (Volumes 2 and 8 relate to the expedition in Missouri.) Lincoln: University of Nebraska Press, 1983–1987.

Moulton, Gary E. *Lewis and Clark in the Middle Missouri.* Lincoln: Nebraska Historical Society, 2001.

Rogers, Ann. *Lewis and Clark in Missouri.* Columbia: University of Missouri Press, 1981.

Kansas

HISTORICAL AND TOURISM ORGANIZATIONS

Kansas State Historical Society | 6425 S.W. 6th Ave., Topeka, 66615 | 785/272–6861 | www.kshs.org.

TOUR COMPANIES

Discovery Expedition. This company has reconstructed the three Corps of Discovery boats and takes excursions of up to a week along parts of the rivers traveled by Lewis and Clark. | 314 S. Main St., St. Charles, MO 63301 | 636/916–5344 | www.lewisandclark.net.

FURTHER READING

Moulton, Gary E., ed. *The Journals of the Lewis and Clark Expedition.* (Volumes 2 and 8 relate to the expedition in Kansas.) Lincoln: University of Nebraska Press, 1983–87.

Nebraska

HISTORICAL AND TOURISM ORGANIZATIONS

National Park Service Midwest Regional Office | 1709 Jackson St., Omaha, 68102-2571 | 402/221–3478.

Nebraska Historical Society | Box 82554, 1500 R St., Lincoln, 68501 | 402/471–4746 | wwww.nebraskahistory.org.

Nebraska Lewis and Clark Bicentennial Commission | 2200 N. 33rd St., Lincoln, 68503 | 402/471–5499 | www.lewisandclarkne.org.

TOUR COMPANIES

Allied Tours, Inc. Tours include 1-, 2-, and 10-day tours through the Lewis and Clark of Iowa, Nebraska, and South Dakota. | 720 E. Norfolk Ave., Norfolk, 68701 | 402/721–8730 | www.alliedtt.com.

Omaha History Tours. The Douglas County Historical Society coordinates a variety of walking and river-cruising tours that incorporate the landing of Lewis and Clark. | 5730 N. 30th St., Omaha, 68111 | 402/455–9990 | www.omahahistory.org.

FURTHER READING

Menard, Orville. *From Rulo to Lynch with Lewis and Clark.* Omaha: Douglas County Historical Society, 2003.

Moulton, Gary E., ed. *The Journals of the Lewis and Clark Expedition.* (Volume 2 relates to Nebraska.) Lincoln: University of Nebraska Press, 1983–1987.

Nebraskaland Magazine, "American Looks West—Lewis and Clark on the Missouri," Vol. 80. Nebraska Game and Parks Commission, 2002.

Ronda, James P. *Lewis and Clark Among the Indians.* Lincoln: University of Nebraska Press, 1984.

Iowa

HISTORICAL AND TOURISM ORGANIZATIONS

Iowa Lewis and Clark Bicentennial Commission | 1520 Morningside Ave., Sioux City, 51106 | 317/232–9628 | www.lewisandclarkne-ia.com.

State Historical Society of Iowa | 600 E. Locust, Des Moines, 50319 | 515/281–5111 | www.iowahistory.org.

TOUR COMPANIES

Allied Tours, Inc. Tours include 1-, 2-, and 10-day tours through the Lewis and Clark of Iowa, Nebraska and South Dakota. | 720 E. Norfolk Ave., Norfolk, 68701 | 402/721–8730 | www.alliedtt.com.

Loess Hills Hospitality Association. Historical and ethnic heritage tours are among the tours that travel the footsteps of early explorers and pioneers of the famous Loess Hills. Personal and motor-coach tours available, along with maps for self-guided tours. Box 51, Moorhead, 51558 | 712/886–5441 or 800/886–5441 | www.loesshillstours.com.

Relive the Journey. This two-day tour organized by the Sioux City Convention and Visitors Bureau begins in Omaha and returns to Sioux City, visiting numerous Lewis and Clark historical sites in the area. | 800/593–2228 | www.siouxcitytourismconvention.com.

FURTHER READING

Moulton, Gary E., ed. *The Journals of the Lewis and Clark Expedition.* (Volume 2 covers Iowa; Volume 9 includes Sergeant Floyd's Journal.) Lincoln: University of Nebraska Press, 1983–1987.

South Dakota

HISTORICAL AND TOURISM ORGANIZATIONS

Great Lakes of South Dakota Association | 320 E. Capitol Ave., Pierre, 57501-0786 | 605/224–4617 or 888/386–4617 | fax 605/224–9913 | www.sdgreatlakes.org.

Preserve South Dakota | 215 W. Sioux Ave., Pierre, 57501 | 605/945–0409.

South Dakota Department of Game, Fish and Parks | 523 E. Capitol Ave., Pierre, 57501-3182 | 605/773–3391.

South Dakota State Historical Society | 900 Governors Dr., Pierre, 57501-2217 | 605/773–3458 | fax 605/773–6041 | www.sdhistory.org.

South Dakota Tourism | 711 E. Wells Ave., Pierre, 57501-3369 | 605/773–3301 | fax 605/773–3256 | www.travelsd.com.

Southeast South Dakota Visitors Association | 800 Mariner La., Suite 104, Yankton, 57078 | 605/665–2435 or 888/353–7382 | fax 605/665–8776.

TOUR COMPANIES

Dakota Sightseeing and Tours. Customized sightseeing tours of the Black Hills and surrounding areas are available for groups or individuals, as well as charters and convention services. | Box 132, Rapid City, 57709 | 605/343–9001 | fax 605/343–9004 | www.dakotasightseeingandtours.com.

Mike Kuchera'a Wild West Expeditions. Choose your own adventure with Wild West Expeditions' customizable and guided tours throughout South Dakota. Possible activities include powwows, horseback riding, wagon trains, fishing, hiking, and canoe rides along the mighty Missouri. | Box 10, Mitchell, 57301 | 605/996–1120 | fax 605/996–1232 | www.wwexpeditions.com.

FURTHER READING

Griffith, Thomas D. *South Dakota.* A comprehensive guidebook exploring the history, evolution, and attractions of South Dakota. New York: Fodor's Travel Publications, Inc., 1994.

Robinson, Doane. *Lewis and Clark in South Dakota.* An account of the expedition's journey through South Dakota, written by South Dakota's most famed state historian. Pierre, SD: South Dakota State Historical Society, 1918.

North Dakota

HISTORICAL AND TOURISM ORGANIZATIONS

North Dakota Indian Affairs Commission | 600 E. Boulevard Ave., 1st floor., J Wing, Bismarck, 58505-2428 | www.health.state.nd.us/ndiac.

North Dakota Tourism Department | 604 E. Boulevard Ave., Bismarck, 58505-5663 | 800/435–5663 | fax 701/328–4878 | www.ndtourism.com.

State Historical Society of North Dakota | 612 E. Boulevard Ave., Bismarck, 58505-0830 | 701/328–2666 | fax 701/328–3710 | www.state.nd.us/hist.

Three Affiliated Tribes Tourism | 336 Main St., New Town, 58763 | 701/627–2870 | www.mhanation.com.

TOUR COMPANIES

Satrom Travel & Tour. Satrom Travel & Tour conducts a Lewis and Clark Legacy Tour and two Corps of Discovery Tours that are more in-depth. All the tours originate out of Bismarck. | Provident Building, 316 N. 5th St., Bismarck, 68701 | 800/833–8787 | www.satromtours.com.

FURTHER READING

Ahler, Stanley A., Thomas D. Thiessen, and Michael K. Trimble. *People of the Willow: The Prehistory and Early History of the Hidatsa Indians.* Grand Forks: University of North Dakota Press, 1991. The Hidatsa lived in North Dakota thousands of years before Lewis and Clark were in the state, and the Lewis and Clark expedition spent more time with the Hidatsa and Mandan tribes in the Knife and Missouri River areas of central North Dakota than they did with any other Native American tribes along their route to the Pacific.

Dill, C. L. *Early Peoples of North Dakota.* Bismarck, ND: State Historical Society of North Dakota, 1990. This book traces the history of the first people who lived in and traveled across this area from 11,000 years ago to 1858, when the first fort was built in North Dakota.

Heidenreich, Virginia. *The Fur Trade in North Dakota.* Bismarck, ND: State Historical Society of North Dakota, 1990. The impact of the fur trade on American Indian cultures in North Dakota from the 1730s to 1880s is captured in four essays by W. Raymond Wood, C. L. Dill, Gregory S. Camp, and Jacqueline C. Peterson, which detail the people, companies, and forts that dominated the era.

North Dakota Historical Society. *North Dakota Blue Book.* Bismarck, ND: Secretary of State's Office, 1899, 1995, 1997, 1999, 2001, 2003. Published every two years, this comprehensive overview covers North Dakota's history, government, and people with special sections on various topics, including famous people from the state, the state bird, and the state flower. The 1999–2001 book has a special section focusing on Lewis and Clark's journey through the state.

Reid, Russell. *Lewis and Clark in North Dakota.* Bismarck, ND: State Historical Society of North Dakota, 3rd printing, 2003. This publication follows Lewis and Clark through North Dakota along the Missouri River, the changing seasons, and encounters with new people and cultures.

Rogers, Ken. *Lewis and Clark: The Dakota Winter.* The *Bismarck Tribune.* 1997. This publication covers the time Lewis and Clark spent in North Dakota at Fort Mandan and the surrounding area the winter of 1804–05.

Reid, Russell, ed. *Lewis and Clark in North Dakota.* A new edition is in the works, edited by Clay S. Jenkinson. It should be available sometime in 2003.

Montana

HISTORICAL AND TOURISM ORGANIZATIONS

Bureau of Land Management BLM Tourism, Box 36800, Billings, 59107 | 406/896–5000 | www.blm.gov.

Custer Country Box 160, Laurel, 59044 | 800/346–1876 | www.custer.visitmt.com.

Glacier Country Box 1035, Bigfork, 59911-1035 | 800/338–5072 | fax 406/837–6231 | www.glacier.visitmt.com.

Gold West Country | 1155 Main, Deer Lodge, 59722 | 800/879–1159 | www.goldwest.visitmt.com.

Lewis and Clark Bicentennial Commission | www.montanalewisandclark.org.

Missouri River Country Box 387, Wolf Point, 59201 | 800/653–1319 | www.missouririver.visitmt.com.

Montana Department of Fish, Wildlife and Parks Box 200701, Helena, 59620-0701 | 406/444–2535 | www.fwp.stat.mt.us.

Montana Historical Society | 225 N. Roberts St., Helena, 59620 | 406/444–2694 or 800/243–9900 | www.montanahistoricalsociety.org.

Montana Tribal Tourism Alliance | www.montanalewisandclark.com/resources/americanindians/mtta.htm.

Russell Country Box 3166, Great Falls, 59403-3166 | 800/527–5348 | www.russell.visitmt.com.

Travel Montana Box 200533, Helena, 59620 | 800/847–4868 | www.visitmt.com.

Yellowstone Country | 1822 W. Lincoln, Bozeman, 59715 | 800/736–5276 | www.yellowstone.visitmt.com.

TOUR COMPANIES

Canoe Montana. Canoe trips through the Wild and Scenic Missouri River include camping at Lewis and Clark sites, reading the journals, and discussing the expedition. Trips run from half a day to seven days, May–October. | 1312 Front St., Fort Benton, 59442 | 406/622–5882 or 800/500–4538 | www.montanariver.com.

Lewis and Clark Trail Adventures. Hiking, biking, and canoe tours for two to seven days. Tour areas include Salmon River, Lochsa, and Alberton Gorge of the Clark Fork, Missouri River, Lolo Trail, and Yellowstone River. | 517 Cleveland, Missoula, 59801 | 406/728–7609 or 800/366–6246.

Montana Rockies Rail Tours. Train tours of seven days, six nights along sections of the Lewis and Clark Trail. Tours offered are Billings and Pompeys Pillar; Livingston to Missoula; Missoula to Lewiston, Idaho, or Pasco, Oregon, to Portland, Oregon, and Fort Clatsop, Oregon. | 2660 Ontario St., Sandpoint, ID 83864 | 800/519–7245.

Off the Beaten Path. Tour of nine days, eight nights follows the Lewis and Clark Trail by ground transportation, canoeing, rafting, and some walking. Group size is 16 people; tours are led by experienced guides and historians. | 27 Main St., Bozeman, 59715 | 406/586–1311 or 800/445–2995.

Rocky Mountain Discovery Tours. Specializing in Lewis and Clark, the company leads motor-coach tours though Montana, Idaho, Washington, and Oregon for the general public and customized tours for groups. Tours include lodging, meals, fees, sites, interpretive centers, speakers, performers, and boat tours of the Missouri and/or Columbia rivers. You can start in any city or state you wish, for as many days as you prefer. | PMB 520 248A, N. Higgins Ave., Missoula, 59802 | 406/721–4821 or 888/400–0048 | www.rmdt.com.

FURTHER READING

Edwards, Judith. *Colter's Run.* Helena, MT: Falcon Press, 1993. The story of John Colter's escape from the Blackfeet; a young people's book for eight and older.

English, Tom, Ella M. Howard, Robert Moritz. *Lewis and Clark Exploration of Central Montana: Marias River to Gates of the Mountains.* Great Falls: Lewis and Clark Interpretive Association, 2000. Although this is a relatively small part of the area the expedition covered, it was rich in discoveries and happenings.

Harris, Burton. *John Colter: His Years in the Rockies.* Lincoln: University of Nebraska Press, 1952, reprinted 1993. Describes Colter's experiences with Lewis and Clark and his life in the frontier of Montana and Wyoming as an explorer and trapper.

Schmidt, Tom; Schmidt, Jeremy. *The Saga of Lewis and Clark into the Uncharted West.* New York: DK Publishing, 1999. A classical account and pictorial presentation of America's greatest quest.

Schullery, Paul. *Lewis and Clark Among the Grizzlies.* Guilford, MT: Falcon Press, 2002. Bear anecdotes from the Lewis and Clark Expedition.

Idaho

HISTORICAL AND TOURISM ORGANIZATIONS

Clearwater-Snake Lewis Clark Bicentennial Committee | Box 871, Lewiston, 83501 | 208/935–7636 | www.lewisclarkidaho.org.

Idaho Chapter Lewis & Clark Trail Heritage Foundation | 804 E. Pennsylvania St., Boise, 83706.

Idaho Department of Commerce Box 83720, Boise, 83720-0093 | 208/334–2470 | www.lewisandclarkidaho.org.

Idaho Department of Parks & Recreation | 5657 Warm Springs Ave., Boise, 83712 | 208/334–4199.

Idaho Lewis & Clark Bicentennial | 415 Main St., Lewiston, 83501 | 208/792–2249 | www.lewisandclarkidaho.org.

Idaho Transportation Department | Box 7129, Boise, 83720 | 208/799–5010.

Lemhi County Lewis&Clark Bicentennial Committee | 200 Main St., Suite 1, Salmon, 83467 | 208/756–3679.

Lemhi Shoshone Box 208, Fort Hall, 83203.

Nez Percé Tribe Box 365, Lapwai, 83540 | 208/843–2553 | www.nezperce.org.

North Central Idaho Travel Association | Box 2018, Lewiston, 83501 | 208/790–1276 | www.idahonwp.org.

TOUR COMPANIES

Clearwater River Company. Jim Cook provides a variety of vacation experiences, including tours down the Clearwater River in replicas of historic longboats. | 208/276–3199 | www.clearwatertrips.com.

Hells Canyon Visitor Association. The association provides information on jet-boat tours into Hells Canyon and Clearwater River tours and links to Idaho Lewis and Clark road tours. | 800 Port Dr., Clarkston, WA 99403 | 509/758–5773 | www.hellscanyonvisitor.com.

Idaho Adventures. White-water adventures down the River of No Return are lead by this outfitter. For the Bicentennial, they have a three-hour float trip that includes a program about Lewis, Clark, and Sacagawea. They also have overnight accommodations. Box 834, Salmon, WA 83467 | 208/756–2986 or 800/789–9283 | www.idahoadventures.com.

Lewis Clark Idaho Road Tours. Historical tours given by this outfitter are designed to be a physical, intellectual, and spiritual experience. | 208/926–7875 | fax 405/681–6442 | www.lewisclarkidaho.com.

Odyssey Tours. With Lewis and Clark scholar Clay Jenkinson, Becky Cawley conducts a motor-coach tour designed specifically for Lewis and Clark enthusiasts. | 208/791–8721 | www.hibek.com.

Triple O Outfitters. Barb and Harlan Opdahl have led horse trips over the Lolo portion of the Lewis and Clark Trail for nearly two decades. The tour takes one week. | 208/464–2349 | www.tripleO-outfitters.com.

FURTHER READING

Aegerter, Mary and Steve F. Russell. *Hike Lewis and Clark's Idaho.* Moscow, ID: University of Idaho Press, 2002. A must for anyone wanting to leave the road for short to long hikes along the trail in Idaho.

Fazio, James R., Mike Venso, Steve F. Russell. *Across the Snowy Ranges—The Lewis & Clark Expedition in Idaho and Western Montana.* Moscow, ID. Woodland Press, 2001. Fazio's free-flowing narrative, Venso's rich photographs, and Russell's accurate and detailed maps make this book the best study of the Lewis and Clark expedition through Idaho.

Washington
HISTORICAL AND TOURISM ORGANIZATIONS

Lewis and Clark Trail Heritage Foundation, Washington Chapter | 886 S. Hwy., 17, Othello, 99344 | 509/488–9074 | www.lcarchive.org/wa_lcthf.html.

Washington State Historical Society | 1911 Pacific Ave., Tacoma, 98402 | 253/272–3500 | www.wshs.org.

Washington State Tourism Office of Trade and Economic Development | 360/725–5052 | fax 360/586–8440 | www.tourism.wa.gov.

TOUR COMPANIES

Columbia River Journeys. Narrated three-hour tours depart from Richland and ply the waters of the Snake River. The company also leads tours into the Hanford Reach National Monument, one of the last free-flowing stretches of the Columbia River and the largest remaining remnant of the shrub-steppe ecosystem that dominated the region when Lewis and Clark made their journey west. | Box 26, Richland, 99352 | 509/734–9941 or 888/486–9119 | www.columbiariverjourneys.com.

Cruise West. A popular tour for the past 10 years, Cruise West's Lewis and Clark–focused tour is "A River Voyage of Discovery," eight days, seven nights round-trip from Portland. Cruises depart in spring and fall. | 2401 4th Ave., Suite 700, Seattle, 98121 | 206/441–8687 or 800/580–0072 | fax 206/441–4757 | www.cruisewest.com.

Lindblad Expeditions, Inc. The Lindblad expedition travel company tours Washington with its "In the Wake of Lewis and Clark Tour." Travelers head up the Columbia River starting in Portland, Oregon, through eastern Washington to Hells Canyon, and back through the gorge to the Washington–Oregon coast. Historians and naturalists are on board the 70-guest ships. Cruises depart in spring and fall. | 1415 Western Ave., Suite 700, Seattle, 98101 | 212/765–7740 or 800/527–6298 | fax 206/403–1501.

Skamokawa Paddle Center. In the heart of the Columbia River estuary about 45 mi east of Long Beach, Skamokawa sits about where Captain William Clark wrote his famous words, "Ocian in View!" Guided "Lewis and Clark Tours" take paddlers of all skill levels on two-day excursions along this famous stretch of the Columbia. | 1391 W. State Hwy. 4, Skamokawa, 98647 | 360/795–8300 or 888/920–2777 | fax 360/795–8304 | www.skamokawakayak.com.

FURTHER READING

Kirk, Ruth, Alexander, Carmela. *Exploring Washington's Past, A Road Guide to History.* This traveler's guide to Washington focuses on the state's rich history. Seattle: University of Washington Press, 1996 (revised).

Nisbet, Jack. *Singing Grass, Burning Sage: Discovering Washington's Shrub-Steppe.* In this book produced with the Nature Conservancy, award-winning writer Jack Nesbit celebrates Washington's wide-open spaces with photographs and essays. North Vancouver: Whitecap Books, 1999.

Ziak, Rex. *In Full View.* A true and accurate account of Lewis and Clark's arrival at the Pacific Ocean and their search for a winter camp along the lower Columbia River. Washington historian and writer Rex Ziak explores the harrowing end of Lewis and Clark's final push to the sea. Astoria, OR: Moffit House Press, 2002.

Oregon

HISTORICAL AND TOURISM ORGANIZATIONS

Lewis and Clark Bicentennial in Oregon | 1230 S.W. Park, Portland, 97205 | 503/306–5222 | www.lcbo.net.

Lewis and Clark Trail Heritage Foundation, Oregon Chapter | 1190 N.E. Birchaire La., Hillsboro, 97140 | 503/640–9493 | www.lcarchive.org/or_lcthf.html.

Oregon Heritage Commission | 1115 Commercial St. N.E. Suite 1, Salem, 97301-1002 | 503/378–4168 | fax 503/378–6447 | ww.oregonheritage.org.

Oregon Historical Society | 1200 S.W. Park Ave., Portland, 97205-2483 | 503/222–1741 | fax 503/221–2035 | www.ohs.org.

Oregon Tourism Commission | 775 Summer St. NE, Salem, 97310 | 800/547–7842 | fax 503/986–0001 | www.traveloregon.com.

TOUR COMPANIES

Adventure Cruises. Naturalists on board the company's yacht-style ship bring the scenery alive for travelers. Spring and summer cruises chart the Snake and Columbia rivers on a 1,000-mi journey following Lewis and Clark's famous voyage through the Pacific Northwest. | 14405 S.E. Ellis St., Portland, 97236 | 503/762–0939 or 800/613–2789 | www.adventurecruises.com.

American West Steamboat Company. With a fleet of three old-fashioned steamboats, American West follows the Lewis and Clark Trail along the Snake and Columbia rivers. Choose from weeklong steamboat excursions, rail/cruise excursions, and shore excursions. Fine dining, live showboat-type entertainment. | 2101 4th Ave., Suite 1150, Seattle, 98121 | 800/434–1232 | www.columbiarivercruise.com.

Ecotours of Oregon. Ecotours leads sightseeing and nature day tours in Oregon and southwest Washington with naturalist guides, including Lewis and Clark on the Lower Columbia. | 3127 S.E. 23rd Ave., Portland, 97202 | 503/245–1428 or 888/808–7733 | fax 503/245–1428 | www.ecotours-of-oregon.com.

Lewis and Clark Columbia River Cruise Tours. Day and overnight cruises on the Columbia River. Narrated tours aboard the Lewis and Clark catamaran excursion boat in April–November. | 2719 N. Hayden Island Dr., Portland, 97217 | 888/464–1805 | www.lewisandclarkcolumbiarivercruises.com.

Sternwheeler *Columbia Gorge*. Cruises departing from Cascade Locks in the Columbia River Gorge ply the waters along the Lewis and Clark trail. The triple-decker paddle wheeler leads narrated sightseeing cruises and meal excursions year-round with a modified schedule November–May. | Box 307, Cascade Locks, 97014 | 541/374–8427 or 800/643–1354 | fax 541/374–8647 | www.sternwheeler.com.

FURTHER READING

Beckham, Steven. *Lewis and Clark in Oregon Country: From the Rockies to the Pacific.* Stunning photos and captivating essays examine what the region was really like when Lewis and Clark explored this uncharted territory. Portland: Graphic Arts Center Publishing Company, 2002.

Duncan, Dayton. *Out West.* Journalist Dayton Duncan embarked on his own epic journey when he set out in his Volkswagon camper to retrace Lewis and Clark's steps from St. Lewis to the Oregon coast. Greenwich: Bison Books Corp., 2000.

McKinney, Sam. *Reach of Tide, Ring of History: A Columbia River Voyage.* Sam McKinney, an historian and founder of the Lewis and Clark Columbia River Trail, sets out to explore the Columbia River aboard his small handmade boat, visiting old Indian village sites and Lewis and Clark camps along the way. Corvallis: Oregon State University Press, 2000.

Moulton, Gary E. and Thomas E., Dunlay, eds. *The Definitive Journals of Lewis & Clark: Down the Columbia to Fort Clatsop, Vol. 6.* An excellent companion to exploring the Lewis and Clark trail, this volume of Lewis's and Clark's journals focuses on the Pacific Northwest portion of the voyage. Greenwich: Bison Books Corp., 2002.

Wells, Gail and Dawn Anzinger. *Lewis and Clark Meet Oregon's Forests: Lessons From Dynamic Nature.* The Oregon Forest Resources Institute commissioned the book to explore the conditions in Oregon's forests at the time of Lewis and Clark. Corvallis: Oregon State University Press, 2002.

Important Numbers and On-line Info

LODGINGS

Adam's Mark	800/444–2326	www.adamsmark.com
Baymont Inns	800/428–3438	www.baymontinns.com
Best Western	800/528–1234	www.bestwestern.com
TDD	800/528–2222	
Budget Host	800/283–4678	www.budgethost.com
Clarion	800/252–7466	www.clarioninn.com
Comfort	800/228–5150	www.comfortinn.com
Courtyard by Marriott	800/321–2211	www.courtyard.com
Days Inn	800/325–2525	www.daysinn.com
Doubletree	800/222–8733	www.doubletree.com
Drury Inns	800/325–8300	www.druryinn.com
Econo Lodge	888/424–6423	www.choicehotel.com
Embassy Suites	800/362–2779	www.embassysuites.com
Exel Inns of America	800/356–8013	www.exelinns.com
Fairfield Inn by Marriott	800/228–2800	www.fairfieldinn.com
Fairmont Hotels	800/257–7544	www.fairmont.com
Four Seasons	800/332–3442	www.fourseasons.com
Hampton Inn	800/426–7866	www.hamptoninn.com
Hilton	800/445–8667	www.hilton.com
TDD	800/368–1133	
Holiday Inn	800/465–4329	www.holiday-inn.com
TDD	800/238–5544	
Howard Johnson	800/446–4656	www.hojo.com
TDD	800/654–8442	
Hyatt & Resorts	800/233–1234	www.hyatt.com
Inns of America	800/826–0778	www.innsofamerica.com
Inter-Continental	800/327–0200	www.intercontinental.com
La Quinta	800/531–5900	www.laquinta.com
TDD	800/426–3101	

Loews	800/235–6397	www.loewshotels.com
Marriott	800/228–9290	www.marriott.com
Master Hosts Inns	800/251–1962	www.reservahost.com
Le Meridien	800/543–4300	www.lemeridien.com
Motel 6	800/466–8356	www.motel6.com
Omni	800/843–6664	www.omnihotels.com
Quality Inn	800/228–5151	www.qualityinn.com
Radisson	800/333–3333	www.radisson.com
Ramada	800/228–2828	www.ramada.com
TDD	800/533–6634	
Red Carpet/Scottish Inns	800/251–1962	www.reservahost.com
Red Lion	800/733–5466	www.redlion.com
Red Roof Inn	800/843–7663	www.redroof.com
Renaissance	800/468–3571	www.renaissancehotels.com
Residence Inn by Marriott	800/331–3131	www.residenceinn.com
Ritz-Carlton	800/241–3333	www.ritzcarlton.com
Rodeway	800/228–2000	www.rodeway.com
Sheraton	800/325–3535	www.sheraton.com
Shilo Inn	800/222–2244	www.shiloinns.com
Signature Inns	800/822–5252	www.signature-inns.com
Sleep Inn	800/221–2222	www.sleepinn.com
Super 8	800/848–8888	www.super8.com
Travelodge/Viscount	800/255–3050	www.travelodge.com
Vagabond	800/522–1555	www.vagabondinns.com
Westin Hotels & Resorts	800/937–8461	www.westin.com
Wyndham Hotels & Resorts	800/996–3426	www.wyndham.com

AIRLINES

Air Canada	888/247–2262	www.aircanada.ca
Alaska	800/426–0333	www.alaska-air.com
American/TWA	800/433–7300	www.aa.com
America West	800/235–9292	www.americawest.com
British Airways	800/247–9297	www.british-airways.com
Continental Airlines	800/525–0280	www.continental.com
Delta	800/221–1212	www.delta.com
Northwest	800/225–2525	www.nwa.com
Southwest	800/435–9792	www.southwest.com
United	800/241–6522	www.ual.com
USAirways	800/428–4322	www.usairways.com

BUSES AND TRAINS

Amtrak	800/872–7245	www.amtrak.com
Greyhound	800/231–2222	www.greyhound.com
Trailways	800/343–9999	www.trailways.com

CAR RENTALS

Advantage	800/777–5500	www.arac.com
Alamo	800/327–9633	www.goalamo.com
Avis	800/331–1212	www.avis.com
Budget	800/527–0700	www.budget.com
Dollar	800/800–4000	www.dollar.com
Enterprise	800/325–8007	www.enterprise.com
Hertz	800/654–3131	www.hertz.com
National	800/328–4567	www.nationalcar.com
Payless	800/237–2804	www.paylesscarrental.com
Rent-A-Wreck	800/535–1391	www.rent-a-wreck.com
Thrifty	800/367–2277	www.thrifty.com

Note: Area codes are changing all over the United States as this book goes to press. For the latest updates, check www.areacode-info.com.

ABOUT OUR WRITERS

✦ **Gina Bacon** is a freelance writer and Pacific Northwest native. Her years fighting forest fires for the U.S. Forest Service instilled in her a deep appreciation of the still-wild West and Lewis and Clark's amazing journey into the unknown.

✦ Black Hills resident **Tom Griffith,** who has served as director of communications for the Mount Rushmore Preservation Fund, wrote the South Dakota chapter. In his busy career he has worked for newspapers in Arizona, Montana, and South Dakota and has written several books, including *America's Shrine of Democracy.*

✦ Writer/photographer **Pat Hansen,** of Avon, Montana, has freelanced for the past 18 years for such publications as *Montana Magazine, Rural Heritage, Range Magazine, GRIT,* and *The Fence Post.* She and her husband enjoy leisurely trips, often visiting off-the-beaten-track points of interest.

✦ The grandparents of **Candi Helseth** came from Norway and traveled by wagon train to North Dakota, where they established a homestead. The Helseth family still lives there, and our North Dakota writer grew up trail riding in the area. Trading in her saddle for a computer, she has written several histories for area cooperatives and has published stories on Lewis and Clark in *American Profile Magazine, North Dakota Living,* and *North Dakota Horizons.*

✦ A contributor to numerous Fodor's titles, **Diana Lambdin Meyer** learned how to spin a mean yarn at the knee of her grandfather, the family genealogist. A Nebraska native who now lives on the Lewis and Clark Trail in Platte County, Missouri, she wrote the Illinois, Missouri, Kansas, Nebraska, and Iowa chapters.

✦ **Carole Simon-Smolinski** is a Pacific Northwest historian and writer. She is on the Washington Governor's Lewis Clark Committee and the Clearwater Snake Lewis Clark Bicentennial Committee and is currently writing a comprehensive history of Hells Canyon and the Middle Snake River.

REGIONAL DIRECTORY

IDAHO

Kamiah, *204–206, 208*
Lewiston, *213–216, 218*
Orofino, *210, 212–213*
Salmon, *200–202*
Weippe, *208–210*

ILLINOIS

Alton, *29–30*
Cahokia, *25, 28–29*
Hartford, *31–33*
Wood River, *30–31*

IOWA

Council Bluffs, *100–102*
Glenwood, *100*
Missouri Valley, *102*
Onawa, *103, 105*
Sidney, *99–100*
Sioux City, *105–108*

KANSAS

Atchison, *70–72*
Highland/White Cloud, *73*
Kansas City, *67–68*
Leavenworth, *68–70*

MISSOURI

Arrow Rock, *54–55*
Augusta, *44–45*
Boonville, *53–54*
Columbia, *49*
Glasgow, *55, 57*

Hermann, *46–47*
Independence, *57–58*
Jefferson City, *47–48*
Kansas City, *59–60*
Lexington, *57*
Marthasville, *45–46*
Parkville and Weston, *61–63*
Rocheport, *49, 51–53*
St. Charles, *41–44*
St. Joseph, *63–64*
St. Louis, *37–41*

MONTANA

Billings, *188–192*
Bozeman, *184–186*
Dillon, *178–181*
Fort Benton, *165–168*
Fort Peck, *163*
Great Falls, *168, 170–171*
Helena, *171–174*
Lewistown, *164–165*
Livingston, *186, 188*
Miles City, *192–193*
Missoula, *181–183*
Sidney, *160, 162*
Three Forks, *174–176*
Whitehall, *176–178*

NEBRASKA

Bellevue, *82–83*
Blair, *86–88*
Brownville, *79, 81–82*
Crofton, *91–93*
Decatur, *88–90*

Lynch, *93–95*
Omaha, *83–86*
South Sioux City, *90–91*

NORTH DAKOTA

Bismarck, *139, 141–142*
Fort Yates, *137–138*
Garrison, *146–147*
Mandan, *138–139*
New Town, *147, 149–150*
Stanton, *144–146*
Washburn, *142–144*
Williston, *151–152*

OREGON

Astoria, *263–267*
The Dalles, *254–256*
Hood River, *256–258, 260–261*
Pendleton, *252–254*
Portland, *261–262*
Umatilla, *251–252*

SOUTH DAKOTA

Chamberlain–Oacoma, *121–123*
Elk Point, *113, 115*
Fort Thompson, *123–124*
Gettysburg, *127–128*
Mobridge, *129–131*
Pickstown, *120–121*
Pierre, *124–125, 127*
Vermillion, *115–116*
Yankton, *116–120*

WASHINGTON

Cathlamet, *239–241*
Clarkston, *226, 228*
Dayton, *228–230*
Goldendale, *236–237*
Ilwaco, *242–244*
Kennewick, *232–233*

Long Beach, *241–242*
Pasco, *233–234*
Richland, *234*
Stevenson, *237–238*
Vancouver, *238–239*
Walla Walla, *230–232*

INDEX

Adams Homestead and Nature Preserve (Elk Point, SD), *113, 115*

Ahsahka, ID. *See* Orofino

Akta Lakota Museum and Lakota Visitors Center (Chamberlain–Oacoma, SD), *122*

Alton, IL, *29–30*

Alton Museum of History (Alton, IL), *30*

American Bowman (Parkville and Weston, MO), *62*

American Legacy Expo (Mandan, ND), *139*

Anderson House Museum (The Dalles, OR), *256*

Appaloosa Museum and Heritage Center (Lewiston, ID), *214*

Arabia Steamboat Museum (Kansas City, MO), *59*

Ark Restaurant and Bakery (Long Beach, WA), *241*

Arrival of the Corps (Hartford, IL), *33*

Arrow Rock, MO, *54–55*

Arrow Rock Heritage Crafts Festival (Arrow Rock, MO), *55*

Arrow Rock State Historic Site Visitor Center (Arrow Rock, MO), *54*

Ashland, NE. *See* Bellevue

Asotin, WA. *See* Clarkston

Asotin County Museum (Clarkston, WA), *226*

Astoria, OR, *263–267*

Astoria Inn (Astoria, OR), *266–267*

Astoria Regatta Festival (Astoria, OR), *266*

Atchison, KS, *70–72*

Atchison County Historical Society Museum (Atchison, KS), *71*

Audubon National Wildlife Refuge (Garrison, ND), *146*

Augusta, MO, *44–45*

Bailey's Place (The Dalles, OR), *256*

Baldwin Saloon Historic Restaurant and Bar (The Dalles, OR), *256*

Bancroft, NE. *See* Decatur

Bannack State Historic Park (Dillon, MT), *179–180*

Barrister (Helena, MT), *173*

Beacon Rock State Park (Stevenson, WA), *237*

Beall Mansion (Alton, IL), *30*

Bear Medison Island Marker (Parkville and Weston, MO), *61*

Beaverhead County Museum (Dillon, MT), *180*

Beaverhead Rock State Park (Dillon, MT), *180*

Bellefontaine Cemetery (St. Louis, MO), *38*

Bellevue, NE, *82–83*

Benjamin Young Inn (Astoria, OR), *267*

Berkley River Front Park (Kansas City, MO), *59*

Bertran's Salmon Valley Brewery (Salmon, ID), *202*

Beulah, ND. *See* Stanton

Beyond York (St. Louis, MO), *40*

Bicentennial Concert Series (Alton, IL), *30*

Big Bend Dam–Lake Sharpe (Fort Thompson, SD), *123–124*

Big Hole National Battlefield (Dillon, MT), *180*

Billings, MT, *188–192*

Bird Woman Missouri River Adventures (Washburn, ND), *142*

Bismarck, ND, *139, 141–142*

Blackbird Hill (Decatur, NE), *89*

Blair, NE, *86–88*

Bojack's Broiler Pit (Lewiston, ID), *216*

Bonaparte's (St. Charles, MO), *44*

Bonner Springs, KS. *See* Kansas City

Bonneville Lock and Dam (Hood River, OR), *257*

Boone's Lick Trail Inn (St. Charles, MO), *44*

Boonville, MO, *53–54*

Boonville, MO. *See* Rocheport

Boonville, MO. *See* St. Charles

Boreas Bed & Breakfast (Long Beach, WA), *242*

Borgman's Bed & Breakfast (Arrow Rock, MO), *55*

Botanical Gardens (Omaha, NE), *83–84*

Boyer Chute National Wildlife Refuge (Blair, NE), *86–87*

Bozeman, MT, *184–186*

Bozeman, MT. *See* Three Forks

Bradley House, The (Cathlamet, WA), *240*

Brownville, NE, *79, 81–82*

Brownville State Recreation Area (Brownville, NE), *81*

Bucking Horse Sale (Miles City, MT), *193*

Cable's Riverview Ridge B&B (Chamberlain–Oacoma, SD), *123*

Cahokia, IL, *25, 28–29*

Cahokia Courthouse State Historic Site (Cahokia, IL), *28*

Cahokia Mounds Historic Site (Cahokia, IL), *28*

Camp Dubois (Hartford, IL), *33*

Camp Dubois (Wood River, IL), *31*

Camp Dubois Rendezvous (Wood River, IL), *31*

Camp Rulo River Club (Brownville, NE), *82*

Canoe Camp (Orofino, ID), *210, 212*

Canyon Ferry Recreation Area (Helena, MT), *172*

Cathedral Park (Portland, OR), *261*

Cathlamet, WA, *239–241*

Cattleman's Club (Pierre, SD), *127*

Celilo Park (The Dalles, OR), *255*

Center, ND. *See* Washburn

Center for Arts & History (Lewiston, ID), *214*

Chamberlain, SD. *See* Chamberlain–Oacoma

Chamberlain–Oacoma, SD, *121–123*

Charles M. Russell National Wildlife Refuge (Lewistown, MT), *164*

Charlie Russell Chew-Choo (Lewistown, MT), *164*

Charlie Russell Manor (Great Falls, MT), *171*

Chief Joseph & Lawyer Powwow (Lewiston, ID), *216*

Chief Lookingglass Powwow (Kamiah, ID), *206*

Chief Plenty Coups State Park (Billings, MT), *189–190*

Chief War Eagle Monument (Sioux City, IA), *106*

China Beach Retreat (Ilwaco, WA), *243–244*

Church of the Holy Family, The (Cahokia, IL), *28*

City Market (Kansas City, MO), *59*

Civil War Festival (Gettysburg, SD), *128*

Clark Bottom Rendezvous (Billings, MT), *191*

Clark County Historical Museum (Vancouver, WA), *238*

Clark Days (Billings, MT), *191*

Clark on the Yellowstone (Billings, MT), *192*

Clark's Eastward Journey, MT, *183–184*

Clark's Hill/Norton State Historic Site (Jefferson City, MO), *47*

Clark's Lookout State Park (Dillon, MT), *180*

Clark's Point (Kansas City, MO), *60*

Clark's Yellowstone River Camps (Billings, MT), *191*

Clarkston, WA, *226, 228*

Clearwater Historical Museum (Orofino, ID), *212*

Clearwater National Forest (Kamiah, ID), *204–205*

Colbert House Museum (Ilwaco, WA), *243*

Coleharbor, ND. *See* Garrison

Collins Mansion B&B (Great Falls, MT), *171*

Collinsville, IL. *See* Cahokia

Columbia, MO, *49*

Columbia Gorge Discovery Center (The Dalles, OR), *255*

Columbia Gorge Hotel (Hood River, OR), *260*

Columbia Gorge Interpretive Center (Stevenson, WA), *238*

Columbia River Estuary Tours (Astoria, OR), *263*

Columbia River Exhibition of History, Science, and Technology Museum (Richland, WA), *234*

Columbia River Inn Bed and Breakfast (Astoria, OR), *267*

Columbia River Journeys (Richland, WA), *234*

Columbia River Maritime Museum (Astoria, OR), *263*

Confluence Interpretive Center (Williston, ND), *151*

Conqueror's Stones (Mobridge, SD), *129*

Corps of Discovery Welcome Center (Crofton, NE), *92*

Cottonwood Cove (South Sioux City, NE), *90*

Council Bluffs, IA, *100–102*

Country Homestead Bed & Breakfast, The (Onawa, IA), *105*

Cow Island Marker (Parkville and Weston, MO), *61*

Craig, NE. *See* Blair

Cramer-Kenyon Heritage Home (Yankton, SD), *117*

Crofton, NE, *91–93*

Cross J Ranch Bed and Breakfast (Lynch, NE), *95*

Cross Ranch Centennial State Park (Washburn, ND), *143*

Cross Ranch Nature Conservancy Preserve (Washburn, ND), *143*

Crow Creek Sioux Tribe Annual Powwow (Fort Thompson, SD), *124*

Crow Flies High Butte Historical Site (New Town, ND), *149*

Crown Point State Scenic Corridor and Vista House (Hood River, OR), *257*

Czech Days (Yankton, SD), *119*

Dakota City, NE. *See* South Sioux City

Dakota Sunset Museum (Gettysburg, SD), *128*

Dakota Territorial Museum (Yankton, SD), *117*

Dakota/Thurston County Fair (South Sioux City, NE), *91*

Dalles, The, OR, *254–256*

Dalles Dam and Lake Celilo, The (The Dalles, OR), *255–256*

Daniel Boone Home & Boonesfield Village (St. Charles, MO), *41*

DAR Historical Marker (Highland/White Cloud, KS), *73*

Dayton, WA, *228–230*

Dayton Historic Depot (Dayton, WA), *229*

Dayton's Depot Days (Dayton, WA), *229*

De Voto Memorial Cedar Grove (Kamiah, ID), *205*

Decatur, NE, *88–90*

Decision Point Overlook (Fort Benton, MT), *165*

Defiance, MO. *See* St. Charles

Delta Queen Steamboat Company (St. Louis, MO), *38*

Departure from Fort Mandan (Washburn, ND), *144*

DeSoto National Wildlife Refuge (Blair, NE), *87*

DeSoto National Wildlife Refuge (Missouri Valley, IA), *102*

Dillon, MT, *178–181*

Dillon Visitor Center (Dillon, MT), *181*

Discover Travelers' Rest (Missoula, MT), *182*

Discovery Center (Kansas City, MO), *60*

Dorothy Pecaut Nature Center (Sioux City, IA), *107*

Double Ditch Indian Village State Historic Site (Bismarck, ND), *141*

Down Over Bed & Breakfast (Arrow Rock, MO), *55*

Drury Plaza Hotel (St. Louis, MO), *40*

Durham Western Heritage Museum (Omaha, NE), *84–85*

Dworshak Dam and Reservoir (Orofino, ID), *212*

Dworshak National Fish Hatchery (Orofino, ID), *212–213*

Ecola State Park (Astoria, OR), *263–264*

Elk Point, SD, *113, 115*

Elk Point Heritage Days (Elk Point, SD), *115*

English Landing Park (Parkville and Weston, MO), *61–62*

Explore the Big Sky (Great Falls, MT), *171*

Farm Island State Recreation Area (Pierre, SD), *125*

Father Flanagan's Boys and Girls Town (Omaha, NE), *85*

Festival of Discovery (Orofino, ID), *213*

First Missouri State Capitol State Historic Site (St. Charles, MO), *43*

First Tribal Council (Blair, NE), *88*

Five Nations Art and Gift Shop (Mandan, ND), *138*

Flavel House (Astoria, OR), *264*

Foley Station (Pendleton, OR), *253*

Fond Farewell, A (Stanton, ND), *145*

Fontenelle Forest Nature Center (Bellevue, NE), *82*

Fort Abraham Lincoln State Park (Mandan, ND), *138*

Fort Atkinson State Historical Park (Blair, NE), *87*

Fort Belle Fontaine County Park (St. Louis, MO), *38*

Fort Benton, MT, *165–168*

Fort Benton Levee (Fort Benton, MT), *165–166*

Fort Benton Summer Celebration (Fort Benton, MT), *167*

Fort Buford Encampment (Sidney, MT), *162*

Fort Buford 6th Infantry Encampment (Williston, ND), *152*

Fort Buford State Historic Site (Williston, ND), *151*

Fort Calhoun, NE. *See* Blair

Fort Canby State Park (Ilwaco, WA), *243*

Fort Charrette (Augusta, MO), *45*

Fort Clark State Historic Site (Stanton, ND), *144–145*

Fort Clatsop National Memorial (Astoria, OR), *264*

Fort Dalles Museum (The Dalles, OR), *256*

Fort Leavenworth (Leavenworth, KS), *69*

Fort Mandan (Washburn, ND), *140, 143*

Fort Manuel Site (Mobridge, SD), *129*

Fort Omaha Intertribal Powwow (Omaha, NE), *86*

Fort Osage (Independence, MO), *58*

Fort Peck, MT, *163*

Fort Peck Assiniboine and Sioux Culture Center and Museum (Fort Peck, MT), *163*

Fort Peck Hotel (Fort Peck, MT), *163*

Fort Peck Hotel Restaurant (Fort Peck, MT), *163*

Fort Pierre, SD. *See* Pierre

Fort Randall Dam (Pickstown, SD), *120*

Fort Randall Powwow (Pickstown, SD), *121*

Fort Stevens State Park (Astoria, OR), *264*

Fort Stevenson Military Days (Garrison, ND), *147*

Fort Stevenson State Park (Garrison, ND), *146*

Fort Thompson, SD, *123–124*

Fort Union Living History (Sidney, MT), *162*

Fort Union Rendezvous (Sidney, MT), *162*

Fort Union Trading Post Historic Site (Sidney, MT), *162*

Fort Union Trading Post National Historic Site (Williston, ND), *151*

Fort Union Trading Post Rendezvous (Williston, ND), *151*

Fort Vancouver National Historic Reserve (Vancouver, WA), *238–239*

Fort Walla Walla Museum (Walla Walla, WA), *230*

Fort Walla Walla Park (Walla Walla, WA), *230*

Fort Yates, ND, *137–138*

Four Bears Casino and Lodge (New Town, ND), *150*

Four State Lookout (Highland/White Cloud, KS), *73*

Frank Church–River of No Return Wilderness (Salmon, ID), *201*

Franklin County Historical Museum (Pasco, WA), *233*

Fremont County Historical Museum (Sidney, IA), *100*

Frontier Discovery Games (Wood River, IL), *31*

Frontier Music Festival (Kamiah, ID), *206*

Frontier Park (St. Charles, MO), *42–43*

Frontier Return to Nature Cabins (Lynch, NE), *95*

Gallatin County Pioneer Museum (Bozeman, MT), *184*

Gallatin Gateway, MT. *See* Bozeman

Gallatin Gateway Inn (Bozeman, MT), *185*

Garrison, ND, *146–147*

Garrison Dam Overlook Historical Site (Garrison, ND), *146–147*

Gass Election Monument (Elk Point, SD), *115*

Gates of the Mountains Boat Tours (Helena, MT), *172*

Gateway Arch (St. Louis, MO), *39*

Gateway to the West Parade (Blair, NE), *88*

Geery's Bed & Breakfast (St. Charles, MO), *44*

George Henry's (Billings, MT), *192*

George Shannon Statue (Crofton, NE), *92*

George Shannon Trail (Crofton, NE), *92*

Gettysburg, SD, *127–128*

Giant Springs State Park and Trout Hatchery (Great Falls, MT), *170*

Glasgow, MO, *55, 57*

Glasgow, MT. *See* Fort Peck

Glenwood, IA, *100*

Glore Psychiatric Museum (St. Joseph, MO), *63*

Golden Belle Restaurant (Billings, MT), *192*

Golden Valley, ND. *See* Stanton

Goldendale, WA, *236–237*

Goldsmith's Bed & Breakfast (Missoula, MT), *182*

Goodner House Bed & Breakfast Inn (Pierre, SD), *127*

Grand Union Grille (Fort Benton, MT), *167*

Grand Union Hotel (Fort Benton, MT), *167–168*

Great Falls, MT, *168, 170–171*

Great Falls Historic Trolley (Great Falls, MT), *170*

Great Pacific Wine and Coffee Company (Pendleton, OR), *254*

Great Plains Black Museum (Omaha, NE), *85*

Great Plains Resource Center (Chamberlain–Oacoma, SD), *122*

Great River Road National Scenic Byway (Cahokia, IL), *28*

Green Gables Inn (Walla Walla, WA), *232*

Greenwood (Pickstown, SD), *121*

Greenwood, SD. *See* Pickstown

Grey House Inn (Salmon, ID), *202*

Gunderson's Cannery Cafe (Astoria, OR), *266*

Hamburg, IA. *See* Sidney

Harley Park Overlook (Boonville, MO), *53*

Harrison County Historical Village (Missouri Valley, IA), *102*

Hartford, IL, *31–33*

Hat Rock State Park (Umatilla, OR), *251*

Hatchery House (Parkville and Weston, MO), *62–63*

Headwaters Heritage Museum (Three Forks, MT), *175*

Hearthstone Lodge (Kamiah, ID), *208*

Helena, MT, *171–174*

Hells Gate State Park (Lewiston, ID), *214*

Heritage Day (Pasco, WA), *234*

Heritage Days (Boonville, MO), *53*

Heritage Outbound Adventure (Washburn, ND), *144*

Heritage Weekend (Miles City, MT), *193*

Hermann, MO, *46–47*

High Noon Saloon and Brewery (Leavenworth, KS), *69*

Highland/White Cloud, KS, *73*

Hilger's Gulch and Governor's Grove (Pierre, SD), *125*

Historic Arrow Rock Tavern (Arrow Rock, MO), *55*

Historic Columbia River Highway (Hood River, OR), *257*

Historic Headwaters Restaurant (Three Forks, MT), *176*

Historic Marker (Hartford, IL), *33*

Historical Home Tours (Dayton, WA), *229*

Home Spirit Café and Restaurant (Astoria, OR), *266*

Hood River, OR, *256–258, 260–261*

Hood River Hotel (Hood River, OR), *260–261*

Hood River Valley Blossom Festival (Hood River, OR), *260*

Horsethief Lake State Park (Goldendale, WA), *236*

Howell Territorial Park (Portland, OR), *261–262*

Huber's Ferry Bed & Breakfast (Jefferson City, MO), *48*

Huran Indian Cemetery (Kansas City, KS), *68*

Ilwaco, WA, *242–244*

Ilwaco Heritage Museum (Ilwaco, WA), *243*

Independence, MO, *57–58*

Independence Creek Site (Atchison, KS), *71*

Independence Park (Atchison, KS), *71*

Indian Arts Showcase (Sidney, MT), *162*

Indian Cave State Park (Brownville, NE), *81*

Indian Hills Resort (Garrison, ND), *147*

Inn at Blackberry Creek (Walla Walla, WA), *232*

Inn of the White Salmon (Goldendale, WA), *237*

Interpretive Marker and Kiosk (Marthasville, MO), *46*

Ionia Volcano (South Sioux City, NE), *90–91*

Jarrot Mansion State Historic Site (Cahokia, IL), *29*

Jedediah Smith Monument (Mobridge, SD), *129*

Jefferson City, MO, *47–48*

Jefferson Landing State Historic Site (Jefferson City, MO), *47*

Jefferson National Expansion Park (St. Louis, MO), *38–39*

Jentell Brees Conservation Area (St. Joseph, MO), *63*

John Bozeman Bistro (Bozeman, MT), *185*

John Colter Run (Three Forks, MT), *176*

John G. Neihardt Center (Decatur, NE), *89*

Jonathan's (Lewiston, ID), *216*

Joslyn Art Museum (Omaha, NE), *85*

Journey Fourth, A (Atchison, KS), *71*

Journey Fourth, A (Kansas City, KS), *68*

Journey Fourth, A (Kansas City, MO), *60*

Journey of Discovery (Whitehall, MT), *178*

Kahill's (South Sioux City, NE), *91*

Kamiah, ID, *204–206, 208*

Kamiah Riverfront Park (Kamiah, ID), *206*

Kansas City, KS, *67–68*

Kansas City, MO, *59–60*

Kansas City Museum (Kansas City, MO), *60*

Kanza Territory, KS, *65, 67*

Katy Trail (St. Charles, MO), *42*

Katy Trail Bike Ride (Rocheport, MO), *53*

Katy Trail State Park (Rocheport, MO), *51–53*

Kaw Point (Kansas City, KS), *68*

Kaw Point Commemoration (Kansas City, KS), *68*

Kenel Memorial Day Wacipi (Mobridge, SD), *130*

Kennewick, WA, *232–233*

Kirkwood, MO. *See* St. Louis

Klein Museum (Mobridge, SD), *130*

Klickitat County Historical Museum (Goldendale, WA), *236*

Knife River Indian Villages National Historic Site (Stanton, ND), *145, 148–149*

Knife River Ranch (Stanton, ND), *145*

Kooskia, ID. *See* Kamiah

Kooskia Kiosk (Kamiah, ID), *206*

Kreycik Elk and Bison Ranch (Crofton, NE), *92*

La Grande, OR. *See* Pendleton

Laclède's Landing (St. Louis, MO), *39*

LaFramboise Island (Pierre, SD), *125*

Lake Andes National Wildlife Refuge (Pickstown, SD), *121*

Lake Manawa State Park (Council Bluffs, IA), *101*

Lake Sakakawea State Park (Garrison, ND), *147*

Landing Reenactment (Cahokia, IL), *29*

Last Chance Train Tour (Helena, MT), *172–173*

Leavenworth, KS, *68–70*

Leavenworth Landing (Leavenworth, KS), *69*

Lee G. Simmons Wildlife Safari Park (Bellevue, NE), *82–83*

Lemhi County Historical Museum (Salmon, ID), *201*

Lemhi Shoshone Meeting Lewis and Clark Reenactment (Dillon, MT), *181*

Lewis & Clark Resort (Kamiah, ID), *208*

Lewis and Clark: An American Adventure (Sioux City, IA), *106*

Lewis and Clark Annual Symposium (Lewiston, ID), *216*

Lewis and Clark at the Confluence (Sidney, MT), *162*

Lewis and Clark Boat House (St. Charles, MO), *43*

Lewis and Clark Cave (Rocheport, MO), *52–53*

Lewis and Clark Caverns (Three Forks, MT), *175*

Lewis and Clark Center (St. Charles, MO), *43*

Lewis and Clark Columbia River Tours (Portland, OR), *262*

Lewis and Clark Council Bluff Interpretive Monument (Blair, NE), *87*

Lewis and Clark Days (Clarkston, WA), *228*

Lewis and Clark Days (Walla Walla, WA), *231*

Lewis and Clark Days (Washburn, ND), *144*

Lewis and Clark Discovery Faire (Lewiston, ID), *216*

Lewis and Clark Encampment (Three Forks, MT), *176*

Lewis and Clark Expedition Tours (Billings, MT), *190*

Lewis and Clark Festival (Crofton, NE), *93*

Lewis and Clark Festival (Dillon, MT), *181*

Lewis and Clark Festival (Great Falls, MT), *171*

Lewis and Clark Festival (Onawa, IA), *105*

Lewis and Clark Festival (Vermillion, SD), *116*

Lewis and Clark Festival (Yankton, SD), *119*

Lewis and Clark Goosefest and Bad River Gathering (Pierre, SD), *127*

Lewis and Clark: Great Journey West (St. Louis, MO), *40*

Lewis and Clark Heritage Days (St. Charles, MO), *43*

Lewis and Clark Interpretive Center (Chamberlain–Oacoma, SD), *122*

Lewis and Clark Interpretive Center (Ilwaco, WA), *243*

Lewis and Clark Interpretive Center (Sioux City, IA), *106*

Lewis and Clark Interpretive Center (Washburn, ND), *143*

Lewis and Clark Kayaking (Washburn, ND), *144*

Lewis and Clark Lake Visitor Center (Crofton, NE), *92*

Lewis and Clark Landing (Omaha, NE), *85*

Lewis and Clark Monument Park (Council Bluffs, IA), *101*

Lewis and Clark Motor Coach Tours (Crofton, NE), *93*

Lewis and Clark Mural (Washburn, ND), *143*

Lewis and Clark National Back Country Byway & Adventure Road (Salmon, ID), *201–202*

Lewis and Clark National Historic Trail Interpretive Center (Great Falls, MT), *170*

Lewis and Clark National Signature Event (St. Charles, MO), *43*

Lewis and Clark Recreation Area (Yankton, SD), *117*

Lewis and Clark Rediscovery Festival (Mobridge, SD), *130–131*

Lewis and Clark Riverboat (Bismarck, ND), *141*

Lewis and Clark Rock Fort Site (The Dalles, OR), *256*

Lewis and Clark Scenic Byway (Decatur, NE), 89

Lewis and Clark State Historic Site (Hartford, IL), 32–33

Lewis and Clark State Park (Hood River, OR), 257–258

Lewis and Clark State Park (Onawa, IA), 103

Lewis and Clark State Park (Parkville and Weston, MO), 62

Lewis and Clark State Park (Williston, ND), 152

Lewis and Clark: The National Bicentennial Exhibition (St. Louis, MO), 40

Lewis and Clark Tradin' Days (Parkville and Weston, MO), 62

Lewis and Clark Trail State Park (Dayton, WA), 229

Lewis and Clark Wagon Train (Mandan, ND), 139

Lewis and Clark's Public House (St. Charles, MO), 44

Lewis-Clark State College (Lewiston, ID), 214–215

Lewiston, ID, 213–216, 218

Lewiston Gateway (Lewiston, ID), 215

Lewistown, MT, 164–165

Lexington, MO, 57

Lexington Heritage Tours (Lexington, MO), 57

Liberty Bell of the West (Cahokia, IL), 29

Little Bighorn Battlefield National Monument (Billings, MT), 190

Little Knife Outfitters (Williston, ND), 152

Little Shell Powwow and Four Bears Celebration (New Town, ND), 150

Living History Days (Blair, NE), 88

Livingston, MT, 186, 188

Lochsa Historical Ranger Station (Kamiah, ID), 205

Lochsa Lodge Restaurant (Kamiah, ID), 206, 208

Lochsa River (Kamiah, ID), 205

Lodge at Prairie Knights (Fort Yates, ND), 138

Loess Hills Scenic Byway (Onawa, IA), 103

Lolo, ID. See Kamiah

Lolo, MT. See Missoula

Lolo Hot Springs Resort (Missoula, MT), 182–183

Lolo Motorway (Kamiah, ID), 205

Lolo Pass Visitor Center (Kamiah, ID), 205–206

Lom, MT. See Fort Benton

Loma, MT. See Fort Benton

Long Beach, WA, 241–242

Louisiana Territory Land Transfer Commemoration (St. Charles, MO), 43

Louisville, NE. See Omaha

Lower Brule Sioux Tribe Annual Fair and Powwow (Fort Thompson, SD), 124

Lower Granite Lock and Dam (Lewiston, ID), 215

Lynch, NE, 93–95

Ma Hush Kah Museum (Highland/White Cloud, KS), 73

Macy, NE. See Decatur

Madison Buffalo Jump State Park (Three Forks, MT), 175

Maifest (Hermann, MO), 46

Majestic House, The (Atchison, KS), 72

Mandan, ND, 138–139

Mandaree Powwow (New Town, ND), 150

Marc, The (Walla Walla, WA), 231

Marcus Whitman Hotel and Conference Center (Walla Walla, WA), 232

Marthasville, MO, 45–46

Martin-Boismenue House State Historic Site (Cahokia, IL), 29

Maryhill Museum of Art (Goldendale, WA), 237

McLean County Historical Society Museum (Washburn, ND), 144

McNary Lock and Dam (Umatilla, OR), 252

Meridian Bridge (Yankton, SD), 118

Meriwether Lewis (Brownville, NE), 81

Meriwether's (St. Louis, MO), 40

Meriwether's Restaurant (Lewiston, ID), 216

Miami, MO. See Arrow Rock

Midway Expo Center Tipi (Columbia, MO), 49

Miles City, MT, 192–193

Mill Creek Inn (Walla Walla, WA), 232

Mills County Historical Museum (Glenwood, IA), 100

Milton York Restaurant (Long Beach, WA), 241–242

Mission Creek Ranch Bed and Breakfast (Livingston, MT), 186, 188

Missoula, MT, 181–183

Missouri Breaks National Back Country Byway (Lewistown, MT), 164–165

Missouri Headwaters State Park (Three Forks, MT), 175–176

Missouri History Museum (St. Louis, MO), 39

Missouri Information Center (Jefferson City, MO), 48

Missouri National Recreation Scenic River Resource and Education Center (South Sioux City, NE), 91

Missouri River Basin Lewis and Clark Interpretive Center (Brownville, NE), 81

Missouri River Breaks Lewis and Clark Encampment (Lewistown, MT), 165

Missouri River Lodge (Stanton, ND), 146

Missouri River Overlook (Glasgow, MO), 57

Missouri Storytelling Festival (St. Charles, MO), 43

Missouri Valley, IA, 102

Mobridge, SD, 129–131

Monona County Arboretum (Onawa, IA), 103

Monona County Historical Museum (Onawa, IA), 103, 105

Montana Historical Society Museum (Helena, MT), 173

Montana State Capitol (Helena, MT), 173

Moose River Grill (Kamiah, ID), 208

Moscow, ID. See Lewiston

Mother-In-Law House (St. Charles, MO), *44*

Mount Hood Scenic Railroad and Dinner Train (Hood River, OR), *258*

Multnomah Falls (Hood River, OR), *258*

Murray Hotel, The (Livingston, MT), *188*

Museum of Art and Archaeology (Columbia, MO), *49*

Museum of Military History (Jefferson City, MO), *48*

Museum of the Rockies (Bozeman, MT), *184–185*

Museum of the Upper Missouri and Old Fort Benton (Fort Benton, MT), *166*

Museum of Westward Expansion (St. Louis, MO), *39*

My Just Desserts (Alton, IL), *30*

Nahcotta, WA. *See* Long Beach

Napoleon's Retreat B&B (St. Louis, MO), *40–41*

National Frontier Trails Center (Independence, MO), *58*

National Professional Rodeo Association's Edge of the West Rodeo (Bismarck, ND), *142*

National Signature Event (Hartford, IL), *33*

Native American Festival (Bellevue, NE), *83*

Native American Heritage Museum (Highland/White Cloud, KS), *73*

Native American Scenic Byway (Fort Thompson, SD), *124*

Native American/French Fête (Cahokia, IL), *29*

Neahkahnie Mountain (Astoria, OR), *264*

Nebraska City, NE. *See* Brownville

New Franklin, MO. *See* Boonville

New Orleans, MO. *See* St. Louis

New Town, ND, *147, 149–150*

Nez Percé County Museum (Lewiston, ID), *215*

Nez Percé National Historical Park–Spalding Site (Lewiston, ID), *215*

Nez Percé Wolf Education and Research Center (Lewiston, ID), *215*

Niobrara, NE. *See* Crofton

Niobrara, NE. *See* Lynch

Niobrara State Park (Crofton, NE), *92–93*

North Dakota Heritage Center (Bismarck, ND), *141*

North Fork, ID. *See* Salmon

North Fork Store & Cafe (Salmon, ID), *202*

North Sioux City, SD. *See* Elk Point

Northern Hotel (Billings, MT), *192*

Northern Plains Indian Culture Festival (Stanton, ND), *145*

Nux-Bah-Ga Powwow (New Town, ND), *150*

Oakland, IA. *See* Onawa

Oceti Sakowin (Chamberlain–Oacoma, SD), *122–123*

Off the Beaten Path (Bozeman, MT), *185*

Officers' Row (Vancouver, WA), *239*

Old Baldy (Lynch, NE), *94–95*

Old Courthouse (St. Louis, MO), *39*

Old Time Autumn (Brownville, NE), *82*

Omaha, NE, *83–86*

Omaha History Tours (Omaha, NE), *85*

Omaha Reservation (Decatur, NE), *89*

Omaha Tribal Harvest Celebration (Decatur, NE), *90*

On-A-Slant Indian Village (Mandan, ND), *139*

Onawa, IA, *103, 105*

Opera Omaha (Omaha, NE), *85*

Oregon Historical Society (Portland, OR), *262*

Oregon Maritime Center and Museum (Portland, OR), *262*

Orofino, ID, *210, 212–213*

Oscar Howe Indian Murals (Mobridge, SD), *130*

Outpost 1806 Steakhouse (Stanton, ND), *145*

Oysterville (Long Beach, WA), *241*

Park University Lecture Series (Parkville and Weston, MO), *62*

Parker House (Pendleton, OR), *254*

Parkville, MO. *See* Parkville and Weston

Parkville and Weston, MO, *61–63*

Parshall, ND. *See* New Town

Pasco, WA, *233–234*

Paul Broste Rock Museum (New Town, ND), *149–150*

Peacock Alley Bar and Grill (Bismarck, ND), *142*

Pearson Air Museum (Vancouver, WA), *239*

Pelican Point State Recreation Area (Blair, NE), *87*

Pendleton, OR, *252–254*

Pendleton Round-Up (Pendleton, OR), *253*

Pendleton Underground Tours (Pendleton, OR), *252*

Pendleton Woolen Mills (Pendleton, OR), *252–253*

Petroglyphs (Clarkston, WA), *226, 228*

Pickstown, SD, *120–121*

Picotte Center (Decatur, NE), *89*

Pictograph Cave State Park (Billings, MT), *190*

Pierre, SD, *124–125, 127*

Pioneer Lodge Motel (Fort Benton, MT), *168*

Pioneer Park (Kansas City, MO), *60*

Plant Life of the Expedition (St. Louis, MO), *40*

Platte Creek State Recreation Area (Pickstown, SD), *120–121*

Platte River State Park (Omaha, NE), *85–86*

Plattsmouth, NE. *See* Bellevue

Pompeys Pillar National Monument (Billings, MT), *190–191*

Ponca State Park (South Sioux City, NE), *91*

Ponca Tribal Powwow (Crofton, NE), *93*

Ponca Tribe Museum (Crofton, NE), *93*

Poplar, MT. *See* Fort Peck

Porch Swing Bed & Breakfast, The (Parkville and Weston, MO), *63*

Portland, OR, *261–262*

Portland Art Museum (Portland, OR), *262*

Powder Valley Conservation Nature Center (St. Louis, MO), *39*

Powwows (Fort Yates, ND), *138*

Prairie du Pont, IL. *See* Cahokia

Prairie Queen Bed & Breakfast (Leavenworth, KS), *70*

Purple House Bed and Breakfast (Dayton, WA), *229–230*

Quarry Steak House & Lounge, The (Yankton, SD), *120*

Range Riders Museum (Miles City, MT), *193*

Raphael's (Pendleton, OR), *254*

Redfern Farm Bed and Breakfast (Cathlamet, WA), *240–241*

Reeder's Alley (Helena, MT), *173*

Reflections Inn (Kamiah, ID), *208*

Retreat at Someday Ranch, The (Weippe, ID), *209–210*

Return of the Sternwheeler Days (Hood River, OR), *260*

Return to the Home of Sakakawea (New Town, ND), *150*

Rex (Billings, MT), *192*

Richland, WA, *234*

River Boat Cruises (Alton, IL), *30*

River City Star (Omaha, NE), *86*

River Life Interpretive Center (Cathlamet, WA), *240*

River Towne Resort (St. Joseph, MO), *64*

River's Edge Trail (Great Falls, MT), *170*

Rivercene Bed & Breakfast (Boonville, MO), *53–54*

Riverdale, ND. *See* Garrison

Riverfest (Kamiah, ID), *206*

Riverfest (Leavenworth, KS), *69*

Riverfest (Pierre, SD), *127*

Riverfront Heritage Trail (Kansas City, MO), *59–60*

Riverhouse Restaurant, The (Atchison, KS), *71*

Riverside Grill (Council Bluffs, IA), *102*

Rocheport, MO, *49, 51–53*

Rooster Rock State Park (Hood River, OR), *258*

Root Feast (Kamiah, ID), *206*

Round-Up Hall of Fame Museum (Pendleton, OR), *253*

Rulo, NE. *See* Brownville

Running Water (Yankton, SD), *119*

Running Water, SD. *See* Yankton

Rushville, MO. *See* Parkville and Weston

Sacagawea Heritage Days (Salmon, ID), *202*

Sacagawea Interpretive, Cultural & Education Center (Salmon, ID), *202*

Sacagawea Monument (Mobridge, SD), *130*

Sacagawea Select Inn (Lewiston, ID), *218*

Sacajawea Heritage Trail (Kennewick, WA), *233*

Sacajawea Hotel (Three Forks, MT), *176*

Sacajawea State Park (Pasco, WA), *234*

Salmon, ID, *200–202*

Salt Works (Astoria, OR), *264, 266*

Sanders-Helena's B&B (Helena, MT), *174*

Santa-Cali-Gon Days (Independence, MO), *58*

Santee Sioux Tribal Powwow (Crofton, NE), *93*

Sarpy County Historical Museum (Bellevue, NE), *83*

Schilling Wildlife Management Area (Bellevue, NE), *83*

Seaview, WA. *See* Long Beach

Sergeant Floyd Memorial Encampment (Sioux City, IA), *108*

Sergeant Floyd Monument (Sioux City, IA), *106–107*

Sergeant Floyd Welcome Center and Museum (Sioux City, IA), *107*

Settler's Inn (Boonville, MO), *53*

Shelburne Inn (Long Beach, WA), *242*

Shoalwater Restaurant (Long Beach, WA), *242*

Sibley, MO. *See* Independence

Sidney, IA, *99–100*

Sidney, MT, *160, 162*

Signing of the Louisiana Purchase (Jefferson City, MO), *48*

Sioux City, IA, *105–108*

Sioux City Art Center (Sioux City, IA), *107*

Sioux City Public Museum (Sioux City, IA), *107*

Sitting Bull Monument (Mobridge, SD), *130*

Sitting Bull Stampede Rodeo and Celebration (Mobridge, SD), *130*

63 Ranch (Livingston, MT), *188*

Skamokawa, WA. *See* Cathlamet

Skamokawa Paddle Center (Cathlamet, WA), *240*

Snake Creek State Recreation Area (Pickstown, SD), *121*

Snyder Bend County Park (Onawa, IA), *105*

Solaas Bed & Breakfast (Salmon, ID), *202*

South Dakota Cultural Heritage Center (Pierre, SD), *125*

South Dakota National Guard Museum (Pierre, SD), *125*

South Sioux City, NE, *90–91*

Spalding, ID. *See* Lewiston

Spirit Mound (Vermillion, SD), *116*

Spirit of Brownville (Brownville, NE), *81*

Spirit of the Plains Gallery (Bismarck, ND), *141*

Springfield, SD. *See* Yankton

Springfield Discovery Day (Yankton, SD), *120*

Springfield Historical Society Museum (Yankton, SD), *119*

St. Charles, MO, *41–44*

St. Charles Historic District (St. Charles, MO), *43*

St. Joseph, MO, *63–64*

St. Joseph Museum (St. Joseph, MO), *64*

St. Joseph's Indian School Powwow (Chamberlain–Oacoma, SD), *122*

St. Louis, MO, *37–41*

Standing Rock (Fort Yates, ND), *137*

Standing Rock Agency Stockade (Fort Yates, ND), *137*

Stanton, ND, *144–146*

State Capitol (Pierre, SD), *127*

State Capitol Building (Jefferson City, MO), *48*

Sternwheeler Columbia Gorge (Hood River, OR), *258*

Stevenson, WA, *237–238*

Stone State Park (Sioux City, IA), *107*

Stonehouse Restaurant (Helena, MT), *173*

Stroud's (Kansas City, MO), *60*

Struck by the Ree's Grave (Pickstown, SD), *121*

Stump Island Encampment (Glasgow, MO), *57*

Sunset Grill (St. Joseph, MO), *64*

Tamastslikt Cultural Institute (Pendleton, OR), *253*

Tavern Cave (Augusta, MO), *45*

Tekamah, NE. *See* Decatur

Terrace Park (Yankton, SD), *119*

Thomas Jefferson's Original Gravemarker (Columbia, MO), *49*

Three Affiliated Tribes Museum (New Town, ND), *150*

Three Forks, MT, *174–176*

Threshing Bee (Mobridge, SD), *131*

Timber Lake, SD. *See* Gettysburg

Timber Lake and Area Museum (Gettysburg, SD), *128*

Timberline Café (Weippe, ID), *209*

Time of Renewal and Exchange (Bismarck, ND), *142*

Tobacco Garden Resort and Marina (Williston, ND), *152*

Touch the Trail of Lewis and Clark (Fort Benton, MT), *167*

Trails West! (St. Joseph, MO), *64*

Trapper's Kettle (Williston, ND), *152*

Travelers' Rest National Historic Landmark and State Park (Missoula, MT), *181–182*

Treaty of 1858 Monument (Pickstown, SD), *121*

Trial at Kaw Point (Kansas City, KS), *68*

Turin, IA. *See* Onawa

Twin Buttes Celebration (New Town, ND), *150*

Two Rivers Park (Kennewick, WA), *233*

Two Rivers Saloon and Hotel (Lynch, NE), *95*

Ulm Pishkun State Park (Great Falls, MT), *170–171*

Umatilla, OR, *251–252*

Umatilla County Historical Society Museum (Pendleton, OR), *253*

Union County Museum (Elk Point, SD), *115*

United Tribes Indian Art Expo and Market (Bismarck, ND), *141*

United Tribes International Powwow (Bismarck, ND), *141*

University of Missouri (Columbia, MO), *49*

Upper Missouri National Wild and Scenic River (Fort Benton, MT), *166*

Upper Missouri River Keelboat Co (Fort Benton, MT), *166–167*

Valley County Pioneer Museum (Fort Peck, MT), *163*

Van Meter State Park (Arrow Rock, MO), *54*

Vancouver, WA, *238–239*

Verdigre, NE. *See* Lynch

Verendrye Monument (Pierre, SD), *127*

Vermillion, SD, *115–116*

Vintage Inn (Vancouver, WA), *239*

Virgelle Merc and Missouri River Canoe Company (Fort Benton, MT), *167*

Virgelle Mercantile (Fort Benton, MT), *168*

Visitor Center (Hartford, IL), *33*

Voss Inn (Bozeman, MT), *185–186*

W. H. Over State Museum (Vermillion, SD), *116*

Wahkiakum County Historical Society Museum (Cathlamet, WA), *240*

Walk of Fame (St. Louis, MO), *39*

Walla Walla, WA, *230–232*

Walthill, NE. *See* Decatur

Ward Indian Village Overlook (Bismarck, ND), *141*

Wasco County Historical Museum (The Dalles, OR), *255*

Washburn, ND, *142–144*

Washington County Historical Museum (Blair, NE), *87*

Waterfront Renaissance Trail (Vancouver, WA), *239*

Waubonsie State Park (Sidney, IA), *100*

Weinhard Café (Dayton, WA), *229*

Weinhard Hotel (Dayton, WA), *230*

Weippe, ID, *208–210*

Weippe Camas Festival (Weippe, ID), *209*

Weippe Discovery Center (Weippe, ID), *209*

West Whitlock Recreation Area (Gettysburg, SD), *128*

Western Heritage Center (Billings, MT), *191*

Western Historic Trails Center (Council Bluffs, IA), *101*

Weston, MO. *See* Parkville and Weston

Weston Bend State Park (Parkville and Weston, MO), *62*

White Catfish Encampment (Council Bluffs, IA), *101*

White Cloud, KS. *See* Highland/White Cloud

White House Hotel (Hermann, MO), *46–47*

White Salmon, WA. *See* Goldendale

Whitehall, MT, *176–178*

Whitehall Lewis and Clark Bicentennial Murals (Whitehall, MT), *178*

Whitehouse-Crawford Restaurant (Walla Walla, WA), *231*

Whitman Mission National Historic Site (Walla Walla, WA), *231*

William Clark's Birthday Party (Blair, NE), *88*

Williston, ND, *151–152*

Winchester Lake State Park (Lewiston, ID), *216*

Winnebago, NE. *See* Decatur

Winnebago Buffalo Herd and Monument (Decatur, NE), *89*

Winnebago Cultural Learning Center and Museum (Decatur, NE), *90*

Winnebago Tribal Powwow (Decatur, NE), *90*

Wood River, IL, *30–31*

Wood River Museum (Wood River, IL), *31*

Working Girls Hotel (Pendleton, OR), *254*

Wyandotte County Historical Museum (Kansas City, KS), *68*

Yankton, SD, *116–120*

Yankton Riverboat Days (Yankton, SD), *119*

Yellowstone, MT. *See* Miles City

Yellowstone Gateway Museum of Park County (Livingston, MT), *186*

NOTES

NOTES

NOTES

Travel Back in Time